ASIAN DEVELOPMENT OUTLOOK

SEPTEMBER 2024

ASIAN DEVELOPMENT BANK

ADB

© 2024 Asian Development Bank
6 ADB Avenue, Mandaluyong City, 1550 Metro Manila, Philippines
Tel +63 2 8632 4444; Fax +63 2 8636 2444
www.adb.org

Some rights reserved. Published in 2024.

ISBN 978-92-9270-906-8 (print); 978-92-9270-907-5 (PDF); 978-92-9270-908-2 (ebook)
ISSN 0117-0481 (print), 1996-725X (PDF)
Publication Stock No. FLS240452-3
DOI: http://dx.doi.org/10.22617/FLS240452-3

The views expressed in this publication are those of the authors and do not necessarily reflect the views and policies of the Asian Development Bank (ADB) or its Board of Governors or the governments they represent.

ADB does not guarantee the accuracy of the data included in this publication and accepts no responsibility for any consequence of their use. The mention of specific companies or products of manufacturers does not imply that they are endorsed or recommended by ADB in preference to others of a similar nature that are not mentioned.

By making any designation of or reference to a particular territory or geographic area in this document, ADB does not intend to make any judgments as to the legal or other status of any territory or area.

Corrigenda to ADB publications may be found at http://www.adb.org/publications/corrigenda.

Notes:
In this publication, "$" refers to US dollars, "¥" refers to yen, "A$" refers to Australian dollars, "AF" refers to afghanis, "B" refers to baht, "CNY" refers to yuan, "K" refers to kina, "NZ$" refers to New Zealand dollars, "RM" refers to ringgit, "SI$" refers to Solomon Islands dollars, "TJS" refers to somoni, "Tk" refers to taka, and "VND" refers to dong.
ADB recognizes "China" as the People's Republic of China; "Hong Kong" as Hong Kong, China; "Korea" as the Republic of Korea; "Lao" and "Laos" as the Lao People's Democratic Republic; "Russia" as the Russian Federation; and "Vietnam" as Viet Nam.

Cover design by Anthony Victoria.

Cover artwork rendered by Samantha Ty licensed exclusively to ADB © 2024 "Collision" Samantha Ty.

CONTENTS

FOREWORD

Asia and the Pacific experienced robust growth and easing inflation in the first half of 2024. Strong domestic demand and recovering exports drove the expansion, while tight monetary policies and declining global food prices helped reduce inflationary pressures.

The *Asian Development Outlook September 2024* raises its 2024 growth forecast for Asia and the Pacific to 5.0% from 4.9% in April. This reflects stronger-than-expected economic expansions in the Caucasus and Central Asia, East Asia, and the Pacific. The region still faces challenges but remains resilient. We project growth to remain solid in 2025, at 4.9%.

At the same time, there are looming risks that require vigilance. Escalating trade tensions and protectionist measures could pose challenges to the region's export-oriented economies and hamper global progress on the green transition. Policymakers should redouble efforts to preserve the benefits of free trade and support continued global and regional integration.

The report also highlights how climate-related risks—from extreme weather to cyclical patterns such as La Niña—can pose macroeconomic challenges to the economies of Asia and the Pacific. Policymakers must integrate climate-related risks into macroeconomic analyses and country development plans so that the region can build resilience against these threats.

This edition introduces a macro-focused analytical chapter. It examines the spillovers of data-driven monetary policy in the United States for economies in our region. This chapter can be useful to central bankers and other policymakers as they assess how new data in the United States can shift expectations about monetary policy, and thus move exchange rates, capital flows, and financial markets—similar to what we saw in early August 2024.

I am pleased that the Asian Development Bank can share this report as we work with our stakeholders to strengthen resilience in our region.

MASATSUGU ASAKAWA
President
Asian Development Bank

ACKNOWLEDGMENTS

Asian Development Outlook (ADO) September 2024 was prepared by staff of the regional departments and resident missions of the Asian Development Bank (ADB) under the guidance of the Economic Research and Development Impact Department. Representatives of these departments met regularly as the Regional Economic Outlook Task Force to coordinate and develop consistent forecasts for the region.

Abdul Abiad, director of the Macroeconomics Research Division led the production of this report, assisted by Priscille Villanueva and Editha Laviña. Emmanuel Alano, Shiela Camingue-Romance, David Keith De Padua, Nedelyn Magtibay-Ramos, Jesson Pagaduan, Melanie Quintos, Pilipinas Quising, Mia Andrea Soriano, Dennis Sorino, Michael Timbang, and Mai Lin Villaruel provided technical and research support. Economic editorial advisors Robert Boumphrey, Eric Clifton, Joshua Greene, and Reza Vaez-Zadeh made substantial contributions to the subregional sections.

The support and guidance of ADB Chief Economist Albert Park, Deputy Chief Economist Joseph E. Zveglich Jr., and Deputy Director General Chia-Hsin Hu are gratefully acknowledged.

Authors who contributed the sections are bylined in each chapter. The regional leads and subregional coordinators were Kiyoshi Taniguchi, Kenji Takamiya, and Rene Cris Rivera for the Caucasus and Central Asia; Akiko Terada-Hagiwara and Dorothea Ramizo for East Asia; Rana Hasan for South Asia; James Villafuerte and Dulce Zara for Southeast Asia; and Kaukab Naqvi, Cara Tinio, and Kayleen Gene Calicdan for the Pacific.

Peter Fredenburg, Guy Sacerdoti, and Eric Van Zant edited *ADO September 2024*. Prince Nicdao and Glenda Cortez did the typesetting and graphics. Art direction for the cover was by Anthony Victoria, with artwork from Samantha Ty. Kevin Nellies designed the landing page for ADO. Heili Ann Bravo, Dyann Buenazedacruz, Fermirelyn Cruz, Eugene Creely Ingking, and Elenita Pura provided administrative and logistical support. A team from the Department of Communications and Knowledge Management, led by David Kruger and Terje Langeland, planned and coordinated the dissemination of *ADO September 2024*.

DEFINITIONS AND ASSUMPTIONS

The economies discussed in *Asian Development Outlook September 2024* are classified by major analytic or geographic group. For the purposes of this report, the following apply:

- **Association of Southeast Asian Nations** (ASEAN) comprises Brunei Darussalam, Cambodia, Indonesia, the Lao People's Democratic Republic, Malaysia, Myanmar, the Philippines, Singapore, Thailand, and Viet Nam. ASEAN 4 are Indonesia, Malaysia, the Philippines, and Thailand.

- **Developing Asia** comprises the 46 members of the Asian Development Bank, listed below by geographic group.

- **Caucasus and Central Asia** comprises Armenia, Azerbaijan, Georgia, Kazakhstan, the Kyrgyz Republic, Tajikistan, Turkmenistan, and Uzbekistan.

- **East Asia** comprises the People's Republic of China; Hong Kong, China; Mongolia; the Republic of Korea; and Taipei,China.

- **South Asia** comprises Afghanistan, Bangladesh, Bhutan, India, Maldives, Nepal, Pakistan, and Sri Lanka.

- **Southeast Asia** comprises Brunei Darussalam, Cambodia, Indonesia, the Lao People's Democratic Republic, Malaysia, Myanmar, the Philippines, Singapore, Thailand, Timor-Leste, and Viet Nam.

- **The Pacific** comprises the Cook Islands, Fiji, Kiribati, the Marshall Islands, the Federated States of Micronesia, Nauru, Niue, Palau, Papua New Guinea, Samoa, Solomon Islands, Tonga, Tuvalu, and Vanuatu.

Unless otherwise specified, the symbol "$" and the word "dollar" refer to US dollars.

A number of assumptions have been made for the projections in *Asian Development Outlook September 2024*. The policies of national authorities are maintained. Real effective exchange rates remain constant at their average from 1 August–5 September 2024. The average price of oil is $83/barrel in 2024 and $81/barrel in 2025. The US federal funds rate averages 5.20% in 2024 and 4.20% in 2025, the European Central Bank refinancing rate averages 4.10% in 2024 and 3.10% in 2025, and the Bank of Japan's overnight call rate averages 0.25% in 2024 and 0.40% in 2025.

All data in *Asian Development Outlook September 2024* were accessed from 1 August–5 September 2024.

ABBREVIATIONS

ADO	Asian Development Outlook
AI	artificial intelligence
AIS	Automatic Identification System
ASEAN	Association of Southeast Asian Nations
BDI	Baltic Dry Index
BNM	Bank Negara Malaysia
CDS	credit default swap
COFA	Compact of Free Association
COVID-19	coronavirus disease
CPI	consumer price index
EU	European Union
FDI	foreign direct investment
FOMC	Federal Open Market Committee
FSM	Federated States of Micronesia
FY	fiscal year
GDP	gross domestic product
H	half
HCP	honorary citizenship program (Vanuatu)
IMF	International Monetary Fund
Lao PDR	Lao People's Democratic Republic
LNG	liquefied natural gas
MSCI	Morgan Stanley Capital International
MSME	micro, small, and medium enterprise
NFRK	National Fund for the Republic of Kazakhstan
NOAA	National Oceanic and Atmospheric Administration
OPEC+	Organization of the Petroleum Exporting Countries and partners or their agreement
PBOC	People's Bank of China
PCE	personal consumption expenditures
PMI	purchasing managers' index
PNG	Papua New Guinea
PRC	People's Republic of China
Q	quarter
QE	quantitative easing
ROK	Republic of Korea
RPC	Regional Processing Centre (Nauru)
saar	seasonally adjusted annualized rate
SBV	State Bank of Vietnam
The Fed	US Federal Reserve Bank
US	United States
VIX	volatility index
yoy	year on year

Growth in developing Asia remained robust during the first half of 2024, as domestic demand and the continued recovery in exports supported economies in the region. High-income technology exporters benefited as global sales of semiconductors rose amid strong demand for artificial intelligence products. Inflation declined further, mainly as the lagged effects of tight monetary policy took hold and global food prices eased. This update revises the region's 2024 growth forecast up slightly to 5.0%, from 4.9% in April, on stronger-than-expected expansions in East Asia, Caucasus and Central Asia, and the Pacific. The update continues to forecast 4.9% growth for 2025. The inflation forecast is revised downward to 2.8% for 2024, from 3.2% in April, as food prices in the People's Republic of China (PRC) bottom out more slowly than expected. Expected inflation in 2025 is revised down slightly to 2.9%, from 3.0% in April. Policymakers in the region need to stay vigilant to keep growth and inflation on track, however. Downside risks include a rise in protectionism that could occur depending on the outcome of the United States (US) presidential election, worsening geopolitical tensions, a fragile PRC property market, and adverse weather conditions.

This edition of the *Asian Development Outlook* also introduces a new analytical chapter delving into how financial markets across the world react to data-driven US monetary policy changes. Calculations based on the chapter's results suggest that an unexpected return of US inflation to its July level of 2.9% by end-2024 could push other economies' bond yields up as much as 70 basis points, depreciate currencies by almost 4% vis-à-vis the US dollar, and reduce stock market values by 5.5%. These effects are driven by shifts in US monetary policy expectations, as higher inflation prompts investors to revise down the anticipated number of interest rate cuts by the Federal Reserve. Conversely, a deeper-than-expected cooling of the US economy would lead investors to expect more rate cuts, substantially easing global financial conditions. The analysis underscores that maintaining economic resilience can help economies reduce spillovers from external developments.

Albert F. Park
Chief Economist
Asian Development Bank

Solid Growth as Inflation Eases, Yet Risks Loom

- **Developing Asia maintained robust economic growth during the first half of 2024, despite sluggish domestic consumption in the People's Republic of China (PRC).** Strong global demand for electronics continued to support the region's exports, but growth patterns differed. In the PRC, protracted property sector weakness weighed on consumer sentiment and household spending, awlthough higher investment supported by monetary and fiscal stimulus partially offset it. Meanwhile, India's expansion slowed in the first half of 2024 but remained solid on the back of strong domestic demand, confirming South Asia's position as the fastest-growing subregion. Economic activity in most high-income technology exporters also expanded solidly. Association of Southeast Asian Nation economies remained resilient, supported by higher consumption and investment and improvements in net exports.

- **Inflation continued to retreat across developing Asia, but the disinflation process remains uneven.** Price pressures continue to moderate on the lagged effects of monetary tightening and falling global commodity prices. Energy inflation returned to pre-pandemic levels, while food inflation remains slightly elevated relative to its pre-pandemic level, albeit also on a declining trend. Better harvests and crop production helped to significantly reduce food prices in India, but weather disruptions in the PRC pushed food prices into positive territory for the first time in more than a year. Core inflation in the region has now eased to below pre-pandemic levels.

- **Exports from developing Asia continue to increase steadily, led by high-income technology exporters.** Goods exports have regained momentum, recovering from a 3% contraction in March to 8% growth in July. High-income technology exporters and the PRC drove the rebound. Goods exports from the rest of developing Asia are also growing, albeit more moderately. Services export growth has remained steady and is primarily underpinned by tourism.

- **Global demand for electronics has supported export growth in the region, but non-electronics exports have also been expanding.** High-income technology exporters continue to benefit from the upturn in the global semiconductor cycle, driven by surging investment in artificial intelligence. Electronics exports also increased in the Philippines and, to a lesser extent, in Thailand, which are involved in lower value-added segments such as assembly, testing, and packaging. Exports of non-electronic goods remained mostly robust, although low mineral prices held back export revenues in some commodity exporters. Exports of cars and ships were key contributors to export growth in the PRC and the Republic of Korea. Mongolia's exports of coal soared on higher demand from the PRC but falling commodity prices have reduced the export value of various commodities from Indonesia, India, Malaysia, and Georgia.

- **Regional financial markets remain resilient, with currencies holding steady.** The Chicago Board Options Exchange's Volatility Index, which measures the expected volatility of the United States (US) stock market and proxies global risk aversion, spiked sharply in early August to its highest level since June 2020. Driven by investor concerns about US growth prospects and weaker-than-expected earnings by major global technology firms, a broad sell-off out of risky assets also affected Asian markets. But financial markets quickly regained lost ground. Apart from this brief period of elevated volatility, equity markets in the region rallied throughout the year, risk premiums narrowed, and net portfolio inflows increased, supported by anticipated easing of monetary policy in the US, which eventually materialized in September. Meanwhile, Asian currencies held roughly steady, experiencing marginal depreciations against the US dollar.

- **The 2024 growth outlook for major advanced economies is revised slightly upward to 1.5% on faster-than-expected US growth.** Stronger-than-expected private consumption and investment in the first half despite tight monetary policy conditions underpins the upward revision to 2024 US growth. Meanwhile, higher consumption and investment in green and digital infrastructure will support growth in the euro area. In Japan, the growth forecast is marginally lowered in 2024 as high inflation has weighed on consumption. The growth forecast for 2025 is retained for most of these economies. Among commodities, oil prices are expected to remain broadly stable and rice prices to decline from current elevated levels.

- **Developing Asia's 2024 growth forecast is raised slightly to 5.0% from 4.9% in April 2024 and maintained at 4.9% for 2025.** In East Asia, growth is revised to 4.6% from 4.5% due to higher-than-expected external demand for semiconductors from the Republic of Korea and Taipei,China. The outlook in the Caucasus and Central Asia is also a better-than-expected 4.7% on stronger domestic demand, bolstered by remittances in some economies. The growth forecast for the Pacific is revised upward to 3.4%, driven by the increase in tourist arrivals. In South Asia, the growth outlook is unchanged at 6.3% for 2024 on solid growth in India, while a decline in public investments and slower-than-expected export recovery imply a slight downward revision to growth in Southeast Asia.

- **The inflation forecast for the region is revised down to 2.8% for 2024 and 2.9% for 2025.** In the PRC, domestic demand has been weaker than expected and food prices have bottomed out more slowly than expected, underpinning the downward revision for 2024. The inflation forecast for the Caucasus and Central Asia is also lowered, as currencies have appreciated and with the lagged impact of previous monetary tightening. The inflation outlook in the Pacific is also revised downward on weaker-than-expected inflation in the first half of 2024. South Asia's inflation projection is unchanged in 2024 but has been revised upward in 2025 due to supply disruptions in Bangladesh. Currency depreciation in the Lao People's Democratic Republic and Myanmar contributed to an upward revision to Southeast Asia's inflation forecast.

- **Lower inflation is creating conditions for eventual monetary policy easing.** With inflation running below or close to target in most of the inflation-targeting economies, some central banks are easing policy rates to support economic activity. This is mostly taking place in the Caucasus and Central Asia, where interest rates have been high. Elsewhere in the region, continued progress on disinflation is creating space for reducing rates. Economies with negative or low interest rate differentials relative to the US have held rates steady during the year given depreciation concerns. However, downward pressure on US yields and the US dollar during August, on elevated expectations of US monetary policy easing at that time, contributed to appreciation of many Asian currencies and created greater scope for lowering rates. Further room is anticipated given the 50 basis point rate cut by the Federal Reserve in September, marking the start of its easing cycle.

- **Fiscal deficits in the region are narrowing, but vulnerabilities remain.** Improvements in fiscal balances have materialized for most economies facing large fiscal deficits. While robust growth is set to drive the regional average government debt-to-GDP ratio to 47% this year, after peaking at 50% in 2020, pockets of vulnerability remain. Some economies are facing a combination of elevated public debt and high shares of interest payments relative to fiscal revenues, including Pakistan and Sri Lanka. This will challenge their capacity for productive public spending and investment.

- **Depending on the outcome of the US presidential election, an increase in protectionism and trade fragmentation could materialize.** The election could result in higher blanket tariffs by the US on all global imports, and a broad-based and steep increase in tariffs on all US imports from the PRC. This would significantly escalate US-PRC trade tensions, with potential negative spillovers to developing Asia through real and financial channels.

- **Escalating geopolitical tensions due to wider conflict in the Middle East and Russia's war in Ukraine remain concerning.** A wider conflict in the Middle East, in particular, could further disrupt shipping routes or draw in major oil producers. This could raise oil prices and thus, potentially, the prices of other commodities, including metals. Amplified geopolitical tensions more broadly could trigger negative spillovers to investor and consumer sentiment and worsen the outlook.

- **Growth prospects in the PRC could be weakened by further deterioration in its property market.** The current downturn in the property market could become more severe or more disorderly, negatively impacting overall economic activity. This could be compounded by indirect effects through a worsening of consumer and investor sentiment, as well as its implications for local government revenues. The rest of the region could also be affected through several channels, including on the real side via lower PRC demand for imports.

- **Adverse weather conditions and the impacts of climate change could undermine food and energy security and lead to volatile commodity prices.** The US National Oceanic and Atmospheric Administration's Climate Prediction Center currently estimates a 70% likelihood of La Niña developing during the third quarter (Q) of 2024, persisting into Q1 2025. La Niña could bring higher precipitation to the region, especially in South and Southeast Asia, and a good amount of rainfall can boost production in rice and palm-oil producing economies and increase water resources. However, too much rainfall can also increase the risk of flooding and landslides and damage agriculture and livelihoods.

Letting the Data Speak: Global Spillovers from Data-Dependent Federal Reserve Monetary Policy

- **This chapter examines how data-driven US monetary policy affects international financial markets, introducing a novel methodological approach.** The pace of the ongoing US Federal Reserve (Fed) easing cycle remains uncertain and dependent on incoming data. While it is well recognized that the Fed's decisions are highly data-dependent, the effects of data-driven US monetary policy changes remain unexplored. Traditionally, research has focused on market reactions to Fed meetings, but this chapter shows that significant market effects occur around key data releases, as investors anticipate their influence on Fed policy. The chapter investigates the reaction of key financial variables—such as government bond yields, exchange rates, stock market prices, and default probabilities—across a large sample of 108 economies. The analysis specifically targets the spillover effects that arise around the time of US data releases, particularly those related to inflation and employment.

- **The analysis relies on newly constructed measures to gauge the Fed's data dependency and attentiveness to inflation and employment data.** These measures show that the degree of Fed data dependency and its relative attentiveness to inflation and employment data fluctuate significantly over time. Periods of low interest rates, such as those following the global financial crisis and during the COVID-19 pandemic, were characterized by lower data dependency, while the post-pandemic period saw heightened Fed data dependency. Attentiveness to inflation data rises when inflation is more distant from the Fed's 2% target, while attentiveness to employment increases the further unemployment is from its natural rate. Recognizing these patterns, the empirical analysis accounts for fluctuations in data dependency and relative attentiveness to inflation and employment data to properly identify data-driven changes in expectations about future Fed policy at the time of data releases.

- **Results indicate that inflation-driven Fed policy changes affect debt, currency, and equity markets in other economies.** When the Fed is highly attentive to inflation data, as it was in the first half of 2024, a 1-standard deviation inflation surprise—where inflation is 0.1 percentage points higher than expected—causes foreign short-term government bond yields to increase 2 basis points, currencies to depreciate 0.1% vis-à-vis the US dollar, stock markets to decline 0.2%, and government default probabilities to increase 0.1 percentage points, on average. A negative inflation surprise of the same magnitude produces effects that mirror these outcomes.

- **Employment-driven Fed policy changes primarily affect debt and currency markets, with limited effects on equity markets.** When the Fed is highly attentive to employment data, a 1-standard-deviation employment surprise—equivalent to the release of the nonfarm payroll job creation data being 100,000 higher than expected—causes currencies to depreciate 0.2% against the US dollar, and short-term and long-term bond yields to increase about 4 basis points. Effects on stock markets and default probabilities are not statistically significant.

■ **Using the estimated coefficients, the chapter explores the potential impact of a scenario in which inflation gradually rises from its current level of 2.5% to 2.9% by the end of 2024.** Investors currently expect inflation to remain at 2.5% through the end of 2024, which has led to expectations of significant Fed rate cuts in 2024–2025. However, if inflation gradually climbs back to its July 2024 level of 2.9%, investors would likely revise their expectations, reducing the anticipated rate cuts by more than 150 basis points. As a result, short-term bond yields in foreign markets could rise 70 basis points, currencies could depreciate nearly 4% against the US dollar, stock markets could decline 5.5%, and default probabilities could increase 3.3 percentage points.

■ **A scenario where the US economy cools more than currently anticipated would lead to a substantial easing of financial conditions.** Specifically, the chapter considers the effects of US inflation dropping to 2.1%—lower than the expected 2.5%—by the end of 2024, coupled with stagnant net employment creation for the remainder of the year, as opposed to the +129,000 monthly net job gains expected by investors. If this scenario materializes, short- and long-term foreign bond yields could decrease approximately 95 and 30 basis points, respectively. It could also lead to a 4.5% appreciation of currencies against the US dollar, a 5% rise in stock markets, and a reduction in government default probabilities of nearly 3 percentage points.

■ **An economy's macroeconomic conditions can amplify or mitigate spillovers from data-driven US monetary policy.** The analysis finds that larger external debts, higher inflation, and weaker current account and fiscal balances amplify the effects of data-driven US monetary policy. To give a concrete example, the empirical estimates suggest that in a scenario where US inflation were to unexpectedly rise to 2.9% by the end of 2024, an economy in the bottom quartile of current account performance could see its short- and long-term bond yields increase about 70 basis points more than an economy in the top quartile. This suggests that policymakers who can maintain macroeconomic stability and sound fiscal management can buffer their economies from the adverse effects of shifts in US monetary policy, particularly in times of high Fed data dependency.

Gross Domestic Product Growth Rate, % per year

	2023	2024		2025	
		April	September	April	September
Developing Asia	**5.1**	**4.9**	**5.0**	**4.9**	**4.9**
Developing Asia excluding the PRC	**5.1**	**5.0**	**5.1**	**5.3**	**5.2**
Caucasus and Central Asia	**5.3**	**4.3**	**4.7**	**5.0**	**5.2**
Armenia	8.3	5.7	6.0	6.0	6.0
Azerbaijan	1.1	1.2	2.7	1.6	2.6
Georgia	7.5	5.0	7.0	5.5	5.5
Kazakhstan	5.1	3.8	3.6	5.3	5.1
Kyrgyz Republic	6.2	5.0	6.3	4.5	5.8
Tajikistan	8.3	6.5	6.5	6.5	6.5
Turkmenistan	6.3	6.5	6.5	6.0	6.0
Uzbekistan	6.0	5.5	6.0	5.6	6.2
East Asia	**4.7**	**4.5**	**4.6**	**4.2**	**4.2**
People's Republic of China	5.2	4.8	4.8	4.5	4.5
Hong Kong, China	3.3	2.8	2.8	3.0	3.0
Republic of Korea	1.4	2.2	2.5	2.3	2.3
Mongolia	7.4	4.1	5.5	6.0	6.0
Taipei,China	1.3	3.0	3.5	2.7	2.7
South Asia	**6.8**	**6.3**	**6.3**	**6.6**	**6.5**
Afghanistan	−6.2	...	...	...	...
Bangladesh	5.8	6.1	5.8	6.6	5.1
Bhutan	4.0	4.4	5.5	7.0	7.0
India	8.2	7.0	7.0	7.2	7.2
Maldives	4.1	5.4	5.0	6.0	5.4
Nepal	2.0	3.6	3.9	4.8	4.9
Pakistan	−0.2	1.9	2.4	2.8	2.8
Sri Lanka	−2.3	1.9	2.6	2.5	2.8
Southeast Asia	**4.1**	**4.6**	**4.5**	**4.7**	**4.7**
Brunei Darussalam	1.4	3.7	3.7	2.8	2.8
Cambodia	5.0	5.8	5.8	6.0	6.0
Indonesia	5.0	5.0	5.0	5.0	5.0
Lao People's Democratic Republic	3.7	4.0	4.0	4.0	3.7
Malaysia	3.6	4.5	4.5	4.6	4.6
Myanmar	0.8	1.2	0.8	2.2	1.7
Philippines	5.5	6.0	6.0	6.2	6.2
Singapore	1.1	2.4	2.6	2.6	2.6
Thailand	1.9	2.6	2.3	3.0	2.7
Timor-Leste	1.9	3.4	3.1	4.1	3.9
Viet Nam	5.1	6.0	6.0	6.2	6.2
The Pacific	**3.4**	**3.3**	**3.4**	**4.0**	**4.1**
Cook Islands	14.0	9.1	15.0	5.2	7.5
Fiji	7.5	3.0	3.4	2.7	2.9
Kiribati	4.2	5.3	5.8	3.5	4.1
Marshall Islands	−0.6	2.7	2.0	1.7	3.0
Federated States of Micronesia	0.8	3.1	3.1	2.8	3.5
Nauru	1.6	1.8	2.0	2.0	2.5
Niue	...	...	...	...	...
Palau	−0.2	6.5	6.5	8.0	8.0
Papua New Guinea	2.0	3.3	3.2	4.6	4.5
Samoa	8.0	4.2	11.0	4.0	8.0
Solomon Islands	3.0	2.2	2.5	2.2	2.5
Tonga	2.2	2.6	2.0	2.3	2.3
Tuvalu	3.9	3.5	3.5	2.4	2.4
Vanuatu	1.0	3.1	1.9	3.6	2.4

... = not available, ADB = Asian Development Bank, PRC = People's Republic of China.

Notes: The current uncertain situation permits no forecasts for Afghanistan over 2024–2025. ADB placed on hold its regular assistance to Afghanistan effective 15 August 2021. Effective 1 February 2021, ADB placed a temporary hold on sovereign project disbursements and new contracts in Myanmar.

Source: *Asian Development Outlook* database (accessed 5 September 2024).

Inflation, % per year

	2023	2024		2025	
		April	September	April	September
Developing Asia	**3.4**	**3.2**	**2.8**	**3.0**	**2.9**
Developing Asia excluding the PRC	**6.3**	**5.1**	**5.1**	**4.4**	**4.5**
Caucasus and Central Asia	**10.5**	**7.9**	**6.9**	**7.0**	**6.2**
Armenia	2.0	3.0	0.8	3.5	2.5
Azerbaijan	8.8	5.5	2.1	6.5	3.8
Georgia	2.5	3.5	2.5	4.0	3.5
Kazakhstan	14.5	8.7	8.5	6.3	6.1
Kyrgyz Republic	10.8	7.0	6.8	6.5	6.2
Tajikistan	3.8	5.5	5.5	6.5	6.5
Turkmenistan	5.9	8.0	5.0	8.0	5.0
Uzbekistan	10.0	10.0	9.5	9.5	9.0
East Asia	**0.6**	**1.3**	**0.8**	**1.6**	**1.3**
People's Republic of China	0.2	1.1	0.5	1.5	1.2
Hong Kong, China	2.1	2.3	1.8	2.3	2.3
Republic of Korea	3.6	2.5	2.5	2.0	2.0
Mongolia	10.4	7.0	6.8	6.8	7.2
Taipei,China	2.5	2.3	2.3	2.0	2.0
South Asia	**8.4**	**7.0**	**7.0**	**5.8**	**6.1**
Afghanistan	10.8	...	...	...	...
Bangladesh	9.0	8.4	9.7	7.0	10.1
Bhutan	4.2	4.5	4.6	4.2	4.2
India	5.4	4.6	4.7	4.5	4.5
Maldives	2.9	3.2	2.8	2.5	2.3
Nepal	7.7	6.5	5.4	6.0	5.5
Pakistan	29.2	25.0	23.4	15.0	15.0
Sri Lanka	17.4	7.5	3.8	5.5	5.5
Southeast Asia	**4.2**	**3.2**	**3.3**	**3.0**	**3.2**
Brunei Darussalam	0.4	1.1	0.4	1.0	1.0
Cambodia	2.1	2.0	0.5	2.0	2.5
Indonesia	3.7	2.8	2.8	2.8	2.8
Lao People's Democratic Republic	31.2	20.0	25.0	7.0	21.5
Malaysia	2.5	2.6	2.4	2.6	2.7
Myanmar	27.0	15.5	20.7	10.2	15.0
Philippines	6.0	3.8	3.6	3.4	3.2
Singapore	4.8	3.0	2.6	2.2	2.2
Thailand	1.2	1.0	0.7	1.5	1.3
Timor-Leste	8.4	3.5	3.4	2.9	2.9
Viet Nam	3.3	4.0	4.0	4.0	4.0
The Pacific	**3.0**	**4.3**	**3.6**	**4.1**	**4.1**
Cook Islands	13.2	2.3	4.5	2.3	4.0
Fiji	2.4	3.7	5.0	2.6	2.6
Kiribati	9.3	4.0	4.5	3.0	3.0
Marshall Islands	7.3	5.5	5.8	3.7	4.6
Federated States of Micronesia	6.2	4.1	4.1	3.5	3.5
Nauru	5.2	10.3	5.0	3.5	3.5
Niue	8.6	...	...	...	...
Palau	12.4	5.5	5.5	1.0	1.0
Papua New Guinea	2.3	4.5	3.0	4.8	4.8
Samoa	12.0	4.5	3.6	4.3	3.2
Solomon Islands	5.1	3.2	3.2	2.7	2.7
Tonga	9.7	4.5	4.6	4.2	4.2
Tuvalu	7.2	3.0	2.5	3.0	3.0
Vanuatu	11.2	4.8	4.8	2.9	2.9

... = not available, ADB = Asian Development Bank, PRC = People's Republic of China.

Notes: The current uncertain situation permits no forecasts for Afghanistan over 2024–2025. ADB placed on hold its regular assistance to Afghanistan effective 15 August 2021. Effective 1 February 2021, ADB placed a temporary hold on sovereign project disbursements and new contracts in Myanmar.

Source: *Asian Development Outlook* database (accessed 5 September 2024).

1

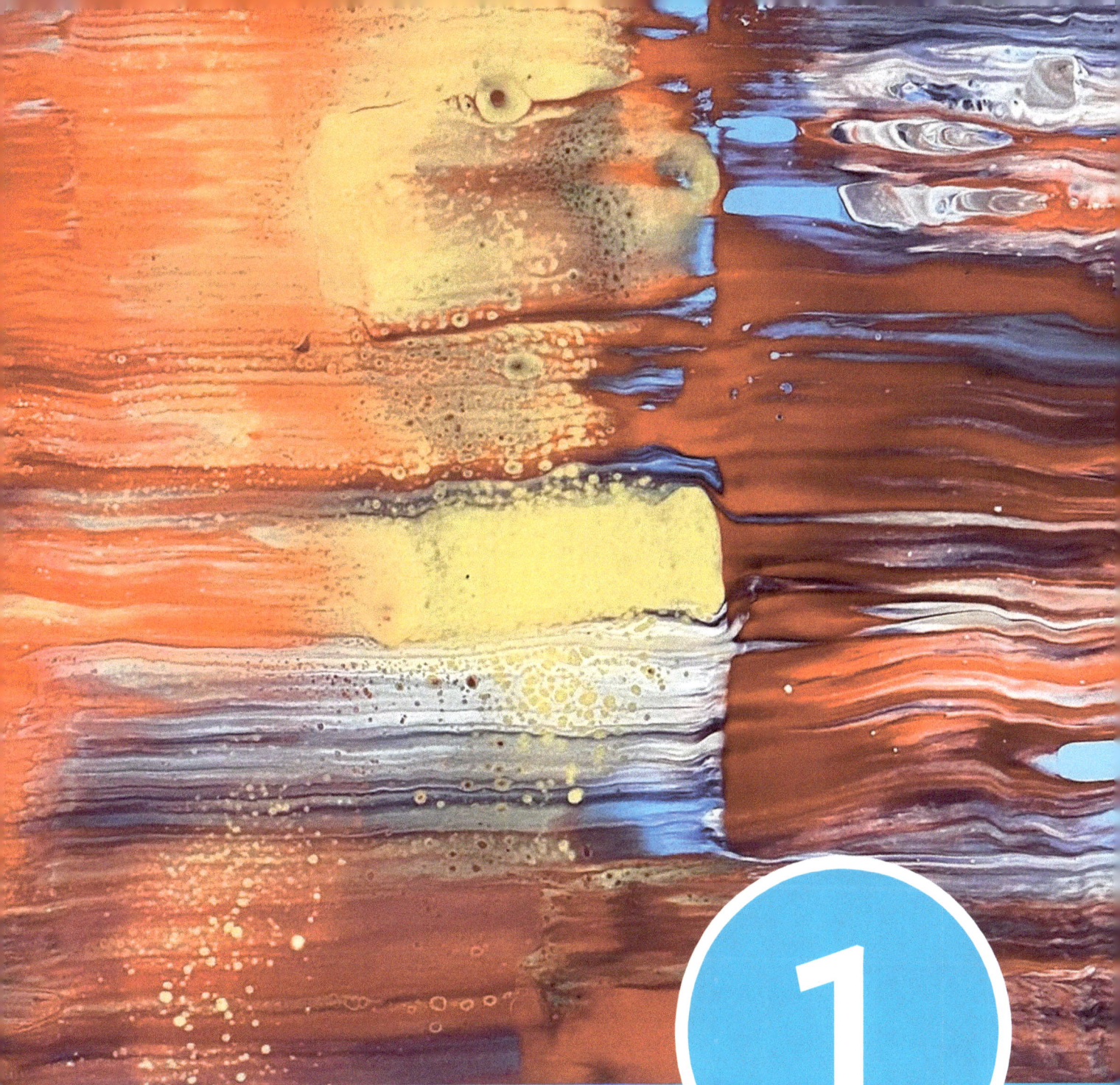

SOLID GROWTH
AS INFLATION EASES,
YET RISKS LOOM

SOLID GROWTH AS INFLATION EASES, YET RISKS LOOM

Growth in developing Asia remained strong during the first half of 2024, supported by domestic demand and continued recovery in exports. *High-income technology exporters benefited from rising global semiconductor sales driven by strong demand for artificial intelligence products. Regional financial markets remained resilient amid episodes of global volatility. Meanwhile, inflation continued to decline, driven by the lagged effects of tight monetary policy and easing global food prices. This creates the conditions for more central banks in the region to lower policy rates to support economic activity.*

The growth outlook for developing Asia has been revised slightly upward to 5.0% for 2024 from 4.9% in April. *This reflects stronger-than-expected growth in East Asia, the Caucasus and Central Asia, and the Pacific. The 2025 growth projection remains at 4.9%. Inflation in the region is forecast at 2.8% for 2024, down from 3.2% in April, due to currency appreciation in the Caucasus and Central Asia and slower-than-expected bottoming out of food prices in the People's Republic of China (PRC). The inflation forecast for 2025 is revised down marginally to 2.9%, compared to 3.0% in April.*

Downside risks persist. *Rising protectionism, depending on the outcome of the presidential election in the United States, could lead to negative real and financial spillovers in developing Asia. Other risks to the outlook relate to escalating geopolitical tensions, a deterioration in the PRC's property market, and adverse weather conditions.*

This section was written by Abdul Abiad, John Beirne (lead), Shiela Camingue-Romance, David Keith De Padua, Jaqueson K. Galimberti, Jules Hugot, Matteo Lanzafame (colead), Nedelyn Magtibay-Ramos, Madhavi Pundit, Melanie Grace Quintos, Pilipinas Quising, and Mai Lin Villaruel of the Economic Research and Development Impact Department, ADB, Manila.

Growth Momentum Continued on Stronger Exports

Developing Asia's growth momentum remained robust overall during the first half of 2024, despite sluggish domestic consumption in the People's Republic of China (PRC) (Figure 1.1.1, panel A). Robust global demand for electronics continued to support exports in the region. In the PRC, growth remained strong, despite deceleration in domestic consumption during the first half (H1) of 2024. Lingering weakness in the property sector, which affected consumer sentiment, retail sales, and household spending, was partially offset by higher investment, supported by stimulatory monetary and fiscal policies. India's gross domestic product (GDP) expanded 7.2% in H1 2024, due in part to a surge in government spending and private consumption. Though slower compared to H2 2023, India's expansion remained solid, reaffirming South Asia as the fastest-growing subregion. Economic activity in high-income technology-exporting economies also expanded solidly, except for Hong Kong, China, where overall activity declined in the first half even as net exports surged. Exports also accounted for a substantial share of H1 2024 growth in the Republic of Korea. In Taipei,China, firms raised their capital outlay plans on solid export momentum. Large Association of Southeast Asian Nation (ASEAN) economies remained resilient, supported by strong private consumption and investment, particularly in electronics and automobile-related sectors, and public infrastructure projects. Growth expanded rapidly in Malaysia as net exports became less negative, while growth in H1 2024 in Indonesia held steady as lower investment was balanced by election-related boosts to consumption.

Industrial activity remained robust in H1 2024, due to solid expansion in the PRC and other technology exporters, while services improved significantly in many economies. In the PRC, the manufacturing sector posted solid growth—particularly high-tech products, new-energy vehicles, and electronics—supported by increased production capacities and targeted government policy support (Figure 1.1.1, panel B). Meanwhile, industrial growth in India slowed somewhat, as rising input prices reduced margins in the manufacturing sector, offsetting gains in mining and construction. Industrial performance in ASEAN-4 (Indonesia, Malaysia, the Philippines, and Thailand) economies was likewise robust, with Malaysia and the Philippines benefiting from substantial gains in machinery, metallic products, and electronics, along with increased construction activity. Meanwhile, Thailand's industrial sector, which had been hampered by persistent challenges in automobile production, returned to growth in H1 2024 owing to solid increases in mining and electricity and gas. Industrial growth was solid in the Republic of Korea and Taipei,China as well, while in Singapore, industry was mostly negative in the first half because of weakness in the biomedical manufacturing and precision engineering sectors. These trends are mirrored in industrial production growth figures, with Thailand and Singapore in negative territory through June (Figure 1.1.2). Meanwhile, services growth remained strong overall in the first half of 2024 compared to the second half of 2023, as increased domestic activity continued to boost finance, information and technology, retail, and tourism-related sectors. Services in Singapore increased the most in H1 2024, largely due to a concert-driven boost to retail and tourism sectors in the first quarter (Q1) 2024.

Purchasing managers' indexes (PMI) remained in expansion territory for most regional economies. Most economies recorded PMI readings above 50 in August 2024, with 3 experiencing solid manufacturing expansion for 8 straight months since January 2024 (Table 1.1.1). In Indonesia and the PRC, the index dropped to below 50 in July, while in Malaysia it stayed below the threshold during most of the year. Figure 1.1.3 shows the distance of Standard and Poor's (S&P) PMI, a survey-based indicator of business conditions, from the 50 threshold and the weighted contribution to overall distance of

Figure 1.1.1 Contributions to Gross Domestic Product Growth

A. Demand-Side

Developing Asia's growth remained strong in H1 2024.

Legend:
- Total consumption
- Total investment
- Net exports
- ○ Gross domestic product growth, %

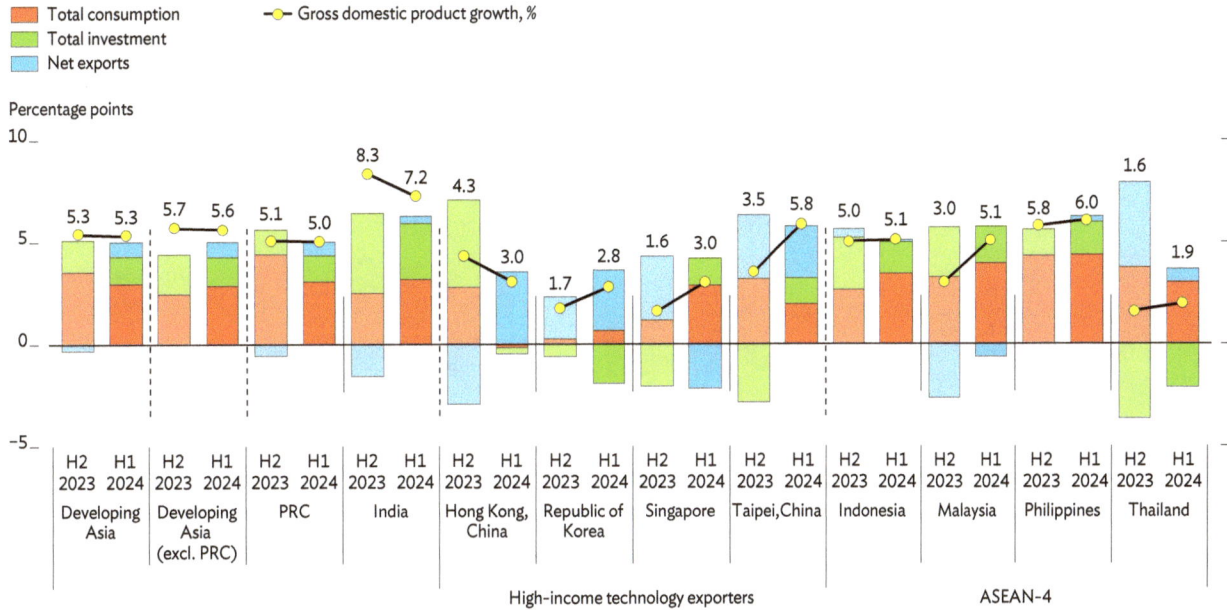

B. Supply-Side

Industrial activity generally improved on manufacturing gains across economies.

Legend:
- Agriculture
- Industry
- Services
- ○ Gross domestic product growth, %

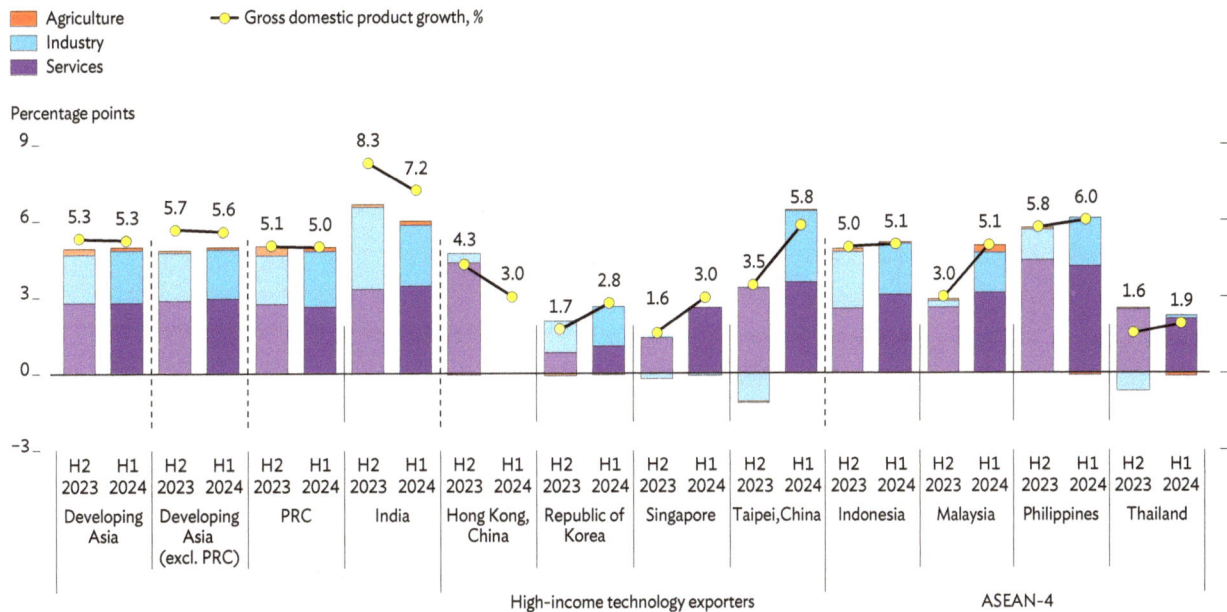

ASEAN = Association of Southeast Asian Nations, GDP = gross domestic product, H = half-year, PRC = People's Republic of China.

Notes: Economies included are those that have quarterly GDP figures with demand-side breakdown, which account for about 90% of developing Asia. Components do not add up to total due to statistical discrepancy and the chain-linking method of GDP estimation and reporting. The regional average is calculated using GDP purchasing power parity shares as weights. All data are in calendar years and in non-seasonally adjusted terms. High-income technology exporters include Hong Kong, China; Republic of Korea; Singapore; and Taipei,China. ASEAN-4 includes Indonesia, Malaysia, Philippines, and Thailand.

Source: Haver Analytics; CEIC Data Company.

Figure 1.1.2 Industrial Production Index, Selected Economies

Industrial production picked up in many economies, moderated in some due to weaker performance in some sectors.

A. High-Income Technology Exporters

— Republic of Korea   — Taipei,China
— Singapore

% change year on year, seasonally adjusted, 3-month moving average

B. South and Southeast Asia

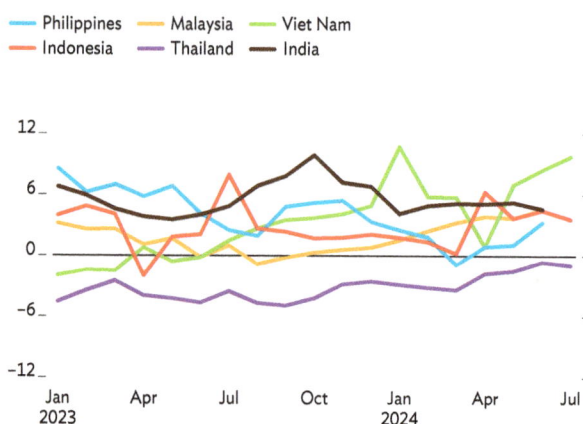

— Philippines   — Malaysia   — Viet Nam
— Indonesia   — Thailand   — India

Source: CEIC Data Company.

Table 1.1.1 Purchasing Managers' Index, Selected Asian Economies

Manufacturing PMIs generally improved through June, reflecting better operating conditions, but reversed by July in some economies, while services PMI remained robust, except in the Philippines.

Manufacturing PMI, seasonally adjusted

	2023					2024							
	Q3		Q4			Q1			Q2			Q3	
Economy	Aug	Sep	Oct	Nov	Dec	Jan	Feb	Mar	Apr	May	Jun	Jul	Aug
India	58.6	57.5	55.5	56.0	54.9	56.5	56.9	59.1	58.8	57.5	58.3	58.1	57.5
Viet Nam	50.5	49.7	49.6	47.3	48.9	50.3	50.4	49.9	50.3	50.3	54.7	54.7	52.4
Thailand	48.9	47.8	47.5	47.6	45.1	46.7	45.3	49.1	48.6	50.3	51.7	52.8	52.0
Republic of Korea	48.9	49.9	49.8	50.0	49.9	51.2	50.7	49.8	49.4	51.6	52.0	51.4	51.9
Taipei,China	44.3	46.4	47.6	48.3	47.1	48.8	48.6	49.3	50.2	50.9	53.2	52.9	51.5
Philippines	49.7	50.6	52.4	52.7	51.5	50.9	51.0	50.9	52.2	51.9	51.3	51.2	51.2
Singapore	49.9	50.1	50.2	50.3	50.5	50.7	50.6	50.7	50.5	50.6	50.4	50.7	50.9
PRC	51.0	50.6	49.5	50.7	50.8	50.8	50.9	51.1	51.4	51.7	51.8	49.8	50.4
Malaysia	47.8	46.8	46.8	47.9	47.9	49.0	49.5	48.4	49.0	50.2	49.9	49.7	49.7
Indonesia	53.9	52.3	51.5	51.7	52.2	52.9	52.7	54.2	52.9	52.1	50.7	49.3	48.9

Services PMI, seasonally adjusted

Economy	Aug	Sep	Oct	Nov	Dec	Jan	Feb	Mar	Apr	May	Jun	Jul	Aug
India	60.1	61.0	58.4	56.9	59.0	61.8	60.6	61.2	60.8	60.2	60.5	60.3	60.4
PRC	51.8	50.2	50.4	51.5	52.9	52.7	52.5	52.7	52.5	54.0	51.2	52.1	...
Sri Lanka	57.6	54.7	56.2	59.4	58.9	60.1	53.0	67.7	56.7	55.0	63.5	71.1	...
Philippines	53.0	53.2	50.1	50.0	56.2	52.0	50.9	51.8	55.8	54.6	54.0	47.4	...

... = not available, PMI = purchasing managers' index, PRC = People's Republic of China, Q = quarter.

Notes: Pink to red indicates deterioration (< 50) and white to green indicates improvement (> 50). Series for the Philippines, Singapore, and Sri Lanka are not seasonally adjusted.

Source: CEIC Data Company; Philippine Institute for Supply Management; Singapore Institute of Purchasing and Materials Management.

Figure 1.1.3 S&P Manufacturing PMI, by Components, Selected Developing Asia

PRC's Caixin General Manufacturing PMI returned to above 50 in August, after falling below that threshold in July, while momentum continued in India, high-technology exporting economies, and ASEAN-5.

- New orders index
- Employment index
- Stocks of purchases index
- Output index
- Suppliers' delivery times index
- ◆ Headline PMI

A. People's Republic of China

Distance from the
50-point threshold

B. India

Distance from the
50-point threshold

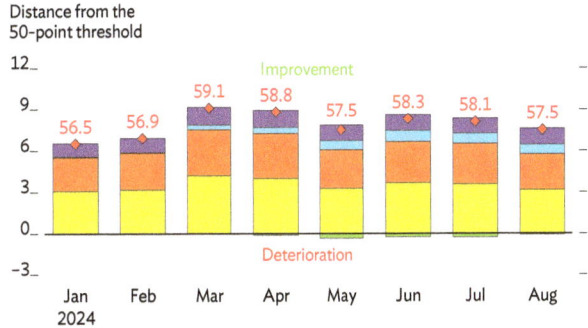

C. High-Income Technology Exporters

Distance from the
50-point threshold

D. ASEAN-5

Distance from the
50-point threshold

ASEAN = Association of Southeast Asian Nations; ASEAN-5 = Indonesia, Malaysia, Philippines, Singapore, and Thailand; PMI = purchasing managers' index; S&P = Standard & Poor's.

Notes: Distance from threshold is calculated as the PMI Index or subindex minus 50, while the contributions are the distance multiplied by weight. Positive distance or readings above 50 indicate improvement, while negative distance or readings below 50 indicate deterioration. The series for Hong Kong, China; and Singapore refers to the whole economy. ASEAN-5 is the weighted average PMI for Indonesia, Malaysia, the Philippines, Thailand, and Viet Nam. High Income Technology Exporters (HITE) is the weighted average PMI for Hong Kong, China; the Republic of Korea; Singapore; and Taipei,China.

Source: CEIC Data Company.

different components. This provides a more refined breakdown of changes in the PMI. PRC's Caixin General Manufacturing PMI dropped from 51.8 in June to 49.8 in July, its first decline in 9 months, due to weaker manufacturing output (orange bar) and reduced new orders (yellow bar). Although this covers only smaller private businesses and exporters, the reading aligns with National Bureau of Statistics (NBS) Manufacturing PMI, which covers a broader range of enterprises, such as state-owned enterprises and larger companies. While the Caixin PMI returned to above 50

in August, NBS manufacturing PMI still lingered below 50 as seasonal factors, lower orders, and challenges in the real estate sector continued to weigh on production activities of a wider range of manufacturers. In Indonesia and Malaysia, sluggish demand was the principal factor pushing firms to scale down production. Conversely, India's PMI declined slightly in August, from 58.1 in July, but remained above 50 indicating continued growth. August PMI also dropped fractionally in high-income technology exporters, Thailand, and Viet Nam, but remained above 50, on softer upticks in new orders, output, and improved suppliers' delivery times (green bar), which has turned positive since April 2024. Services PMI in the PRC and India remained strong, driven by higher demand for services such as travel and recreation and supported by solid economic growth and easing inflation, while in the Philippines, it slid below 50 in July as poor weather conditions affected services operations in many areas.

Inflation continued to retreat across developing Asia (Figure 1.1.4). Headline inflation in January to July 2024 for the region, including and excluding PRC, continued to decline toward pre-pandemic levels (Figure 1.1.4, panel B), driven by the impact of past monetary tightening and easing global commodity price pressures. Energy inflation is now back at pre-pandemic levels, while food inflation is still slightly elevated relative to its pre-pandemic level, albeit also on a declining trend. Crude oil prices averaged around $83 per barrel in the 8 months to August 2024 and were broadly stable, apart from episodes of volatility.

Meanwhile, rice prices remained elevated, despite decreasing by 12% from the 16-year peak of $669 per metric ton during the last week of January to $589 on 22 August 2024. Core inflation in the region, including and excluding the PRC, continued to ease on the back of lower prices of retail goods and services and is now lower than the pre-pandemic average. On the other hand, increased shipping volumes and congestion at the Mediterranean and Asian ports, related to the lingering conflict in the Red Sea, have amplified shipping costs and delays. These developments, however, have not significantly affected inflation in the region (Box 1.1.1).

The disinflation process, however, has been uneven (Figure 1.1.5). By subregion, inflation in the Caucasus and Central Asia, and South Asia declined faster in January to July 2024 but that was offset by increases in the rest of the region, due largely to upward pressure from food prices. In South Asia, improved harvests and crop production contributed

Figure 1.1.4 Contributions to Inflation, Developing Asia

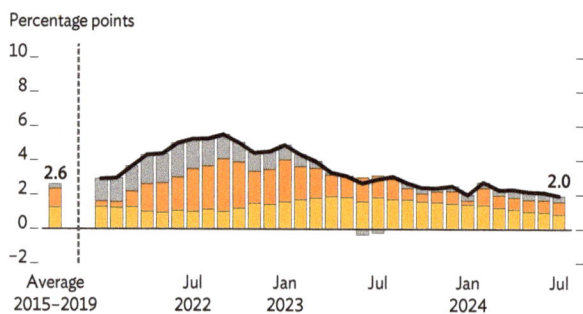

Inflation in Asia continues to retreat towards pre-pandemic levels.

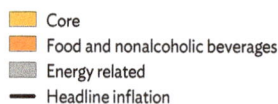

- ▢ Core
- ▢ Food and nonalcoholic beverages
- ▢ Energy related
- ▬ Headline inflation

A. Developing Asia

B. Developing Asia Excluding the People's Republic of China

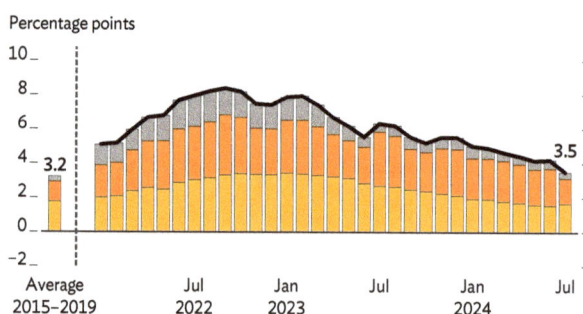

Notes: Core inflation excludes food and energy sectors. For some economies, core is estimated as the residual between overall inflation and the sum of food and non-alcoholic beverages and energy-related items. For lack of a more disaggregated breakdown, energy-related consumer prices for most economies include housing, water, and nonfuel transport. Regional averages are calculated using gross domestic product purchasing power parity shares as weights, and includes data for 22 economies. Data are as of July 2024.

Sources: Asian Development Bank estimates using data from Haver Analytics; CEIC Data Company; official sources.

Box 1.1.1 Shipping Rates Have Surged Again, But Inflation Is Unlikely to Follow Suit

Shipping costs have been on the rise again in recent months. Since January 2024, global shipping has been under pressure due to the conflict in the Red Sea. This has forced ships to avoid the Suez Canal and the Bab El-Mandeb Strait and instead navigate around the Cape of Good Hope, increasing travel times and freight costs significantly. Meanwhile, lower water levels in the Panama Canal, which reduced the number of vessels allowed to pass through (see Box 1.1.2), also added upward pressure to shipping costs. A temporary increase in demand may be playing a role as well. With the outcome of the US presidential election uncertain through early November, it is possible that shipments are being brought forward to lock in supplies as a precaution against renewed United States–People's Republic of China (US–PRC) trade frictions and higher tariffs.

As a result of these supply and demand factors, the Drewry's World Container Index, which tracks freight rates on eight major trade routes, rose from less than $1,700 per 40-foot equivalent unit at end-2023 to above $5,800 in July 2024 (box figure 1). While substantial, this increase is still smaller than the increase in shipping costs experienced during the pandemic, when they rose from $1,600 in May 2020 to a high of $10,100 in October 2021, and remained above $9,000 until March 2022.

While significant, the spike in shipping costs is unlikely to renew price pressures globally or in developing Asia. This is due to several factors, some of which distinguish the current episode from the 2021–2022 surge in shipping rates:

- **Shipping costs account for a small share of household final consumption.** This share is just 0.11% in the US, 0.22% in the Euro area, and below 0.50% for most economies in Asia and the Pacific. Even for Asian economies where they matter the most—such as Singapore; Hong Kong, China; and the Pacific economies Fiji and Maldives—shipping costs only account for 0.47% to 1.25% of household consumption (box figure 2).

2 Value of Shipping Services Embodied in Household Final Consumption, 2023

Shipping costs account for a relatively small portion of household final consumption.

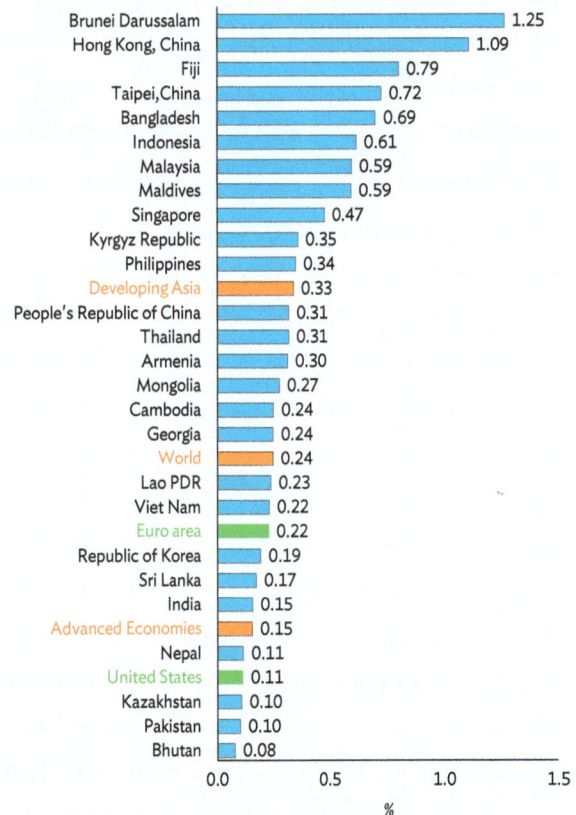

1 World Container Index

Container shipping costs have risen in recent months due to the conflict in the Red Sea and drought-induced disruptions in the Panama Canal.

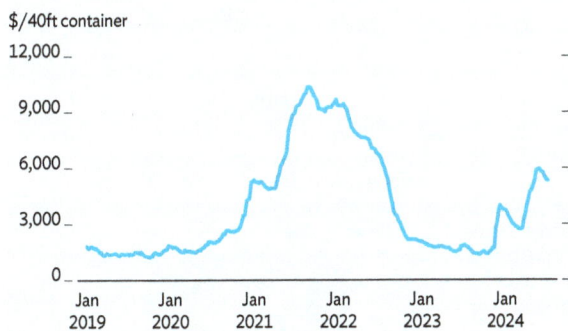

Notes: Drewry World Container Index reports actual spot container freight rates for major east–west trade routes. The Index consists of eight route-specific indices representing individual shipping routes and a composite index. All indices are reported in US dollar per 40-foot container. Data is as of 22 August 2024.

Source: Bloomberg.

Lao PDR = Lao People's Democratic Republic.

Note: Advanced economies refer to the weighted average of Australia, New Zealand, Japan, United Kingdom, Euro area, Canada, and the US.

Source: Asian Development Bank calculations using ADB Multiregional Input-Output Tables (July 2024 version).

continued on next page

Box 1.1.1 *Continued*

- **While container freight rates increased this year, other shipping costs, particularly for bulkers and tankers, rose much less or even declined.** Box figure 3 (green line) shows movements of the Baltic Dry Index (BDI), which tracks the cost of shipping dry bulk cargo—or commodities in loose, unpackaged form—on over 23 standard routes including the Suez Canal. After spiking briefly in January 2024, the BDI stood at around 1,800 as of end-August 2024, down 7% year to date and below its long-run average. Similar to the BDI, the Baltic Dirty Tanker Index and the Baltic Clean Tanker Index—covering, respectively, tankers transporting crude oil and refined products—also declined this year (see box figure 3, blue and orange lines).

- **The water level in the Panama Canal is now back to its historical average.** In response, the Panama Canal Authority lifted restrictions on vessel traffic on 26 August, increasing the canal's maximum draft to 50 feet and raising the number of vessels allowed to transit per day from 24 at the height of the drought to 36. This is expected to help ease the bottlenecks for shipping routes from Asia to the East Coast of North America.

3 Baltic Exchange Dry and Tanker Indices

Freight rates for bulkers and tankers rose much less than the World Container Index in early 2024 and then declined, falling below their January values in August.

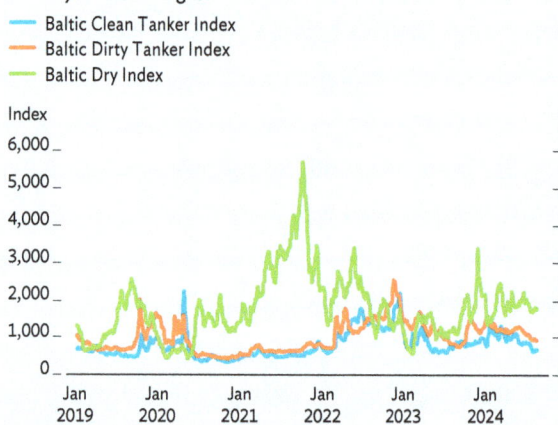

Note: Data are as of 30 August 2024.
Source: CEIC Data Company.

- **Stimulus-driven demand pressure in the US and Europe, which was a key contributor to inflationary pressures in 2021–2022, is now absent.** Large stimulus measures, plus a shift in demand away from services and toward goods, raised demand substantially in the US and the EU in 2021–2022. In combination with various supply constraints, including port closures, this boosted demand-side price pressures. This can be seen in box figure 4, which shows survey-based measures of excess demand in the US and European Union. Excess demand pressures have subsided over the past 2 years as household transfer stimulus measures were withdrawn and rapid (albeit delayed) monetary policy tightening took hold. As the US economy continues to cool and growth in the EU remains modest, excess demand pressures of the kind in 2021–2022 are no longer present.

4 Excess Demand, United States and European Union

Excess demand in the US and the EU declined from the third quarter of 2022 onwards as fiscal and monetary policies tightened.

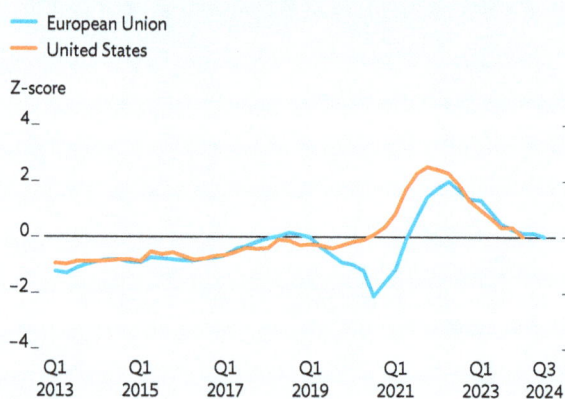

Q = quarter.
Notes: Using data from business surveys, excess demand is constructed as the difference between the percentage of manufacturing firms saying that supply constraints limit their production (i.e., shortage of material or equipment) versus the share of firms saying it is insufficient demand. The Z-scores are expressed as the ratio of the difference between excess demand and series mean to standard deviation: i.e., Z score = {(excess demand − series mean)/ standard deviation}.
Source: Asian Development Bank calculations using data from the US Census Bureau and the European Commission.

continued on next page

Box 1.1.1 *Continued*

- **Shipping costs did not increase for key routes toward Asia.** Global shipping cost indexes mask important variations across economies. Most of the increase in shipping costs has been for shipments from Asia to the rest of the world (box figure 5), implying that inflationary pressures in the region from freight rate increases are likely to be minimal. This is compounded by the fact that energy and food prices—key drivers of regional inflationary pressure, as opposed to shipping costs—are expected to stabilize and moderate, respectively, during the remainder of 2024.

This box was written by Abdul D. Abiad, Matteo Lanzafame, Shiela Romance of the Economic Research and Development Impact Department (ERDI), ADB, Jesson Pagaduan, and Michael Timbang, ERDI consultants.

5 World Container Index, by Trade Routes

Most of the increase in shipping costs has been for shipments from Shanghai—the world's busiest container port—to the rest of the world, while those toward Shanghai barely moved or declined.

- Shanghai to LA
- Shanghai to NY
- Shanghai to Genoa
- Shanghai to Rotterdam
- Shanghai to Shanghai
- LA to Shanghai

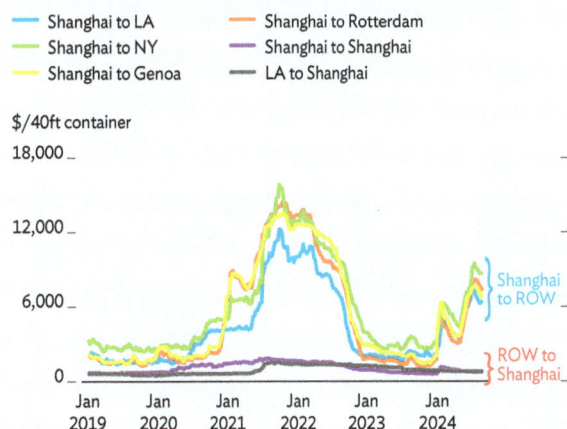

LA = Los Angeles, NY = New York, ROW = rest of the world.
Notes: See box figure 1.
Source: Bloomberg.

Box 1.1.2 Using Automatic Identification System Data to Track Shipping Disruptions from Asia: An Update

The Automatic Identification System (AIS) is crucial in monitoring and managing global maritime trade. The AIS helps vessels communicate during navigation and was originally designed to prevent collisions. Vessels equipped with AIS send location and other information every 2 to 10 seconds, allowing real-time tracking of vessel movements and trade routes, making AIS valuable for monitoring disruptions in global maritime trade. The Global Movements Data, developed by the Asian Development Bank, processes and aggregates AIS data to monitor trade disruptions like the Panama Canal drought and the conflict in the Red Sea (ADB 2023, 2024). Indicators from the Global Movements Data include daily transit counts for major passageways, transit times for key trade routes, and port activity metrics.

Disruptions in major global trade routes have been causing significant shifts in shipping patterns. The Panama Canal, a crucial trade route connecting the Atlantic and Pacific oceans, was the primary pathway for 57.5% of all container ship

cargo from Asia to the United States East Coast in 2022 (Panama Canal Authority 2023). However, severe drought linked to the El Niño phenomenon had affected the canal since early 2023, affecting the canal's daily operations. Similarly, the Suez Canal, a 193.3 kilometer artificial waterway in Egypt that connects the Mediterranean Sea to the Red Sea and on to the Indian Ocean, has experienced disruptions. This key trade route between Europe and Asia has seen a significant drop in daily transits due to the conflict in the Red Sea, which has also impacted the adjacent Bab El-Mandeb Strait (ADB 2023). Consequently, with both the Panama Canal and the Suez Canal facing operational challenges, ships have been increasingly rerouting through longer passages. For instance, vessels traveling from Asia to Europe or the United States are navigating around the Cape of Good Hope, significantly extending their journeys.

Recent disruptions in key maritime trade routes highlight their varying impacts on global shipping stability. The aftermath of the November 2023

continued on next page

Box 1.1.2 *Continued*

conflict in the Red Sea resulted in persistently low transit levels in both the Suez Canal and the Bab El-Mandeb Strait, with no recovery observed during the second quarter of 2024 (box figure 1, panels a and b). The Strait of Hormuz, a critical oil chokepoint between Oman and Iran, handles about 30% of the world's oil trade. Despite recent geopolitical tensions and Iran's suggestion in April 2024 of potentially closing the strait, daily transits have remained stable. The consistent ship traffic levels (box figure 1, panel c) mirror patterns from previous years, demonstrating the strait's resilience and its importance as an economic lifeline for Iran, which likely explains the absence of significant disruptions so far. The Panama Canal had been severely impacted by drought, causing the Panama Canal Authority to reduce allowable transits throughout 2023. Despite improved water levels in 2024 and the lifting of transit limits, daily transits have only slightly increased and remain below pre-drought levels (box figure 1, panel d).

Transit times and shipping costs remain elevated on certain routes. Ships traveling from Shanghai to Rotterdam typically use the Suez Canal or the Panama Canal. Ongoing disruptions in these canals have forced vessels to take longer alternative routes, leading to sustained shipping delays and elevated transit times (box figure 2, panel a). Similarly, transit times for ships traveling from Shanghai to New York or New Jersey, which usually rely on the Panama Canal for the quickest route, remain high as conditions in the Panama Canal have yet to return to pre-drought capacity (box figure, panel b). In contrast, the median transit time for ships traveling from Shanghai to Los Angeles has remained unchanged since 2023, as this route has not been affected by the Panama Canal restrictions or the conflict in the Red Sea. Further, the panels show that median transit times and route-specific shipping costs are correlated, indicating that shipping delays contribute to higher costs. However, the recent increase in shipping costs for the Shanghai to Los Angeles route occurred despite stable transit times. The high correlation of Drewry World Container Index across different routes suggests that global factors are at play. Increased global shipping demand, driven by purchasers advancing holiday shipments as a precautionary measure, has led to increased shipping rates across all routes.

1 Automatic Identification System-Based Daily Transits Along Major Passageways

Post-2023 conflict in the Red Sea, transit is still low in the Suez Canal and Bab El-Mandeb, stable in the Strait of Hormuz despite tensions, and slowly recovering in the Panama Canal after the drought.

A. Suez Canal

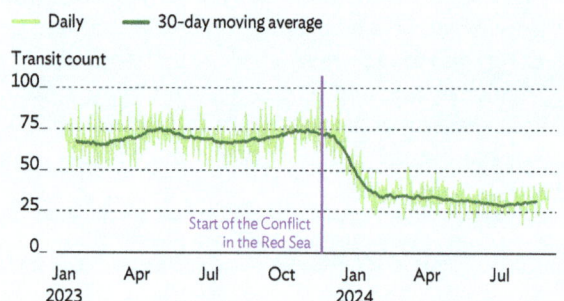

B. Bab El-Mandeb Strait

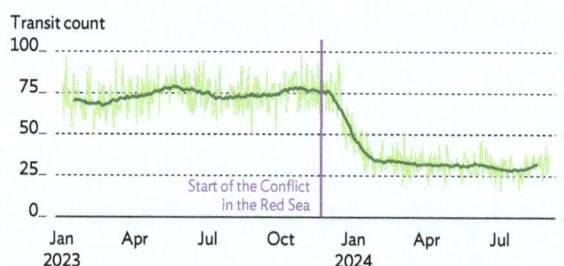

C. Strait of Hormuz

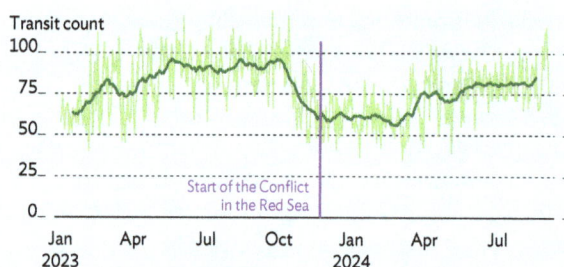

D. Panama Canal

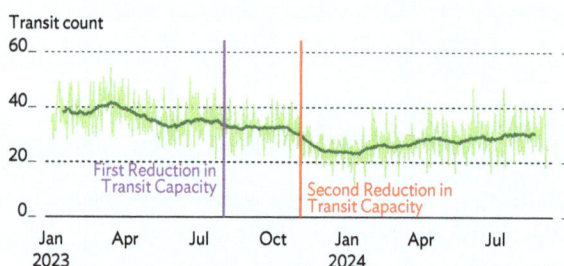

Note: Data are up to 31 August 2024.
Sources: Asian Development Bank calculations using United Nations Global Platform for Official Statistics. 2024; AIS data.

continued on next page

Box 1.1.2 *Continued*

2 Median Transit Time and World Container Index, by Trading Routes,

Transit times from Shanghai to Rotterdam and New York have increased due to canal disruptions, while the Shanghai to Los Angeles route remains unaffected.

A. Shanghai to Rotterdam

B. Shanghai to New York/New Jersey

C. Shanghai to Los Angeles

Note: Data is as of 31 August 2024.

Sources: Asian Development Bank calculations using United Nations Global Platform for Official Statistics. 2024; Bloomberg.

In addition to monitoring maritime passageways, major global ports are tracked using AIS data. A key example is the Port of Odesa in Ukraine, the country's largest seaport and a major hub in the Black Sea region. The Russian invasion of Ukraine in February 2022 had an adverse impact on maritime operations at the port, as evidenced by the sharp decline in the daily count of unique ships in box figure 3 panel (a) in the figure. Although the overall number of ships has not yet returned to pre-invasion levels, the situation for cargo ships tells a different story (box figure 3, panel b). Recently, Ukraine has significantly increased its production and exports, which is reflected in the surge of cargo ships at the

3 Daily Unique Count of Ships in the Port of Odesa

While overall ship numbers remain below pre-invasion levels, cargo ship activity has surged in 2024, surpassing pre-invasion figures.

A. All Ships

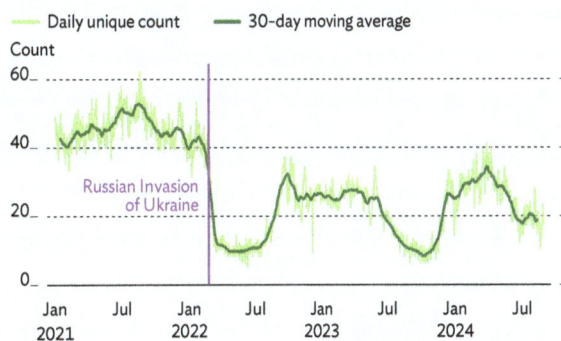

B. Cargo Ships

Note: Data is up to 31 August 2024.

Sources: Asian Development Bank calculations using United Nations Global Platform for Official Statistics. 2024; AIS data.

continued on next page

Box 1.1.2 *Continued*

Port of Odesa in 2024, with numbers even surpassing pre-invasion levels. Given that Ukraine is one of the world's largest producers and exporters of wheat, this increased activity at the port could have significant implications for the supply and price of wheat in developing Asia. As many economies in the region rely heavily on wheat imports, a boost in Ukraine's export capacity could help stabilize or even lower wheat prices, enhancing food security and supporting inflation management across developing Asia.

References:
ADB (Asian Development Bank). 2023. *Methodological Framework for Unlocking Maritime Insights Using Automatic Identification System Data: A Special Supplement of Key Indicators for Asia and the Pacific 2023.*
——. 2024. Using Automatic Identification System Data to Track Shipping Disruptions from Asia. *Asian Development Outlook April 2024.* Manila.
Panama Canal Authority. 2023. Weekly Update on Transits through the Panama Canal.

This box was written by Mahinthan Mariasingham of the Economic Research and Development Impact Department (ERDI), ADB, Cherryl Chico, Ed Kieran Reyes, and Zhaowen Wang, ERDI consultants.

to easing food prices, bringing headline inflation down in July to almost a 5-year low in India and to a 2-year low in Pakistan. Food prices in Pakistan normalized and returned toward zero during May to July, driven by base effects and improved agricultural production. In the Caucasus and Central Asia, the decline in food prices took place in almost all economies in the subregion, except for Turkmenistan, in line with declines in global commodity prices. Meanwhile, rising food prices contributed to small increases in headline inflation in the PRC, Southeast Asia, and the Pacific. In the PRC, inflation reached 0.5% in July, as weather

disruptions lifted food prices into positive territory for the first time in 13 months (Figure 1.1.5, panel C). Adverse weather conditions and supply constraints also affected local food production and kept food and energy prices elevated in Fiji and Tonga in the Pacific. Higher food prices, including those for vegetables and meat, in the Philippines, Thailand, and Viet Nam, also contributed to increases in average food inflation for Southeast Asia. Meanwhile, energy inflation increased in the Caucasus and Central Asia and some Pacific economies since the start of the year, and is now higher than pre-pandemic levels.

Figure 1.1.5 Contributions to Inflation, by Subregion

The disinflation process in the region varies due to differences across economies.

- Core
- Food and nonalcoholic beverages
- Energy-related
- Headline inflation

A. Caucasus and Central Asia

Percentage points

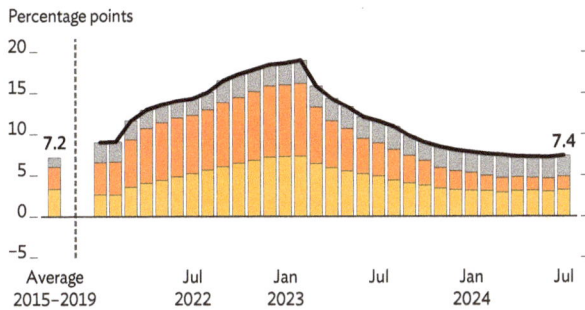

B. East Asia, Excluding the People's Republic of China

Percentage points

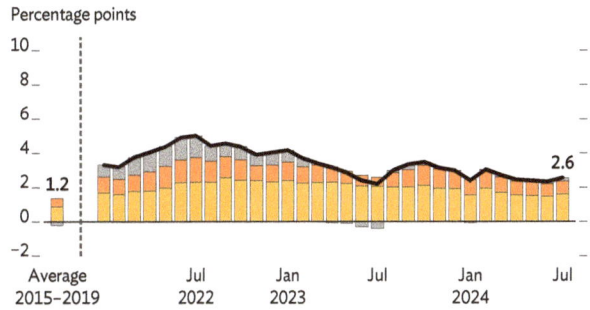

C. People's Republic of China

Percentage points

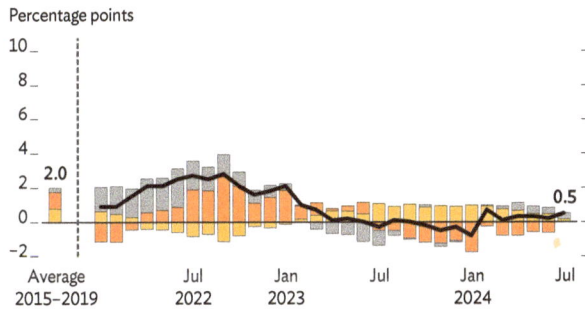

D. South Asia

Percentage points

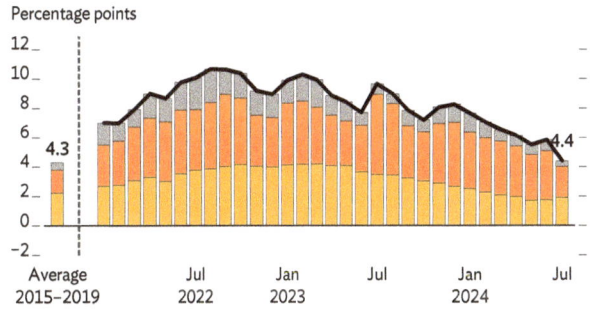

E. Southeast Asia

Percentage points

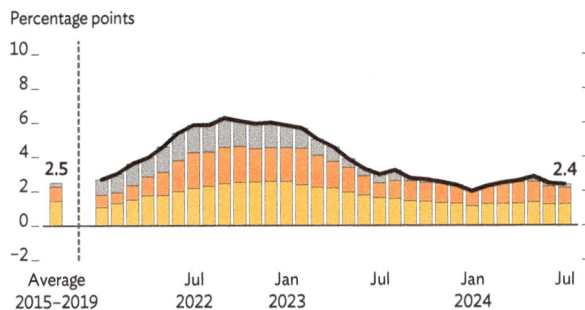

F. The Pacific

Percentage points

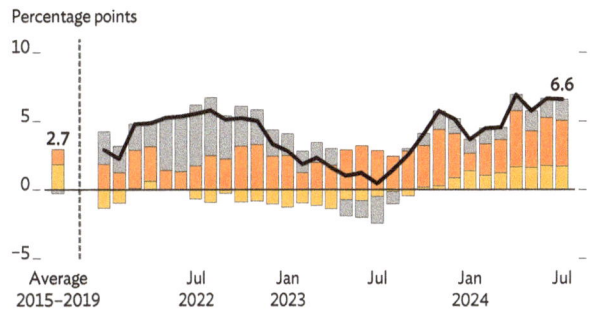

Notes: Core inflation excludes food and energy sectors. For some economies, core is estimated as the residual between overall inflation and the sum of food and nonalcoholic beverages and energy-related items. For lack of a more disaggregated breakdown, energy-related consumer prices for most economies includes housing, water, and nonfuel transport. Subregional averages are calculated using gross domestic product purchasing power parity shares as weights, and includes the following economies: Central Asia = Armenia, Georgia, and Kazakhstan; East Asia = People's Republic of China; Hong Kong, China; Republic of Korea; Mongolia; Taipei,China; South Asia = India, Pakistan, Maldives, Nepal, and Sri Lanka; Southeast Asia = Cambodia, Indonesia, Lao People's Democratic Republic, Malaysia, Philippines, Singapore, and Thailand; and the Pacific = Fiji and Tonga.

Sources: Asian Development Bank estimates using data from Haver Analytics; CEIC Data Company; official sources.

Strong Export Growth Supported by Global Demand for Electronics

Exports in developing Asia continue to grow, led by high-income technology exporters.
High-income technology exporters recorded the fastest growth in in nominal goods exports in the region, at 9.9% in July (Figure 1.1.6). Following an 8.6% year-on-year decline in the PRC's exports in March—statistically driven by the high base from last year's border reopening—PRC goods exports grew robustly, at 7.4% in July. Exports are also recovering well in the rest of developing Asia, where growth of 7.7% was recorded in July.

Figure 1.1.6 Growth in Nominal Goods Exports in Developing Asia

Exports continued to grow strongly, led by high-income technology exporters.

— People's Republic of China
— Rest of developing Asia
— High-income technology exporters
— Developing Asia

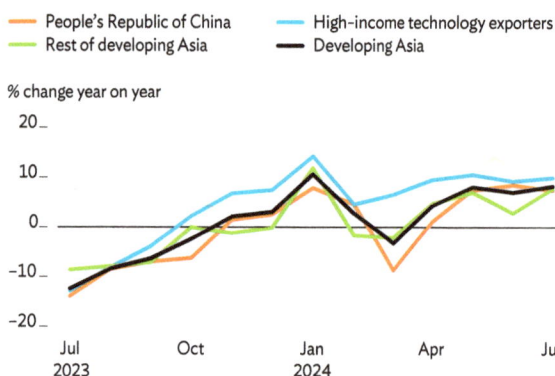

Note: High-income technology exporters include Hong Kong, China; the Republic of Korea; Singapore; Taipei,China.
Source: CEIC Data Company.

Exports are also higher in real terms, especially from the PRC. Apart from the March 2024 blip, export volumes from the PRC have been growing strongly since August 2023, while export prices continue to decrease (Figure 1.1.7). The decline in the PRC's export prices, especially for basic metals likely reflects subdued domestic demand, in part due to the prolonged adjustment in its housing market. However, low-priced exports from the PRC could aid price stabilization efforts in destination markets. Export volume from the rest of emerging Asia trended upward, while export prices are generally stabilizing.

Figure 1.1.7 Volume and Unit Value Export Growth from the People's Republic of China and Emerging Asia

PRC real exports grew strongly as export prices declined.

— PRC (volume)
-- PRC (unit value)
— Emerging Asia ex PRC (volume)
-- Emerging Asia ex PRC (unit value)

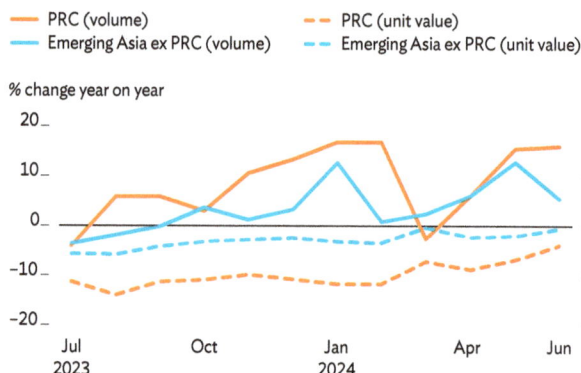

GDP = Gross domestic product, PRC = People's Republic of China.
Note: Emerging Asia ex-PRC includes India, Indonesia, Malaysia, Pakistan, the Philippines, Thailand, and Viet Nam, which account for 70.4% of developing Asia's GDP, excluding the PRC.
Sources: CEIC Data Company and CPB Netherlands Bureau for Economic Policy Analysis.

Electronics have continued to support export growth in developing Asia. High-income technology-exporting economies continue to benefit from the upturn in the global semiconductor cycle, driven in part by rising investment in artificial intelligence (AI), which is causing spillovers along the industry's value-chain. Electronics are the largest contributor to goods export growth in a number of economies (Figure 1.1.8). Taipei,China; Hong Kong, China; and the Republic of Korea top the list, with electronics adding 11.7, 9.8 and 7.2 percentage points to export growth, respectively. The contribution of electronics to export growth is also high in the Philippines and Singapore, 5.4 and 4.6 percentage points, respectively. The Philippines is benefiting from its continued involvement in lower value-added segments such as assembly, testing, and packaging. Meanwhile, electronics exports contracted in Cambodia, Georgia, and Malaysia. Cambodia, Indonesia, and Thailand have not yet benefited from the AI-related semiconductors upcycle as they do not specialize in high-tech products. Malaysia's performance may also partly reflect a failed attempt to climb the value chain. It established local wafer fabrication and chip design but had difficulty capturing markets for them. The growth in electronics in Thailand came from telecom equipment.

Figure 1.1.8 Contributions to Goods Export Growth by Product, 2024 to Date

Global demand for electronics boosted exports from the region.

- Minerals and metals (incl. precious)
- Electronics
- Agriculture, food, and garments
- Machinery and other electrical
- Vehicles, ships, and aircraft
- Other
- Total exports change

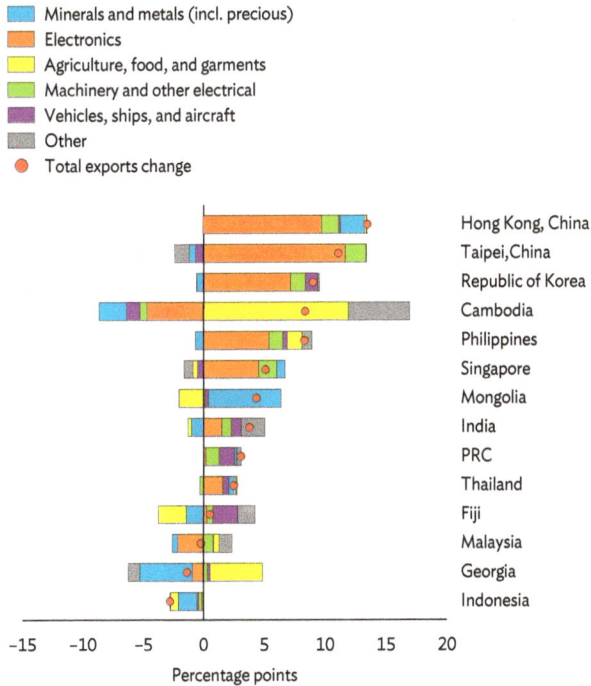

PRC = People's Republic of China.
Note: Year-to-date export growths are based on 2023 and 2024 total exports from January to April for India, January to May for Fiji and the Philippines, January to July for Georgia and Malaysia, and January to June for the remaining economies.
Sources: UN Comtrade; International Trade Centre.

Figure 1.1.9 Contributions to Goods Export Growth by Destination, 2024 to Date

Intraregional trade and strong demand from the US supported export growth.

- PRC
- Developing Asia
- United States
- European Union
- Russian Federation
- Rest of the world
- Total exports change

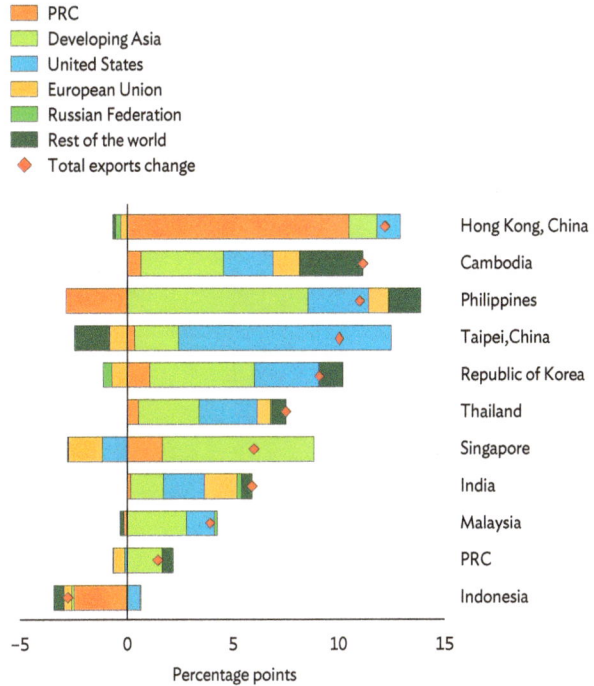

PRC = People's Republic of China.
Note: Developing Asia excludes the PRC. Year-to-date export growth rates are based on 2023 and 2024 total exports from January to April for the Philippines and Cambodia; from January to May for India; from January to July for Taipei,China; and from January to June for the remaining economies.
Source: CEIC Data Company.

Exports of nonelectronic goods remain mostly robust. Cambodia's exports were boosted by agriculture and garments exports as shipping bottlenecks eased and the labor market stabilized with fewer strikes. Agriculture and food also increased Georgia's export growth by 4.3 percentage points, mainly due to beverages and spirits, but the country's total exports were dragged down by a significant decrease in exports of copper ores to the PRC. Minerals and metals contributed significantly to export growth in Mongolia and, to a lesser extent, in Hong Kong, China. In Mongolia, coal was the main driver of export growth, adding 4.6 percentage points, while gold added 2.0 percentage points to export growth of Hong Kong, China. Minerals subtracted from export growth in India, Indonesia, and Malaysia. Declining commodity prices have lowered the

export value of coal from Indonesia, oil and gas from Malaysia, and oil from India. Exports of cars and ships were key contributors to export growth in PRC and Republic of Korea, while aircrafts and parts thereof added to export growth in India and Fiji.

Exports to developing Asia contributed significantly to goods export growth in most Asian economies. The Philippines and Singapore benefited from strong growth in trade with developing Asia, with 8.5 percentage points and 7.1 percentage points added to their export growth rates, respectively (Figure 1.1.9). Exports to the United States (US) benefited most economies, especially Taipei,China, where exports to the US contributed 10.1 percentage points. The PRC is the primary contributor to Hong Kong, China's export growth, adding 10.5 percentage points. Exports to the PRC dragged down growth in Indonesia and the Philippines. Except for Indonesia, intra-regional exports contributed positively to goods export growth in the selected economies. Hong Kong, China and Singapore gained most from intra-regional trade, which added 11.8 percentage points and 8.8 percentage points to export growth, respectively. While extra-regional exports significantly contributed to growth in Taipei,China (7.7 percentage points) and Cambodia (6.7 percentage points).

Services exports expanded in Q1, underpinned by growth of travel and recreation in most economies. Boosted by tourism, the largest travel and recreation contributions were observed in Malaysia (17.9 percentage points), Indonesia (10.6 percentage points), and the Philippines (6.6 percentage points), (Figure 1.1.10). Travel and recreation dragged down services export growth in Pakistan, whereas telecoms and information technology drove services exports to

positive growth. Transport services were the largest contributor in Singapore and Uzbekistan on the back of strong growth in freight services.

Tourist arrivals are moving beyond pre-pandemic levels. This year more economies breached the 2019 level of international tourist arrivals, notably Maldives, Fiji, Cook Islands, Viet Nam, Nepal, and Sri Lanka, ranked from highest to lowest (Figure 1.1.11). On the other hand, tourist arrivals dropped in Samoa, though remaining close to pre-pandemic levels. Tourist arrivals in the other economies continue to increase, with Viet Nam improving the most.

Figure 1.1.11 International Tourist Arrivals in Developing Asian Economies

Tourist arrivals continue to converge toward pre-pandemic levels.

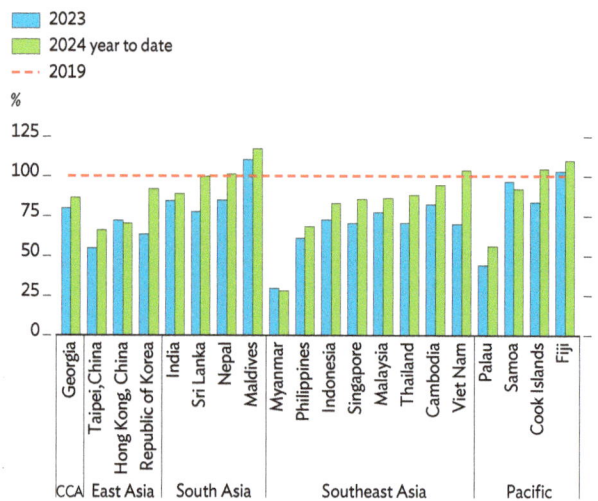

Figure 1.1.10 Sectoral Contributions to Nominal Services Export Growth

Receipts from tourism, transportation, and IT services improved.

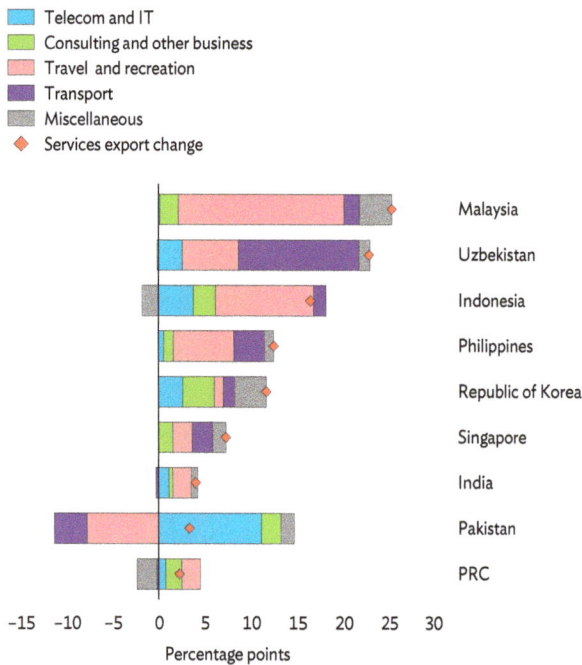

CCA = Caucasus and Central Asia.
Sources: CEIC Data Company and official sources.

IT = information technology, PRC = People's Republic of China.
Notes: Growth rate is for the first quarter of 2024, year on year change. Miscellaneous refers to intellectual property, construction, financial, government, insurance and pensions, maintenance and repair, and manufacturing services.
Source: CEIC Data Company.

Personal transfers continue to provide a significant source of income in many developing Asian economies. For most economies, personal transfers as a percent of GDP increased steadily over the last 5 plus years through Q1 2024 (Figure 1.1.12). A favorable external economic environment shaped by tight labor market conditions and a deceleration in inflation helped improve migrants' savings, boosting remittance flows to the region. Recent data points show that personal transfers as a percent of GDP increased significantly in Fiji, Georgia, Nepal, and the Philippines, surpassing pre-pandemic levels. In Georgia, remittances from the US, European Union (EU), and

Europe's Schengen States have risen, which could be due to the visa liberalization deal made with the EU and Georgia in 2017. In Armenia and Kyrgyz Republic, personal transfers dropped considerably below the 2019 level. This is possibly due to a slowdown of

money transfers from the Russian Federation to its neighboring countries and migrants returning to their home countries due to Russia's war in Ukraine.

Favorable Monetary Easing Conditions but Lingering Fiscal Vulnerabilities

Lower inflation is creating space for monetary easing. Inflation is now within or below target for 12 out of 17 inflation-targeting economies in the region (Figure 1.1.13). The exceptions are Bangladesh and Kazakhstan, where inflation remains roughly 4 percentage points above their respective targets. In Pakistan, inflation slowed substantially from 28% at the start of the year to 11% July, bringing it slightly below target. Armenia, the PRC, and Thailand saw deflation at the start of the year; inflation has returned in recent months, but it remains below target in these economies.

Favorable conditions point to more monetary policy easing on the horizon. With inflation pressures waning, 12 economies in the region have cut rates so

Figure 1.1.12 Personal Transfers

Personal transfers remain healthy on stable flow of remittances.

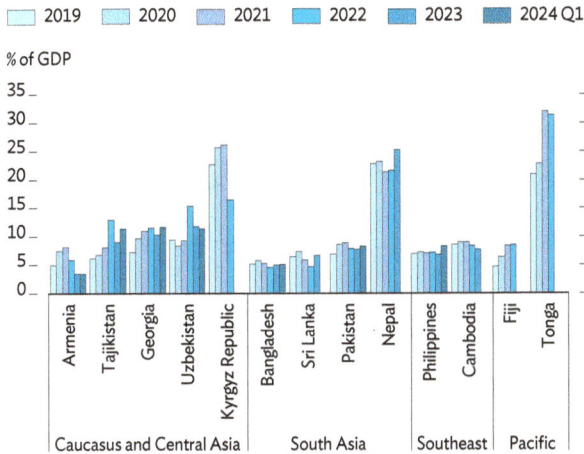

GDP = gross domestic product, Q = quarter.
Note: Data for Kyrgyz Republic, Fiji, and Tonga is up to 2022, Sri Lanka and Nepal up to 2023, and the other economies up to Q1 2024.
Source: CEIC Data Company.

Figure 1.1.13 Inflation and Inflation Targets

Inflation is within target for most inflation targeting economies.

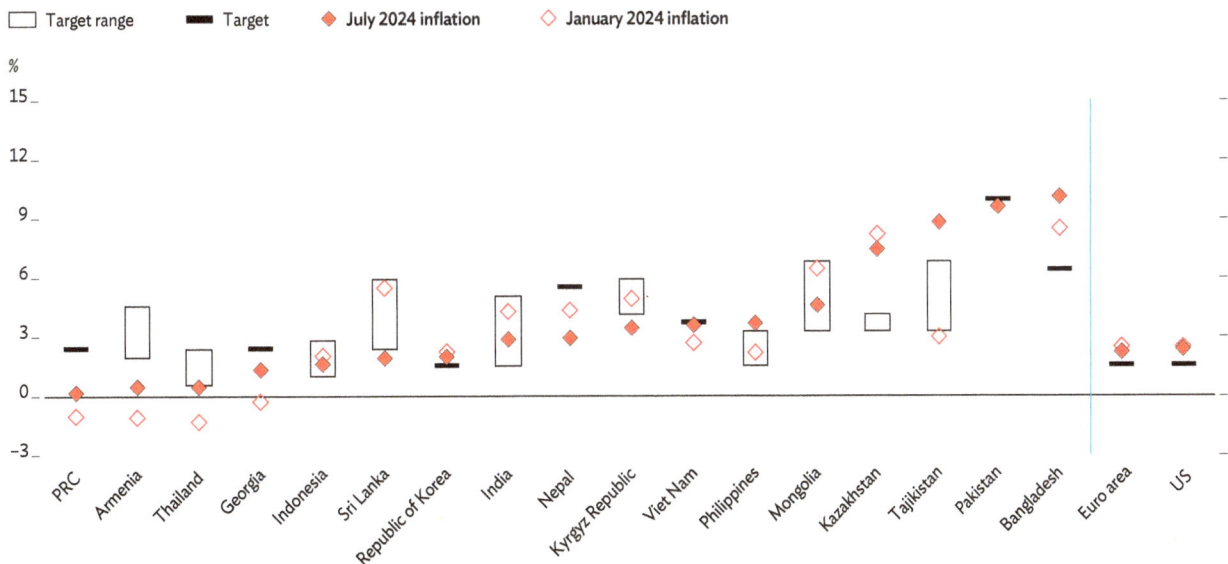

PRC = People's Republic of China, US = United States.
Note: January inflation for Pakistan was 28.3% and is omitted due to the axis scale. Latest data for Armenia and Tajikistan are for June, all other economies use July data.
Sources: CEIC Data Company and official sources.

far this year, with most of the easing in the Caucasus and Central Asia. Nevertheless, most other central banks have been holding policy rates steady as easing would widen interest rate differentials vis-à-vis the US and potentially lead to capital outflows and exchange rate depreciations. At the end of July, however, weaker US employment data and lower inflation raised expectations of Fed easing. This drove US bond yields down and many regional currencies relative to the US dollar up (Figure 1.1.14). The Fed's 50 basis point rate cut in September, together with the continued progress on disinflation, increases the scope for more central banks in the region to also commence easing.

Fiscal balances are improving, but a few vulnerabilities remain. Fiscal positions in most economies with large deficits are expected to improve in 2024 (Figure 1.1.15), with notable exceptions such as Maldives, where the deficit is expected to widen to 12.2% of GDP from 11% in 2022. Fiscal positions are expected to worsen for roughly half of the economies in the region but deficits will remain relatively small, with an average deficit of 3% of GDP. The average government debt-to-GDP ratio for developing Asia is projected to decline marginally to around 47% this year as robust growth continues to offset upward pressure from primary deficits and higher borrowing costs. Lao PDR struggles with high public debt and debt service payments, and low foreign exchange reserves which are causing persistent currency depreciation, inflationary pressure, and economic difficulties. In Pakistan, public debt is forecast to decline as a percent of GDP in 2024, but risks remain as interest payments rose to close to 60% of fiscal revenues (Figure 1.1.16). Interest payments as a share of fiscal revenues also increased for most other economies in the region relative to their pre-pandemic average, but most of these rises were not large.

Figure 1.1.14 Change in Exchange Rates and Yield Differentials, 1 August–3 September

Appreciating exchange rates and growing yield differentials with the US suggest more easing on the horizon.

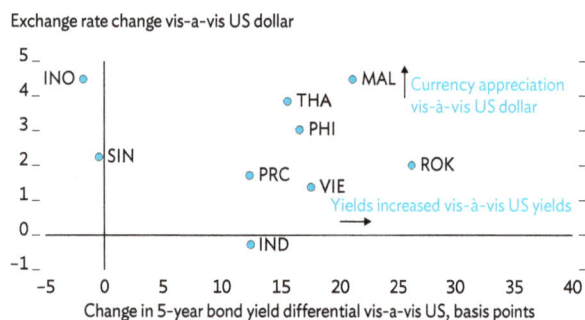

IND = India, INO = Indonesia, MAL = Malaysia, PHI = Philippines, PRC = People's Republic of China, ROK = Republic of Korea, SIN = Singapore, THA = Thailand, US = United States, and VIE = Viet Nam.

Source: Asian Development Bank calculations using data from Bloomberg.

Figure 1.1.15 Fiscal Balances

Fiscal balances improved in most economies with large deficits.

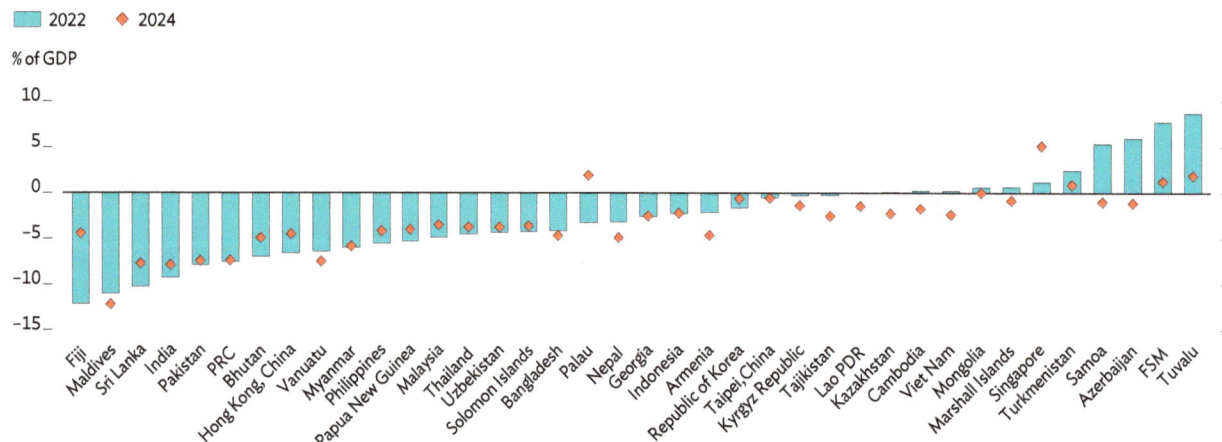

FSM = Federated States of Micronesia, GDP = gross domestic product, Lao PDR = Lao People's Democratic Republic, PRC = People's Republic of China.
Source: International Monetary Fund. World Economic Outlook April 2024 database.

Figure 1.1.16 Public Debt and Interest Payments, 2023

Some economies are facing high public debt and interest payments.

Interest payments as share of fiscal revenues, %

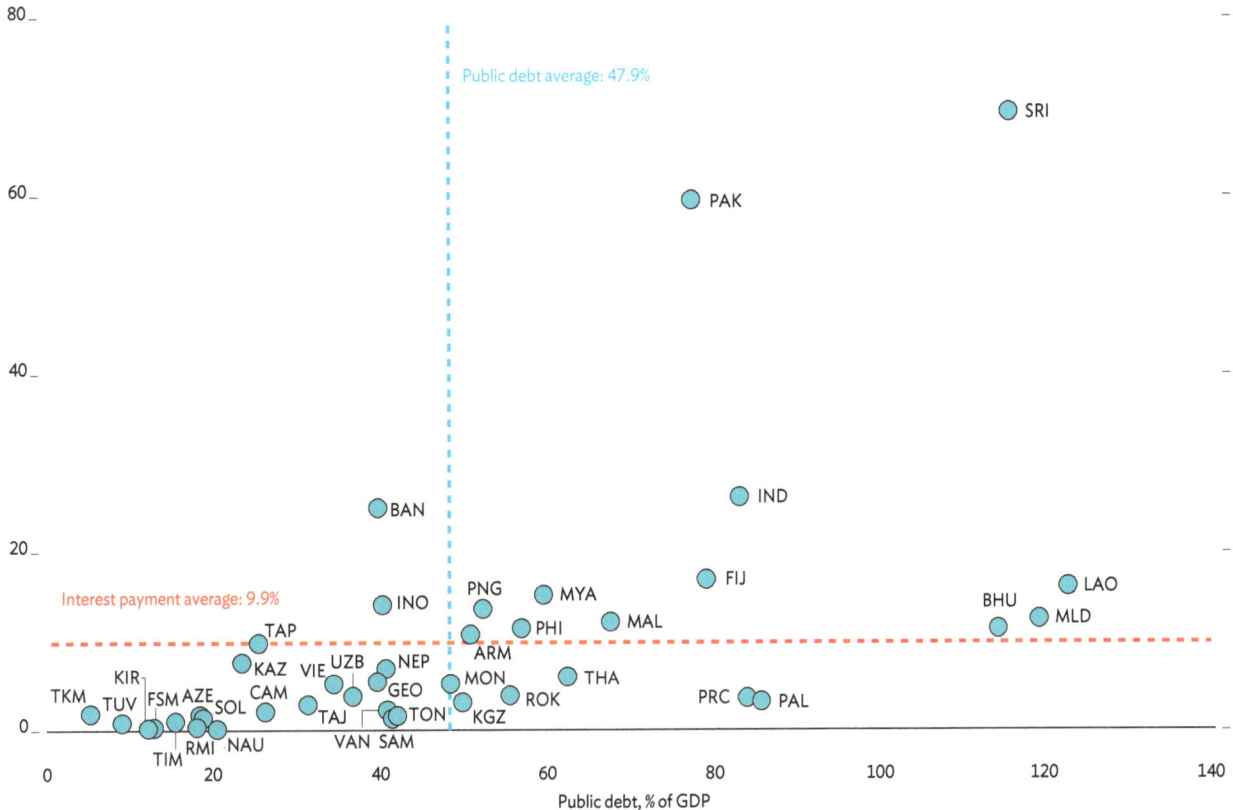

ARM = Armenia; AZE = Azerbaijan; BAN = Bangladesh; BHU = Bhutan; BRU = Brunei Darussalam; CAM = Cambodia; FIJ = Fiji; FSM = Federated States of Micronesia; GDP = gross domestic product; GEO = Georgia; IND = India; INO = Indonesia; KAZ = Kazakhstan; KIR = Kiribati; KGZ = Kyrgyz Republic; LAO = Lao People's Democratic Republic; MAL = Malaysia; MLD = Maldives; RMI = Marshall Islands; MON = Mongolia; MYA = Myanmar; NAU = Nauru; NEP = Nepal; PAK = Pakistan; PAL = Palau; PNG = Papua New Guinea; PHI = Philippines; PRC = People's Republic of China; ROK = Republic of Korea; SAM = Samoa; SOL = Solomon Islands; SRI = Sri Lanka; TAP = Taipei,China; TAJ = Tajikistan; THA = Thailand; TIM = Timor-Leste; TON = Tonga; TRK = Turkmenistan; TUV = Tuvalu; UZB = Uzbekistan; VAN = Vanuatu; VIE = Viet Nam.

Source: Asian Development Bank. Asian Sovereign Debt Monitor database.

Regional Financial Markets Remain Resilient, with Currencies Holding Steady

For most of the year, regional financial conditions have remained solid, bolstered by easing inflation and signals of impending monetary easing by the US which ultimately commenced in September 2024. Market turbulence at the end of July led to temporary volatility in both global and regional markets, but this subsided relatively quickly. Overall, regional equity markets continue to be robust, long-term bond yields continue to decline,

and risk premiums have mostly narrowed. In addition, cumulative net portfolio inflows across the region were recorded, and Asian currencies depreciated only marginally against the US dollar.

Equity markets in the region continued to rally during 2024, overcoming a brief episode of market volatility at the end of July. Then, Asian equity markets fluctuated following a sell-off in global technology stocks—particularly those related to AI—due to over-valuation concerns. Market volatility at that time was triggered by weaker-than-expected US employment data and a largely unexpected interest rate hike by the Bank of Japan that raised the cost of funding in Japanese yen and led to the unwinding of carry trades. These factors triggered a broader sell-off of risky assets, including those in Asian markets (Figure 1.1.17). Meanwhile, the Chicago Board Options Exchange's Volatility Index (VIX), a gauge of uncertainty and risk aversion, surged to 38.6 on 5 August, its highest level since June 2020 and

well above an average reading of 13.9 from January to July 2024. However, this spike was short-lived, and Asian equity markets began to recover within the week. Despite the market volatility, developing Asia's market-weighted return has increased by 11.2% in 2024, buoyed by expectations of rate cuts by the US Federal Reserve, which materialized in September as the monetary policy easing cycle commenced.

Figure 1.1.17 Equity Performance

Equity markets in developing Asia have been on an upward trend, but with occasional pockets of volatility.

CBOE = Chicago Board Options Exchange, VIX = volatility index.
Note: Developing Asia includes Bangladesh; People's Republic of China; Hong Kong, China; India; Indonesia; Kazakhstan; Republic of Korea; Malaysia; Pakistan; Philippines; Singapore; Sri Lanka; Taipei,China; Thailand; and Viet Nam. Data is as of 5 September 2024.
Source: Asian Development Bank calculations using data from Bloomberg.

Long-term bond yields began declining in the middle of 2024 as expectations of US monetary policy easing gathered pace. Ten-year government bond yields declined in selected Asian economies since the end of June on the expectation that the Federal Reserve would cut the federal funds rate in the latter months of this year, which it actually did in September (Figure 1.1.18). Among the economies in the region, bond yields in Hong Kong, China; Singapore; and the Philippines declined most, in line with the trajectory of US yields. Moderating inflation also contributed to the decline in bond yields, especially in Indonesia, Malaysia, and Singapore. On the other hand, the weighted average regional risk premium—measured by J.P. Morgan's Emerging Markets Bond Index Global stripped spreads—widened in July to early August largely due to elevated financial market volatility experienced at the end of

Figure 1.1.18 10-Year Government Bond Yield, Difference 30 June and Year to Date

Long-term government bond yields have mostly declined since the end of June.

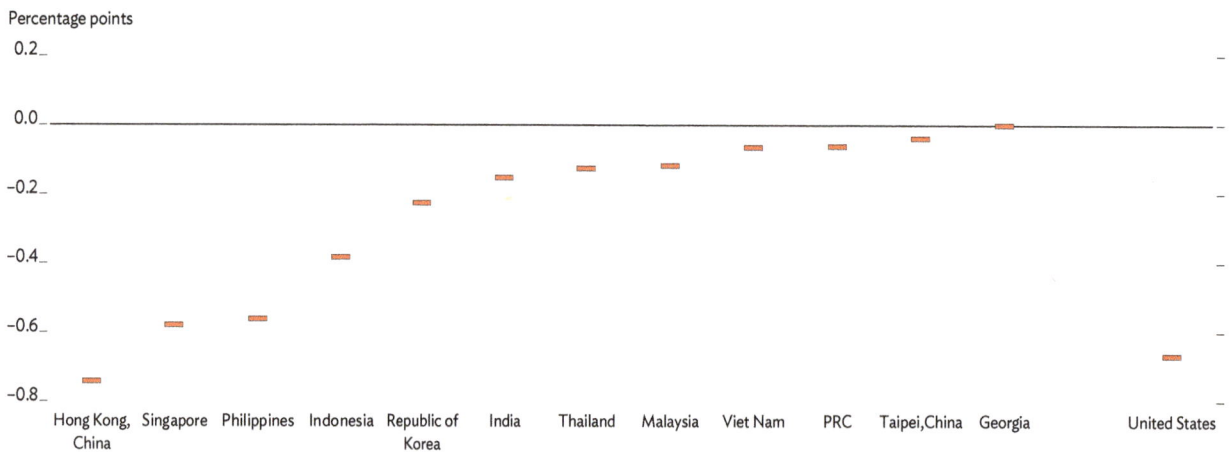

Note: Data is as of 5 September 2024.
Source: Asian Development Bank calculations using data from Bloomberg.

Figure 1.1.19 JP Morgan EMBI Stripped Spreads, by Subregion

Risk premiums widened in July to early August but are still down year to date.

- 1 January to 30 June
- 1 July to 5 August
- 5 August to date
- ◆ 1 January to date

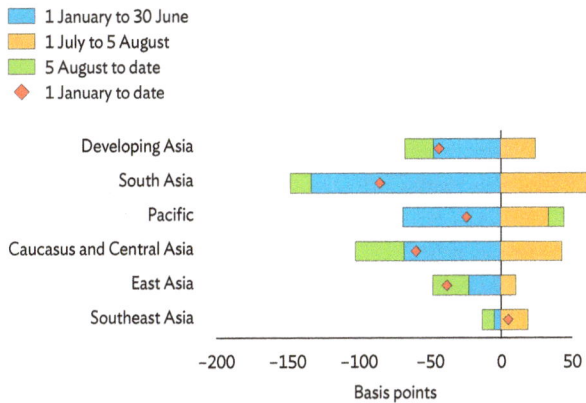

Notes: Caucasus and Central Asia includes Armenia, Azerbaijan, Kazakhstan, Tajikistan. East Asia includes People's Republic of China, Republic of Korea, and Mongolia. South Asia includes India, Pakistan, and Sri Lanka. Southeast Asia includes Indonesia, Malaysia, Philippines, and Viet Nam. Pacific includes Papua New Guinea. Subregional bond spreads are aggregated using gross domestic product purchasing power parity shares as weights. Data is as of 5 September 2024.
Source: Asian Development Bank calculations using data from Bloomberg.

Figure 1.1.20 Exchange Rate Movement Against the US Dollar, by Subregion

Due to market expectations for interest rate cuts by the Federal Reserve and uncertainty about the US economy, regional currencies appreciated in August.

- Change, 1 January to 31 July 2024
- Change, 1 August 2024 to date

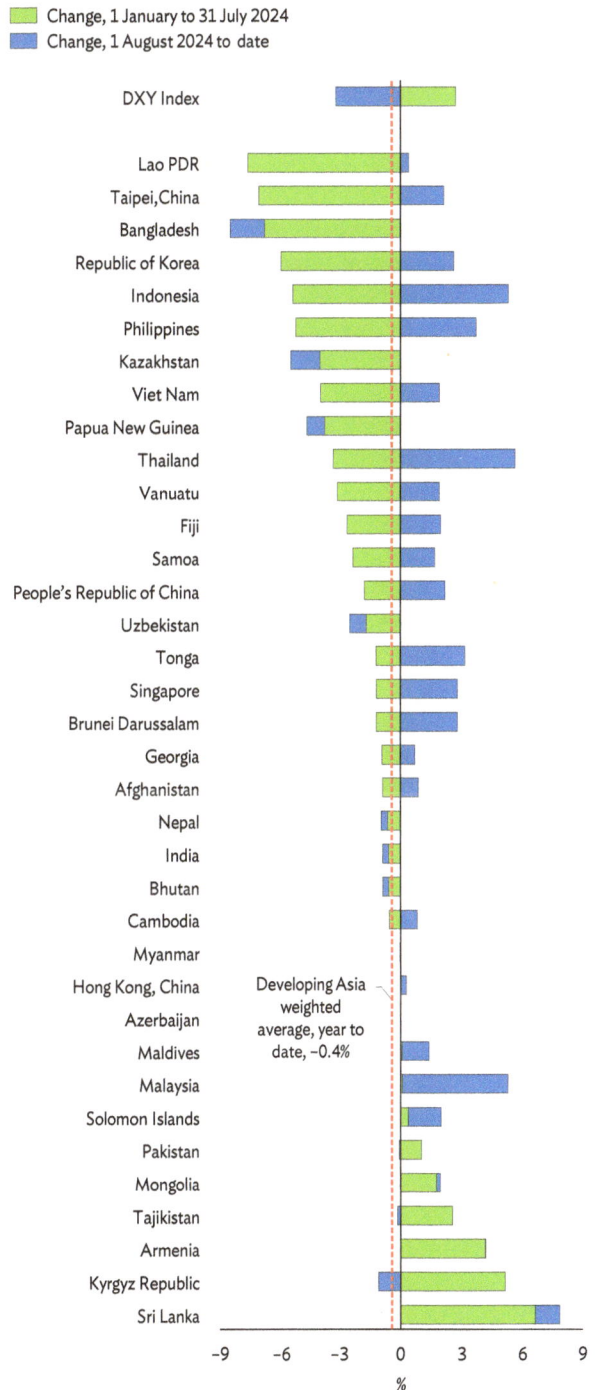

DXY = US dollar index, Lao PDR = Lao People's Democratic Republic, US = United States.
Notes: Changes in exchange rates are aggregated using gross domestic product purchasing power parity shares as weights. Data is as of 5 September 2024.
Source: Asian Development Bank calculations using data from Bloomberg.

July. South Asian bond spreads widened the most, 62.1 basis points, during this period, followed by Caucasus and Central Asia, where spreads widened 42.8 basis points (Figure 1.1.19). From 5 August onwards, when market volatility subsided, bond spreads narrowed. During 2024 across the region as a whole, a narrowing in the risk premium materialized, reflecting improved bond market sentiment.

Most regional currencies began to appreciate against the US dollar after the US Fed hinted at monetary easing during the July Federal Open Market Committee meeting. The DXY index, which measures the strength of the US dollar against a basket of major currencies, continued on an upward trajectory up to July due to stronger-than-expected economic growth and persistently high Federal Reserve interest rates, leading to a slight weakening of many Asian currencies relative to the US dollar (Figure 1.1.20). Currency losses were significant in Lao PDR due to external debt concerns; Taipei,China's currency was affected by the global tech stock sell-off; while Bangladesh's currency depreciated following the introduction of a more flexible "crawling peg" exchange rate system. However, by the end of July, regional currencies strengthened as the Fed signaled potential rate cuts for September, while concerns about the strength of the US economy at that time also impacted the US dollar's strength. Of the 27 currencies that depreciated from 1 January to 31 July, 19 appreciated from 1 August, with the Thai baht recording the largest gains due to favorable domestic economic conditions. For 2024 as a whole, GDP-weighted currencies across developing Asia have depreciated a marginal 0.4% against the US dollar.

Developing Asia recorded cumulative net portfolio inflows into the region since January, despite a setback in August. Portfolio net inflows into Asia were robust in the first quarter of 2024, bolstered by a less hawkish monetary policy stance by the US Fed and a more favorable economic outlook in the region. However, this positive momentum stalled in the second quarter as market expectations shifted towards the possibility of prolonged higher interest rates in the US. This was particularly notable in April, with outflows driven by portfolio rebalancing by investors in response to anticipated delays in US monetary easing. Portfolio flows rebounded in subsequent months, however. In August 2024, the region experienced portfolio withdrawals largely driven by the PRC over uncertainties about its growth outlook and concerns in the property sector (Figure 1.1.21). Portfolio inflows to developing Asia excluding the PRC increased overall in August, despite some volatility at the start of month. Nevertheless, the cumulative net inflow into the region for the year was recorded at $27.9 billion.

Figure 1.1.21 Cumulative Net Portfolio Inflows in the Region

The region recorded net portfolio inflows of $27.9 billion in 2024.

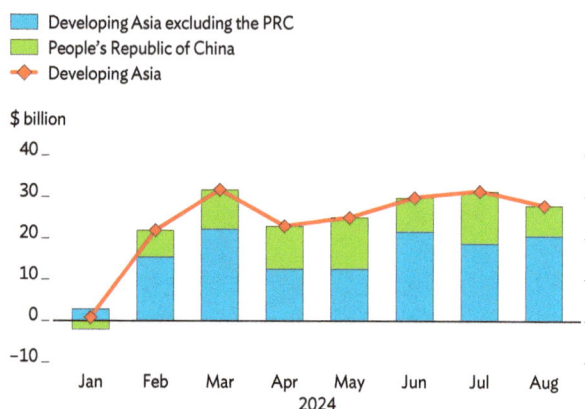

PRC = People's Republic of China.
Note: Data is as of 29 August.
Source: Institute of International Finance.

Improved Regional Growth and Inflation Outlook

Global Conditions Expected to Stabilize

The growth outlook for 2024 in major advanced economies is revised up from April projections, primarily due to a stronger-than-expected US economy. The US GDP growth forecast for 2024 is raised to 2.4%, reflecting robust private consumption and investment especially in the first half of the year, despite tight monetary conditions (Table 1.1.2). Growth is expected to slow to 1.7% in 2025 as still-high borrowing costs affect investment and as the labor market worsens. The US Federal Reserve commenced easing monetary policy in September 2024, cutting rates by 50 basis points to support the labor market, with further rate cuts expected this year and next. In the euro area, the growth projection for 2024 is raised slightly to 0.8%, rising to 1.4% in 2025 on recovering consumption, investment in green and digital infrastructure, and continued easing by the European Central Bank as disinflation progresses. Japan's growth forecast is lowered to 0.4% in 2024, as persistent high inflation has weighed on consumption. However, the growth outlook for 2025 is revised up to 1.0% driven by expected improvement in consumption as inflation moderates and wages increase.

Table 1.1.2 Baseline Assumptions on the International Economy

The growth outlook is raised for 2024 and maintained for 2025, with inflation forecasts revised up for both years.

	2023	2024		2025	
		April	September	April	September
Gross domestic product growth, %					
Major advanced economies[a]	**1.7**	**1.3**	**1.5**	**1.5**	**1.5**
United States	2.5	1.9	2.4	1.7	1.7
Euro area	0.5	0.7	0.8	1.4	1.4
Japan	1.9	0.6	0.4	0.8	1.0
People's Republic of China	5.2	4.8	4.8	4.5	4.5
Inflation, %					
Major advanced economies[a]	**4.5**	**2.4**	**2.7**	**2.0**	**2.2**
United States	4.1	2.6	2.9	2.2	2.2
Euro area	5.4	2.4	2.5	2.0	2.3
Japan	3.3	1.9	2.4	1.3	1.9

GDP = gross domestic product.

[a] Average growth rates are weighted by GDP purchasing power parity.

Sources: CEIC Data Company; Haver Analytics; IMF World Economic Outlook; Asian Development Bank estimates.

Oil prices are expected to remain broadly stable, with some upside risks. Brent crude oil prices averaged $83 from January to August 2024 and are expected to hover around this level through the end of the year (Figure 1.1.22). Oil prices will remain constrained by the slowdown in PRC, high global interest rates, and the unwinding of production cuts by the Organization of the Petroleum Exporting Countries and its partners (OPEC+). Upward pressure on oil prices could materialize in a scenario of heightened geopolitical tensions and wider conflict in the Middle East that draws in major oil producers. For 2025, oil prices are expected to decline to $81/barrel as the International Energy Agency forecasts that oil supply will rise faster than demand with the unwinding of OPEC+ production cuts.

Figure 1.1.22 Commodity Prices

Oil prices are forecast at $83/barrel in 2024, while rice prices will decline from current elevated levels.

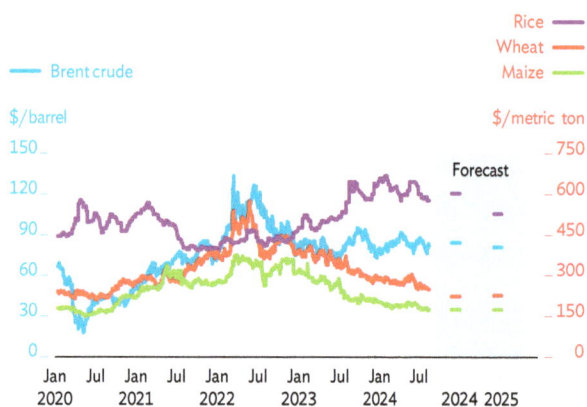

Note: Rice price refers to 5% broken, white rice, milled from Thailand.
Sources: Bloomberg; FocusEconomics.

Rice prices are expected to decline from their current high levels. Compared to the start of the year, rice prices dropped 9.3%, wheat 5.5%, and maize 5.2% as of early September, and may ease further as supply rises. The Food and Agriculture Organization of the United Nations expects rice production to reach a new record in 2024/2025 as El Niño dissipates. The easing of India's export restrictions on rice as stocks surge could also dampen price pressures. The high probability of La Niña developing later this year could also benefit water-intensive crops such as rice and wheat. However, excessive rainfall associated with La Niña also raises the risk of flooding, which could potentially damage agricultural crops and put upward pressure on food prices (Box 1.1.3).

Box 1.1.3 La Niña's Looming Impact on Developing Asia

La Niña is set to replace El Niño. The transition to La Niña is now anticipated. El Niño, which peaked in December 2023 as one of the five strongest on record, has given way to this new phase. According to the World Meteorological Organization, La Niña typically follows strong El Niño events and can last from 6 months to 2 years. It is associated with increased risk of heavy rainfall and flooding in some regions, while others may experience drought due to reduced rainfall.

Past La Niña events have had severe impacts. Historical data from the past 50 years show over 10 moderate-to-severe La Niña events (see box figure). Among these, the 2010–2012 La Niña event was particularly intense, causing severe flooding, particularly in Pakistan and Thailand, where millions were affected (FAO 2020, World Bank 2012).

Southern People's Republic of China experienced one of its worst droughts in decades, while Mongolia faced harsh winters that caused widespread livestock deaths (Sun and Yang 2012; Fernandez-Gimenez, Batjav, and Baival 2012). The Western Pacific saw an increase in strong tropical cyclones, affecting the Philippines and other regions (Boening, et al. 2012, NOAA 2011). The agricultural sector was heavily impacted, with both excessive rainfall and drought damaging crops. The economic toll was substantial, especially in Thailand, where the 2011 floods disrupted global supply chains and caused widespread damage (World Bank 2012). During the triple-dip La Niña from 2020 to 2023, several Pacific economies experienced flooding, landslides, and storm surges. These events led to significant destruction of infrastructure and crops, as well as the loss of lives and livestock (SPREP 2023).

continued on next page

Box 1.1.3 *Continued*

Weather Cycles and Commodity Prices

Over the years, various notable weather events have significantly impacted commodity prices.

Food price index ▬▬
Energy price index ▬▬
Metals and minerals price index ▬▬

■ El Niño Southern Oscillation (ENSO) index

% change year on year   Index

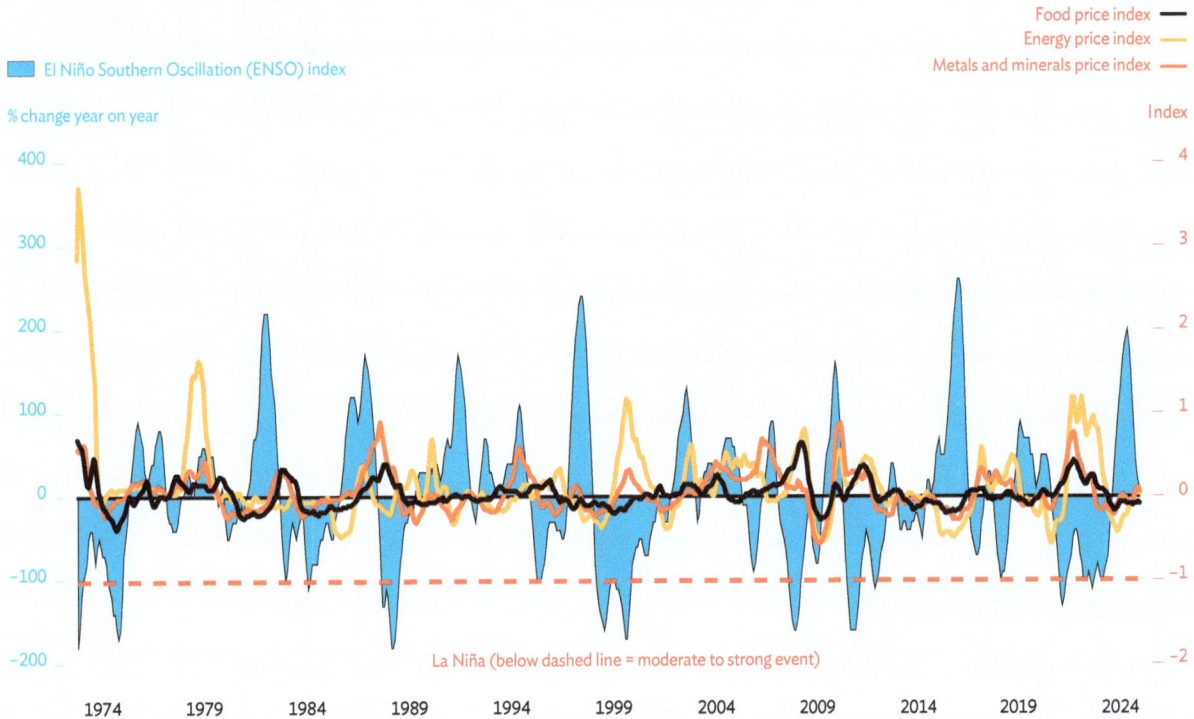

La Niña (below dashed line = moderate to strong event)

Note: Data used for the indexes are 3-month moving averages.
Sources: Climate Prediction Center - ONI (National Oceanic and Atmospheric Administration Climate Prediction Center); World Bank Commodity Pink Sheets.

While La Niña brought many challenges, it also had positive effects. Since La Niña frequently follows strong El Niño events, it counteracts the adverse effects of El Niño by bringing cooler temperatures and increased rainfall to regions that experienced drought and heat during previous El Niño events. La Niña offers the benefit of enhanced rainfall and improved monsoon conditions, which lead to increased irrigation and higher crop yields (CGIAR 2019; Deepak et al. 2018; Shuai et al. 2013; Li, Strapasson, and Rojas 2020). A study by Bertrand et al. (2020) also noted improved fish catches during La Niña years due to increased nutrient availability in cooler waters. These effects helped stabilize food supplies and support food security.

The upcoming La Niña could bring volatility to global commodity markets. In a recently released note, S&P Global Commodity Insights lists several

potential effects of La Niña on global commodity markets (Sadden and Style 2024). In Asia and the Pacific, countries such as India (producing rice, wheat, and sugarcane), Indonesia and Malaysia (producing palm oil and rice), and Australia (producing barley and canola) are likely to experience substantial increases in agricultural output. This boost is expected to lower commodity prices and help alleviate inflation risks in these areas. Conversely, La Niña is predicted to diminish agricultural yields in North and South America due to droughts and cold spells, particularly affecting wheat and soybeans. Other non-cereal crops will also be vulnerable to weather fluctuations. In livestock markets, improved pasture growth in Australia and New Zealand could enhance beef and dairy production, potentially increasing exports. However, the risk of heavy rainfall leading to waterlogging and disease outbreaks could harm overall livestock health. For the metals

continued on next page

Box 1.1.3 *Continued*

sector, heavier and more frequent rainfall can disrupt the transport and extraction of key minerals in Southeast Asia, Africa, and Australia. La Niña exacerbates the risk of flooding and landslides in Indonesia, where the mining of coal, copper, nickel, and bauxite already experiences frequent disruptions due to heavy seasonal rainfall. In the energy sector, La Niña's effects can be evident on both the supply and demand sides. The increased frequency and intensity of hurricanes, particularly in the Atlantic basin, pose significant risks to US Gulf Coast energy infrastructure which could affect global energy markets. The National Oceanic and Atmospheric Administration (NOAA) has warned of a potentially very active hurricane season, predicting 17 to 24 tropical storms, 8 to 13 hurricanes, and 4 to 7 major hurricanes compared to an average of about 14 storms, 7 hurricanes, and 3 major hurricanes during neutral seasons (NOAA 2024). On the demand side, La Niña often leads to colder-than-average winter temperatures in North America and North Asia, driving short-term increases in the demand for thermal coal and natural gas. On a more positive note, the Panama Canal is expected to recover its water level after a year of drought and logistical challenges, which should alleviate some pressure on global freight operations.

The effects of La Niña are highly contingent on the event's strength and duration. Historical data show that La Niña's impact on commodity prices varies; some events cause price increases due to supply reductions or higher production costs from extreme weather, while others lead to lower prices if increased production in certain regions offsets disruptions elsewhere. Broader economic conditions, sector-specific factors, and government policies also influence La Niña's impact. Governments can mitigate these effects by enhancing early warning systems, improving infrastructure resilience, managing water resources, supporting vulnerable populations, and coordinating disaster preparedness efforts.

References:

Bertrand, A., Lengaigne, M., Takahashi, K., Avadí, A., Poulain, F. & Harrod, C. 2020. El Niño Southern Oscillation (ENSO) effects on fisheries and aquaculture. *FAO Fisheries and Aquaculture Technical Paper* No. 660. Rome: FAO.

Boening, C., et al. 2012. The 2011 La Niña: So Strong, the Oceans Fell. Geophysical Research Letters 39 (19).

CGIAR (Consultative Group on International Agricultural Research). 2019. Managing El Niño and La Niña in Agriculture in Southeast Asia.

Deepak, S.N., J. Chowdary, A. Dandi, G. Srinivas, A. Parekh, C. Gnanaseelan, and R.K. Yadav. 2018. Impact of Multiyear La Niña events on the South and East Asian Summer Monsoon Rainfall in Observations and CMIP5 Models. *Climate Dynamics*.

FAO (Food and Agriculture Organization of the United Nations). 2020. FAO 2020–2021 La Niña Advisory.

Fernandez-Gimenez, M., B. Batjav, and B. Baival. 2012. Lessons from the Dzud: Adaptation and Resilience in Mongolian Pastoral Social-Ecological Systems.

Li, Y., A. Strapasson, and O. Rojas. 2020. Assessment of El Niño and La Niña Impacts on China: Enhancing the Early Warning System on Food and Agriculture. *Weather and Climate Extremes* 27.

NOAA (National Oceanic and Atmospheric Administration). 2024. NOAA 2024 Atlantic Hurricane Season Outlook. August.

———. 2011. 2010 Climate Events Connected to El Niño or La Niña.

Sadden, E. and G. Style. 2024. Commodities Markets Brace for La Niña Weather Impacts. S&P Commodity Insights. 16 July.

Shuai, J., ZX Zhang, D. Sun, F. Tao, and P. Shi. 2013. ENSO, Climate Variability and Crop Yields in China. *Climate Research* 58: 133–148.

SPREP (Secretariat of the Pacific Regional Environmental Programme). 2023. La Niña Impacts Felt throughout the Pacific.

Sun, C. and S. Yang. 2012. Persistent Severe Drought in Southern China during Winter-Spring 2011: Large Scale Circulation Patterns and Possible Impacting Factors. *Journal of Geophysical Research* 117(D10).

World Bank. 2012. Thailand Floods 2011: Rapid Assessment for Resilient Recovery and Reconstruction Planning.

This box was written by Pilipinas Quising of the Economic Research and Development Impact Department, ADB, Manila.

Regional Growth Remains Steady

Developing Asia's 2024 growth forecast is revised up slightly to 5.0%, from 4.9% in April ADO 2024, and maintained at 4.9% in 2025 (Figure 1.1.23). Exports will play a significant role in driving growth, with technology exporters benefiting the most, particularly from semiconductor exports, fueled by a surge in demand for AI processing and cloud computing applications. Domestic demand will remain firm, bolstered by further easing of price pressures. For 2024, the upward revisions in Caucasus and Central Asia, East Asia, and the Pacific have offset the slightly lower forecasts in Southeast Asia. Excluding the PRC, much of the region has now returned to pre-pandemic average growth rates.

The growth forecast for the PRC is retained at 4.8% in 2024 and 4.5% in 2025 (Table 1.1.3). The economy is expected to remain stable despite the prolonged downturn in the property sector, which is likely to persist throughout the year. Government measures, including expansionary fiscal policies, increased subsidies for trade-in schemes, and initiatives promoting large-scale equipment renewal and upgrades, are anticipated to spur consumption and investment. Amid foreign trade tensions, such as tariff hikes imposed by the US and EU, the PRC's price competitiveness and rising global demand for semiconductors and low-carbon technologies will help sustain export growth.

Exports will bolster growth in developing Asia's high-income technology-exporting economies this year. The momentum in global electronics demand that has driven growth in Hong Kong, China; Republic of Korea; Singapore; and Taipei,China in the first half of the year is expected to continue. In June 2024, the World Semiconductor Trade Statistics raised its projections for semiconductor billings, with growth of 77% forecast this year for memory chips, a key component in AI applications. Growth forecasts for the Republic of Korea and Taipei,China for 2024 are revised upward to 2.5% and 3.5%, respectively, on stronger-than-expected exports of semiconductors and AI-related goods in the first half of the year. For 2025, growth forecasts for the Republic of Korea and Taipei,China remain unchanged at 2.3% and 2.7%, respectively. Singapore's 2024 growth forecast is revised up to 2.6%, driven by increased demand for electronics and financial services, and is expected to remain steady at 2.6% in 2025. Growth projections for Hong Kong, China are retained at 2.8% in 2024 and 3.0% in 2025.

Figure 1.1.23 Growth Forecasts in Developing Asia

Growth in developing Asia is expected to remain steady and, excluding the PRC, most of the region has returned to pre-pandemic rates.

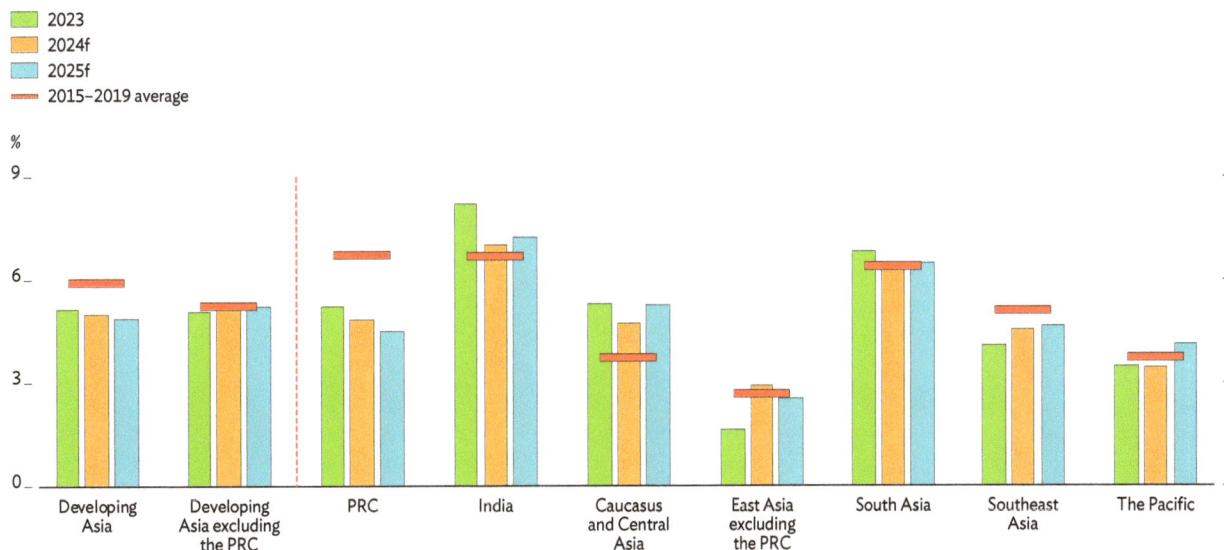

f = forecast; PRC = People's Republic of China.

Source: *Asian Development Outlook* database (accessed 5 September 2024).

Table 1.1.3 Gross Domestic Product Growth Rate and Inflation, %

Subregion/Economy	Gross Domestic Product Growth					Inflation				
	2023	2024f		2025f		2023	2024f		2025f	
		Apr	Sep	Apr	Sep		Apr	Sep	Apr	Sep
Developing Asia	**5.1**	**4.9**	**5.0**	**4.9**	**4.9**	**3.4**	**3.2**	**2.8**	**3.0**	**2.9**
Developing Asia excluding the PRC	**5.1**	**5.0**	**5.1**	**5.3**	**5.2**	**6.3**	**5.1**	**5.1**	**4.4**	**4.5**
Caucasus and Central Asia	**5.3**	**4.3**	**4.7**	**5.0**	**5.2**	**10.5**	**7.9**	**6.9**	**7.0**	**6.2**
Armenia	8.3	5.7	6.0	6.0	6.0	2.0	3.0	0.8	3.5	2.5
Azerbaijan	1.1	1.2	2.7	1.6	2.6	8.8	5.5	2.1	6.5	3.8
Georgia	7.5	5.0	7.0	5.5	5.5	2.5	3.5	2.5	4.0	3.5
Kazakhstan	5.1	3.8	3.6	5.3	5.1	14.5	8.7	8.5	6.3	6.1
Kyrgyz Republic	6.2	5.0	6.3	4.5	5.8	10.8	7.0	6.8	6.5	6.2
Tajikistan	8.3	6.5	6.5	6.5	6.5	3.8	5.5	5.5	6.5	6.5
Turkmenistan	6.3	6.5	6.5	6.0	6.0	5.9	8.0	5.0	8.0	5.0
Uzbekistan	6.0	5.5	6.0	5.6	6.2	10.0	10.0	9.5	9.5	9.0
East Asia	**4.7**	**4.5**	**4.6**	**4.2**	**4.2**	**0.6**	**1.3**	**0.8**	**1.6**	**1.3**
People's Republic of China	5.2	4.8	4.8	4.5	4.5	0.2	1.1	0.5	1.5	1.2
Hong Kong, China	3.3	2.8	2.8	3.0	3.0	2.1	2.3	1.8	2.3	2.3
Republic of Korea	1.4	2.2	2.5	2.3	2.3	3.6	2.5	2.5	2.0	2.0
Mongolia	7.4	4.1	5.5	6.0	6.0	10.4	7.0	6.8	6.8	7.2
Taipei,China	1.3	3.0	3.5	2.7	2.7	2.5	2.3	2.3	2.0	2.0
South Asia	**6.8**	**6.3**	**6.3**	**6.6**	**6.5**	**8.4**	**7.0**	**7.0**	**5.8**	**6.1**
Afghanistan	−6.2	...	...	...	...	10.8	...	...	...	...
Bangladesh	5.8	6.1	5.8	6.6	5.1	9.0	8.4	9.7	7.0	10.1
Bhutan	4.0	4.4	5.5	7.0	7.0	4.2	4.5	4.6	4.2	4.2
India	8.2	7.0	7.0	7.2	7.2	5.4	4.6	4.7	4.5	4.5
Maldives	4.1	5.4	5.0	6.0	5.4	2.9	3.2	2.8	2.5	2.3
Nepal	2.0	3.6	3.9	4.8	4.9	7.7	6.5	5.4	6.0	5.5
Pakistan	−0.2	1.9	2.4	2.8	2.8	29.2	25.0	23.4	15.0	15.0
Sri Lanka	−2.3	1.9	2.6	2.5	2.8	17.4	7.5	3.8	5.5	5.5
Southeast Asia	**4.1**	**4.6**	**4.5**	**4.7**	**4.7**	**4.2**	**3.2**	**3.3**	**3.0**	**3.2**
Brunei Darussalam	1.4	3.7	3.7	2.8	2.8	0.4	1.1	0.4	1.0	1.0
Cambodia	5.0	5.8	5.8	6.0	6.0	2.1	2.0	0.5	2.0	2.5
Indonesia	5.0	5.0	5.0	5.0	5.0	3.7	2.8	2.8	2.8	2.8
Lao People's Democratic Republic	3.7	4.0	4.0	4.0	3.7	31.2	20.0	25.0	7.0	21.5
Malaysia	3.6	4.5	4.5	4.6	4.6	2.5	2.6	2.4	2.6	2.7
Myanmar	0.8	1.2	0.8	2.2	1.7	27.0	15.5	20.7	10.2	15.0
Philippines	5.5	6.0	6.0	6.2	6.2	6.0	3.8	3.6	3.4	3.2
Singapore	1.1	2.4	2.6	2.6	2.6	4.8	3.0	2.6	2.2	2.2
Thailand	1.9	2.6	2.3	3.0	2.7	1.2	1.0	0.7	1.5	1.3
Timor-Leste	1.9	3.4	3.1	4.1	3.9	8.4	3.5	3.4	2.9	2.9
Viet Nam	5.1	6.0	6.0	6.2	6.2	3.3	4.0	4.0	4.0	4.0
Pacific	**3.4**	**3.3**	**3.4**	**4.0**	**4.1**	**3.0**	**4.3**	**3.6**	**4.1**	**4.1**
Cook Islands	14.0	9.1	15.0	5.2	7.5	13.2	2.3	4.5	2.3	4.0
Fiji	7.5	3.0	3.4	2.7	2.9	2.4	3.7	5.0	2.6	2.6
Kiribati	4.2	5.3	5.8	3.5	4.1	9.3	4.0	4.5	3.0	3.0
Marshall Islands	−0.6	2.7	2.0	1.7	3.0	7.3	5.5	5.8	3.7	4.6
Federated States of Micronesia	0.8	3.1	3.1	2.8	3.5	6.2	4.1	4.1	3.5	3.5
Nauru	1.6	1.8	2.0	2.0	2.5	5.2	10.3	5.0	3.5	3.5
Niue	...	...	...	...	...	8.6	...	...	...	...
Palau	−0.2	6.5	6.5	8.0	8.0	12.4	5.5	5.5	1.0	1.0
Papua New Guinea	2.0	3.3	3.2	4.6	4.5	2.3	4.5	3.0	4.8	4.8
Samoa	8.0	4.2	11.0	4.0	8.0	12.0	4.5	3.6	4.3	3.2
Solomon Islands	3.0	2.2	2.5	2.2	2.5	5.1	3.2	3.2	2.7	2.7
Tonga	2.2	2.6	2.0	2.3	2.3	9.7	4.5	4.6	4.2	4.2
Tuvalu	3.9	3.5	3.5	2.4	2.4	7.2	3.0	2.5	3.0	3.0
Vanuatu	1.0	3.1	1.9	3.6	2.4	11.2	4.8	4.8	2.9	2.9

... = not available, f = forecast.

Source: *Asian Development Outlook* database (accessed 5 September 2024).

South Asia's growth forecast for 2024 is maintained at 6.3%, fueled by solid growth in India. India's growth forecasts are retained at 7.0% for fiscal year (FY) 2024 and 7.2% for FY2025, in line with April projections, supported by broad-based expansion across sectors. Bhutan's 2024 growth outlook is revised to 5.5%, up from 4.4% in April, driven by the earlier-than-expected completion of the Punatsangchhu II hydropower plant, which will boost electricity generation. The growth forecast for 2025 is maintained at 7.0%. Nepal's economy expanded 3.9% in FY2024, driven by higher agricultural output, increased tourist arrivals, and greater electricity generation. The growth forecast for 2025 has been slightly raised to 4.9%, as the government ramps up infrastructure spending and considers further monetary easing. Pakistan's economy expanded by 2.4% in FY2024, driven by higher consumption following the government's economic stabilization and reform program. Growth is projected to further improve to 2.8% in FY2025, supported by a revival in private investment. Sri Lanka's growth forecast is adjusted upwards to 2.6% in 2024 and 2.8% in 2025, supported by progress on debt restructuring and effects of monetary policy easing. However, these gains were partially offset by downward revisions in Bangladesh largely due to supply disruptions caused by the political unrest in July and August 2024, and in Maldives as the construction sector is anticipated to decline further due to planned reductions in public sector investment.

Subdued government capital spending and slower-than-expected export recovery will weigh on growth in Southeast Asia this year. The subregional growth outlook for 2024 is revised down to 4.5%, driven by downward revisions in Myanmar, Thailand, and Timor-Leste. Lower-than-expected government spending and weaker-than-expected export recovery underpinned the downward adjustment in Thailand's growth outlook to 2.3% in 2024 and 2.7% in 2025, down 0.3 percentage points from April's projections. Again, lower public spending due to delays in capital-intensive projects led to the revision for Timor-Leste to 3.1% in 2024 and 3.9% in 2025. In Myanmar, macroeconomic instability, rising input costs and declining investment amid the ongoing conflict resulted in a downward revision of the growth forecast to 0.8% in 2024 and 1.7% in 2025. Meanwhile, the growth projection is retained for the rest of Southeast Asia's economies, apart from Singapore, where higher export growth led to an upward revision.

In the Caucasus and Central Asia, growth projections are higher for both 2024 and 2025, driven by stronger-than-expected domestic demand. The subregion is now expected to grow by 4.7% in 2024 and 5.2% in 2025, up by 0.4 and 0.2 percentage points, respectively, from April's estimates. In Armenia, the 2024 growth forecast is adjusted upward to 6.0% on account of a first half performance driven by industry, while remaining unchanged in 2025 at 6.0%. Azerbaijan's projections are raised to 2.7% in 2024 and 2.6% in 2025, fueled by higher public spending on reconstruction. Georgia recorded faster-than-expected growth in the first half of 2024, on robust domestic consumption, and supported by strong credit growth, exports, and tourism receipts. Consequently, growth is revised up to 7.0% in 2024 while remaining at 5.5% in 2025. Similarly, in the Kyrgyz Republic, consumption is expected to drive growth, with higher forecasts at 6.3% in 2024 and 5.8% in 2025, supported by remittances and improved prospects in agriculture and industry sectors. In Uzbekistan, steady growth in consumption and investment, particularly in infrastructure and machineries and equipment, is projected to boost growth to 6.0% in 2024 and 6.2% in 2025. In contrast, Kazakhstan's growth forecast is lowered to 3.6% in 2024 and 5.1% in 2025, due to reduced oil production in line with the OPEC+ agreement. Meanwhile, the growth projections for Tajikistan and Turkmenistan for 2024 and 2025 remain unchanged from April's forecasts.

Tourism is expected to remain a key driver of growth in the Pacific. The subregional growth forecasts are raised to 3.4% for 2024 and 4.1% for 2025, up by 0.1 percentage point from April estimates. Forecasts for this year and next for Cook Islands, Fiji, Kiribati, Nauru, Samoa, and Solomon Islands are better than initially estimated in April, due to sustained growth in visitor arrivals and an increase in public sector wages in some economies. However, downward adjustments in the 2024 growth numbers of Marshall Islands, Papua New Guinea, Tonga, and Vanuatu have partially weighed on overall subregional growth. Papua New Guinea's 2024 growth outlook is slightly revised down to 3.2% due to lower-than-expected output in the resource sector. Tonga's growth outlook is also lowered to 2.0% on weaker-than-expected agricultural output due to El Niño. The liquidation of Air Vanuatu dampened economic activity in Vanuatu, while there were downward data revisions for the Marshall Islands.

Looking ahead to 2025, subregional growth forecast for the Pacific is expected to increase to 4.1% driven primarily by higher visitor arrivals.

Inflation Further Moderates in Developing Asia

While regional inflation is expected to ease further, some economies still face price pressures. The inflation forecast for the region is lowered to 2.8% for 2024 and 2.9% for 2025, from 3.2% and 3.0% in April, driven largely by the downward revision in the PRC. Excluding the PRC, the inflation forecast for the region is at 5.1% for 2024, unchanged from April's estimates, with the inflation projected to remain high in Lao PDR, Myanmar, and Pakistan amid economic and political tensions (Figure 1.1.24).

Declining food and property prices due to weak domestic demand will continue to suppress the PRC's inflation. The 2024 inflation forecast for the PRC has been adjusted downwards from 1.1% in the April ADO 2024 to 0.5%, due to delayed bottoming out of food prices and the ongoing property sector

weakness. In addition, price competition in industries such as semiconductors, electric vehicles, solar photovoltaics, and steel may add to deflationary pressures. For 2025, inflation is projected at 1.2%, down from 1.5% in April, as domestic demand remains subdued. In July 2024, the People's Bank of China reduced several key interest rates, including the seven-day reverse repo rate by 10 basis points to 1.7% and the medium-term lending facility rate by 20 basis points to 2.3%, to boost economic recovery.

Inflation will further moderate in the region's high-income technology exporters. The forecast for Hong Kong, China is revised down to 1.8% in 2024, from April's 2.3%, reflecting slower-than-anticipated inflation in H1 2024 on subdued domestic demand. Inflation is expected to reach 2.3% in 2025. In Singapore, the outlook for 2024 has been lowered to 2.6%, as currency appreciation is expected to moderate imported inflation throughout the year. The inflation forecast for 2025 is unchanged at 2.2%. In the Republic of Korea, inflation is expected to moderate to 2.5% in 2024 and 2.0% in 2025, similar to April's projections. For Taipei,China, inflation will decelerate to 2.3% in 2024 and 2.0% in 2025, following a rate hike in March 2024 and the easing of global price pressures.

Figure 1.1.24 Inflation Forecasts for 2024 for Selected Developing Asian Economies

Regional inflation will further moderate, but price pressures will remain elevated in Lao PDR, Myanmar, and Pakistan.

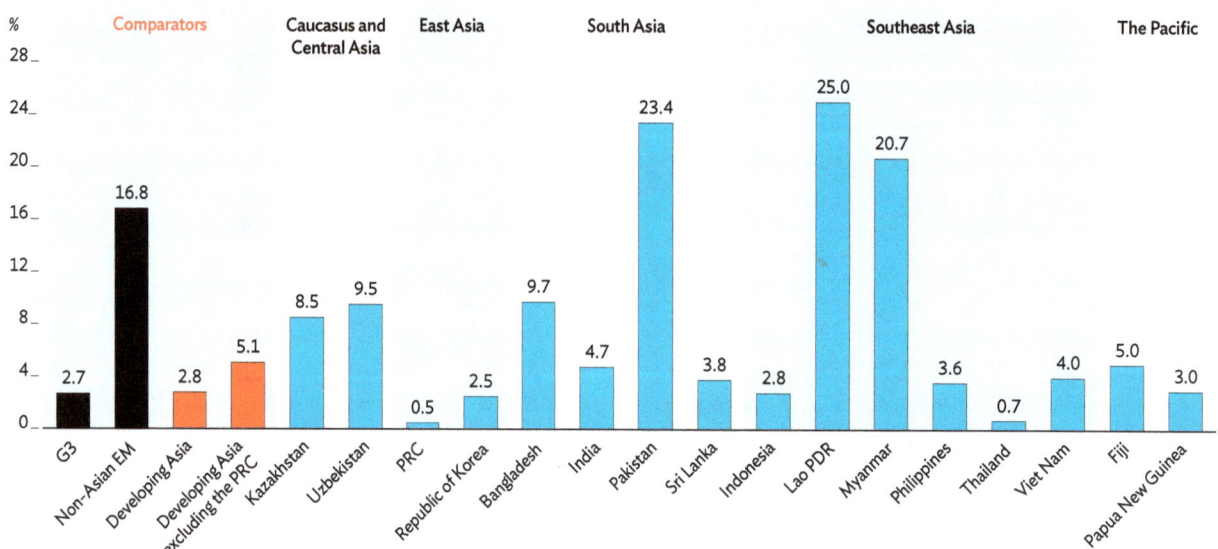

EM = emerging market; G3 = euro area, Japan, United States; Lao PDR = Lao People's Democratic Republic; PRC = People's Republic of China.
Source. *Asian Development Outlook* database (accessed 5 September 2024).

In South Asia, inflation projections are maintained for 2024 and raised for 2025. Headline inflation for the subregion is expected to moderate to 7.0% in 2024 from 8.4% in 2023, and further to 6.1% in 2025. There are notable revisions among the economies. India's inflation is revised up to 4.7% by 0.1 percentage points in 2024, owing to higher-than-expected food inflation from adverse weather conditions. For 2025, the inflation forecast is maintained at 4.5%. In Bangladesh, inflation rose to 9.7% in FY2024, driven primarily by high food prices. The FY2025 forecast is up 3.1 percentage points from April estimates, to 10.1% due to supply chain disruptions and rising import costs due to currency depreciation. Pakistan's inflation slowed to 23.4% in FY2024 mainly on lower food inflation resulting from higher agriculture production. Inflation in 2025 is expected to moderate to 15.0%, supported by a tighter monetary policy and more stable global commodity prices. Sri Lanka's inflation is revised down 3.7 percentage points to 3.8% in 2024, due to significant reductions in utility prices and weak domestic demand resulting in slower-than-expected inflation in the first half of the year. Inflation is expected to pick up to 5.5% in 2025 as growth recovers.

Currency depreciations in the Lao PDR and Myanmar have contributed to upward revisions in the inflation forecast for Southeast Asia. The 2024 inflation forecast for the subregion has been revised upward to 3.3% from 3.2% in April. Lao PDR's forecast has surged to 25.0%, the highest among all 46 economies in developing Asia, while Myanmar's has risen to 20.7%, both driven by the depreciation of their currencies, which has intensified domestic inflationary pressures. On the other hand, inflation was revised downward for some economies, including Brunei Darussalam, Cambodia, Malaysia, the Philippines, Singapore, Thailand, and Timor-Leste. A stronger-than-expected easing of global commodity prices, as well as currency appreciation in some cases, were contributory factors. For 2025, the inflation projection for the subregion is raised to 3.2%.

Tight monetary policy and currency appreciation will further drive down inflation in the Caucasus and Central Asia. Inflation for the subregion is adjusted to 6.9% in 2024 and 6.2% in 2025, down by 1.0 and 0.8 percentage points from April's estimates, respectively. In Azerbaijan, the inflation forecast for 2024 is significantly lower at 2.1%, from 5.5% in April, due to easing of global commodity prices and the impact of a series of monetary tightening measures. The central bank cut its key policy rate by 50 basis points from January to July to 7.25% to spur consumption, and this is expected to partly offset downward pressures on inflation in the near term. In Turkmenistan, projections are also lowered, to 5.0%, in 2024 and 2025, from 8.0% previously, amid tight monetary policy and exchange rate and price control measures. The inflation forecast for Uzbekistan is revised down to 9.5% in 2024 due to better-than-expected supply of agricultural products and lower cost of imported goods. In July 2024, the central bank reduced its key policy rate by 50 basis points to 13.5% as inflation moderated. Currency appreciation contributed to the downward revision in the inflation forecasts of Kazakhstan and Kyrgyz Republic.

Slower-than-expected inflation in H1 2024 in the Pacific led to a downward revision to 3.6% for 2024. The subregion's forecast for 2024 is lowered mainly due to revisions in Nauru, Papua New Guinea, Samoa, and Tuvalu. In Papua New Guinea, inflation fell more than expected in H1 due to lower prices of alcoholic beverages, tobacco, betelnut, household equipment and communication costs. Similarly, in Samoa and Tuvalu, inflation slowed more than expected due to subdued food and transportation costs. Communication costs are anticipated to decline further in Nauru following a recent agreement that will introduce fee-based public access to the internet. These outweighed upward adjustments in Cook Islands, Fiji, Kiribati, Marshall Islands, and Tonga. For 2025, the inflation forecast is unchanged at 4.1%.

Several Downside Risks Cloud the Regional Outlook

Risks to the outlook for developing Asia remain skewed to the downside. While regional economic growth remains robust and inflation continues to trend downward, several risks persist. These include a rise in protectionism depending on the outcome of the US presidential election in November, geopolitical tensions, further weakening of the PRC's property market, and more severe weather-related events than anticipated.

Depending on the outcome of the US presidential election, an increase in protectionism and trade fragmentation could materialize. The election could result in higher blanket tariffs by the US on all global imports, and a broad-based and steep increase in tariffs on all US imports from the PRC. This would significantly escalate US-PRC trade tensions, with potential negative spillovers to developing Asia through real and financial channels. Sharp shifts in US trade policies, foreign relations, or economic strategies post-election could impact global trade flows and investment patterns, adding another layer of complexity to the economic outlook. Rising protectionism could also lead to elevated volatility in global financial markets, and capital outflows from the region. These outflows could trigger currency depreciation in emerging economies, higher borrowing costs, and increased difficulty in financing debt, which could further strain economies already under pressure. The US administration of 2017 to 2021 was marked by aggressive trade actions, most notably the trade tensions with the PRC, which included substantial tariffs on PRC goods. If a similar approach is pursued, it could lead to renewed trade tensions, potentially affecting not only the PRC but other Asian economies closely tied to global supply chains.

Escalating geopolitical tensions due to wider conflict in the Middle East and Russia's war in Ukraine remain concerning. The war in Ukraine remains fluid, with ongoing military and diplomatic developments, thus still posing significant risks to the global economy. These include potentially disrupting energy supplies, exacerbating inflation, and destabilizing international trade networks. Likewise, the conflict in Red Sea since mid-November has caused most container lines to reroute around Africa—rather than through the Suez Canal and into the Mediterranean—adding nearly 6,000 miles and 2 weeks to their journeys (Box 1.1.2). Consequently, average weekly port calls through the Suez dropped 86% in the first 7 months of 2024 compared to the same period last year. A.P. Moller-Maersk A/S, a major shipping and logistics company, reported on 6 May that fuel consumption per journey had increased 40% and charter rates were three times higher than usual. One of the primary risks associated with an escalation of the wider conflict in the Middle East is the potential disruption of crucial oil shipping routes, such as the Strait of Hormuz, through which a significant portion of the world's oil supply is transported. While this waterway has never been fully closed to traffic, it has faced multiple threats to its accessibility. Any blockage or interference in this route, akin to the disruptions currently being experienced in other routes, could drastically reduce global oil supply, driving up prices and impacting energy costs. Furthermore, broader conflicts in the region could heighten geopolitical risks, prompting businesses to delay expansion and consumers to reduce spending, which may dampen economic activity and increase financial market volatility as investors seek safer assets.

Growth prospects in the PRC could be weakened by further deterioration in its property market. The current downturn in the property market could become more severe or more disorderly, negatively impacting overall economic activity. This could be compounded by indirect effects through a worsening of consumer and investor sentiment, and the implications on local government revenues due to declining land sales to property developers. These effects could also lead to higher borrowing costs, making it more challenging for businesses to access credit and for local governments to finance public investment and infrastructure projects. In addition, the rest of the region could be affected through several channels, including on the real side via lower PRC demand for imports. This reduction in demand could affect industries heavily reliant on Chinese consumption, such as manufacturing and tourism, leading to lower export revenues and economic contractions.

Adverse weather conditions and the impacts of climate change could undermine food and energy security and lead to volatile commodity prices. In September, the US National Oceanic and Atmospheric Administration's Climate Prediction Center forecasts that there is currently a 71% likelihood of La Niña developing between September and November and persisting into Q1 2025. The August 2024 climate forecast from the International Research Institute for Climate and Society shows elevated probabilities of above-normal precipitation in Central America and Caribbean regions, Southwestern parts of the Arabian Peninsula, South Asia, Southeast Asia, parts of the PRC, and Australia during the three forecast

seasons (August–October, September–November, and October–December 2024) (Figure 1.1.25). In contrast, parts of South America, the western and central US, Mexico, and the Middle East are expected to experience below-normal rainfall, especially as La Niña develops. The anticipated return of the La Niña climate phenomenon, along with its effects on global weather patterns and temperature extremes, could introduce a new wave of disruption and volatility to major global commodity markets (see Box 1.1.3).

The higher precipitation associated with La Niña may provide relief to coffee, sugar, and rice producers in Asia who have faced dry conditions over the past year. However, excessive rainfall could also elevate the risk of flooding and landslides, potentially threatening agriculture and livelihoods. Conversely, drier-than-expected conditions in South America and the US might severely impact the production of key agricultural commodities like wheat, soybeans, corn, coffee, and sugar, which are vital to global supply. Beyond agriculture, La Niña could disrupt mining operations and increase the risk of damage to energy infrastructure.

Figure 1.1.25 Forecast Precipitation October–December 2024

La Niña alters rainfall patterns across various regions of the world.

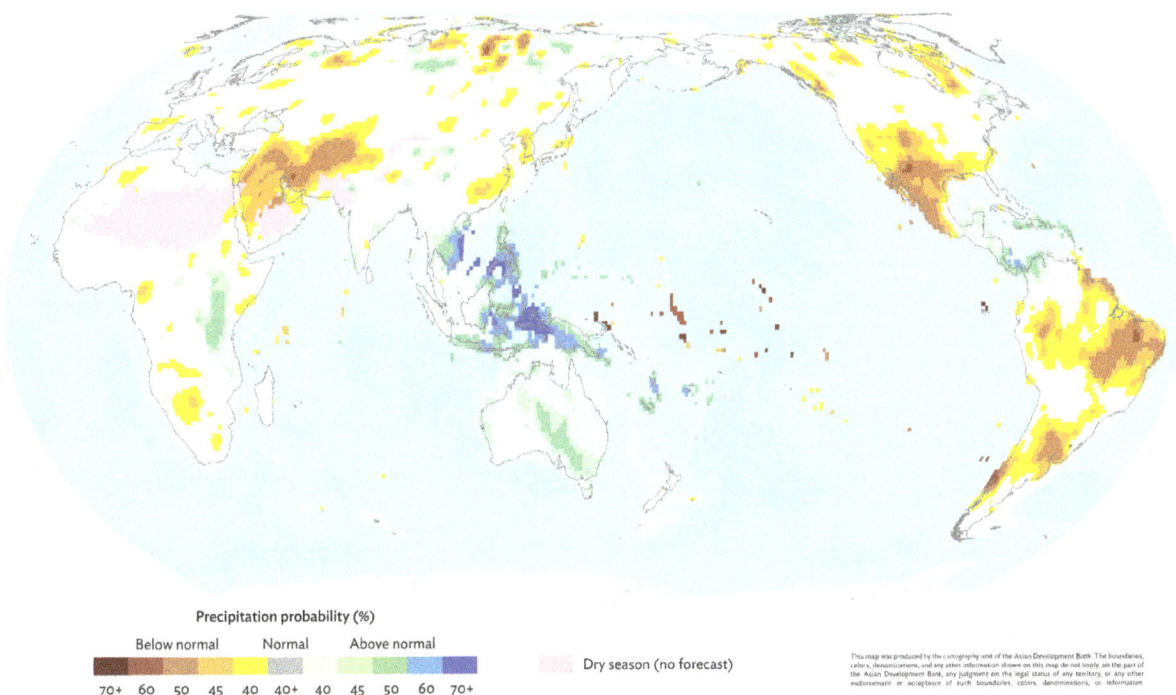

Note: White areas indicate grid points where all three categories are equally likely.

Source: Adapted from Columbia Climate School International Research Institute for Climate and Society. 2024. IRI Multi-Model Probability Forecast for Precipitation for October–November–December 2024. August.

Resilient Growth in Major Economies, Despite Geopolitical Risks

Aggregate growth forecasts for the major industrial economies of the United States, the euro area, and Japan are upgraded to 1.5% in 2024 and retained at 1.5% in 2025 (Table A.1). US data has remained resilient despite tight monetary conditions, but a slowdown is expected as the labor market weakens and private consumption and investment wanes. In the euro area, private consumption supported by wage increases and rising public investment in green and digital infrastructure will boost activity. Similarly, consumption in Japan will drive growth as wages increase and inflation slows.

Table A.1 Baseline Assumptions on the International Economy

	2023	2024		2025	
		April	September	April	September
Gross domestic product growth, %					
Major advanced economies[a]	1.7	1.3	1.5	1.5	1.5
United States	2.5	1.9	2.4	1.7	1.7
Euro area	0.5	0.7	0.8	1.4	1.4
Japan	1.9	0.6	0.4	0.8	1.0
Inflation, %					
Major advanced economies[a]	4.5	2.4	2.7	2.0	2.2
United States	4.1	2.6	2.9	2.2	2.2
Euro area	5.4	2.4	2.5	2.0	2.3
Japan	3.3	1.9	2.4	1.3	1.9
Brent crude spot prices, average, $/barrel	83	82	83	79	81
Interest rates					
United States federal funds rate, average, %	5.00	5.20	5.15	4.20	3.97
European Central Bank refinancing rate, average, %	3.90	4.20	4.10	3.10	3.10
Bank of Japan overnight call rate, average, %	0.00	0.00	0.25	0.10	0.40

GDP = gross domestic product.

[a] Average growth rates are weighted by GDP purchasing power parity.

Sources: CEIC Data Company; Haver Analytics; International Monetary Fund. World Economic Outlook; Asian Development Bank estimates.

This annex was written by John Beirne, Gabriele Ciminelli, Jaqueson Galimberti, Jules Hugot, Matteo Lanzafame, Pilipinas Quising, and Dennis Sorino of the Economic Research and Development Impact Department (ERDI), ADB, Manila, and Emmanuel Alano, Jesson Pagaduan, and Michael Timbang, ERDI consultants.

Recent Developments in the Major Advanced Economies

United States

The US economy grew faster than expected in the second quarter of 2024. After growing 1.4% in the first quarter (Q1) in seasonally adjusted annualized terms (as assumed for all quarterly growth rates in this *Annex* unless otherwise stated), the economy more than doubled that pace to 3.0% in Q2 (Figure A.1). A rebound in private spending growth contributed 2.0 percentage points to overall GDP growth, leading the robust expansion. Private investment also increased notably, growing 7.5% due to higher nonresidential investment and private inventories. Government spending added 0.5 percentage points to GDP growth, primarily due to a 4.9% increase in national defense spending. However, net exports subtracted 0.8 percentage points from growth as imports grew faster than exports.

Despite positive GDP growth, several forward-looking economic indicators point to underlying weaknesses. The ISM manufacturing purchasing managers' Index (PMI) revised to 47.2 in August,

Figure A.1 Demand-Side Contributions to Growth, United States

Growth in Q2 was faster than expected, driven by private expenditure and investment.

- Private expenditure
- Private investment
- Government expenditure and investment
- Exports
- Imports
- Gross domestic product growth, %

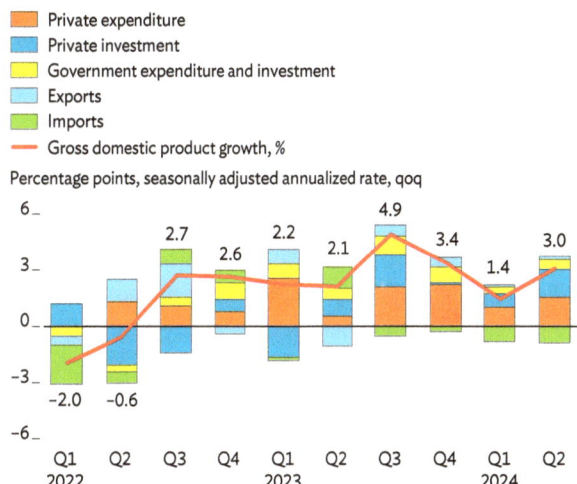

Q = quarter, qoq = quarter on quarter.
Sources: Department of Commerce. Bureau of Economic Analysis; Haver Analytics.

marking the fifth consecutive month of contraction in manufacturing activity (Table A.2). This slowdown was attributed to weak demand, declining output, and contracting employment. The ISM Services PMI fell sharply to 48.8 in June, the lowest since May

Table A.2 Consumer, Business, and Employment Indicators, United States

| | Annual Average | | | 2024 | | | | | | | |
	2021	2022	2023	Jan	Feb	Mar	Apr	May	Jun	Jul	Aug
Business											
Manufacturing PMI, 50 = no change	60.6 ▲	53.5 ▲	47.1 ▼	49.1 ▼	47.8 ▼	50.3 ▲	49.2 ▼	48.7 ▼	48.5 ▼	46.8 ▼	47.2 ▲
Service PMI, 50 = no change	62.4 ▲	56.1 ▲	52.8 ▲	53.4 ▲	52.6 ▲	51.4 ▲	49.4 ▼	53.8 ▲	48.8 ▼	51.4 ▲	51.5 ▲
Industrial production index, 2017 = 100	99.3 ▲	102.7 ▲	102.9 ▲	101.5 ▼	102.7 ▲	102.5 ▼	102.5 ↔	103.3 ▲	103.5 ▲	102.9 ▼	...
Consumer											
Consumer confidence, 1985 = 100	112.7 ▲	104.5 ▼	105.4 ▲	110.9 ▲	104.8 ▼	103.1 ▼	97.5 ▼	101.3 ▲	97.8 ▼	101.9 ▲	103.3 ▲
Consumer sentiment, Q1 1966 = 100	77.6 ▲	59.0 ▼	65.4 ▲	79.0 ▲	76.9 ▼	79.4 ▲	77.2 ▼	69.1 ▼	68.2 ▼	66.4 ▼	67.9 ▲
Retail Sales, $ billion	542.6 ▲	586.8 ▲	601.3 ▲	601.9 ▼	606.7 ▲	610.1 ▲	608.5 ▼	610.0 ▲	608.5 ▼	615.0 ▲	...
Employment											
Unemployment rate, %	5.4 ▼	3.6 ▲	3.6 ▼	3.7 ↔	3.9 ▲	3.8 ▼	3.9 ▲	4.0 ▲	4.1 ▲	4.3 ▲	4.2 ▼
Nonfarm payrolls, thousand	604 ▲	377 ▼	251 ▼	256 ▲	236 ▼	310 ▲	108 ▼	216 ▲	118 ▼	89 ▼	142 ▲
Job openings, million	10.0 ▲	11.2 ▲	9.4 ▼	8.7 ▼	8.8 ▲	8.4 ▼	7.9 ▼	8.2 ▲	7.9 ▼	7.7 ▼	...

... = data not available.
Notes: For PMI, ▲ is greater than 50, ▼ is less than 50, and ↔ equals 50. For other indicators, ▲ is increasing, ▼ is decreasing, and ↔ remains the same.
Source: Haver Analytics.

2020, but rebounded moderately in July and August, driven by a recovery in orders and employment. These developments suggest that certain sectors of the economy are starting to face challenges.

Households feel the pressure of higher prices amid a cooling labor market. Consumer sentiment remained on the weak side, with the University of Michigan's index adjusted to 67.9 in August. Consumer price index (CPI)-deflated retail sales were 5.2% below the peak reached in April 2022. The labor market continued to soften with nonfarm payrolls growing 142,000 in August, while the unemployment rate stood at to 4.2%. Inflation edged down to 2.9% in July, marking the lowest rate since June 2023 (Figure A.2). High core inflation, at 3.2% in July, mainly drove the persistently high inflation rate, primarily due to higher costs in housing and transport services. The US Federal Reserve had kept its policy rate target range on hold at 5.25%–5.50% since July 2023, the peak of this hiking cycle. In September 2024, the target range was reduced by 50 basis points, while the Fed continues to emphasize a data-dependent approach.

Growth is expected to slow to 2.4% in 2024 and 1.7% in 2025, while inflation will slow to 2.9% in 2024 and 2.2% in 2025. The economy has so far proven resilient to the tight monetary conditions, but a slowdown is imminent. Private consumption is

expected to lose steam as the job market cools and consumer sentiment remains low. Investment is also expected to slow as high interest rates hamper credit growth and as policy uncertainty mounts amid the presidential election. In the external sector, imports will continue to outpace exports as global demand remains weak while importers build inventories amid rising geopolitical uncertainty and fears of a potential strike in East Coast ports. As the Fed continues the monetary easing cycle, business confidence and growth will rebound in 2025. Inflation will continue softening as the labor market eases and the persistence in housing inflation fades away.

Risks to the forecast are balanced. The upcoming presidential elections pose downside risks in the near term and beyond. If policy uncertainties continue to rise in the run-up to the elections, businesses may further hold back planned investments. Beyond 2024, loose fiscal policy may reignite inflation and monetary tightening, while restrictive trade and immigration policies may hamper growth prospects. The timing of the monetary easing cycle is another risk to the outlook. While inflationary surprises may lead the Fed to slow down the pace of monetary easing, recession fears may trigger a faster-than-expected loosening of monetary conditions. Global demand and geopolitical uncertainties also pose balanced risks to the outlook. Although the impact of heightened uncertainty is already apparent in business decisions, an escalation in trade tensions and geopolitical conflicts can have a negative impact on growth, while de-escalation would impact the outlook positively.

Euro area

The economy has picked up steam, supported by a strong labor market and increased external demand. After tepid growth in the second half of 2023, the euro area GDP expanded 1.3% (0.5% year on year) in Q1 of 2024 and 0.8% (0.6% year on year) in Q2. The expansion was supported by an increase in net exports. These contributed 3.4 and 2.0 percentage points to Q1 and Q2 growth rates, offsetting a large negative contribution of investment (Figure A.3). Services trade recovered as the tourism sector continued its rebound. Although energy prices have decreased, output in energy-intensive sectors continues to decline, bringing down overall industrial production, which is still well below record 2022 levels.

Figure A.2 Inflation, United States

Inflation persists above target, driven by housing and transportation services costs.

- Food
- Energy
- Core: Housing
- Core: Transportation services
- Core: Others
- Headline

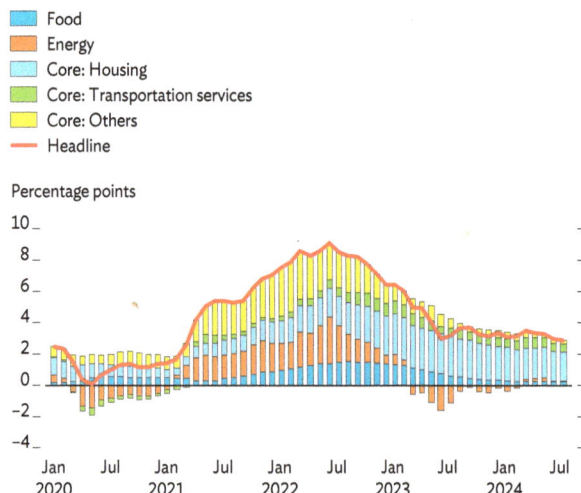

Percentage points

Sources: Asian Development Bank estimates; Haver Analytics.

Figure A.3 Demand-Side Contributions to Growth, Euro Area

Net exports boosted Q1 and Q2 growth.

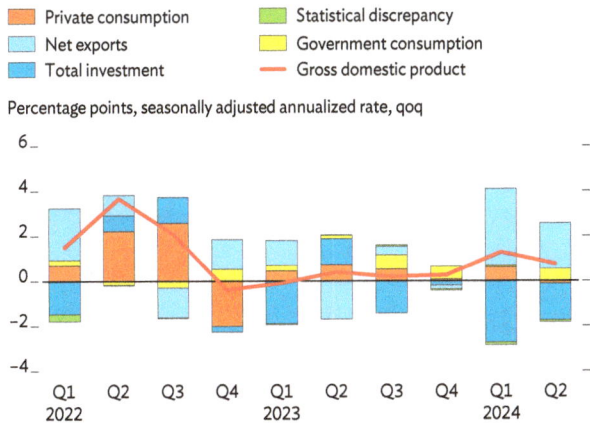

- Private consumption
- Net exports
- Total investment
- Statistical discrepancy
- Government consumption
- Gross domestic product

Percentage points, seasonally adjusted annualized rate, qoq

Q = quarter, qoq = quarter on quarter.
Source: Haver Analytics.

Figure A.4 Purchasing Managers' Index, Euro Area Aggregate and Selected Countries, August 2024

Leading indicators suggest expansion in the services sector and continued contraction in manufacturing activity.

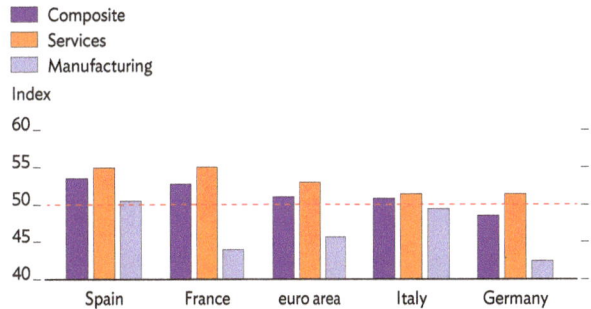

- Composite
- Services
- Manufacturing

Index

Note: An index reading < 50 signals deterioration, > 50 improvement.
Source: S&P Global.

Financial conditions have eased somewhat, but credit standards remain tight and demand for loans continues to decline.

Leading PMI indicators point to diverging prospects between services and manufacturing sectors and between core and peripheral countries. The euro area manufacturing PMI stabilized just below 46 in August 2024, well below 50, the expansion threshold, while the services PMI remained expansionary, settling above 53, up from less than 52 in June. Composite PMI indicators suggest contraction in Germany and expansions in France, Spain, and Italy (Figure A.4). Record-low ratios of unemployed people to job

vacancies and high rates of vacancies opened per total jobs suggest that the labor market will remain strong, continuing to support healthy wage growth.

The impulse from the macroeconomic policy mix will be broadly neutral (Figure A.5). The European Central Bank cut interest rates for the first time in 5 years in June. But interest rates are still high, and the nascent easing cycle will be gradual and contingent on sustained disinflationary progress, which has slowed somewhat since the beginning of 2024. After declining rapidly from over 10% in October 2022, largely thanks to energy prices either falling or stabilizing, headline inflation has hovered at around 2.5% between February and July 2024, before declining further to

Figure A.5 Primary Budget Balance and ECB Main Refinancing Rate

Monetary policy will become more accommodative, while fiscal policy will become more restrictive.

A. Primary Budget Balance

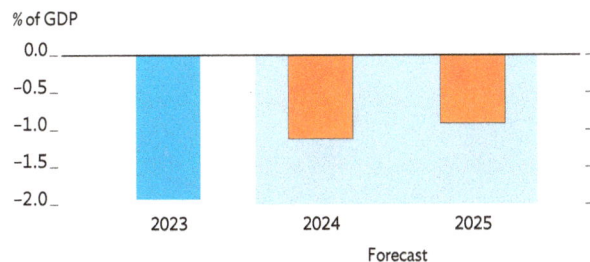

B. ECB Main Refinancing Rate

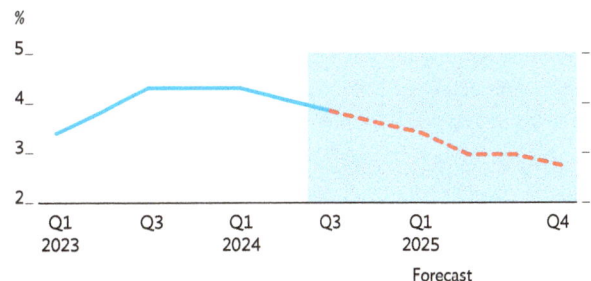

ECB = European Central Bank, GDP = gross domestic product, Q = quarter.
Source: European Commission AMECO database and Asian Development Bank estimates.

2.2% in August. Growth in government real current expenditures is expected to moderate as authorities withdraw previous energy price support schemes and multiannual deficit reduction plans kick in, drawn up according to new European Union (EU) fiscal rules. At the same time, public investment will continue to increase, partly financed by EU-wide common debt issuance through the Next Generation EU scheme. Rising government capital expenditures will partly counterbalance declining current expenditures, so that the fiscal impulse will be only slightly negative.

GDP growth is forecast to settle at around 0.8% in 2024, and then accelerate to 1.4% in 2025. Private consumption will be supported by wage increases in tight labor markets and increasing real incomes as inflation settles below wage growth. Rising public investment in green and digital infrastructure will further support economic activity and may crowd in private investment. GDP is forecast to keep expanding by about 1.1% in the remaining two quarters of 2024, but yearly GDP growth will be only 0.8% in 2024 due to a weak carry-over from 2023. Growth is expected to increase more robustly into 2025 as declining interest rates help ease credit conditions and the external environment improves. If successful, ongoing structural reforms may lift potential medium-term growth in the weaker euro area members.

Headline inflation is forecast to stay at 2.5% in 2024 and slow to 2.3% in 2025. Further disinflationary progress may be slow due to sticky services inflation, which has hovered around 4% since the end of last year and is likely to remain elevated in tight labor markets. As services make up almost half of the overall consumption basket, persistently high services inflation may complicate the last steps of disinflation. At the same time, long-term inflation expectations have returned to the close-but-below 2% target of the European Central Bank.

Risks are tilted to the downside. Another spike in geopolitical tensions may push up energy prices, which would dent household purchasing power through higher inflation, prolong the contraction of energy-intensive sectors, and complicate the expected easing of monetary policy. US presidential elections may result in higher tariffs on European exports to the US as well as in higher defense spending needs for European countries. Slow implementation of the

Next Generation EU recovery package may lead to a lower fiscal impulse, while supply side constraints may delay the current investment plans and push inflation temporarily higher.

Japan

Japan's economy expanded in Q2 2024. GDP grew by 2.9% in Q2, after contracting by 2.4% in Q1, driven by domestic demand (Figure A.6). Private consumption rebounded in Q2 following four quarters of contraction. The gradual normalization in automobile production led to strong growth in durable goods consumption as well as corporate non-residential investment. Non-durable goods consumption registered the first quarter-on-quarter growth (0.7%) since Q1 2023, as food inflation continued to ease. In the public sector, both consumption and investment rose. On the external side, exports rose 6.1%, though imports increased at a slightly higher rate of 6.9% (versus –9.6% in Q1), resulting in net exports subtracting from growth.

Figure A.6 Demand-Side Contributions to Growth, Japan

Q2 GDP expands on rebounding private consumption and investment.

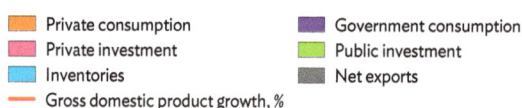

Percentage points, seasonally adjusted annualized rate, qoq

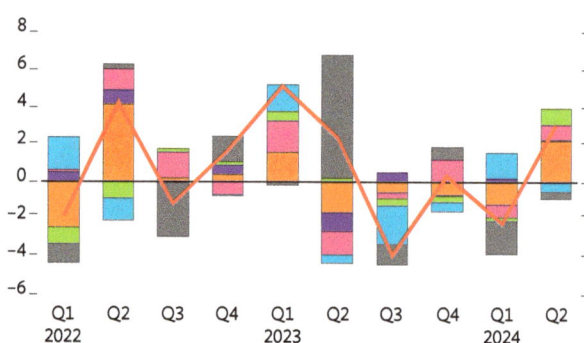

GDP = Gross domestic product, Q = quarter, qoq = quarter on quarter.
Source: CEIC Data Company.

Leading indicators point to an improvement in GDP in the coming quarters. Seasonally adjusted core machinery orders—which cover the private sector, exclude volatile orders, and a leading indicator for capital spending over the coming 3 to 6 months—

rose 2.1% month-on-month in June, up from a 3.2% decline in May. The au Jibun Bank Japan composite PMI rose to 53 in August, from 52.5 in July. The manufacturing PMI edged up to 49.5 after a 4-month low of 49.1 in July, while the services PMI remained above the 50-point threshold. A rebound in "new export orders" in July suggests small gains in export volumes. An upturn in goods exports can be expected as global demand for electronics rises and other major economies grow moderately. Exports increased 9.0% in the first 7 months of 2024 while imports increased 3.0%, narrowing the trade deficit. With the global manufacturing PMI rising to a 2-year high in recent months, Japan's manufacturing sector is expected to improve as well. Further, business surveys still point to healthy growth in business activity and inbound tourism is projected to remain strong.

Inflation remains above target. Headline CPI inflation in July remained at 2.8%, for the third consecutive month, bringing the average for the first 7 months of the year to 2.7% (Figure A.7). This figure is still above the Bank of Japan's inflation target of 2.0%. CPI inflation, which excludes fresh food (the central bank's preferred "core CPI" measure), accelerated to 2.7% in July, up from 2.6% in June and 2.5% in May. Utility prices rose most, up 12.9%, following the end of an energy subsidy program. While the central bank does not target the yen exchange rate, monetary policy action can be warranted if the yen's weakness significantly affects the inflation outlook. Given

sustained price pressures, the Bank of Japan increased short-term policy rates on 31 July 2024 to 0.25% from a range of 0.0%–0.1%. It also announced plans to reduce purchases of Japanese government bonds from around ¥6 trillion per month to around ¥3 trillion per month from 2026.

The growth forecast for Japan is downgraded to 0.4% for 2024 but has been revised upward to 1.0% for 2025. The first-quarter GDP contraction notwithstanding, a rebound is likely in subsequent quarters. Real wages grew again in June after contracting for more than 2 years (Figure A.8). Nominal wage rises in excess of inflation were agreed by large firms in this year's annual spring labor-management wage negotiations. However, persistent inflation, combined with the largely unexpected rate hike at the end of July, is likely to weigh on the fragile recovery in real wages and the consumption outlook for this year, necessitating a downward revision of the GDP forecast.

Figure A.8 Real Wages Growth

Real wages rose in June for the first time in over 2 years.

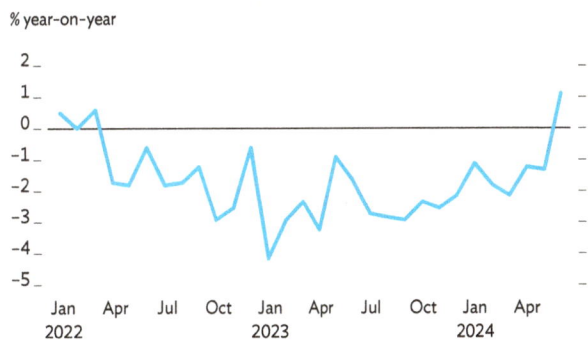

Source: Ministry of Health, Labour and Welfare: Monthly Labour Survey.

Figure A.7 Monthly Inflation

Inflation remains above the Bank of Japan's target.

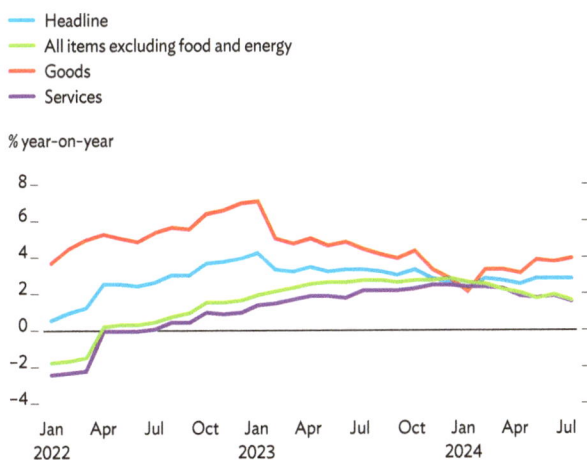

Source: CEIC Data Company.

Inflation forecasts for both 2024 and 2025 are revised upward to 2.4% and 1.9%, respectively, as inflation persists. Inflationary pressures on electricity and gas prices are expected as import prices of liquefied natural gas rebound and amid the phasing out of government subsidies for these utilities. While food inflation has continued to slow, inflation for "other industrial products" has accelerated, supporting the Bank of Japan's concerns that a weaker yen is creating upward pressure on prices, despite appreciation after the central bank's rate hike at the end of July.

Additionally, with producer prices of manufactured goods rising 3.0% year-on-year in July, goods inflation is likely to remain above 2% for the remainder of the year. Services inflation moderated slightly to 1.4% in July, but remains in positive territory, supported by wage increases. Furthermore, early signs indicate that stronger income growth is contributing to an increase in private rental inflation, which has been at 0.3% for the past 4 months—the highest level since the late 1990s. However, hotel inflation is likely to decline sharply in the coming months due to base effects from the spike in charges a year earlier, which should partially offset the rise in electricity and rental inflation. Inflation is expected to decelerate in 2025 as cost-push pressures on consumer prices moderate and depreciating pressure on the yen subsides as monetary policy normalizes.

Recent Developments and Outlook in Other Economies

Australia

Economic growth slowed to 0.5% in Q1 2024 from 1.3% in Q4 2023, due to weak domestic and external demand (Figure A.9). The rise in consumption expenditure in Q1 was offset by a fall in total investment and net trade. Total consumption contributed 1.7 percentage points to growth, with increases in both household spending (1.7%) and government expenditure (4.0%) amid higher spending on essentials and higher social assistance benefits to households. In contrast, fixed investment subtracted 0.8 percentage points from growth, with private and public investment declining over the quarter. On the external side, net trade detracted from growth, as imports of goods and services (21.9%) increased more than total exports (2.8%). Leading indicators suggest activity improved somewhat in Q2. The PMI for services—which make up 80% of Australia's economy—remained expansionary in June, at 51.2, albeit edging down from in 52.5 in May, as growth in new business and activity slowed. In contrast, the contraction in the manufacturing sector worsened, with the manufacturing PMI falling from 49.7 in May to 47.2 in June, marking the worst reading in over 4 years. A sharp fall in new orders mainly drove the decline, due to still-elevated interest rates and soft market conditions.

Figure A.9 Demand-Side Contributions to Growth, Australia

Growth slowed amid weak domestic and external demand.

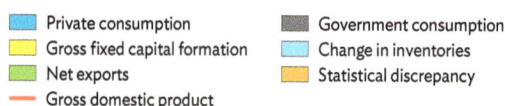

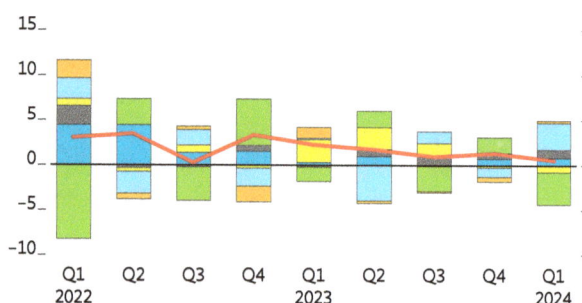

Q = quarter, qoq = quarter on quarter.
Source: Asian Development Bank calculations using data from CEIC Data Company.

Growth will remain subdued this year and next as tight monetary policy continues to constrain demand. Headline inflation jumped to a higher-than-expected 4.0% in May from 3.6% in April, driven by rising price pressures for food, housing, and transport services. In response, the Reserve Bank of Australia held its policy rate unchanged at 4.35% in June. Tight financing conditions and higher unemployment will dampen consumer spending and investment while weak external demand will continue weighing on exports. On 19 July 2024, Consensus Forecasts had GDP growing 1.2% in 2024 and 2.2% in 2025. Inflation was seen at 3.4% this year and 2.8% next year.

New Zealand

Economic growth was unchanged in Q1 2024 at 0.5%, dampened by falling net trade and fixed investment (Figure A.10). The declines in government spending (–1.0%), fixed investment (–5.2%), and exports of goods and services (–1.8%) was partially offset by the strong growth in household consumption expenditure (6.5%), driven by spending on services and nondurable goods. However, economic activity remains weak: GDP per capita fell in Q1 for the sixth consecutive quarter. Leading indicators also point to softening momentum in Q2, as high

Figure A.10 Demand-Side Contributions to Growth, New Zealand

Growth was unchanged in Q1 2024, weighed down by falling net exports and fixed investment.

- Private consumption
- Gross fixed capital formation
- Net exports
- Gross domestic product
- Government consumption
- Change in inventories
- Statistical discrepancy

Percentage points, seasonally adjusted annualized rate, qoq

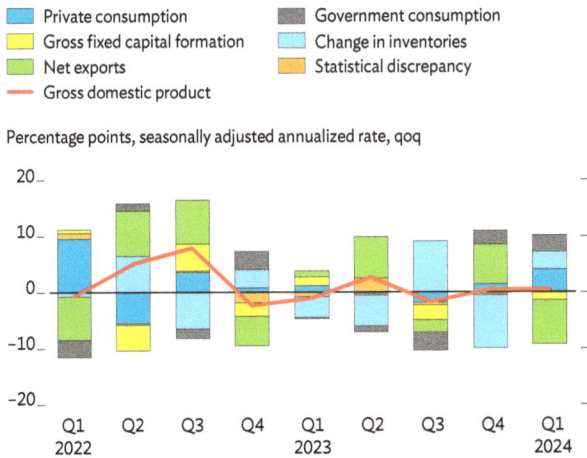

Q = quarter, qoq = quarter on quarter.
Source: Asian Development Bank calculations using data from CEIC Data Company.

interest rates continue to weigh down growth. The business confidence index—the difference between shares of businesses expecting improvement versus worsening—fell to 6.1 from 11.2 in May, driven by weaker sentiment in services and manufacturing. The consumer confidence index fell in the same month to 83.2 from 84.9 in May, suggesting softening private spending in the quarter.

Growth will remain subdued this year, but is seen to recover significantly in 2025, fueled by tourism and declining inflation and interest rates. For the eighth consecutive meeting in July, the Reserve Bank of New Zealand maintained the official cash rate at 5.50%, but signaled a more dovish tone. Headline inflation is still above the central bank's 1%–3% target, but dropped to 4.0% in Q1, from 4.7% in Q4 last year. An increasing population boosted by net migration, recovery in the housing market, expansionary fiscal policy, and rising inbound tourism will support growth this year and next. On the downside, slower growth in Australia and the People's Republic of China, New Zealand's key trading partners, will likely dent export growth and constrain the expansion. As of 19 July 2024, Consensus Forecasts had GDP growing by 0.6% in 2024 and 2.1% in 2025. Inflation is seen at 3.2% this year and 2.2% next year.

Russian Federation

The Russian economy has adapted to international sanctions implemented in response to the Russian invasion of Ukraine. The Russian government has successfully redirected its oil exports from the EU to the PRC and India (Figure A.11), with revenues from energy accounting for 24% of the federal budget as of June 2024, up from 21% in the first half of the previous year (Figure A.12). The Federal State Statistics Service claims that economic activity grew 5.4% year on year in Q1 2024, accelerating from 4.9% in Q4 2023. A recovering mining and quarrying sector, coupled with improved agricultural production, supported this

Figure A.11 Monthly Deliveries of Russian Oil by Region

Oil exports have redirected from the EU to the PRC and India.

- European Union
- US + UK + Japan + Canada
- India
- People's Republic of China
- Türkiye
- Other

Million tons

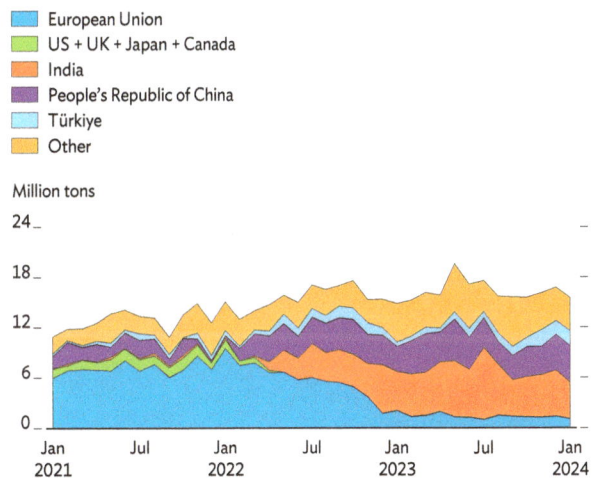

EU = European Union, PRC = People's Republic of China, UK = United Kingdom, US = United States.
Sources: Bruegel. Russian Crude Oil Tracker.

Figure A.12 Oil and Gas Revenues

Revenues from energy resources continue to be an important source of government revenues.

Share in government revenues, %

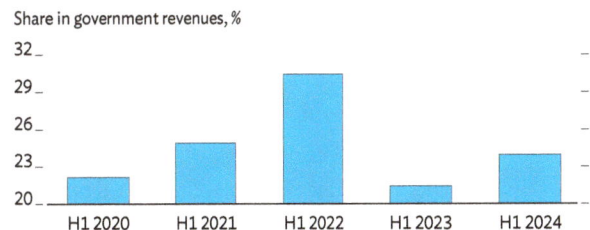

H1 = first half.
Source: Haver Analytics.

upturn in Q1. However, industrial output contracted in April and May, suggesting a slowdown in Q2. In addition, household income deteriorated as real wages decreased in April.

Inflation accelerated to a 16-month high, prompting the central bank to further tighten monetary policy. Inflation surged to 9.1% in July, the highest rate since February 2023, faster price increases for food goods and services outweighed a slower price increase for nonfood goods. Domestic demand will likely continue to rise faster than capacity this year. As a result, average inflation will exceed the central bank's forecast of 6.5% to 7.0%. In this context, the central bank raised its policy rate to 18.0% on 26 July 2024, stating that sustained restrictive policy is necessary to contain inflation.

GDP growth will remain strong this year and in 2025 despite Russia's war in Ukraine. Exports will keep recovering as new economic ties strengthen and sanctions are increasingly circumvented. However, a weakening currency, labor shortages, and deteriorating domestic demand will dampen these tailwinds. Additional sanctions or other adverse geopolitical developments could derail this growth trajectory while a resolution of the war could boost growth. As of 30 August 2024, Consensus Forecasts had GDP growing by 3.3% in 2024 and expanding by 1.7% in 2025.

Oil Prices

Brent crude oil averaged $80.86 per barrel in August, down $4.43 per barrel from July (Figure A.13). Prices fell to $76.49 per barrel on 4 June following the OPEC+ meeting on 2 June, when the group announced that 2.2 million barrels per day of voluntary cuts would gradually be unwound beginning in October. Prices dropped after this announcement as market participants assessed that unwinding production cuts could significantly increase global oil inventories. However, OPEC+ quickly reiterated that the rollback of output reductions would be contingent on market conditions, which somewhat allayed fears of oversupply. Additionally, a better demand outlook for the second half of the year, driven by the onset of summer travel, pushed prices to reach $88.25 per barrel on July 3. Prices then hovered around $86 per

Figure A.13 Brent Crude Oil Prices

Concerns about global demand continue to fuel negative sentiment in oil markets.

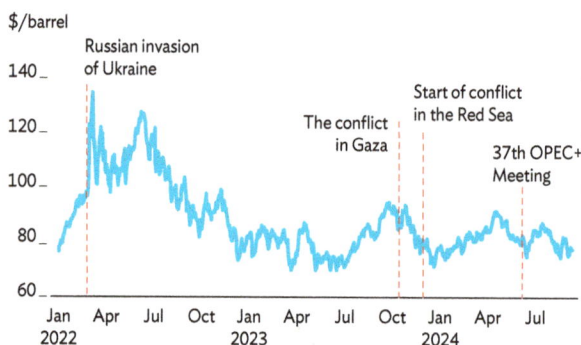

Source: CEIC Data Company.

barrel until the third week of July. By the fourth week of July, Brent started trending downwards, reaching $76.45 by the end of August as expectations of increased supply from OPEC and non-OPEC producers amid signs of weakening global demand pressured prices despite heightened geopolitical tensions and a decline in US crude inventories. The International Energy Agency reported that global oil demand growth in the second quarter slowed to 710,000 barrels per day year-on-year, marking the slowest quarterly increase since the fourth quarter of 2022. This slowdown is attributed to a contraction in PRC consumption, as its post-pandemic rebound has run its course.

Forecasts for Brent crude prices are revised upward to $83/barrel in 2024 and $81/barrel in 2025. Brent crude oil averaged $83.30 per barrel from January to August. It traded around $74 per barrel in the first trading week of September, below its 50-day moving average, signaling short-term weakness. Signs of weakening global demand due largely to the continued weakness in the PRC economy and uncertainties surrounding the unwinding of OPEC+ voluntary cuts contribute to downward pressure on crude oil prices. On 5 September, OPEC+ announced that it will extend voluntary production cuts until the end of November 2024, with a phased monthly reduction starting 1 December and the flexibility to pause or reverse adjustments as needed. Supply constraints arising from geopolitical tensions and possible La Niña-related conditions such as more hurricanes along the Atlantic coast and/or a colder winter provide upward support. Brent crude prices are expected to average around

$82 per barrel in the final 4 months of the year. The International Energy Agency, in August, forecast oil supply growth to outpace demand growth as OPEC+ unwinds its production cuts and non-OPEC+ output rises. This will lead to a fall in oil prices in 2025.

Oil price forecasts remain highly uncertain.
Uncertainty persists due to heightened tensions arising out of the wider conflict in the Middle East, including the conflict in the Red Sea. These situations have significantly disrupted the shipping channel for many oil shipments. While these incidents have not yet directly reduced oil supply, the potential escalation and the lack of any resolution around the conflict in the Red Sea have increased shipping costs and added a risk premium to oil prices. Additionally, the US elections results and subsequent geopolitical ramifications, along with strategic decisions by major oil-producing nations, complicate forecasts.

2

LETTING THE DATA SPEAK:
GLOBAL SPILLOVERS
FROM DATA-DEPENDENT
FEDERAL RESERVE MONETARY POLICY

LETTING THE DATA SPEAK: GLOBAL SPILLOVERS FROM DATA-DEPENDENT FEDERAL RESERVE MONETARY POLICY

"The time has come for policy to adjust. The direction of travel is clear, and the timing and pace of rate cuts will depend on incoming data, the evolving outlook, and the balance of risks."

Jerome H. Powell
Chairman
Board of Governors of the Federal Reserve System
(23 August 2024) (Powell 2024)

When the United States (US) Federal Reserve (the Fed) sets interest rates, it shapes the outlook for financial markets around the world. By setting US interest rates, the Fed affects interest rate differentials between the US and other economies. These differentials influence exchange rates and drive the flow of capital across economies. Capital inflows can improve financial conditions, but they can be volatile, and sudden slowdowns or reversals can have large negative effects through exchange rate depreciations, declining international reserves, tighter credit conditions, and slower or more volatile growth. The dominance of the US dollar in the global economy amplifies the importance of Fed policy actions for foreign economies, since much of global debt and trade is tied to the dollar, and the dollar still accounts for about 60% of official foreign exchange reserves globally.

The pace of the ongoing US monetary policy easing cycle remains uncertain and dependent on incoming data. After a sharp series of contractionary monetary policy actions over 2022–2023 to slow surging inflation in the aftermath of the coronavirus disease (COVID-19) pandemic, the Fed has finally begun to reduce interest rates. The pace at which the Fed will cut rates, however, is still unclear. The Fed has the dual mandate of low and stable inflation and maximum employment and has increasingly emphasized that its future policy actions will depend on how the economic outlook will evolve relative to its objectives. In other words, the expected easing of monetary policy is highly "data-dependent," to use a term that several Fed governors have used in recent years to characterize Fed policy (Figure 2.1.1).

This chapter was written by Abdul Abiad, Gabriele Ciminelli (lead), and David Keith De Padua of the Economic Research and Development Impact Department (ERDI), ADB, Manila, and Emmanuel Alano and Aris Zoleta, ERDI Consultants.

Figure 2.1.1 Frequency of Data-Dependent-Related Keywords in Speeches by Fed Governors

At various times in past years, Fed governors have increasingly stressed that Fed policy is data-dependent.

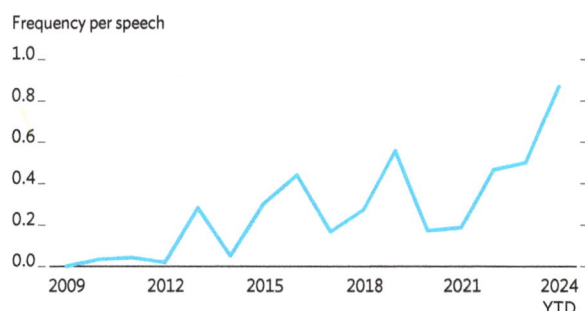

YTD = year to date.

Note: Keywords include "data dependent," "data-dependent," "dependent on data," and "incoming data."

Source: Asian Development Bank calculations.

This chapter studies how US monetary policy changes in response to US economic developments—that is, data-driven changes—affect financial markets across the world. It aims to answer the following questions:

- How do financial variables and capital flows in other economies react to monetary policy actions by the Fed in response to US economic developments?

- Does the Fed's responsiveness to changes in the US economy—what is referred to as Fed's *data dependency*—fluctuate over time? And does the relative attentiveness of the Fed to different kinds of data—particularly regarding inflation and labor market conditions—also fluctuate? If so, how do such fluctuations shape the effects of US economic data releases on financial markets in other economies?

- Do adverse macroeconomic conditions leave certain economies more exposed than others to economic and monetary developments in the US?

A novel approach is used, analyzing the response of financial variables to the release of new US employment and inflation data. This is in contrast to what is done traditionally, which is to focus on the actions taken by the Fed during its monetary policy meetings. The rationale is that, if investors expect the Fed to respond to new data by changing its policies,

they will anticipate the Fed's next moves by reacting at the time of the release of economic data rather than waiting until the Fed formally meets and changes its stance. The reaction of investors to the data release, on expectation that such release will prompt the Fed to change its policy, can thus be seen as the effect of the expected data-driven monetary policy change by the Fed.

US data releases can affect financial variables by influencing both Fed policy expectations and perceptions of the state of the US economy. These two channels could have different effects on financial markets. Employment data indicating that the US labor market is strong could strengthen investor confidence in the health of the US economy and, via trade links, in that of the global economy, which could boost global stock market prices. But if the Fed has indicated that it is *data dependent*, and particularly *attentive* to labor market conditions, the same release may lead investors to think that the Fed is more likely to increase interest rates to cool the labor market and avoid wage-driven inflation. The expectation of higher future US interest rates could in turn lead to a stronger US dollar and reduce global stock market prices.

The chapter constructs new measures of Fed data dependency to disentangle how US data impact global financial markets. These measures capture the Fed's likelihood to respond to economic developments and its attentiveness to inflation and employment data releases. Using these measures, the analysis separates the direct effects of US data releases on global markets working through shifts in perceptions about the state of the US economy from those driven by the expected Fed response. The foreign financial variables considered are government bond yields, exchange rates, stock market prices, and default probabilities across 108 economies, as well as portfolio capital flows in a smaller sample of emerging market economies.

The chapter's main findings are the following:

- **The degree of the Fed data dependency and its relative attentiveness to inflation and employment data varies greatly over time.** Data dependency tends to be low when the Fed policy rate is close to zero, as in the aftermath of the global financial crisis and during the COVID-19 pandemic, and hit all-time highs during the post-pandemic surge in inflation. The Fed paid relatively more attention to employment data during the 2014–2015 monetary policy normalization period and the subsequent hiking cycle, while attentiveness to inflation was highest during 2022–2024.

- **Inflation-driven increases in Fed policy rates lead to a generalized tightening of financial conditions in foreign economies.**[1] When the Fed's data dependency and its attentiveness to inflation are both high, the release of a US inflation report in which inflation is 0.1 percentage points higher than expected leads to a 0.1% depreciation of other economies' currencies vis-à-vis the US dollar, a 0.2% decline in their stock markets, a 2 basis point increase in their short-term government bond yields, and a 0.1 percentage point increase in default probabilities, on average.

- **Employment-driven increases in Fed policy rates also have negative effects for foreign economies, but these are limited to the exchange rate and debt markets.** When the Fed's data dependency and attentiveness to employment are high, the release of a US employment report in which net nonfarm payroll job creation is 100,000 higher than expected results in local currencies depreciating by 0.2% against the US dollar and short-term and long-term bond yields increasing by about 4 basis points, on average. Effects on stock markets and default probabilities are not statistically significant.

- **Strong macroeconomic fundamentals can help economies reduce spillovers.** Among emerging and frontier market economies, running healthy current account and budget balances can help insulate the economy from changes in US monetary policy, while high external debts and inflation rates amplify exposure.

The chapter is structured to first outline the conceptual framework and methodology, then present empirical findings and their policy implications. The next section provides a conceptual framework and a brief survey of the literature. A description of the data and the methodology follows, with technical details left for the Technical Appendix. Stylized facts on the evolution of Fed data dependency are then presented to provide additional context. Empirical results are discussed next, together with a summary of sensitivity analyses and robustness checks. The final section concludes and examines some policy implications derived from the empirical findings.

---

[1] For brevity, throughout the chapter the results are discussed in terms of data-driven increases in Fed policy rates; the effects of data-driven decreases in policy rates are simply the opposite of what is described.

Conceptual Framework and Related Literature

US monetary policy influences foreign financial variables and capital flows through the portfolio-rebalancing, risk-taking, and exchange rate channels. The portfolio-rebalancing channel operates through the effect of Fed monetary policy on US interest rates (Chari, Lundblad, and Stedman 2020). According to this channel, investors shift their portfolios towards US assets when Fed policies raise US interest rates. This negatively affects bond and stock market prices in foreign economies and reduces the value of their currencies vis-à-vis the US dollar, while the opposite holds when the Fed eases policy and interest rates decrease. The risk-taking channel operates through the effect of US monetary policy on risk aversion (Bruno and Shin 2015). According to this channel, Fed contractionary policies increase risk aversion, making investors more reluctant to take on risky positions and leading foreign capital to flow out of less developed markets, which are typically perceived as riskier. Finally, the exchange rate channel works through the direct effect of the Fed's policy on the US dollar exchange rate. A US dollar appreciation because of higher US interest rates increases an economy's debt servicing costs on its US dollar-denominated debt, which may affect its probability of default and reduce the availability of foreign credit.[2]

Recent literature puts forward another channel of US monetary policy—the Fed information effect channel (Romer and Romer 2000; Campbell et al. 2012; Nakamura and Steinsson 2018). Nakamura and Steinsson observe that positive changes in interest rates around Fed meetings are often followed by upward revisions in the private sector forecast of future US gross domestic product (GDP). This is assumed to be only possible if the Fed has superior information relative to investors about the state of the economy, since, according to conventional theory, increases in interest rates should reduce economic activity. Hence, when the Fed meets and decides its monetary policy, it also reveals new information about the economy, which leads investors to revise their forecasts. This may have spillovers to other economies either directly, or indirectly, as investors shift their portfolios in response to the new information about the state of the US economy.[3]

Identifying how data-driven changes in Fed policy impact financial markets is complex due to investor anticipation and the varying level of Fed data dependency. First, if investors have full visibility of US economic developments and have a good understanding of how the Fed reacts to them, they will anticipate data-driven changes to monetary policy as new data is released. Thus, the effects of such changes will be largely felt at the time in which new data is released and not when the Fed meets and decides its policy. Second, investor reaction to data releases depends not only on the (expected) change in Fed policy, but also directly on the economic developments that lead the Fed to change its policies, and these two may affect financial markets in different ways. Third, as documented later in this chapter, the Fed's own communications indicate that there can be substantial

---

[2] While both the exchange rate channel and the portfolio rebalancing channel can influence the value of the US dollar, the exchange rate channel operates directly through changes in interest rates and the immediate impact on currency values. In contrast, the portfolio rebalancing channel operates through investors' decisions to adjust their asset holdings in response to changing returns, which then indirectly impacts the exchange rate. Despite these distinct mechanisms, the two channels are interconnected, as the portfolio rebalancing channel can initiate changes in the exchange rate, which then feed back into the exchange rate channel's effects on the broader economy.

[3] Bauer and Swanson (2023) challenge the Fed information effect literature and emphasize the existence of a Fed-response-to-news channel. Their analysis shows that economic forecast revisions and the change in interest rates around Fed meetings are both driven by the news released before the meetings. This, rather than the Fed-information-effect channel theorized by the earlier literature, explains why positive changes in interest rates around Fed meetings are often followed by upward revisions in the private sector forecast about the US economy. In other words, the Fed and the private sector forecasters both react to the same news.

variation in how sensitive Fed policy is to data (data dependency), and which data the Fed is focused on (relative attentiveness). These two have implications for how the Fed is responsive to economic data.

Figure 2.1.2 illustrates how US economic data, Fed policy adjustments, and investor expectations interact to shape financial markets. As a start, data releases on the US economic outlook influence investors' views of the state of the US economy and of its partners. This, in turn, may immediately affect foreign financial markets. Second, the Fed meets and adjusts its policy stance taking into account the data released since its last meeting. Abstaining for a moment from anticipation effects, this affects US financial variables and, through the three traditional channels of US monetary policy discussed above, foreign financial variables. Third, according to the Fed information effect channel, in adjusting the monetary policy stance, the Fed reveals its superior information about the US economy, which in turn may lead investors to reassess their views on the state of the US economy and therefore have effects on foreign variables. Now, consider anticipation effects: Under rational expectations, investors anticipate how the release of new economic data will affect the Fed's policy stance at the moment the data is released.

Crucially, the degree to which the Fed responds to new data by adjusting its policy stance depends on how much its policy is data dependent. The

degree of data dependency and the type of data to which the Fed pays most attention (i.e., attentiveness to employment versus inflation data) also influence the extent to which investors reassess their expectations of future Fed policy after new data releases.

The chapter's main methodological contribution is its novel approach of examining the effects of data-driven Fed policy changes focusing on the time new data is released, rather than on Fed meetings, as most literature does. This is complemented by the construction of variables that measure the degrees of the Fed's (i) data dependency—how likely is the Fed to change its policy based on incoming data—and (ii) relative attentiveness to inflation and employment data. The latter is important because, given the same level of data dependency, the relative attentiveness of the Fed to different types of data releases may vary depending on where economic outcomes stand relative to Fed goals. When inflation is around target, but unemployment is abnormally high, the Fed is likely to pay more attention to employment than inflation data releases, and vice versa.

The chapter's approach relies on the assumption that investors understand at least partly how the Fed reacts to incoming data (the Fed's reaction function). Bauer and Swanson (2023) argue that investors underestimate how responsive the Fed will be because they lack full information about the Fed's reaction function. They show that financial news

Figure 2.1.2 Transmission Channels of US Economic Data Releases to Foreign Financial Markets

If investors understand and anticipate the Fed's reaction function and the Fed's data dependency is high, US economic data releases impact foreign markets by shifting expectations of Fed policy.

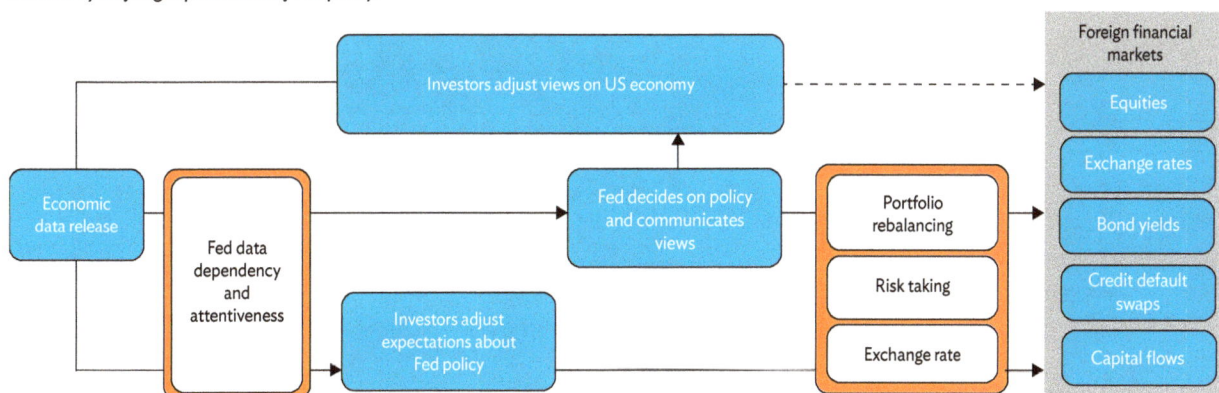

US = United States.

Source: Asian Development Bank.

accounts for a significant share of the change in interest rates around Fed meetings, indicating that investors do not fully anticipate the Fed's response to such news. In contrast, employment and inflation data releases do not have strong predictive power.[4] This suggests that their impact on future monetary policy is already anticipated by investors at the time of release and supports the chapter's focus on data releases rather than Fed meetings to study the effects of data-driven policy changes.

Related Literature

This subsection reviews key studies on the effects of US monetary policy on capital flows and asset prices in emerging markets, focusing on those most relevant to the current analysis. The main points of these closely related studies are summarized in Table 2.1.1. Aizenman, Binici, and Hutchison (2016); Bowman Londono, and Sapriza (2015); and Fratzscher, Lo Duca, and Straub (2018) focus on Fed unconventional policies (including quantitative easing, QE) and find significant spillovers to asset prices in

Table 2.1.1 Literature on Spillover Effects of Federal Reserve Monetary Policy on Emerging Markets

A variety of papers has studied the spillover effects of Fed policy, but none focus on the time of US data releases to identify data-driven changes.

Paper	Type of Monetary Policy Action Considered	Identification	Main Results
Aizenman, Binici, and Hutchinson (2016)	QE announcements	Announcement dummies in a daily panel	QE announcements + QE tapering –
Arteta, Kamin, and Ruch (2023)	Reaction, growth and inflation shocks	Comovement of US interest rates, inflation swap rates and equity prices in a monthly sign-restricted Bayesian VAR	Reaction/inflation shocks – growth shocks +
Bowman, Londono and Sapriza (2015)	QE announcement days	Identification-through-heteroskedasticity method in days of QE announcements	Tightening –
Bruno and Shin (2015)	Monetary policy changes (no distinction)	Change in federal funds rate in a monthly VAR	Tightening –
Chari, Lundblad, and Stedman (2020)	QE announcement days	Change in implied yield on five-year Treasury Futures in 1-day window around QE announcements	Tightening –
Ciminelli, Rogers and Wu (2022)	Reaction shocks and information shocks	Heteroskedasticity-based, partial least squares approach for reaction shocks, information shocks identified as residual (time of FOMC announcements)	Reaction shocks – information shocks neutral
Fratzscher, Lo Duca, and Straub (2018)	QE announcements	Announcement dummies	QE announcements +
Hoek, Kamin and Yoldas (2022)	Reaction and growth shocks	Comovement of 2-year US treasury yields and US equity prices in tight window around FOMC meetings and NFP employment data releases	Growth shocks + reaction/inflation shocks –
Iacoviello and Navarro (2019)	Reaction shocks	Residual in a regression of various controls on change in federal funds rate at quarterly frequency	Tightening –
Pinchetti and Szczepaniak (2024)	Information shocks	Comovement between US equities and interest rates around FOMC meetings	Information shocks +

QE = quantitative easing.

Note: + indicates positive spillovers, – indicates negative spillovers.

Source: Asian Development Bank.

[4] Employment data releases are found to explain part of the change in interest rates around Fed meetings when a sample including unscheduled meetings prior to 1994 is considered. Employment data releases are not found to have any predictive power when post-1994 samples are considered. See the Online Appendix B (Table B3) of Bauer and Swanson (2023).

emerging markets. Iacoviello and Navarro (2019) find that GDP growth in emerging markets drops just about as much as it does in the US when the Fed tightens policy. Fratzscher (2012) finds that crisis events and monetary and fiscal policies in advanced economies can exert large effects on capital flows. Ciminelli, Rogers, and Wu (2022) find that the information effect channel of Fed monetary policy tends to have neutral effects for emerging markets, while Pinchetti and Szczepaniak (2024) find positive spillovers of information shocks to global equity prices, cross-border credit, and global economic activity.[5]

These studies focus on Fed meeting days but overlook the impact of data-driven policy shifts, as investors anticipate future changes when new data is released. Additionally, some of them explicitly focus on changes in US interest rates that are independent of changes in the economic outlook—which can be seen as the result of changes in how the Fed reacts to certain given economic conditions (Fed reaction shocks). This distinction is important given that data-driven changes may spill over to foreign financial variables through different channels than changes in monetary policy that are independent from economic developments.

Arteta, Kamin, and Ruch (2023) and Hoek, Kamin, and Yoldas (2022) are two exceptions, as they study the spillover effects of Fed monetary policy changes in response to economic developments separately from those of Fed reaction shocks. These two studies identify Fed policy changes in response to improving economic conditions as instances in which US government interest rates and the US stock market move in the same direction, after Fed meetings. This approach is problematic because, by design, it excludes from the sample all episodes in which the US stock market decreases in response to a more restrictive Fed policy stance, which should arguably have the most detrimental effects in foreign markets. Both studies find increases in interest rates in response to improving

economic conditions to have benign effects on emerging markets, while rate increases in response to higher inflation or due to reaction shocks are found to have adverse effects. Following the same identification approach, Hoek, Kamin, and Yoldas (2022) additionally focus on employment data releases and classify them into monetary shocks and growth shocks. Growth shocks are again found to have more benign effects than monetary shocks.

Also related to this chapter, Engler, Piazza, and Sher (2023) analyze the effects of US employment and inflation data releases on emerging market financial conditions. Better-than-expected employment releases are found to lead to higher long-term interest rates and an appreciation of the US dollar on average, while inflation releases are not found to have significant effects. Engler, Piazza, and Sher (2023) also find the effects of employment releases to partly work through the contemporaneous change in short-term US government bond yields, which they interpret to be evidence that employment news is partly transmitted to emerging markets through changes in US monetary policy expectations. Their study does not consider variations in the Fed's data dependency or its relative attentiveness to inflation versus employment news.

Finally, a note by Healy and Jia (2024) aligns in spirit to the methodology adopted in this chapter. The note compares the response of Fed policy rate expectations to economic releases. A distinction is made between periods in which the Fed policy interest rate is at its effective lower bound, which are assumed to be periods in which the Fed is less data dependent, and periods in which the policy rate is above the zero lower bound. Healy and Jia (2024) find that US interest rates are more sensitive to economic releases during periods in which the policy rate is above its effective lower bound. Their analysis does not explore the spillovers of data releases to foreign markets.

---

[5] A strand of the literature examines whether certain factors make some economies more exposed than others to changes in US monetary policy. Dahlhaus and Vasishtha (2020) observe that shifts in US monetary policy expectations have highly heterogenous effects across emerging market economies. Aizenman et al. (2024) finds that macroeconomic stability and institutional quality reduce spillovers. Kalemli-Ozcan and Unsal (2024) focus on the role of monetary policy frameworks and find that a stronger framework and lower levels of US-dollar-denominated debt reduce spillovers.

Methodology and Data

The chapter relies on an event study approach to carry out the empirical analysis. An event study consists in analyzing the change in the variable of interest around the time of specific events. Here, the events are the releases of US macroeconomic data, while the variables of interest, or outcome variables, are several, and the analysis is repeated separately for each of them.

Explanatory variables include economic data releases and Fed data dependency, with interaction terms capturing how data dependency affects the impact of economic news on financial markets. Variables expected to affect the outcome variables (or explanatory variables) include those that measure the news content of economic data releases. Economic releases have a direct effect on markets, as they provide information about the state of the US economy. But they also matter because they shape investors' expectations about future Fed policy. The effect of economic releases on expectations also depend on the degree to which the Fed is data dependent. Therefore, the explanatory variables also include a Fed's data dependency variable and the interaction between this variable and the economic news variables. The more the Fed is data dependent, the more economic data releases are going to affect financial markets through their effects on expected future monetary policy. The interaction term accounts for this.

The analysis uses a range of dependent variables to measure the impact of data releases on foreign financial markets, with changes calculated over a 2-day window following data releases to account for time differences. The dependent variables used are each economy's exchange rate vis-à-vis the US dollar; its 2- and 10-year government bond yields; its main stock market index; and its government's default probability. Data on portfolio debt inflows in a set of eight emerging markets is also used. To properly account for time differences across foreign markets relative to the US, and to allow sufficient time for financial market reactions to materialize, the change in the dependent variables is computed in a 2-day window following US macroeconomic data releases.[6] This window ranges from the market close the day before the release to the market close the day following the release.

Given the Fed's dual mandate of low and stable inflation and maximum employment, the chapter focuses on US inflation and employment data releases. The inflation data release considered is the month-on-month change of the headline consumer price index. This is released monthly within the inflation report, usually in the first half of the month, with the data referring to inflation in the month prior.[7] The employment data considered is the change in nonfarm payroll employment. This data point is released the first Friday of every month and measures the net change of

---

[6] US economic data is typically released at 8:30 a.m. Eastern Standard Time (New York time). Given that most equity and bond markets in Asia are already closed at that time, the release of economic data will impact these markets only when they open the following day. A 2-day window is therefore needed to capture the response to US economic release of financial variables across the globe.

[7] The inflation report contains data for headline month-on-month and year-on-year inflation as well as core (excluding food and energy prices) month-on-month and year-on-year inflation. Results in this chapter would be similar if either the headline year-on-year inflation rate or the combination of headline month-on-month and year-on-year inflation rates or the month-on-month core inflation rate were used. See the Technical Appendix for a discussion. The Fed-preferred inflation measure is the one derived from the personal consumer expenditure index rather than the one derived from the consumer price index considered in this analysis. However, data on personal consumer expenditure inflation is usually released at the end of the month, which greatly diminishes its information content for investors, as investors react to data releases that are timely (Gilbert et al. 2017).

the number of nonfarm employees in the US economy during the preceding month. The nonfarm payroll series is more important relative to other labor market data for two reasons. First, the National Bureau of Economic Research uses it as a key indicator to determine whether the economy is in an expansion or a recession. Second, nonfarm payroll releases are very timely, which magnifies their impact on financial markets (Gilbert et al. 2017).

The impact of data releases on financial markets is assessed by focusing on the *surprise* component, the difference between the actual data release and economists' expectations. When new data is released, investors react to the degree to which the actual release deviates from what they expected the release to be. Hence, based on considerable literature (Gürkaynak, Sack, and Swanson 2005; Boyd, Hu, and Jagannathan 2005; Beber and Brandt 2009; Swanson and Williams 2014, and many others), the effects of data releases on financial markets are identified by deriving the surprise component of the releases. This is constructed as the difference between the actual data released and the median of the Bloomberg survey polling economists about their expectations for the release. Surprises are then standardized by their respective standard deviations.

Fed data dependency is measured by the absolute difference between the current Fed policy rate and investor expectations for this rate 1 year ahead, which is heavily influenced by Fed communication. There are periods when the Fed communicates that its policy rate—the federal funds rate—will likely be unchanged for a long period of time, regardless of data developments. This causes the 1-year-ahead expected future federal funds rate to be closely aligned to the current effective federal funds rate. Other times, the Fed communicates that it expects economic conditions to evolve in a manner that will warrant monetary policy changes ahead. This causes the 1-year-ahead expected future federal funds rate to diverge from the current rate. During such times, the Fed must pay close attention to how the economy is evolving, so that it can properly calibrate the timing and pace of monetary policy adjustments.

When the Fed communicates that it expects policy adjustments to be warranted in the future, it also specifies that this expectation is conditional on its assessment of how the outlook will evolve relative to its objectives. Hence, a large difference between the current and the expected future policy rate indicates a general expectation that the Fed will change policy in the next 12 months, but the exact realization will be conditional on how the data evolves. The following quote from Fed Governor Christopher J. Waller's 14 July 2022 speech (Waller 2022) is emblematic of this: "*Based on what we know about inflation today, I expect that further increases in the target range will be needed to make monetary policy restrictive, but that will depend on economic data in the coming weeks and months. Between the end of July and the FOMC's (Federal Open Market Committee) September meeting, we will get two employment and CPI reports with data for July and August. I will be looking for signs that inflation has started its move down toward our 2 percent target on a sustained basis.*" On the other hand, a very small difference between the current and the expected future policy rate indicates that the Fed is "inactive", and data releases provide less information for future monetary policy.

The Fed's focus on inflation versus employment when setting monetary policy shifts over time, with varying attentiveness to these factors affecting how financial markets respond to data releases. This is well illustrated by a wording change between the Fed statements of 12 June and 31 July 2024. A key sentence from the 12 June statement was: "*The economic outlook is uncertain, and the Committee remains highly attentive to inflation risks*". This was dropped from the 31 July statement and replaced with: "*The economic outlook is uncertain, and the Committee is attentive to the risks to both sides of its dual mandate*". This change signaled an important shift. From being mainly attentive to inflation risks during 2022–2024, the Fed was transitioning to being equally attentive to employment and inflation. How much the Fed pays attention to inflation and employment data matters for the response of financial variables to data releases. Even when data dependency is high, inflation/employment data releases may have a low bearing for future monetary policy if the Fed's attentiveness to inflation/employment is low.

Inflation- and employment-specific data dependency variables are created by adjusting the general Fed data dependency measure based on how far inflation and unemployment are from target levels. Two variables to account for the Fed's relative attentiveness to inflation versus employment data releases are first constructed using the distance of actual inflation from the Fed's 2% target and of the unemployment rate from its natural rate (the rate of unemployment arising from structural factors rather than fluctuations in aggregate demand). Then, inflation- and employment-specific data dependency variables are derived by interacting the general Fed data dependency variable, obtained as the difference between the Fed policy rate and the investor expectation 1 year ahead, by these new variables measuring the Fed's relative attentiveness to inflation versus employment. These inflation- and employment-specific data dependency variables are those ultimately used in the regression framework.

The analysis is based on a sample of 108 economies, including MSCI-classified markets and additional ADB developing members, with daily variables measured from April 2009 onward. The sample is made up of 85 economies classified by Morgan Stanley Capital International (MSCI) as developed markets, emerging markets, frontier markets, or standalone markets, plus an additional 23 ADB developing members not covered by MSCI. Variables are measured daily. The time sample ranges from after the global financial crisis (April 2009) to the present, excluding the height of the COVID-19 pandemic (February 2020 to July 2020), when many economies were subject to varying degrees of shutdown and financial market closure. The sample starting period is chosen due to the Fed's increased usage of communication to steer investors' expectations about future policy and emphasis on data dependency since then. More details on the sample, data, sources, transformations, and the construction of the Fed data dependency measures are in the Technical Appendix.

A Review of Fed Communication and Policy Regimes

Over the past 2 decades, the Fed's approach to monetary policy has been significantly transformed. The central bank has increasingly relied on communication to steer investors' expectations about the direction of future monetary policy. This section reviews the evolution of Fed communication and monetary policy. The uninterested reader can move directly to the next section, which provides some stylized facts.

Fed meeting statements have become considerably longer since the global financial crisis, reflecting increased emphasis on explaining current and likely future policy. Statements were almost always below 100 words between January 2000 and the onset of the crisis, notwithstanding important shocks such as the burst of the dot-com bubble and the 9/11 terrorist attack (Figure 2.1.3). Their length increased sharply after the bankruptcy of Lehman Brothers and started increasing again at the end of 2012, when the Fed introduced its third large-scale asset purchase program (or quantitative easing, QE). Statements reached a peak of about 450 words in mid-2014, as the Fed sought to explain the normalization of its

Figure 2.1.3 Simple Word Count of Fed Statements

The length of policy meeting statements has increased substantially since the global financial crisis.

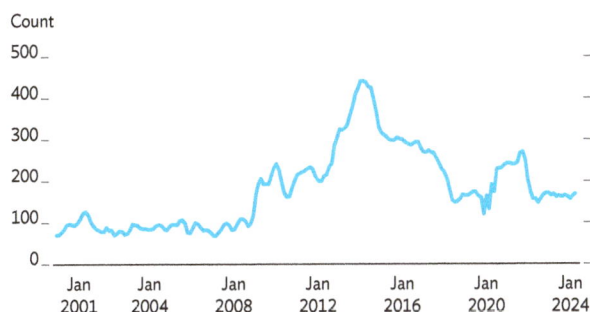

Note: Non-relevant connector words are excluded from the count. 3-month moving average.

Source: Asian Development Bank calculations.

monetary policy following almost 6 years of zero-interest-rate policy. The length of Fed statements gradually decreased as policy normalization was achieved, then increased again during the COVID-19 pandemic, before settling in a range of 150–200 words post-COVID-19.

Soon after the bankruptcy of Lehman Brothers, the Fed lowered the target range for the federal funds rate close to zero and introduced an "open-ended" forward guidance. Specifically, in December 2008 it stated that *"economic conditions are likely to warrant exceptionally low levels of the federal funds rate for some time"*. This forward guidance was modified in the March 2009 statement, as the Fed replaced the expression *"some time"* with *"an extended period"*. This extended-period guidance was repeated until July 2011.

In the summer of 2011, the Fed introduced a calendar date for the likely duration of the zero-interest-rate policy. Specifically, in August 2011 it stated that *"economic conditions are likely to warrant exceptionally low levels for the federal funds rate at least through mid-2013"*. The exact wording was then modified two times to keep indicating a low policy rate for about 2 years. In September 2012, the Fed also announced a third phase of QE, which would last an indefinite period. In the December 2012 statement, the FOMC removed the "calendar-based" guidance and introduced a "threshold-based" guidance, indicating that the zero-interest-rate policy would have been appropriate at least until the unemployment rate had remained above 6.5 percentage points, which was 1.4 points lower than the actual unemployment rate at that time. In the same statement, it also announced an expansion of QE.

The Fed's communication shifted in May 2013, signaling a move toward scaling back QE as economic conditions improved. The Fed first stated that it was *"prepared to increase or reduce the pace of its* purchases to maintain appropriate policy accommodation". That set the stage for the key "taper tantrum" speech given later in the month by then-Chairman Ben Bernanke. Bernanke declared that the Fed "could take a step down in [the] pace of [bond] purchase" (Bernanke 2013). The Fed finally began to scale down QE in January 2014.

As the Fed began scaling down QE, it adjusted its guidance to signal that rate increases would follow the program's end and be contingent on further labor market improvements. First, it stated the intention to maintain the zero-interest-rate policy "for a considerable time" after the end of QE. When bond purchases were completely halted, it stated that it would have been "patient" in beginning to normalize the policy rate. In April 2015, it spelled out some conditions for when it would have been "appropriate" to raise the federal funds rate. Crucially, these included a reference to "further improvement in the labor market". In December 2015, the Fed increased the policy rate by 25 basis points for the first time since before the global financial crisis. It then raised it nine more times by the same amount in the 3 years that followed.

COVID-19 prompted the Fed to introduce guidance signaling sustained low rates until recovery. Worried about persistently low inflation, the Fed had already started a monetary policy easing cycle before COVID-19 hit, but the cycle was sharply accelerated with the pandemic. The policy rate was lowered to close to zero in March 2020 and a guidance was added to signal a low federal funds rate until "the economy has weathered recent events and is on track to achieve its maximum employment and price stability goals".

The post-pandemic inflation surge caused the Fed to rapidly shift course. The Fed had to change its guidance already at the end of 2021, as inflation had risen above its 2% goal. In March 2022, it raised the policy rate for the first time since before COVID-19 and anticipated that "ongoing increases in the target range will be appropriate" to return inflation to its 2% objective. The Fed then raised the target range in 10 additional rapid moves to bring it to 5.25% to 5.50% in July 2023. In September 2024, it cut interest rates for the first time in 4 years, marking the beginning of a new easing cycle. Table 2.1.2 lists key sentences from Fed statements classified according to different monetary policy regimes, as reviewed above.

Table 2.1.2 Key Sentences from Fed Statements in Different Policy Regimes

The changes in Fed communication strategy since the global financial crisis can be characterized as five separate policy regimes.

Forward guidance period (18/03/2009–18/03/2014)	
18/03/2009	Economic conditions are likely to warrant exceptionally low levels of the federal funds rate for an extended period.
13/09/2012	Exceptionally low levels for the federal funds rate are likely to be warranted at least through mid-2015.
12/12/2012	This exceptionally low range for the federal funds rate will be appropriate at least as long as the unemployment rate remains above 6-1/2 percent, inflation between one and two years ahead is projected to be no more than a half percentage point above the Committee's 2 percent longer-run goal, and longer-term inflation expectations continue to be well anchored.
Liftoff period (19/03/2014–15/12/2015)	
19/03/2014	It likely will be appropriate to maintain the current target range for the federal funds rate for a considerable time after the asset purchase program ends.
28/01/2015	Based on its current assessment, the Committee judges that it can be patient in beginning to normalize the stance of monetary policy.
29/04/2015	The Committee anticipates that it will be appropriate to raise the target range for the federal funds rate when it has seen further improvement in the labor market and is reasonably confident that inflation will move back to its 2 percent objective over the medium term.
Hiking cycle (16/12/2015–29/07/2019)	
16/12/2015	The Committee expects that economic conditions will evolve in a manner that will warrant only gradual increases in the federal funds rate; the federal funds rate is likely to remain, for some time, below levels that are expected to prevail in the longer run. However, the actual path of the federal funds rate will depend on the economic outlook as informed by incoming data.
COVID-19 period (30/07/2019–14/12/2021)	
15/03/2020	The Committee expects to maintain this target range until it is confident that the economy has weathered recent events and is on track to achieve its maximum employment and price stability goals.
Inflation surge period (15/12/2021-present)	
02/11/2022	The Committee anticipates that ongoing increases in the target range will be appropriate in order to attain a stance of monetary policy that is sufficiently restrictive to return inflation to 2 percent over time.
14/06/2023	In determining the extent of additional policy firming that may be appropriate to return inflation to 2 percent over time, the Committee will take into account the cumulative tightening of monetary policy, the lags with which monetary policy affects economic activity and inflation, and economic and financial developments.

Source: Federal Open Market Committee, Board of Governors of the Federal Reserve System.

The Evolving Nature of the Fed's Data Dependency

The raw data reveals that Fed data dependency peaked during the post-COVID-19 inflation surge, and economic releases can be as informative as Fed meetings for future monetary policy. This section provides a few stylized facts regarding (i) the evolution of Fed data dependency across the different monetary policy regimes discussed in the previous section, and (ii) the monetary policy information content of inflation and employment news. Its main messages can be summarized as follows. First, data dependency was lowest when the Fed resorted to forward guidance in the aftermath of the global financial crisis and highest in the post-COVID-19 inflation surge period. Second, inflation and employment data releases are as informative for future monetary policy as Fed meetings, and their information content is particularly significant in periods of high data dependency. The rest of the section details these stylized facts, with Fed data dependency measured as the absolute difference between the current federal funds rate and its expected level 1 year ahead, as explained above.

Fed data dependency was low after the global financial crisis, rose during QE tapering and policy normalization, and fell again during COVID-19 (Figure 2.1.4). The Fed usage of various forward guidance statements to cement investors' expectations that the future policy rate would have remained at the zero lower bound for a long time after the global financial crisis lowered data dependency. The degree of data dependency increased when the Fed started to taper QE and prepared the ground to lift the policy rate from the effective zero lower bound, as the Fed made the pace of normalization conditional on further progress in the labor market. Data dependency fell during COVID-19. This fall reflects the fact that (i) the policy interest rate was quickly brought to the effective zero lower bound as the COVID-19 pandemic hit, and (ii) the Fed introduced language to signal that it would have been left at that rate for some time to allow the economy to weather recent events, which contributed to keep down investors' expectations for the future policy rate (Table 2.1.2).

Figure 2.1.4 Average Fed Data Dependency, by Policy Regime and Year

Fed data dependency tends to be low when the Fed's policy rate is close to zero.

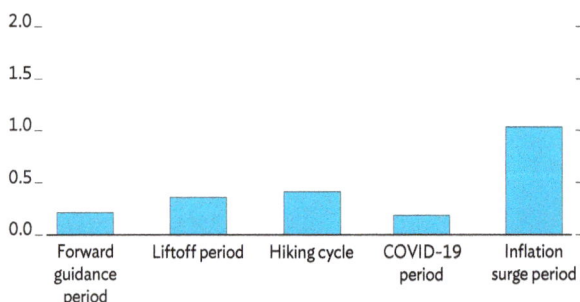

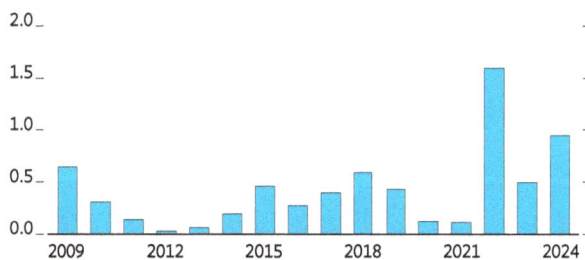

Note: Bars depict averages. Forward guidance period refers to 16/12/2008–18/03/2014; liftoff period to 19/03/2014–15/12/2015; hiking cycle to 16/12/2015–29/07/2019; COVID-19 period to 30/07/2019–14/12/2021; inflation surge period to 15/12/2021–present.

Source: Asian Development Bank calculations based on data from Bloomberg.

Figure 2.1.5 Fed Relative Attentiveness to Inflation and Employment, by Policy Regime and Year

The Fed was particularly attentive to inflation news in the recent inflation surge period.

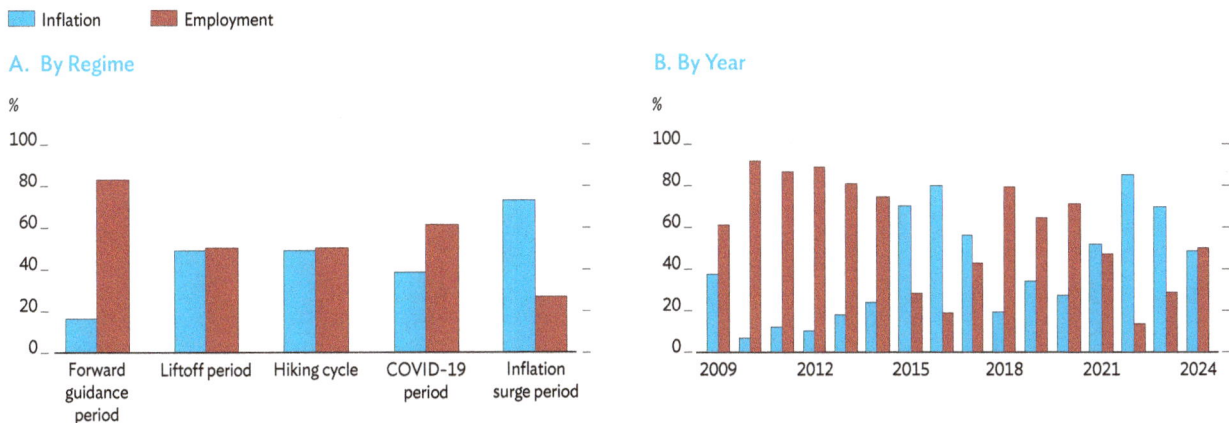

■ Inflation   ■ Employment

A. By Regime

B. By Year

Note: Bars depict averages. Forward guidance period refers to 16/12/2008–18/03/2014; liftoff period to 19/03/2014–15/12/2015; hiking cycle to 16/12/2015–29/07/2019; COVID-19 period to 30/07/2019–14/12/2021; Inflation surge period to 15/12/2021–present. See Technical Appendix for a description of how attentiveness is computed.

Source: Asian Development Bank calculations based on U.S. Congressional Budget Office, U.S. Bureau of Economic Analysis, and U.S. Bureau of Labor Statistics data (retrieved from FRED, Federal Reserve Bank of St. Louis).

The Fed's relative attentiveness to employment data was highest during the forward guidance and COVID-19 regimes, while relative attentiveness to inflation data was highest during the inflation surge regime (Figure 2.1.5). As a result of the global financial crisis, the US unemployment rate increased up to 10% at the end of 2009, far above its natural level, which was estimated to then be around 5%. At the same time, the US inflation rate was just below the Fed's 2% target, which contributed to a low degree of Fed's relative attentiveness to inflation data. The large unemployment gap gradually decreased in the years that followed, as the unemployment rate slowly converged to its natural rate, which it hit sometime in 2017. Inflation kept hovering below the Fed's target so that the central bank's relative attentiveness to inflation and employment is measured to be broadly equal in the hiking cycle of 2016–2019. As COVID-19 began, the unemployment rate spiked, marking a renewed period of higher relative Fed attentiveness to the labor market. But, as the unemployment rate rapidly decreased, while inflation shot up starting in the second half of 2021, the Fed became more attentive to inflation than labor market developments, as can also be shown through a simple word count of inflation- and employment-related keywords in Fed statements.

The 1-year-ahead expected future federal funds rate moves as much in days of inflation and employment data releases as in days of Fed meetings (Figure 2.1.6, blue bars). Future rates move significantly more in days of inflation and employment

Figure 2.1.6 Standard Deviation of the Change in the 1-Year-Ahead Expected Federal Funds Rate

Inflation and employment data releases move monetary policy expectations as much as the Fed's monetary policy meetings.

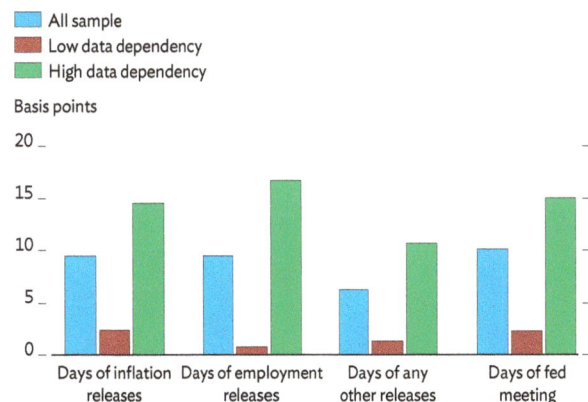

■ All sample
■ Low data dependency
■ High data dependency

Note: The low-data-dependency and high-data-dependency samples are defined as periods in which the data dependency measure is, respectively, below the 25th percentile and above the 75th percentile of its distribution.

Source: Asian Development Bank calculations based on data from Bloomberg.

data releases than in days of other data releases. These findings indicate that inflation and employment data releases are highly informative about future monetary policy. Fed meetings can move interest rate expectations because of data-driven changes in Fed policy but also due to changes in the Fed reaction function. But inflation and employment data releases can only move interest rate expectations precisely because of the expected response of the Fed to these releases.

When Fed data dependency is high, the monetary policy information content of inflation or employment data releases is magnified (Figure 2.1.6, green bars). When Fed data dependency is low the monetary policy information content of these releases is almost null (red bars). At the same time, even Fed meetings themselves are more informative for future policy when data dependency is high and less informative when data dependency is low. As in the full sample, when data dependency is high, employment and inflation data releases are about as informative for future monetary policy as Fed meetings themselves.

The Effects of Data-Driven Changes in Fed Policy on Financial Markets Abroad

This section discusses how data-driven changes in US monetary policy affect foreign financial markets. The discussion draws on the empirical estimates derived using the methodology described above. Since investors form expectations about the upcoming data releases, the estimation focuses on deviations of the actual releases from investors' expectations—referred to as surprises—and does not distinguish between releases that are higher or lower than expected, assuming that they have symmetric effects on financial markets. The estimated coefficients report the impact of a 1-standard-deviation positive surprise—positive meaning that the release is higher than expected. In the case of employment releases, this amounts to the net nonfarm payroll employment creation being about 100,000 higher than expected. A 1-standard-deviation inflation surprise instead amounts to the headline month-on-month inflation release being 0.1 percentage points higher than expected. The effect of releases that are 1 standard deviation below what is expected is simply given by the negative value of the reported coefficients.

The impact of data surprises on the variables of interest is separated into two components: the direct effect of the surprise, and the effect of the expected Fed response to the surprise. The first refers to the change in the variables of interest directly caused by the data surprise, as investors reassess the state of the economy. The latter meanwhile refers to the change in the variables of interest caused by the expected response of the Fed to the surprise. In other words, this component reports the effects of a data-driven change in monetary policy. To interpret the results, the effect working through the Fed's expected response to the surprise is calculated assuming that the Fed is at the 90th percentile of the inflation- and employment-specific data dependency variables. This percentile is chosen to simulate the recent period of heightened inflation data dependency, as it corresponds to the average level of Fed inflation data

dependency that prevailed in the first half of 2024. For employment, the 90th percentile corresponds to the average level in 2018. The sum of the direct effect of the surprise and the effect through the Fed's expected response can be interpreted as the overall impact of economic surprise when the Fed is highly data dependent.

The anticipated Fed responses to positive inflation and employment surprises lead to tighter financial conditions, while the direct effects of surprises are null. An inflation-driven increase of US interest rates leads to higher short-term government bond yields, currency depreciations, declines in stock markets, and higher sovereign default probabilities in other economies. An increase in interest rates in response to faster-than-expected employment growth drives short- and long-term interest rates sharply up, induces a depreciation of foreign currencies, and causes foreign capital to flee emerging market debt. The portfolio-rebalancing channel of monetary policy appears to explain most of these effects, while the risk-taking channel may be important to explain the effects of inflation surprises on stock markets and default probabilities. Data surprises do not have any direct effects—that is, abstaining from the effect working through the expected Fed response.

The expected Fed response to a 1-standard-deviation US inflation surprise leads to a 2-basis-point increase in foreign 2-year bond yields, with no effect on 10-year yields (Figure 2.1.7, panels A and B). The effect of an inflation-driven tightening of US monetary policy on short-term interest rates in foreign markets can be because investors either (i) expect foreign central banks to follow in the footsteps of the Fed, (ii) require a higher return for holding foreign assets, or (iii) a combination of the two. Taken together, these results indicate that an inflation-driven tightening of monetary policy leads to a flattening of foreign yield curves.

Figure 2.1.7 Impacts of US Data Surprises on Financial Markets Abroad, Inflation

An inflation-driven tightening of US monetary policy leads to higher short-term bond yields, foreign currency depreciations, declines in equities, and increased debt default probabilities.

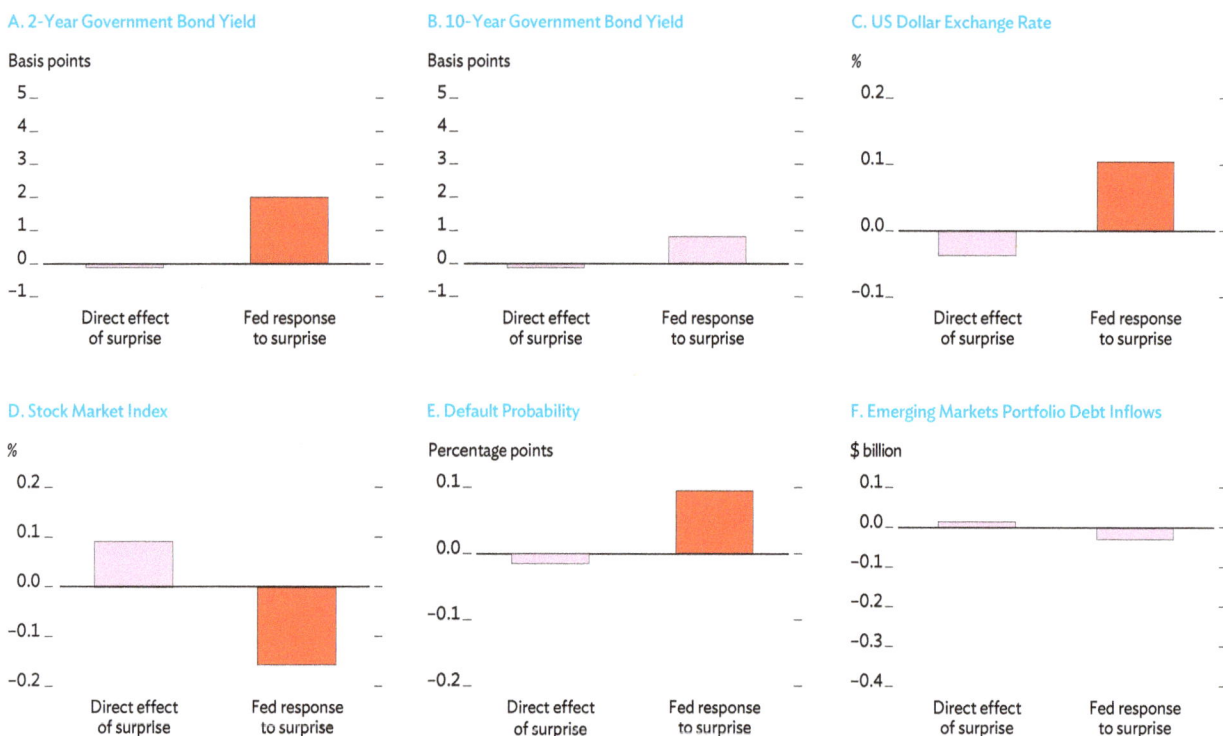

A. 2-Year Government Bond Yield

B. 10-Year Government Bond Yield

C. US Dollar Exchange Rate

D. Stock Market Index

E. Default Probability

F. Emerging Markets Portfolio Debt Inflows

US = United States.

Note: Darker colored bars denote statistically significant coefficients at the 90% confidence level.

Source: Asian Development Bank calculations based on data from Bloomberg and Institute for International Finance.

The Fed response to a 1-standard-deviation inflation surprise leads to an appreciation of the US dollar of about 0.1% on average versus foreign currencies (Figure 2.1.7, panel C). This can be explained by the fact that the Fed response to the inflation news raises the short-term US government bond yield by about 2 basis points more than its foreign equivalent (see Figure 2.9 on US responses). This leads to an interest rate differential between the US and foreign economies that results in an appreciation of the US dollar as capital flows into the US to seek higher returns. Positive inflation surprises have a negative direct effect on the US dollar exchange rate (meaning a depreciation of the US dollar), as should be expected absent a monetary policy response, but the coefficient is not statistically significant.

An inflation-driven tightening of US monetary policy also spills over into foreign stock markets (Figure 2.1.7, panel D). Foreign stock markets decline by about 0.2% on average across economies after a 1-standard-deviation inflation surprise when the Fed is highly data dependent. The stock market index is measured in local currency terms, so that, when considering the US dollar value of the stock market, this effect is on top of the mechanical effect working through the US dollar appreciation. The government default probability also increases, by about 0.1 percentage point (panel E). These effects can be explained by the increase in risk aversion following an inflation-driven tightening of monetary policy, which is discussed in the Technical Appendix. This penalizes riskier investments, such as those in stocks and sovereign debt in emerging and frontier market economies (note that default probability data is mostly unavailable for developed markets).

Figure 2.1.8 Impacts of US Data Surprises on Financial Markets Abroad, Employment

An employment-driven tightening of US monetary policy leads to increases in short- and long-term bond yields, foreign currency depreciations, and capital outflows from emerging markets.

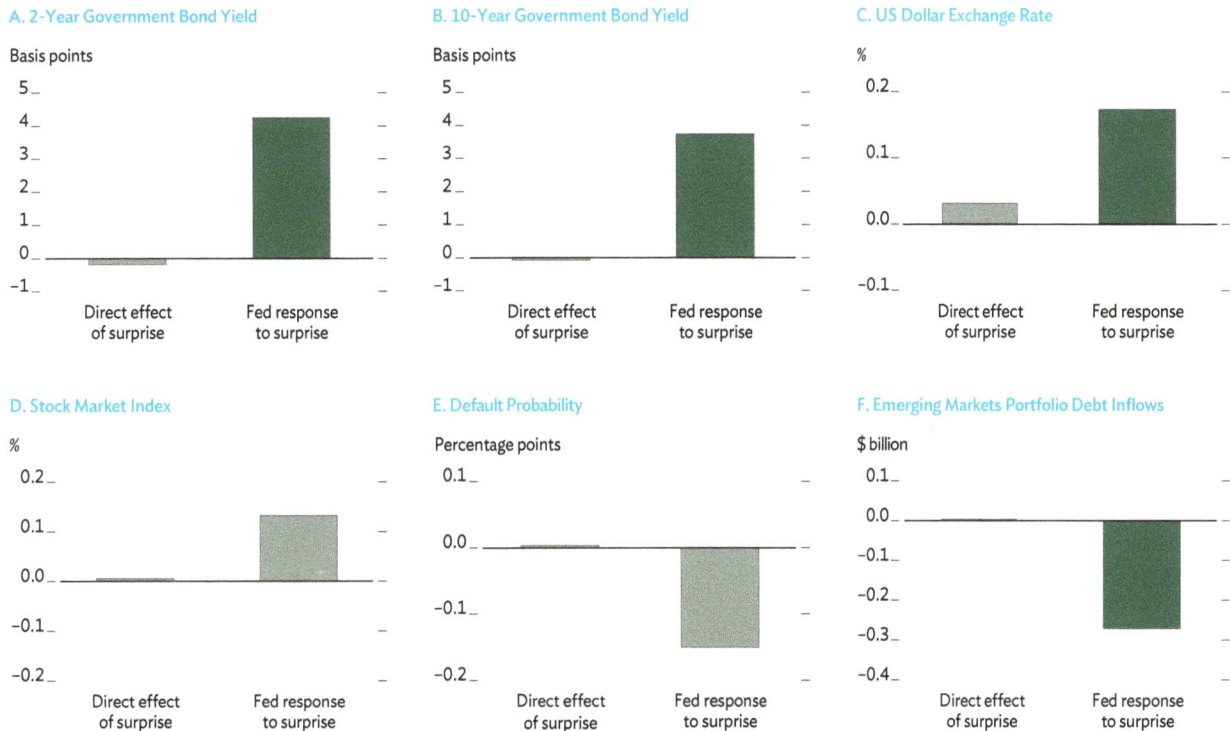

A. 2-Year Government Bond Yield
B. 10-Year Government Bond Yield
C. US Dollar Exchange Rate
D. Stock Market Index
E. Default Probability
F. Emerging Markets Portfolio Debt Inflows

US = United States.

Note: Darker colored bars denote statistically significant coefficients at the 90% confidence level.

Source: Asian Development Bank calculations based on data from Bloomberg and Institute for International Finance.

An employment-driven US monetary tightening raises foreign bond yields, strengthens the US dollar, and triggers emerging market capital outflows (Figure 2.1.8). The expected Fed response to a 1-standard-deviation employment surprise raises short-term bond yields by about 4 basis points, which is about twice as much as the case of an equivalent inflation surprise (Figure 2.1.7), but less than half the effect of the same employment surprise on US government bond yields (shown in Figure 2.1.9 for reference). Unlike the case of an inflation surprise, the expected Fed response to an employment surprise also reverberates in long-term bond yields. This is consistent with the larger impact of employment news on further-ahead federal funds future expectations, which is discussed in the Technical Appendix. Stock markets and default probabilities are not affected by employment surprises.

An employment-driven US monetary tightening creates a large gap between US and foreign bond yields. This causes a substantial appreciation of the US dollar (the estimated effect is about twice as large as in the case of the Fed response to an inflation surprise) and leads foreign capital to leave emerging market debt assets, possibly to be directed towards the US in search of higher yield. The lack of a significant response of foreign stock markets and sovereign default probabilities may be explained by the neutral effect of employment surprises on risk aversion, unlike the case of inflation, as discussed in the Technical Appendix. In other words, the risk-taking channel of monetary policy may operate through an inflation-driven tightening of Fed policy but less so through an employment-driven tightening.

Figure 2.1.9 Impacts of US Data Surprises on US Financial Markets, Inflation and Employment

The effects of inflation- and employment-driven US monetary policy tightenings on bond yields are more than twice as large in the US than abroad.

A. Inflation Surprise

A1. 2-Year Government Bond Yield

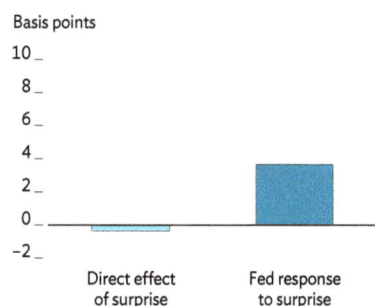

A2. 10-Year Government Bond Yield

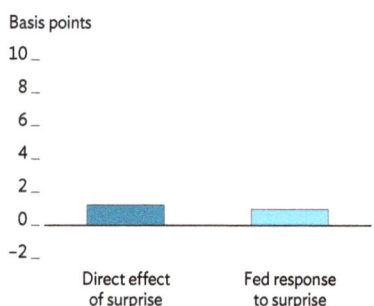

A3. Stock Market Index

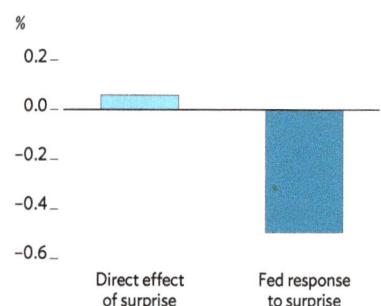

B. Employment Surprise

B1. 2-Year Government Bond Yield

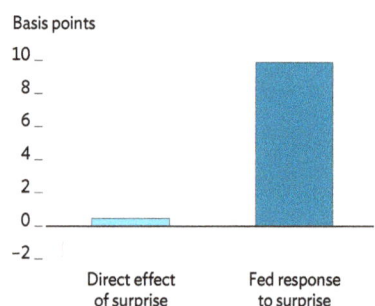

B2. 10-Year Government Bond Yield

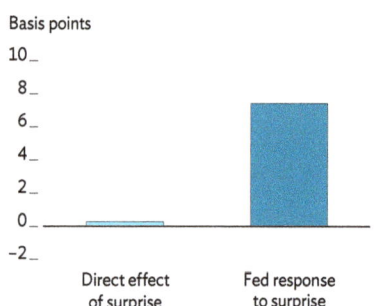

B3. Stock Market Index

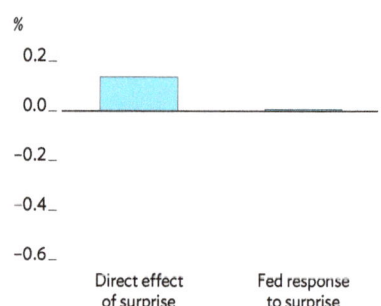

US = United States.
Note: Darker colored bars denote statistically significant coefficients at the 90% confidence level.
Source: Asian Development Bank calculations based on data from Bloomberg.

Robustness and Sensitivity Analyses

Sensitivity analyses confirm the robustness of the baseline results. The section continues by briefly discussing a set of sensitivity analyses performed on the baseline estimations, which overall suggest that the main results are robust. More details and full results from these sensitivity analyses are provided in the Technical Appendix.

As a start, additional variables are included in the empirical regression to control for US economic and financial developments that may also affect asset prices in foreign markets. These variables include measures of (i) uncertainty, such as the VIX index, which is a measure of the expected volatility in the US stock market, and the newspaper-based economic policy uncertainty index (Baker, Bloom, and, Davis 2016); (ii) business conditions, such as

the Aruoba-Diebold-Scotti business conditions index (Aruoba, Diebold, and Scotti 2009), which tracks US high-frequency economic indicators; and (iii) financial stress, such as the Bloomberg financial conditions index, which measures stress in US financial markets. The effective federal funds rate is also included. The inclusion of these variables, both in levels and in changes, does not greatly affect the baseline estimates. This is as expected given that the news variable analyzed in this chapter are constructed as the surprise component of US employment and inflation releases (the actual release minus the investors expectation for that release) and are thus unlikely to co-move with any economic or financial developments.

A second sensitivity analysis accounts for the possible effects of other US macroeconomic data releases beyond inflation and nonfarm payroll employment. These other data releases concern various aspects of the US economy, including consumer and business confidence, industrial production, construction activity as well as other price and labor market developments. Surprise measures are constructed following the same approach used for inflation and employment data releases. These additional surprise variables are introduced in the empirical regression both on their own and interacted with the Fed data dependency variables. The baseline estimates are largely unaffected by the inclusion of these additional macroeconomic news variables.

Another sensitivity analysis is done on the horizon considered, using a 5-day window rather than the 2-day window employed in the baseline estimation. The results using this larger window are qualitatively in line to the baseline 2-day window. Some coefficients lose statistical significance, while others get stronger. This analysis reveals that a large part of the effect estimated is not merely transitory, meaning that it does not fade away after a few days. Other sensitivity analyses are also performed and discussed in the Technical Appendix.

Developed Markets Versus Emerging and Frontier Markets

Data-driven US monetary tightening affects developed and emerging/frontier markets similarly, with some quantitative differences (Figure 2.1.10). The analysis now examines the two separate subsamples of developed market and emerging and frontier market economies and investigates differences in the impact of inflation- and employment-driven US monetary policy tightening on their respective financial variables. The approach is the same as in the baseline estimation. Default probabilities are not considered, as the data is largely unavailable for the sample of developed markets. The effects of inflation and employment news are broadly consistent with what estimated for the full baseline sample, although there exist some quantitative differences across the developed market and emerging and frontier market subsamples.

Figure 2.1.10 Impact of US Data Surprises on Developed, Emerging and Frontier Markets, Inflation and Employment

Developed markets are more affected by data-driven changes in US monetary policy than emerging and frontier markets.

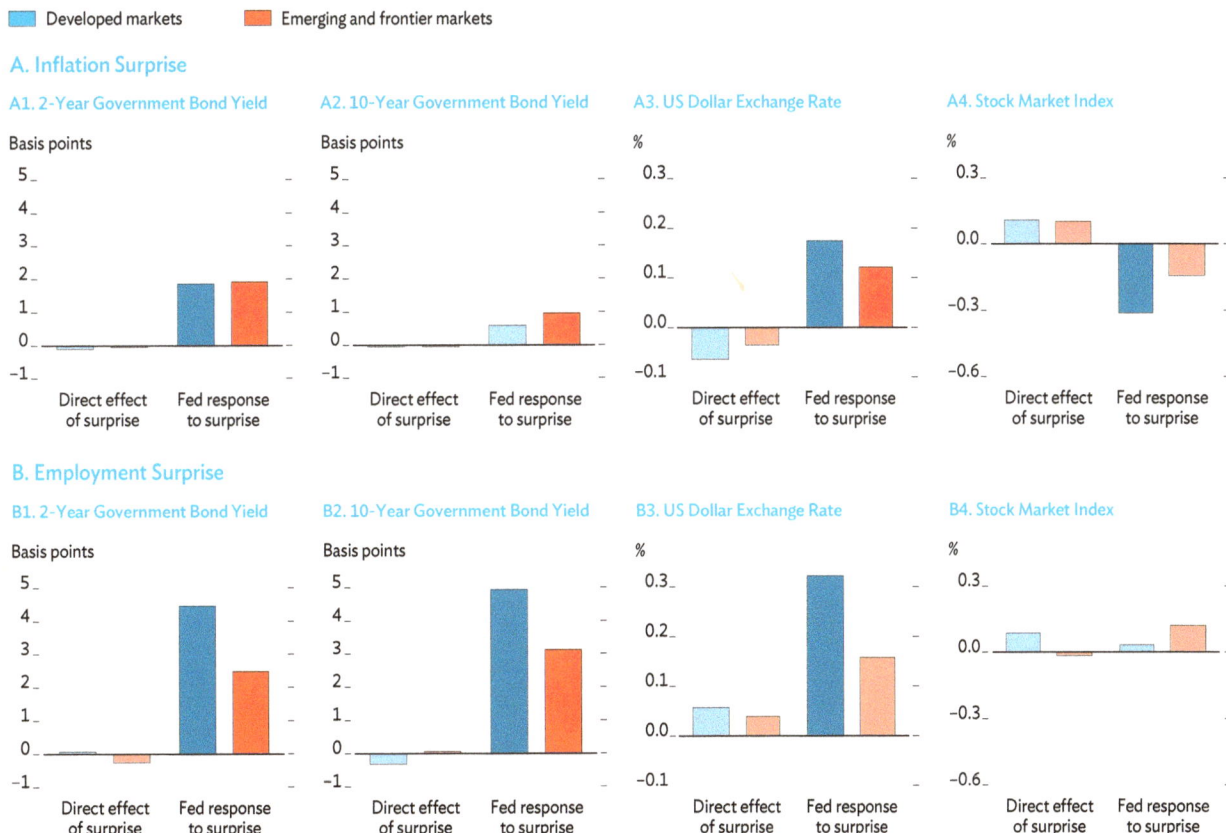

US = United States

Note: Darker colored bars denote statistically significant coefficients at the 90% confidence level.

Source: Asian Development Bank calculations based on data from Bloomberg.

Developed economies are more impacted by a US monetary tightening, especially in exchange rate and stock markets. While the larger sensitivity of developed economies may be surprising at first, it should be considered that their assets are generally more liquid than emerging and frontier market assets, and the capital account is more open in the average developed economy than in its emerging or frontier market counterpart. These factors make the former naturally more sensitive to outside shocks.

ADB developing member economies exhibit responses that are similar to those of emerging and frontier market economies. This is as expected since many ADB developing members fall into this category. Within the subsample of ADB developing member economies, ASEAN-5 economies are those that exhibit the more similar responses to the broader emerging and frontier market economies subsample, while the People's Republic of China exhibits the most muted responses. These subsample results are reported and discussed further in the Technical Appendix.

Role of Macroeconomic Conditions

The chapter next examines how an economy's macroeconomic conditions influence the sensitivity of local financial markets to US monetary policy. This analysis focuses on emerging and frontier market economies. The characteristics considered are the current account deficit as a share of GDP, the fiscal deficit as a share of GDP, the inverse of the GDP growth rate, the inflation rate, the debt denominated in foreign currency as a share of GDP, and the sovereign credit rating. These characteristics are considered separately one at a time. The results are shown in Figure 2.1.11 for inflation surprises and Figure 2.1.12 for employment surprises, only for the effects of the expected Fed response to the surprise. The bars show differences in the estimated responses between economies in the upper and lower quartiles of the distribution of the specific variable considered.

Figure 2.1.11 Differential Effects Across Economies with Different Fundamentals, Fed Response to Inflation Surprises

Current account deficits and external debts increase sensitivity to an inflation-driven tightening of US monetary policy.

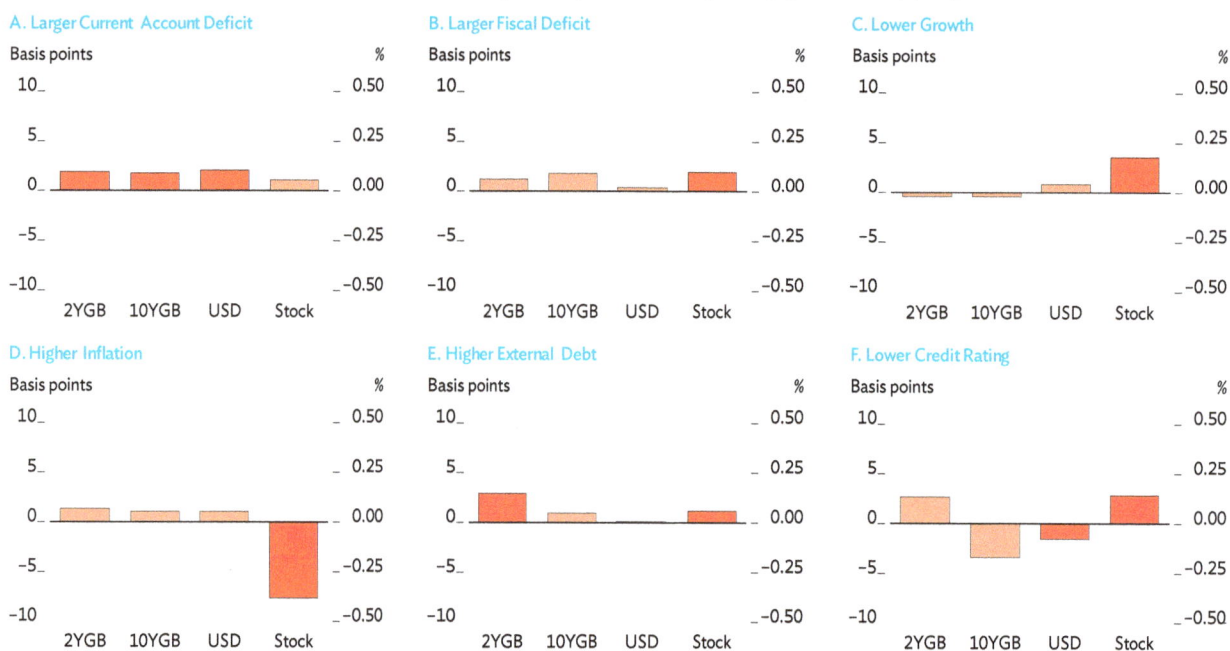

2YGB = 2-year government bond yield, 10YGB = 10-year government bond yield, US = United States, USD = price of the US dollar in local currency units, stock = local currency price of main stock market index.

Note: Bars show differences in estimated effects between economies in the upper and lower quartiles of the distribution of the specific variable considered. Left-hand y-axes report results for 2-year and 10-year government bond yields (2YGB and 10YGB respectively, in basis points). Right-hand y-axes report results for the US dollar exchange rate and the stock market index (USD and stock respectively, in %). The sample includes emerging and frontier markets. Darker colored bars denote statistically significant coefficients at the 90% confidence level.

Source: Asian Development Bank calculations based on data from Bloomberg, the World Economic Outlook of the International Monetary Fund, Moody's, Fitch, and S&P.

Figure 2.1.12 Differential Effects Across Economies with Different Fundamentals, Fed Response to Employment Surprises

A higher inflation rate increases the sensitivity to an employment-driven tightening of US monetary policy.

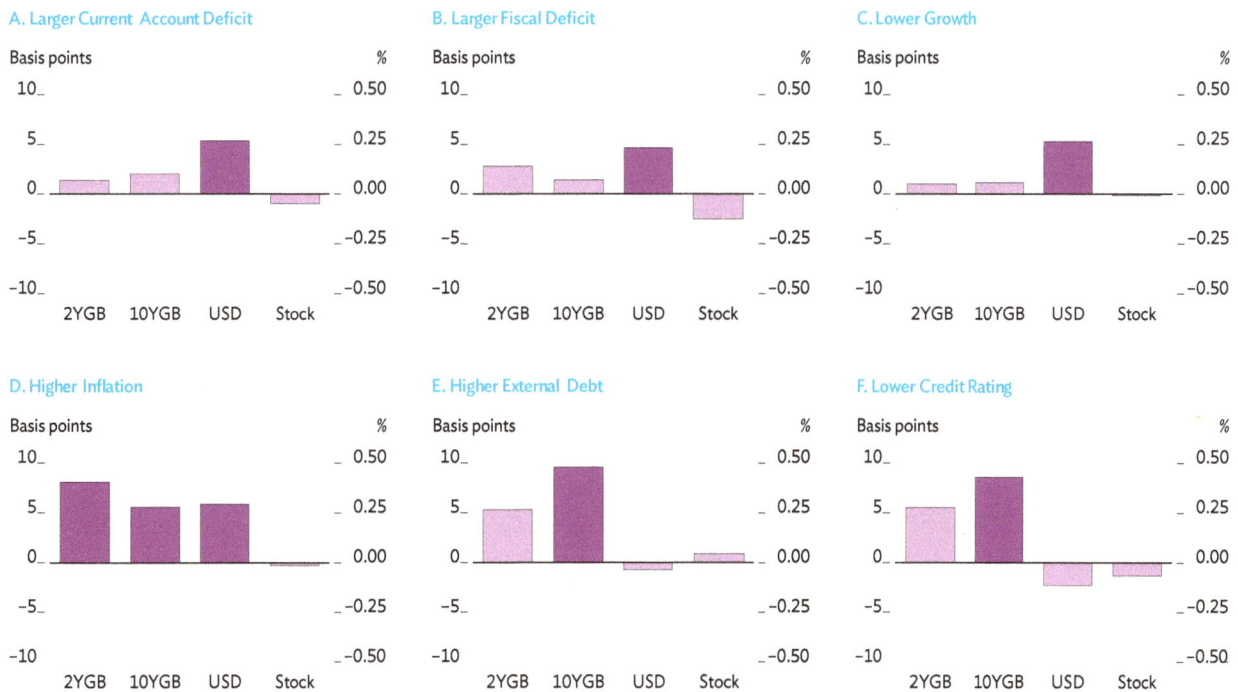

A. Larger Current Account Deficit

B. Larger Fiscal Deficit

C. Lower Growth

D. Higher Inflation

E. Higher External Debt

F. Lower Credit Rating

2YGB = 2-year government bond yield, 10YGB = 10-year government bond yield, US = United States, USD = price of the US dollar in local currency units, stock = local currency price of main stock market index.

Note: Bars show differences in estimated effects between economies in the upper and lower quartiles of the distribution of the specific variable considered. Left-hand Y-axes report results for 2-year and 10-year government bond yields (2YGB and 10YGB respectively, in basis points). Right-hand Y-axes report results for the US dollar exchange rate and the stock market index (USD and Stock respectively, in %). The sample includes emerging and frontier markets. Darker colored bars denote statistically significant coefficients at the 90% confidence level.

Source: Asian Development Bank calculations based on data from Bloomberg, the World Economic Outlook of the International Monetary Fund, Moody's, Fitch, and S&P.

Weaker macroeconomic fundamentals amplify spillovers. The sovereign bond yields of economies with larger current account and budget deficits increase more following an inflation-driven US monetary policy tightening, and their currencies depreciate more after both an inflation- and employment-driven tightening. High inflation, high external debt, and a worse sovereign credit rating make bond yields more responsive to an employment-driven increase in US interest rates.

Conclusion and Policy Implications

This chapter studies the impact of inflation- and employment-driven changes in US interest rates on foreign markets, focusing on the time in which new economic data is released. The Fed has just started an easing cycle. But as Fed Chair Jerome Powell indicated in the quote that opened this chapter, how quickly and by how much interest rates will be reduced depends on the speed at which inflation will durably return close to the Fed target and on labor market developments. When the Fed is highly data dependent, investors scrutinize important data releases and revise their expectations of future monetary policy based on them. Against this background, the chapter studies the impact of data-driven changes in US interest rates examining responses to data releases rather than to Fed meetings. To carry out the analysis, the chapter constructs novel variables measuring the degrees of the Fed's data dependency and relative attentiveness to inflation/employment data releases. These variables determine how such releases shape investors' assessments of the Fed's likely response.

Inflation- and employment-driven increases in US interest rates lead to a significant tightening of financial conditions in other economies. The analysis considers the impact on short-term and long-term bond yields, exchange rates, stock market indices, sovereign default probabilities, and portfolio flows, first across a large sample of 108 foreign economies and then by economy groups. The results strongly suggest that data-driven changes in US monetary policy have important effects for foreign economies. An inflation-driven tightening of monetary policy increases short-term bond yields, leads to a currency depreciation vis-à-vis the US dollar, and causes stock markets to lose value and default probabilities to increase. When US interest rates increase in response to strong employment growth, short- and long-term bond yields go up sharply, foreign currencies depreciate, and foreign capital leaves emerging market debt.

The chapter's empirical results can be used to assess how different US inflation and employment scenarios could shape the current Fed easing cycle, and thereby influence financial markets across the globe. As of 19 September, a majority of economists polled by Bloomberg expects US headline inflation to remain at its current level of 2.5% throughout 2024. At the same time, the US unemployment rate is expected to increase to 4.4% by the end of 2024, while the net monthly change in nonfarm payroll employment is expected to be +129,000 on average in the remainder of 2024. Further, federal funds future rates indicate that investors expect the Fed to lower the policy rate by 50 basis points in total during the November and December 2024 monetary policy meetings.

A rebounding inflation scenario would see investors revising down the expected cuts of Fed policy rates by a total of 150 basis points, causing a sharp tightening of global financial conditions. Specifically, the scenario assumes that inflation gradually returns to its July level of 2.9% by the end of 2024—contrary to investors expectation of remaining at 2.5%. The coefficients estimated in this chapter suggest that short-term foreign bond yields could increase by about 70 basis points, local currencies could depreciate by almost 4% vis-à-vis the US dollar, stock market prices could decline up to 5.5%, and government default probabilities could increase by 3.3 percentage points.[8] Broadly the opposite dynamics would materialize if inflation gradually declined to 2.1% by the end of 2024.

---

[8] These effects are calculated assuming that (i) the difference between the federal funds rate and its 12-months-ahead expectation changes accordingly to the estimated effect of the inflation surprise on the 12-months-ahead federal funds future rate, and (ii) the unemployment rate climbs to 4.4%, as expected by investors.

A worsening of the labor market and falling inflation could substantially lower bond yields, strengthen currencies, boost stock markets, and reduce default risks in foreign markets. Policymakers should also pay attention to US labor market developments and how these would affect future Fed policy. The US unemployment rate has gradually increased over the course of 2024 —from 3.7% at the beginning of the year to 4.2% in August— and is now close to its natural level. The Fed has already signaled that it is paying increasingly more attention to employment data. To get an idea of the effect that a joint decline in inflation and a worsening of the US labor market may have on foreign markets, one can consider the hypothetical case in which there is no net nonfarm job gain in the last four employment report releases of 2024, against the +129,000 figure that investors expect on average. The joint materialization of this scenario, and of inflation falling to 2.1% by the end of 2024, would lead to a reduction of short- and long-term foreign bond yields of about 95 and 30 basis points, respectively, an appreciation of local currencies vis-à-vis the US dollar of about 4.5%, a gain in stock markets of roughly 5%, and a reduction of government default probabilities of 2.7 percentage points.[9]

Maintaining healthy current account balances, low external debts, and stable inflation rates can help economies to reduce exposure to US economic and monetary developments. While emerging and frontier markets will tend to be more affected by changes in US monetary policy as their economies grow and their markets become more liquid and open to foreign capital, there are ways to reduce this exposure. To give a concrete example, the empirical estimates suggest that if US inflation were to unexpectedly return to 2.9% by the end of 2024, an emerging or frontier market economy in the top quartile of current accounts (those with a current account surplus of about 2% or more) could see its short- and long-term bond yields increase by about 70 basis points less than an economy in the worst quartile of current accounts (with a current account deficit of about 4.5% or worse) and its exchange rate could depreciate almost 4 percentage points less.

Future work can analyze whether specific monetary and fiscal policy frameworks can reduce spillovers. This analysis is the first to study the spillover effects of data-driven US monetary policy on international financial markets focusing on the time in which new data is released—which is arguably when the effects of data-driven policy changes should be felt most if investors have rational expectations. The study observes that the degree of Fed's data dependency and relative attentiveness to inflation and employment news vary over time and accounts for that in the empirical analysis. Results suggest that the spillover effects of such data-driven policy changes are large. Future work may consider expanding the analysis to other outcome variables and exploring whether there are specific policy measures that might reduce spillovers.

---

[9] These effects are calculated assuming that (i) the difference between the federal funds rate and its 12-months-ahead expectation does not vary, as the increase produced by the estimated effect of inflation and employment surprises on the 12-months-ahead federal funds future rate is offset by simultaneous interest rate cuts by the Fed and (ii) the unemployment rate gradually rises from the current 4.2% level to 4.6% by the end of 2024.

References

Aizenman, J., M. Binici, and M. M. Hutchison. 2016. The Transmission of Federal Reserve Tapering News to Emerging Financial Markets. *International Journal of Central Banking*. 12 (2). pp. 317–356.

Aizenman et al. 2024. The Performance of Emerging Markets During the Fed's Easing and Tightening Cycles: A Cross-country Resilience Analysis. *Journal of International Money and Finance*. 148.

Arteta, C., S. Kamin, and F. Ruch. 2023. How Do Rising US Interest Rates Affect Emerging and Developing Economies? It Depends. *Policy Research Working Paper* No. 10258. World Bank.

Aruoba, S. B., and T. Drechsel. 2024. Identifying Monetary Policy Shocks: A Natural Language Approach. *NBER Working Paper* 32417. National Bureau of Economic Research.

Aruoba, S. B., F. X. Diebold, and C. Scotti. 2009. Real-Time Measurement of Business Conditions. *Journal of Business & Economic Statistics*. 27 (4). pp. 417–427.

Baker, S. R., N. Bloom, and S. J. Davis. 2016. Measuring Economic Policy Uncertainty. The Quarterly Journal of Economics. 131 (4). pp. 1593–1636.

Bauer, M., and E. Swanson. 2023. An Alternative Explanation for the "Fed Information Effect". *American Economic Review*. 113 (3). pp. 664–700.

Beber, A., and M. W. Brandt. 2009. When it Cannot Get Better or Worse: The Asymmetric Impact of Good and Bad News on Bond Returns in Expansions and Recessions. *Review of Finance*. 14 (1). pp. 119–155.

Bekaert, G., E. Engstrom, N. Xu. 2021. The Time Variation in Risk Appetite and Uncertainty. *Management Science*. 68 (6). pp. 3975-4004

Bernanke, B. 2013a. *Chairman Bernanke's Press Conference, December 18, 2013*. US Federal Open Market Committee.

Bernanke, B. 2013b. *Testimony Before the Joint Economic Committee, May 22, 2013*. US Congress.

Bowman, D., J. M. Londono, and H. Sapriza. 2015. US Unconventional Monetary Policy and Transmission to Emerging Market Economies. *Journal of International Money and Finance*. 55. pp. 27–59.

Boyd, J.H., J. Hu, and R. Jagannathan. 2005. The Stock Market's Reaction to Unemployment News: Why Bad News is Usually Good for Stocks. *The Journal of Finance*. 60 (2). pp. 649–672.

Bruno, V. and H.S. Shin. 2015. Capital Flows and the Risk-taking Channel of Monetary Policy. *Journal of Monetary Economics*. 71. pp. 119–132.

Campbell, J. R., C. L. Evans, J. D. M. Fisher, and A. Justiniano. 2012. Macroeconomic Effects of Federal Reserve Forward Guidance. *Papers on Economic Activity*. 43 (1). The Brookings Institution.

Chari, A., C. Lundblad, and K. D. Stedman. 2020. Taper Tantrums: Quantitative Easing, Its Aftermath, and Emerging Capital Flows. *The Review of Financial Studies*. 34 (3). pp. 1445–1508.

Ciminelli, G., J. Rogers, and W. Wu. 2022. The Effects of US Monetary Policy on International Mutual Fund Investment. *Journal of International Money and Finance*. 127.

Dahlhaus, T., and G. Vasishtha. 2020. Monetary Policy News in the US: Effects on Emerging Market Capital Flows. *Journal of International Money and Finance*. 109.

Engler, P., R. Piazza, and G. Sher. 2023. Spillovers to Emerging Markets from U.S. Economic News and Monetary Policy. *IMF Working Paper 23/107.* International Monetary Fund.

Fratzscher, M. 2012. Capital Flows, Push Versus Pull Factors and the Global Financial Crisis. *Journal of International Economics.* 88 (2). pp. 341–356.

Fratzscher, M., M. Lo Duca, R. Straub. 2018. On the International Spillovers of US Quantitative Easing. *The Economic Journal.* 128 (608). pp. 330–377.

Gilbert, T., C. Scotti, G. Strasser, and C. Vega. 2017. Is the Intrinsic Value of Macroeconomic News Announcements Related to Their Asset Price Impact? *Journal of Monetary Economics.* 92. pp. 78–95.

Gürkaynak, R., B. Sack, and E. Swanson. 2005. The Sensitivity of Long-Term Interest Rates to Economic News: Evidence and Implications for Macroeconomic Models. *American Economic Review.* 95 (1). pp. 425–436.

Healy, C., and C. Jia. 2024. Financial Markets' Perceptions of the FOMC's Data-Dependent Monetary Policy. *Economic Commentary 2024-03.* Federal Reserve Bank of Cleveland.

Hoek, J., S. Kamin, E. Yoldas. 2022. Are Higher US Interest Rates Always Bad News for Emerging Markets? *Journal of International Economics.* 137.

Iacoviello, M. and G. Navarro. 2019. Foreign Effects of Higher US Interest Rates. *Journal of International Money and Finance.* 95. pp. 232–250.

Kalemli-Ozcan, S., and F. Unsal. 2024. Global Transmission of Fed Hikes: The Role of Policy Credibility and Balance Sheets. *NBER Working Paper 32329.* National Bureau of Economic Research.

Nakamura, E., and J. Steinsson. 2018. High-Frequency Identification of Monetary Non-Neutrality: The Information Effect. *Quarterly Journal of Economics.* 133 (3). pp. 1283–1330.

Pinchetti, M. and A. Szczepaniak. 2024. Global Spillovers of the Fed Information Effect. *IMF Economic Review.* 72 (2). International Monetary Fund.

Powell, J. 2024. *Reassessing the Effectiveness and Transmission of Monetary Policy, August 23, 2024.* Economic Symposium of Federal Reserve Bank of Kansas City.

Romer, C. D. and D. Romer. 1989. Does Monetary Policy Matter? A New Test in the Spirt of Friedman and Schwartz. *NBER Macroeconomics Annual* 4. National Bureau of Economic Research.

Romer, C. D. and D. Romer. 2000. Federal Reserve Information and the Behavior of Interest Rates. *American Economic Review.* 90 (3). pp. 429–457.

Romer, C. D. and D. Romer. 2023. Presidential Address: Does Monetary Policy Matter? The Narrative Approach after 35 Years. *American Economic Review* 113 (6). pp. 1395–1423.

Swanson, E. T., and J. C. Williams. 2014. Measuring the Effect of the Zero Lower Bound on Medium- and-Longer-Term Interest Rates. *American Economic Review.* 104 (10). pp. 3154–85.

Waller, C. J. 2022. Monetary Policy in a World of Conflicting Data. *Rocky Mountain Economic Summit, 14 July 2022.* Global Interdependence Center.

Technical Appendix

This Technical Appendix details the data and methodology used for the empirical analysis and provides further empirical results. Section A1 describes the main regression framework. Section A2 discusses the data, including the construction of the macroeconomic news variables and of the variables measuring the extent of Fed data dependency. Section A3 presents results on the effects of US data releases on US monetary policy expectations and risk aversion. Section A4 presents baseline regression results in table format and discusses sensitivity analyses. Section A5 discusses results for the ADB developing members sample.

A1. Regression Framework

To analyze the effects that data-driven changes in US monetary policy have on financial variables in foreign economies, variations of the following regression specification are estimated:

$$y_{i,t+1} - y_{i,t-1} = \alpha_i + \sum_{j=1}^{J} \left(\beta^j News_t^j + \theta^j News_t^j \right. $$
$$\left. *FedDD_{t-1}^j + \sigma^j FedDD_{t-1}^j \right) + \delta X_t + \varepsilon_{i,t} \tag{A1}$$

where subscripts i and t denote the economy and time respectively; $y_{i,t}$ is the financial variable of interest in economy i measured at the end of the trading day t; α_i are economy fixed effects; $News_t^j$ is a variable measuring the news content contained in the release of the US macroeconomic announcement j (with $j=1,..,J$) at time t; $FedDD_t^j$ is a measure of how much future policy decisions by the US Federal Reserve are going to depend on economic data j; X_t is a vector of U.S.-specific control variables.

The β^j and θ^j coefficients are the coefficients of interest to be estimated. β^j measures the direct effect of a 1-standard-deviation surprise in the US macroeconomic announcement j on the 2-day change of financial variable of interest y in economy i, where a

2-day event window is chosen to allow for differences in time zones and trading hours across markets. θ^j measures the effect of the (expected) response of the US Federal Reserve (the Fed) to the same surprise, for the level of Fed data dependency prevailing one day before the data release. The chapter figures are derived using the β^j coefficients to depict the bars denoted by "direct effect of surprise", and the θ^j coefficients, evaluated at the 90th percentile of the data dependency distribution, to depict the bars denoted by "Fed response to surprise".

Equation (A1) is estimated through OLS on a sample of 108 economies. Economies were selected based on whether they satisfied either one of two criteria. The first criterion is to be classified by Morgan Stanley Capital International (MSCI), a firm that provides investment data and analytics services to investors. The second is to be an Asian Development Bank (ADB) developing member. The MSCI classifies economies in four different categories, based on (i) their level of economic development, (ii) whether their financial market assets meet certain minimum investability requirements, and (iii) their level of market accessibility. The four categories are developed markets (DMs), emerging markets (EMs), frontier markets (FMs), and standalone markets (SMs).

The MSCI periodically reclassifies economies. Observations in which an economy is not classified as either DM, EM, FM, or SM are excluded from the sample (unless the economy is an ADB developing member). As of December 2023, the sample included 23 DMs, 24 EMs, 28 FMs, 11 SMs, and 23 economies that MSCI has not classified but that are ADB developing members. The following economies are not included in the sample, despite being ADB developing members, due to a lack of data: Cook Islands, Kiribati, Marshall Islands, Federated States of Micronesia, Nauru, Palau, Tuvalu, and Niue. Table A1 lists all economies in the sample.

The time sample goes from April 2009 to June 2024 and frequency is daily. Equation (A1) is estimated only on days of economic data releases. Standard errors are time clustered.

A2. Dataset

Macroeconomic News

Since market participants form expectations about upcoming macroeconomic announcements, this study follows standard practice in the literature and identifies their unexpected, "surprise", component. Data on the median response to a Bloomberg market survey polling economists about their expectations for each upcoming macroeconomic release is collected. For each announcement j, a surprise variable is then derived as the deviation of the actual release from the median expectation, as follows:

$$Surprise_t^j = Release_t^j - M\left(E_i\left[Release_t^j\right]\right)$$

where the subscript t denotes time; the superscript j denotes the specific announcement considered; $Release_t^j$ is the actual release; $E_i[Release_t^j]$ is the value of the release expected by analyst i; and M is the median operator.

To account for the potential of surprise outliers, for each release, surprises above the 99th percentile and those below the 1st percentile are censored. This amounts to censoring only 2 observations for each release.

In a second step, news variables are derived standardizing the surprise variables by their unconditional standard deviation, $\sigma_{surprise^j}$, so that the ultimate variables used in the analysis ($News_t^j$) is measured in terms of standard deviation surprises in data releases. The standardization is as follows:

$$News_t^j = \frac{Surprise_t^j}{\sigma_{surprise^j}}$$

Given that the Fed has the dual mandate of low and stable inflation and maximum employment, the baseline specification of Equation (A1) is estimated using an inflation and employment news variable. The employment news variable concerns the change in nonfarm payroll employment announcement ($News_t^{NFP}$), while the inflation news variable ($News_t^\pi$) refers to the month-on-month headline consumer price inflation announcement.

For robustness check exercises, other macroeconomic news variables are also considered. These are derived from the following macroeconomic announcements: year-on-year headline consumer price inflation, month-on-month core consumer price inflation, job openings by industry, services and manufacturing purchasing managers' index (PMI), unemployment rate, building permits, personal income, personal consumption expenditures (PCE) inflation, durable goods orders, retail sales, and consumer confidence index. These releases were chosen as they are classified as high-impact economic announcements by Trading Economics, a popular data provider. Data on both the actual release of macroeconomic announcements ($Release_t^j$) and their median expectation ($M(E_i[Release_t^j])$) come from Bloomberg. Table A2 provides descriptive statistics of all the news variables $News_t^j$s.

Fed Data Dependency

The extent of Fed data dependency, how much future policies of the Fed are likely to depend on data, is measured taking the absolute value of the difference between the Fed targeted interest rate (the effective federal funds rate, which is the interest rate charged by banks for unsecured US dollar borrowings among each other) and the market expectation for this rate 1 year ahead. This absolute difference amounts to a measure of how much the Fed is expected to change policy during the following 12 months, without distinguishing between the direction of the change. The idea behind this approach is that a large difference between the current and the expected future policy rate indicates a general expectation that the Fed will change policy, but the exact realization will still be conditional on data (see the main text for a discussion).

Fed Attentiveness to Inflation and Employment Data

The Fed relative attentiveness to inflation and employment data releases is measured as follows. First, data on the US natural rate of unemployment (the rate of unemployment arising from all sources except fluctuations in aggregate demand), the unemployment rate and the PCE index is retrieved from the Federal Reserve Economic Data (FRED) database. Then the absolute values of the difference between (i) the unemployment rate and the natural rate of unemployment (unemployment gap), and (ii) the yearly percent change in the PCE index and the Fed's 2% PCE inflation target (inflation gap) are computed. The relative attentiveness to inflation (employment) variable is derived as the inflation (unemployment) gap divided by the sum of the inflation and the unemployment gaps. Given that economic data is released with a month lag, only the unemployment gap two months prior the nonfarm payroll employment release is known at the time of the release and similarly for inflation releases and the inflation gap. Hence, the analysis uses the 2-month lag of the relative attentiveness variables to construct inflation/employment-specific data dependency variables.

Dependent Variables

The financial variables used to generate the dependent variables in Equation (A1) are the (i) US dollar spot exchange rate (local currency price of the US dollar), (ii) 2-year government bond yield, (iii) 10-year government bond yield, (iv) the main stock market index, (v) credit default swap (CDS) on the 5-year government bond, and (vi) portfolio debt inflows into a set of eight emerging market economies, measured in US dollar billions.[1] Variables (i)-(v) are economy- and time-varying and are thus collected for all economies for which they are available. Variable (vi) is time-varying only.

Before being used in Equation (A1) as $y_{i,t}$, the variables mentioned above are first transformed. For the US dollar spot exchange rate and the stock market index, the log is first taken and then this is multiplied by 100. Hence, for these cases, the dependent variable

$y_{i,t+1} - y_{i,t-1}$ in Equation (A1) measures a 2-day percent change. The 2-year and 10-year government bond yields are multiplied by 100 so that $y_{i,t+1} - y_{i,t-1}$ measures a 2-day basis points change. Portfolio inflows are standardized by the US price level. Given that this is a flow rather than stock variable, the dependent variable is constructed differently than for the other variables. Instead of $y_{i,t+1} - y_{i,t-1}$, the dependent variable is $y_{i,t+1} + y_{i,t}$, which measures inflows over a 2-day window in real US dollar billion. Finally, the CDS spread variable is transformed in an implied probability of default. This is done according to the following formula:

$$PrDef = 1 - e^{\frac{S*T}{1-R}}$$

where S is the annual CDS spread (in basis points), T is the time horizon, in years, of the CDS (5 in this case), R is the recovery rate, which is assumed to be 40%, and subscripts are removed for simplicity. The resulting variable is then used to generate the dependent variable $y_{i,t+1} - y_{i,t-1}$ in Equation (A1), which expresses the percentage point change in the probability of default.

To control for the presence of outliers that may bias the empirical estimates, the dependent variables are cleaned censoring their upper 99.9th and lower 0.1st percentiles. Government bond yield variables are further cleaned by censoring observations in which yield levels are below -2% and above 50%. Table A3 provides relevant descriptive statistics, while Table A4 lists the number of economies covered by each variable.

Data on portfolio debt inflows are sourced from the Institute of International Finance. The other variables are sourced from Bloomberg.

United States Financial Variables

Further variables are collected, to be used either as alternative dependent variables, to study the transmission channels through the US economic news and the (expected) Fed response to this news spillover to foreign markets, or as control variables to be included in the vector X_t in Equation (A1) in sensitivity analyses.

---

[1]   The portfolio-debt-inflows variable measures inflows into Hungary, India, Indonesia, Mexico, Poland, South Africa, Thailand, and Ukraine.

These variables, all sourced from Bloomberg, include the (i) VIX index, a popular measure of expected US stock market volatility; (ii) a measure of risk aversion estimated from the VIX index by Bekaert, Engstrom, and Xu (2021); (iii) the current as well as the 1-month, 6-months and 12-months-ahead expected federal funds rates; (iv) the Bloomberg US financial conditions index, which tracks the overall level of financial stress in the US money, bond, and equity markets; (v) the Aruoba-Diebold-Scotti business conditions index of Aruoba, Diebold, and Scotti (2009), which tracks high-frequency economic indicators; and (vi) the economic policy uncertainty index of Baker, Bloom, and Davis (2016). Table A5 provides relevant descriptive statistics.

Foreign Macroeconomic Conditions

An additional set of variables are collected to measure macroeconomic conditions in the 108 foreign economies considered. These are the gross domestic product (GDP) growth rate, the current account balance as a share of GDP, the government budget balance as a share of GDP, the debt denominated in foreign currency as a share of GDP, the inflation rate, and the government credit rating. These variables are collected at the yearly frequency. The first five are sourced from the World Economic Outlook of the International Monetary Fund. The government credit rating is constructed as the average of the credit rating of three different agencies: Moody's, Fitch, and S&P. The data is downloaded from the website of these agencies.

A3. Responses of United States Monetary Policy Expectations and Risk Aversion

This section investigates how US economic surprises and the expected Fed response to them affect US monetary policy expectations, proxied by changes in federal funds future rates 1-, 6- 12- and 24-months ahead, and investors' aversion to risk. The latter is derived through a decomposition of the VIX index.

The Fed response to an inflation surprise does not have any effects on the 1-month-ahead expected federal funds rate, but it drives up expectations for the longer-term federal funds rate (Figure A1, panels A1–A4).

This is consistent with the fact that the Fed considers multiple data releases so that its response to economic data is calibrated on longer-term trends and underlying macroeconomic conditions and not just on a single data release before its monetary policy meeting. The largest effect is on the 12-months-ahead expectation. Inflation releases explain about 50% of the variation of the 12-months expected federal funds future rates in days of inflation releases, when variation in Fed data dependency is accounted for. Inflation surprises also affect 24-months-ahead expectations.

As in the case of inflation, the expected Fed response to employment surprises drives up the expected federal funds rate (Figure A1, panels B1–B4). The effects of employment surprises, however, are much more concentrated on the 12-month- and 24-month-ahead expectations. In other words, the Fed is expected to respond to employment surprises more strongly but with a delay relative to inflation surprises. An inflation-driven tightening of monetary policy increases risk aversion, whereas the effects of an employment-driven tightening are null (panels A5 and B5).

A4. Robustness and Sensitivity Analyses

This section (i) reports full baseline regression results in Table A6, and (ii) assesses the sensitivity of these baseline results. This is assessed by checking how results vary after changing the main regression specification. The first check involves including additional explanatory variables in the regression to control for US economic and financial developments that may also affect asset prices in foreign markets. These variables are the (i) VIX index, which is a measure of expected volatility in the US stock market; (ii) the effective federal funds rate, which is the interest rate targeted by the Fed; (iii) the economic policy uncertainty index (Baker, Bloom, and Davis 2016), a newspaper-based measure of economic uncertainty; (iv) the Bloomberg financial conditions index, which measures stress in US financial markets; and (v) the Aruoba-Diebold-Scotti business conditions index (Aruoba, Diebold, and Scotti 2009), which tracks US high-frequency economic indicators, and is thus a good measure of overall business conditions. These variables are included first in levels and then in changes.

A second set of sensitivity analyses involves including other US macroeconomic data news, which could also affect foreign asset prices and capital flows into EMs, in the regression. The additional data news considered are those stemming from the core CPE inflation, JOLTS job openings, ISM services purchasing manager index, ISM manufacturing purchasing manager index, unemployment rate, building permits, personal income, personal consumption expenditures, durable goods orders, University of Michigan consumer confidence and retail sales. These additional economic news variables are introduced in the regression first on their own and then interacted with the Fed data dependency variables. The third set of sensitivity analyses involves using alternative variables to measure the degree of Fed data dependency, using the absolute difference between the current effective federal fund rate and the 6-months-ahead (rather than 12-months) expected future rate.

Results from these analyses are shown in Figures A2 and A3 for inflation and employment. Each panel focuses on a different dependent variable, where the bars report the new estimates obtained for the sensitivity analyses described above. For convenience, the baseline estimate is also reported. Light colors denote coefficients that are not statistically different from 0 at the 90% confidence interval. The new estimates are generally in line with the baseline ones. The most notable differences are for the sensitivity on the variable used to measure Fed data dependency. When the alternative variable is used, the estimates are qualitatively in line, although considerably weaker, to those obtained using the preferred variable. When including additional news as controls, some of the estimated effects for employment news lose statistical significance.

Another sensitivity analysis is performed on the construction of the inflation news variable. The baseline analysis considers the month-on-month headline inflation release. This sensitivity considers the year-on-year headline inflation, the combination (meaning the sum) of month-on-month and year-on-year headline inflation, as well as the month-on-month core inflation rates. Considering these alternative measures does not significantly alter the results (Figure A4).

A final sensitivity analysis is done on horizon considered for the US macroeconomic news to impact foreign financial markets and capital inflows to emerging markets, using a 5-day window rather than the 2-day window employed in the baseline estimation. Blue bars report baseline (2-day window) coefficients, red bars report new estimates using the larger 5-day window. The results using this larger window are qualitatively in line with the baseline 2-day window. Some coefficients lose statistical significance, while others get stronger (Figure A5).

A5. Developing Asia Results

This section discusses results for the subsample of developing members of the Asian Development Bank (developing Asia), which are shown in Figure A6. To ease comparison, given that many developing Asia economies are either emerging or frontier market economies, the figure also reports results for this subsample. Additionally, the figure reports results for the two largest developing Asia economies—the People's Republic of China (PRC) and India—as well as for the ASEAN-5 group (Indonesia, Malaysia, Philippines, Singapore, and Thailand).

Overall, responses estimated for the developing Asia sample do not differ much from the emerging and frontier market sample. The main difference is the lower responsiveness of government bond yields and exchange rates to an inflation-driven tightening of US monetary policy. Looking at the responses of the PRC, India and the group of ASEAN-5 economies, the latter are the most responsive to inflation- and employment-driven changes in US monetary policy. The PRC is the least responsive, as the only statistically significant response that is estimated is the one of the exchange rate to an inflation-driven tightening. India falls in the middle between these two cases.

Appendix Figures

Figure A1 Impact of US Data Surprises on Monetary Policy Expectations and Risk Aversion, Inflation and Employment

A. Inflation Surprise

A1. 1M Fed Future

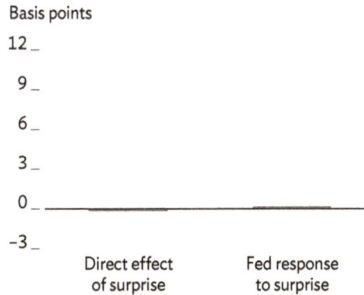

A2. 6M Fed Future

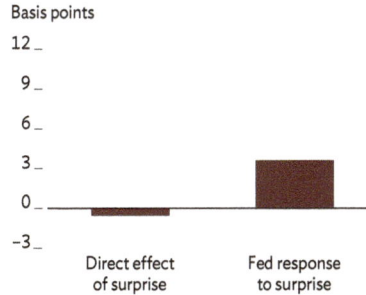

A3. 12M Fed Future

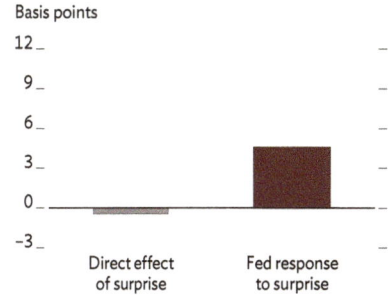

A4. 24M Fed Future

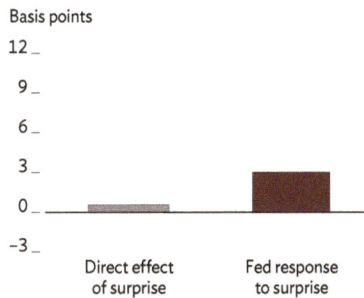

A5. Risk Aversion

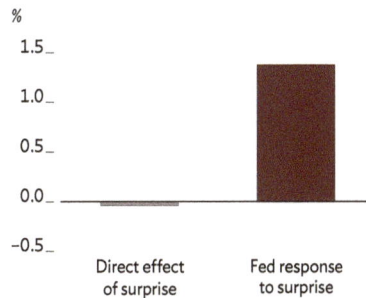

B. Employment Surprise

B1. 1M Fed Future

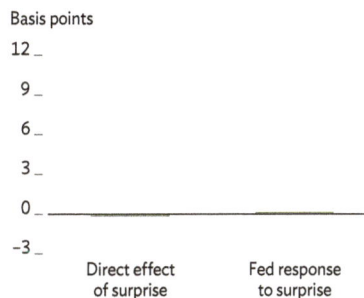

B2. 6M Fed Future

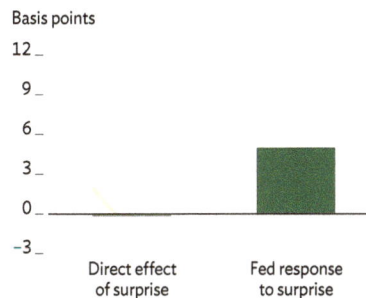

B3. 12M Fed Future

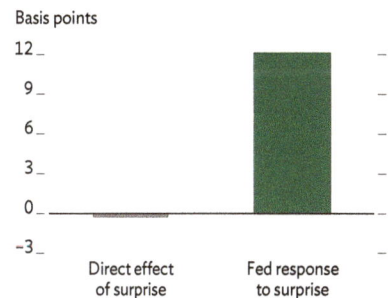

B4. 24M Fed Future

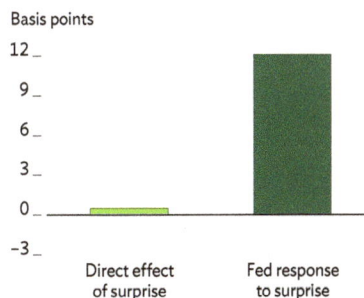

B5. Risk Aversion

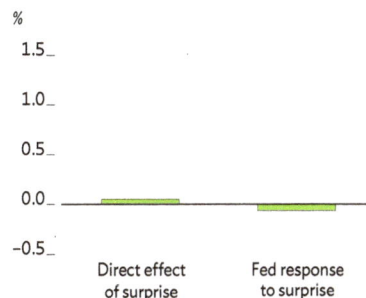

US = United States.

Note: 1M, 6M, 12M, 24M Fed future respectively denote the 1-month, 6-month, 12-month, 24-month ahead federal funds future rates. Darker colored bars denote statistically significant coefficients at the 90% confidence level.

Source: Asian Development Bank calculations based on data from Bloomberg and Bekaert, Engstrom and Xu (2021).

Figure A2 Sensitivity Analysis on Impact of US Data Surprises on Financial Markets Abroad, Inflation

A. Direct Effect of Surprise

A1. 2-Year Government Bond Yield

Basis points

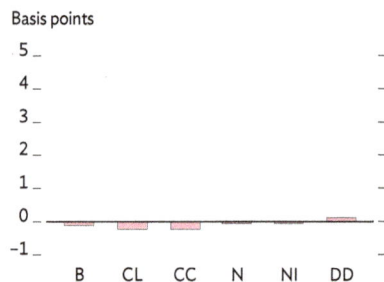

A2. 10-Year Government Bond Yield

Basis points

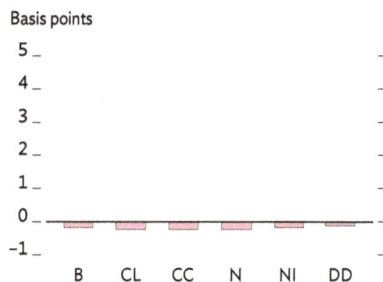

A3. US Dollar Exchange Rate

%

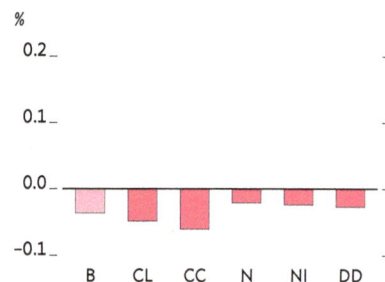

A4. Stock Market Index

%

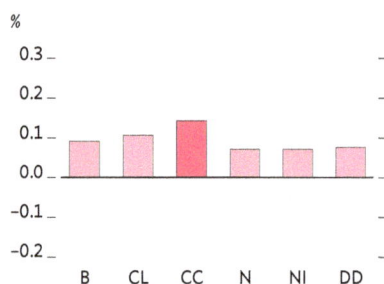

A5. Default Probability

Percentage points

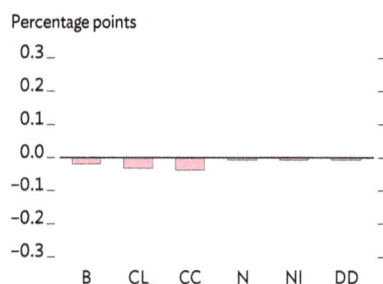

A6. Emerging Markets Portfolio Debt Inflows

$ billion

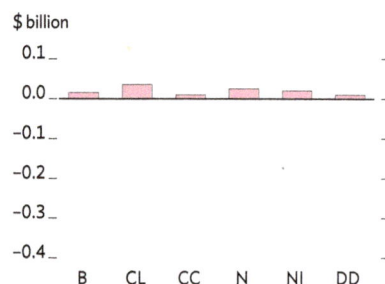

B. Fed Response to Surprise

B1. 2-Year Government Bond Yield

Basis points

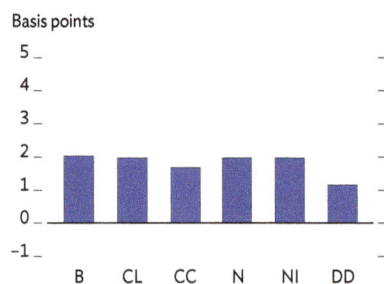

B2. 10-Year Government Bond Yield

Basis points

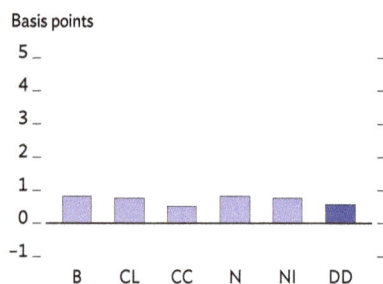

B3. US Dollar Exchange Rate

%

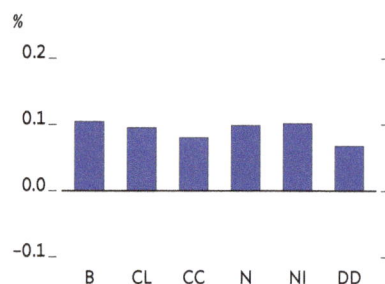

B4. Stock Market Index

%

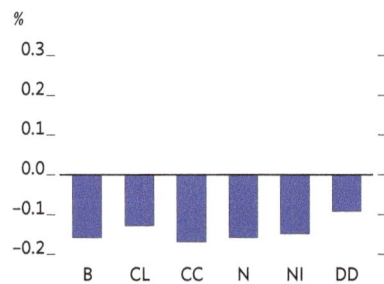

B5. Default Probability

Percentage points

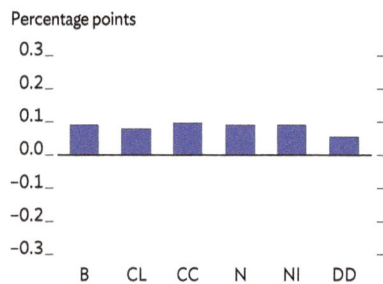

B6. Emerging Markets Portfolio Debt Inflows

$ billion

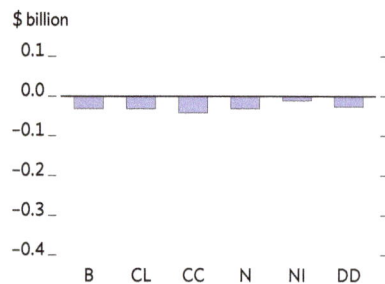

B = baseline; CL = US financial and economic controls, levels; CC = US financial and economic controls, changes; DD = Fed data dependency; N = US macroeconomic news; NI = US macroeconomic news interacted with Fed data dependency; US = United States.

Note: Bars report estimated coefficients from different sensitivity analyses. Darker colored bars denote statistically significant coefficients at the 90% confidence level.

Source: Asian Development Bank calculations based on data from Bloomberg and Institute for International Finance.

Figure A3 Sensitivity Analysis on Impact of US Data Surprises on Financial Markets Abroad, Employment

A. Direct Effect of Surprise

A1. 2-Year Government Bond Yield

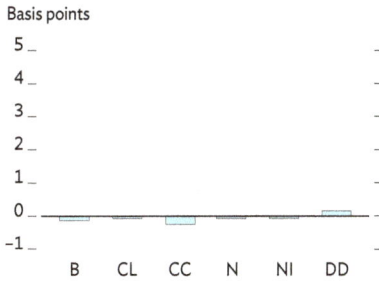

A2. 10-Year Government Bond Yield

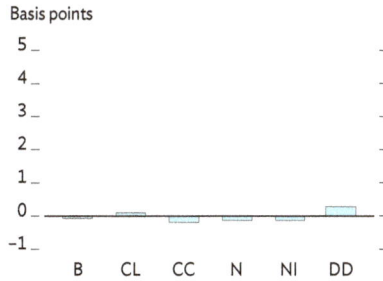

A3. US Dollar Exchange Rate

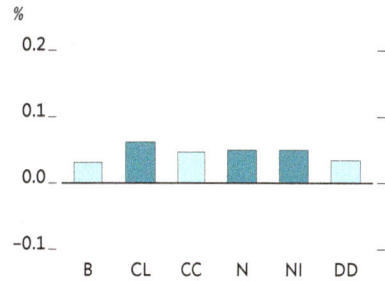

A4. Stock Market Index

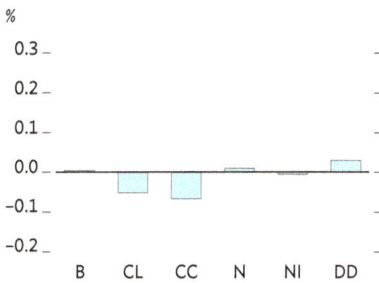

A5. Default Probability

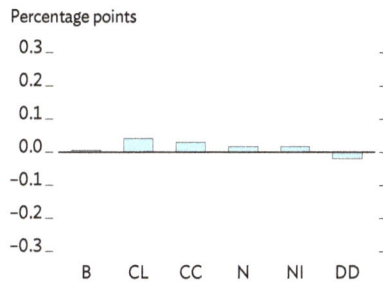

A6. Emerging Markets Portfolio Debt Inflows

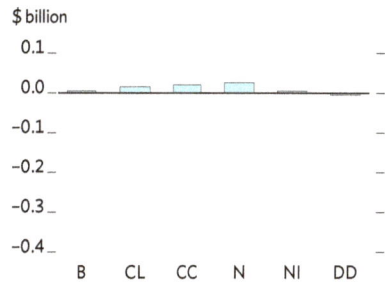

B. Fed Response to Surprise

B1. 2-Year Government Bond Yield

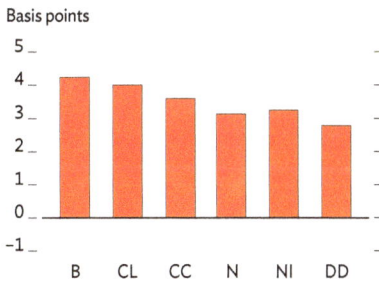

B2. 10-Year Government Bond Yield

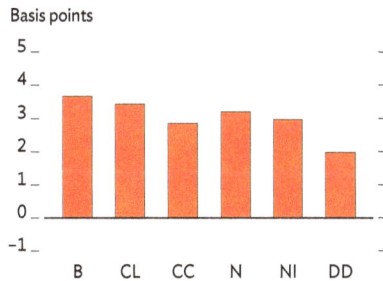

B3. US Dollar Exchange Rate

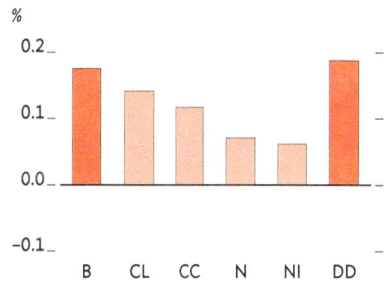

B4. Stock Market Index

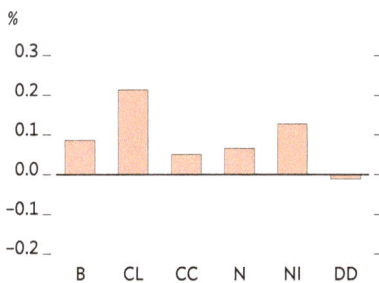

B5. Default Probability

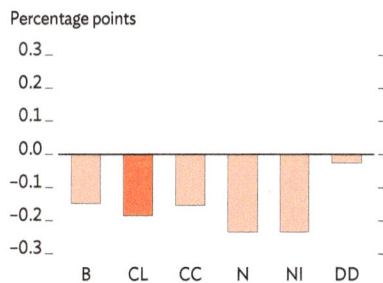

B6. Emerging Markets Portfolio Debt Inflows

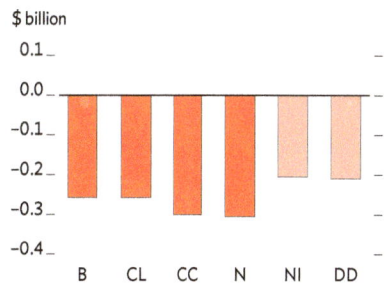

B = baseline; CL = US financial and economic controls, levels; CC = US financial and economic controls, changes; DD = Fed data dependency
N = US macroeconomic news; NI = US macroeconomic news interacted with Fed data dependency; US = United States.

Note: Bars report estimated coefficients from different sensitivity analyses. Darker colored bars denote statistically significant coefficients at the 90% confidence level.

Source: Asian Development Bank calculations based on data from Bloomberg and Institute for International Finance.

Figure A4 Sensitivity Analysis on Impact of US Data Surprises on Financial Markets Abroad, Inflation Measure

A. Direct Effect of Surprise

A1. 2-Year Government Bond Yield

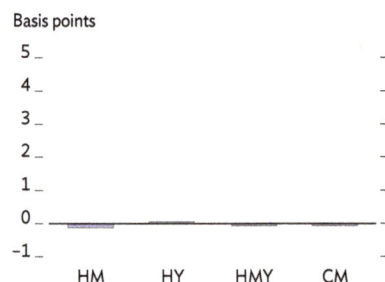

A2. 10-Year Government Bond Yield

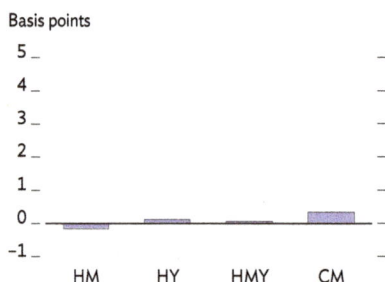

A3. US Dollar Exchange Rate

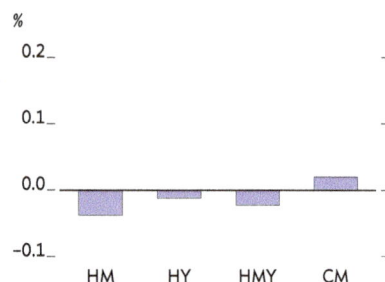

A4. Stock Market Index

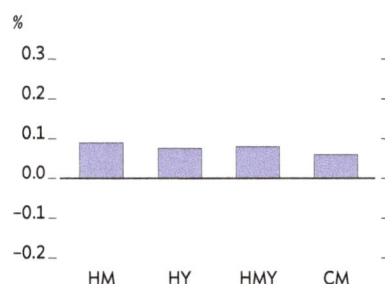

A5. Default Probability

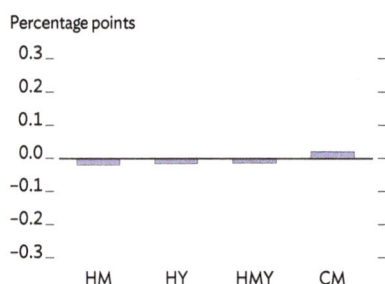

A6. Emerging Markets Portfolio Debt Inflows

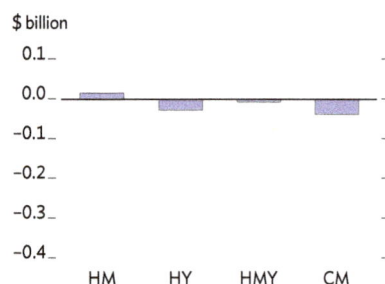

B. Fed Response to Surprise

B1. 2-Year Government Bond Yield

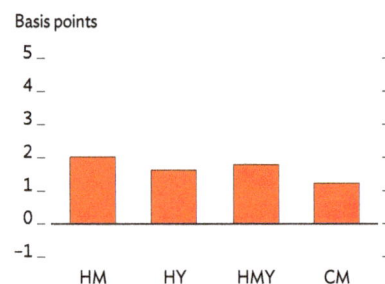

B2. 10-Year Government Bond Yield

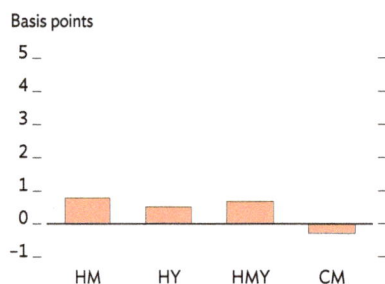

B3. US Dollar Exchange Rate

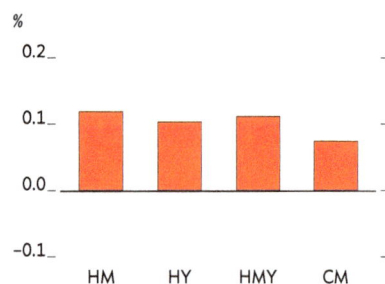

B4. Stock Market Index

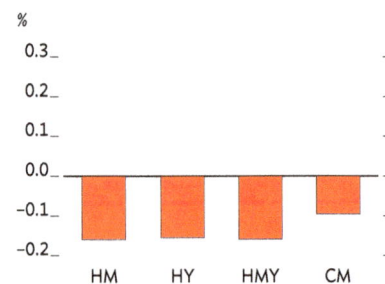

B5. Default Probability

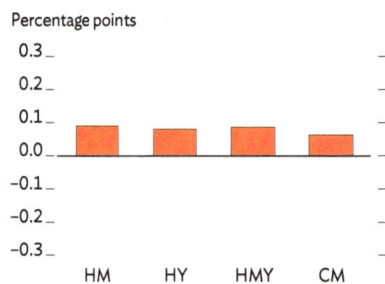

B6. Emerging Markets Portfolio Debt Inflows

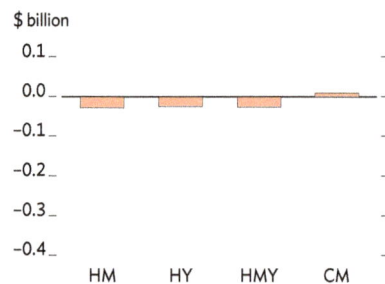

US = United States.

Note: HM, HY, HMY, and CM, respectively, denote month-on-month headline, year-on-year headline, sum of month-on-month and year-on-year headline, and month-on-month core inflation. Darker colored bars denote statistically significant coefficients at the 90% confidence level.

Source: Asian Development Bank calculations based on data from Bloomberg and Institute for International Finance.

Figure A5 Sensitivity Analysis on Impact of US Data Surprises on Financial Markets Abroad, Window of Dependent Variable, Inflation and Employment

■ Baseline (2-day window)　■ 5-day window

A. Inflation Surprise

A1. 2-Year Government Bond Yield

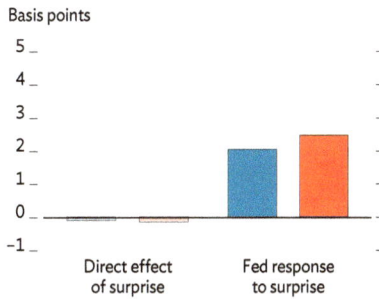

Basis points

A2. 10-Year Government Bond Yield

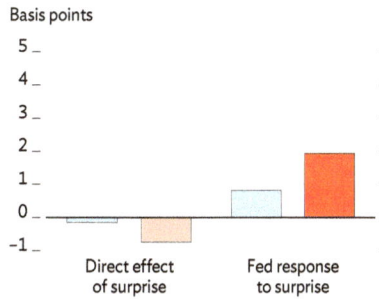

Basis points

A3. US Dollar Exchange Rate

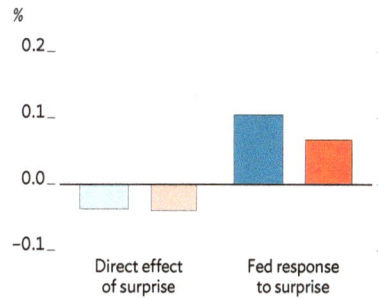

%

A4. Stock Market Index

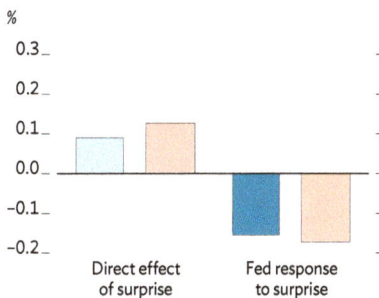

%

A5. Default Probability

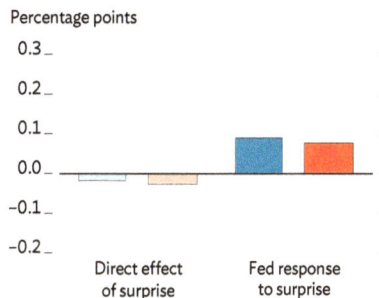

Percentage points

A6. Emerging Markets Portfolio Debt Inflows

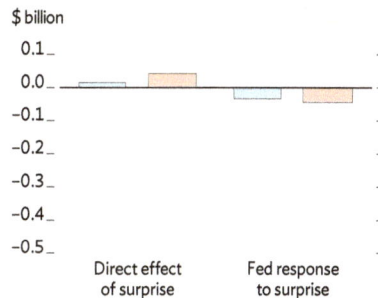

$ billion

B. Employment Surprise

B1. 2-Year Government Bond Yield

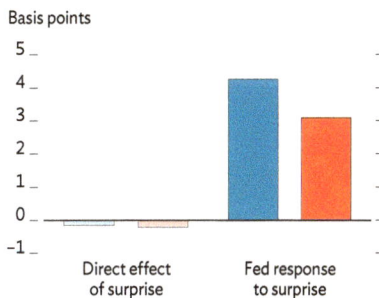

Basis points

B2. 10-Year Government Bond Yield

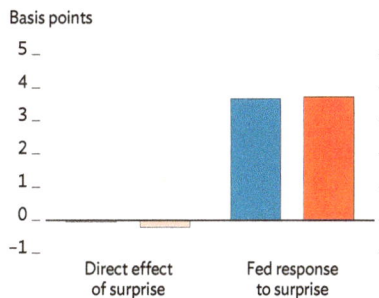

Basis points

B3. US Dollar Exchange Rate

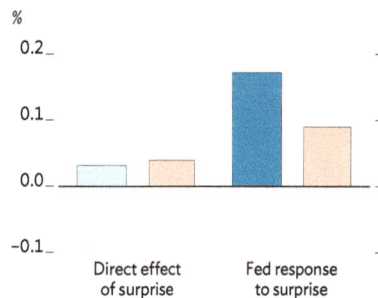

%

B4. Stock Market Index

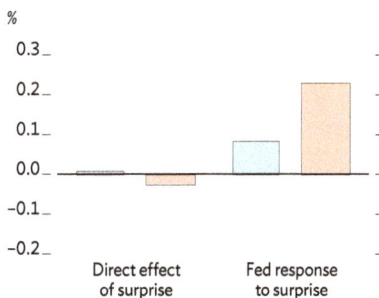

%

B5. Default Probability

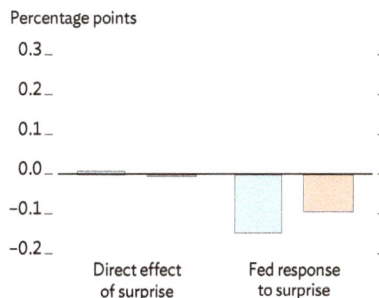

Percentage points

B6. Emerging Markets Portfolio Debt Inflows

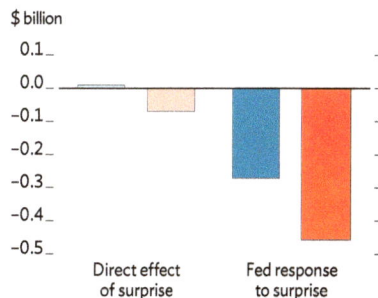

$ billion

US = United States.

Notes: Darker colored bars denote statistically significant coefficients at the 90% confidence level.

Source: Asian Development Bank calculations based on data from Bloomberg and Institute for International Finance.

Figure A6 Impact of US Data Surprises on Financial Markets in Developing Asia, Inflation and Employment

■ Emerging and frontier markets   ■ ADB developing members   ■ People's Republic of China   ■ India   ■ ASEAN-5

A. Inflation Surprise

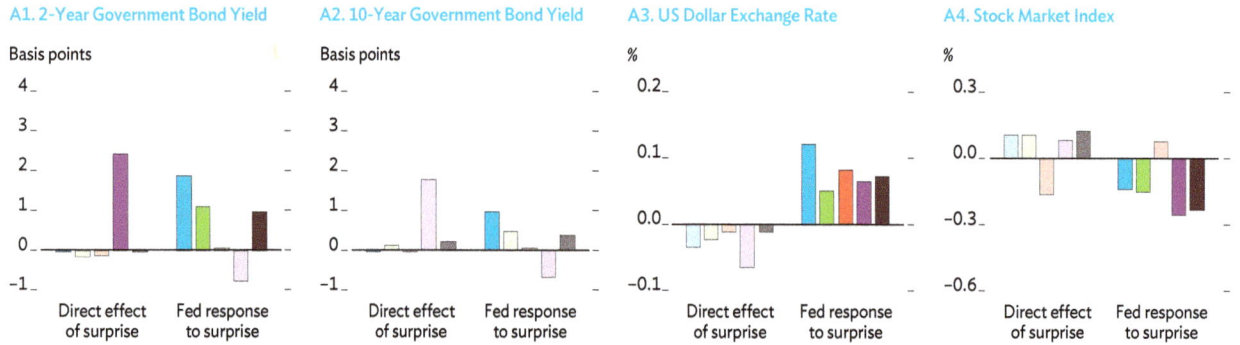

A1. 2-Year Government Bond Yield

A2. 10-Year Government Bond Yield

A3. US Dollar Exchange Rate

A4. Stock Market Index

B. Employment Surprise

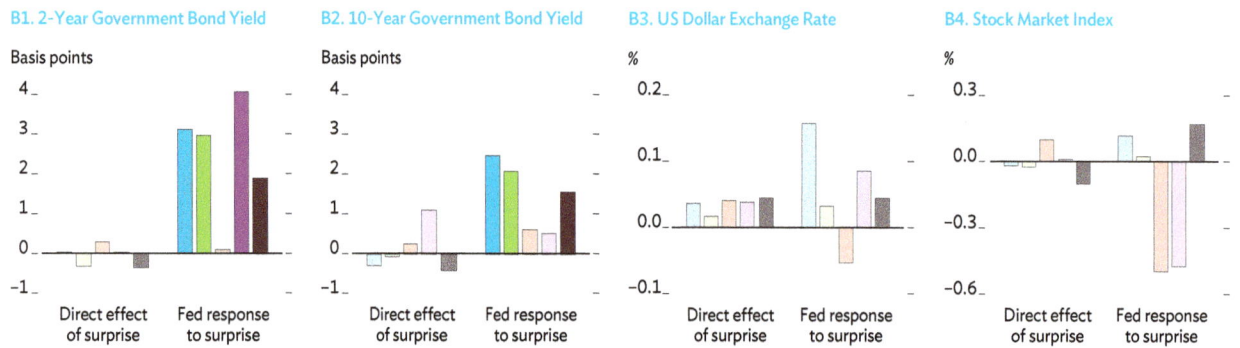

B1. 2-Year Government Bond Yield

B2. 10-Year Government Bond Yield

B3. US Dollar Exchange Rate

B4. Stock Market Index

US = United States.

Notes: Darker colored bars denote statistically significant coefficients at the 90% confidence level.

Source: Asian Development Bank calculations based on data from Bloomberg and Institute for International Finance.

Appendix Tables

Table A1 Morgan Stanley Capital International Classification of Economies, as of December 2023

Developed Markets (23)	Emerging Markets (24)	Frontier Markets (28)	Standalone Markets (11)	Other ADB Developing Members (23)
Australia	Brazil	Bahrain	Argentina	Afghanistan
Austria	Chile	Bangladesh	Bosnia and Herzegovina	Armenia
Belgium	People's Republic of China	Benin	Botswana	Azerbaijan
Canada	Colombia	Burkina Faso	Bulgaria	Bhutan
Denmark	Czech Republic	Cote D'Ivoire	Jamaica	Brunei Darussalam
Finland	Egypt	Croatia	Lebanon	Cambodia
France	Greece	Estonia	Malta	Fiji
Germany	Hungary	Iceland	Panama	Georgia
Hong Kong, China	India	Jordan	Trinidad and Tobago	Kyrgyz Republic
Ireland	Indonesia	Kazakhstan	Ukraine	Lao PDR
Israel	Korea, Republic of	Kenya	Zimbabwe	Maldives
Italy	Kuwait	Latvia		Mongolia
Japan	Malaysia	Lithuania		Myanmar
Netherlands	Mexico	Mali		Nepal
New Zealand	Peru	Mauritius		Papua New Guinea
Norway	Philippines	Morocco		Samoa
Portugal	Poland	Niger		Solomon Islands
Singapore	Qatar	Nigeria		Tajikistan
Spain	Saudi Arabia	Oman		Timor-Leste
Sweden	South Africa	Pakistan		Tonga
Switzerland	Taipei,China	Romania		Turkmenistan
United Kingdom	Thailand	Senegal		Uzbekistan
United States	Türkiye	Serbia		Vanuatu
	United Arab Emirates	Slovenia		
		Sri Lanka		
		Togo		
		Tunisia		
		Viet Nam		

ADB = Asian Development Bank, Lao PDR = Lao People's Democratic Republic.

Note: Russian Federation excluded from the MSCI index (Standalone Markets) on 1 March 2023. Data for Cook Islands, Kiribati, Marshall Islands, Federated States of Micronesia, Nauru, Palau, Tuvalu, and Niue (all ADB developing members) are not available and thus these economies are not included in the sample.

Source: Asian Development Bank.

Table A2 Summary Statistics of US Macroeconomic News

Variable	Obs.	Mean	Median	Min	Max
Nonfarm Payrolls	177	0.05	0.11	−4.94	3.25
Inflation	176	0.003	0.00	−2.04	4.60
Core CPE inflation, MoM	177	−0.17	0.00	−2.94	2.94
JOLTS, Job Openings	158	0.29	0.10	−2.43	3.49
ISM Services	177	0.10	0.10	-2.60	2.44
ISM Manufacturing	177	0.09	0.06	-2.72	2.34
Unemployment rate	178	−0.26	0.00	−4.40	1.88
Building permits	175	0.16	0.05	−1.97	3.33
Personal income	175	0.07	0.00	−3.14	4.32
Personal consumption expenditures	177	0.02	0.00	−2.45	3.06
Durable goods orders	176	−0.02	0.00	−4.45	4.66
UoM Consumer Confidence	176	0.27	0.27	-2.32	2.85
Retail sales	176	−0.02	0.00	−3.19	7.09

US = United States.

Notes: MoM is short for month-on-month growth. Standard deviations are equal to 1 for all variables (by construction).

Source: Asian Development Bank calculations based on data from Bloomberg.

Table A3 Summary Statistics of Dependent Variables

Variable	Obs.	Mean	Median	Min	Max	Std. dev.
Exchange rate (LCU/USD)	296,849	0.02	0.00	−4.06	5.34	0.71
2-year government bond yield	171,401	0.16	−0.10	−157.80	202.20	12.38
10-year government bond yield	145,385	0.06	−0.10	−164.70	169.90	11.86
Stock market index	315,712	0.07	0.06	−8.40	8.36	1.45
Government default probability	90,211	−0.01	−0.01	−20.10	19.96	0.91
Capital inflows to emerging markets	3,716	0.17	0.13	−3.11	3.65	0.62

Notes: The table reports summary statistics of the dependent variables $y_{i,t+1} - y_{i,t-1}$ in Equation (A1). The exchange rate and stock market index are in percent changes, the default probability is in percentage point changes, 2-year and 10-year government bond yields are basis point changes, capital inflows are in real US dollar.

Source: Asian Development Bank calculations based on data from Bloomberg and Institute for International Finance.

Table A4 Coverage of Dependent Variables, as of December 2023

Variable	DMs	EMs	FMs	SMs	ADB Developing Members	Total
Exchange rate (LCU/USD)	13	21	17	9	21	81
2-year government bond yield	23	17	5	0	1	46
10-year government bond yield	19	16	3	2	1	41
Stock market index	23	24	27	7	2	83
Government default probability	5	15	1	2	0	23

Note: DMs, EMs, FMs, SMs respectively indicate developed markets, emerging markets, frontier markets, and standalone markets. For euro area and West African economies, the exchange rate is considered only once.

Source: Asian Development Bank calculations based on data from Bloomberg and Institute for International Finance.

Table A5 Summary Statistics of Other US Variables

Variable	Obs.	Mean	Median	Min	Max	Std. dev.
Effective Fed Funds Rate	3,727	1.10	0.17	0.04	5.33	1.61
1-month ahead Fed funds future	3,873	1.10	0.18	0.06	5.34	1.61
6-month ahead Fed funds future	3,873	1.24	0.29	0.04	5.66	1.65
12-months-ahead Fed funds future	3,873	1.32	0.64	0.00	5.43	1.48
VIX index	3,751	18.28	16.72	9.14	48.00	6.14
Risk aversion	3,561	2.97	2.84	2.43	6.45	0.44
Bloomberg US financial conditions	3,807	−0.02	0.13	−5.86	1.22	0.85
Aruoba-Diebold-Scotti business conditions	3,798	−0.06	−0.07	−2.33	4.42	0.51
Economic policy uncertainty	3,807	115.06	99.63	3.32	1,026.38	67.89

US = United States

Source: Asian Development Bank calculations based on data from Bloomberg.

Table A6 Impacts of US Data Surprises on Financial Markets Abroad, Inflation and Employment, Full Regression Results

	(1) 2YGB	(2) 2YGB	(3) 10YGB	(4) 10YGB	(5) USD	(6) USD	(7) Stock	(8) Stock	(9) CDS	(10) CDS	(11) Flows	(12) Flows
$News^{NFP}$	0.82**	−0.16	0.81**	−0.05	0.07**	0.03	0.02	0.01	−0.02	0.01	−0.06	0.01
	(0.38)	(0.35)	(0.37)	(0.38)	(0.03)	(0.03)	(0.05)	(0.05)	(0.03)	(0.03)	(0.05)	(0.05)
$News^{NFP}*FedDD^{NFP}$		8.74***		7.58***		0.36*		0.17		−0.31		−0.56**
		(2.02)		(1.92)		(0.21)		(0.34)		(0.23)		(0.28)
$News^{\pi}$	1.40***	−0.13	0.62	−0.15	0.04	−0.04	−0.04	0.09	0.06	−0.02	−0.03	0.02
	(0.51)	(0.24)	(0.43)	(0.38)	(0.03)	(0.03)	(0.08)	(0.10)	(0.04)	(0.04)	(0.04)	(0.06)
$News^{\pi}*FedDD^{\pi}$		4.20***		1.68		0.22***		−0.33**		0.19***		−0.06
		(0.76)		(1.18)		(0.05)		(0.14)		(0.06)		(0.08)
	15,605	15,514	13,199	13,122	27,049	26,903	28,724	28,562	8,295	8,238	338	338
	0.007	0.027	0.005	0.015	0.008	0.022	0.002	0.012	−0.000	0.014	0.001	0.049

US = United States.

Notes: The first column and second row respectively indicate the explanatory and the dependent variables. 2YGB, 10YGB, USD, Stock, CDS, Flows denote, respectively, the 2-year government bond yield, 10-year government bond yield, price of the USD in local currency units, stock market index, credit default swap price on the 5-year government bond, portfolio debt inflows into a set of large EMs. ***, **, * indicate statistical significance at, respectively, the 99%, 95%, and 90% confidence intervals, based on time-clustered standard errors (in parentheses).

Source: Asian Development Bank calculations based on data from Bloomberg and Institute for International Finance.

3

ECONOMIC TRENDS
AND PROSPECTS
IN DEVELOPING ASIA

CAUCASUS AND CENTRAL ASIA

Growth projections for the Caucasus and Central Asia are raised for both 2024 and 2025 from those presented in *Asian Development Outlook, April 2024*. Inflation forecasts for both years are lowered. Most subregional economies achieved robust growth and experienced low inflation or deflation mostly in the first half of 2024. Several subregional hydrocarbon exporters achieved current account surpluses during this period, while the four net importers of hydrocarbons recorded deficits.

Subregional Assessment and Prospects

Subregional growth projections for the Caucasus and Central Asia are revised up, mainly because the majority of the countries registered robust economic growth during the first half of 2024. The growth forecast for 2024 is raised from 4.3% in *Asian Development Outlook, April 2024 (ADO April 2024)* to 4.7% and for 2025 from 5.0% to 5.2% (Figure 3.1.1). These upward adjustments reflect higher growth projections for five of the eight subregional economies: Armenia, Azerbaijan, Georgia, the Kyrgyz Republic, and Uzbekistan. Even though these five exhibited robust growth in the first 6 months of 2024, causes for robust growth vary across economies. Growth projections for Kazakhstan, the subregion's largest economy, are revised down because of damage from major floods from March to May 2024 and a cap on oil production imposed by the Organization for the Petroleum Exporting Countries and its partners (OPEC+) in an agreement reached in June 2024. Growth forecasts remain unchanged for Tajikistan and Turkmenistan.

In the three Caucasus economies, growth rates during the first half of 2024 were higher than projected in *ADO April 2024*. Georgia estimated growth at 9.0% during this period, reflecting rapid expansion in services. On the demand side, growth was driven by consumption and domestic investment,

Figure 3.1.1 Gross Domestic Product Growth in the Caucasus and Central Asia

Growth projections for a majority of subregional economies are adjusted up following robust performances in the first half of 2024.

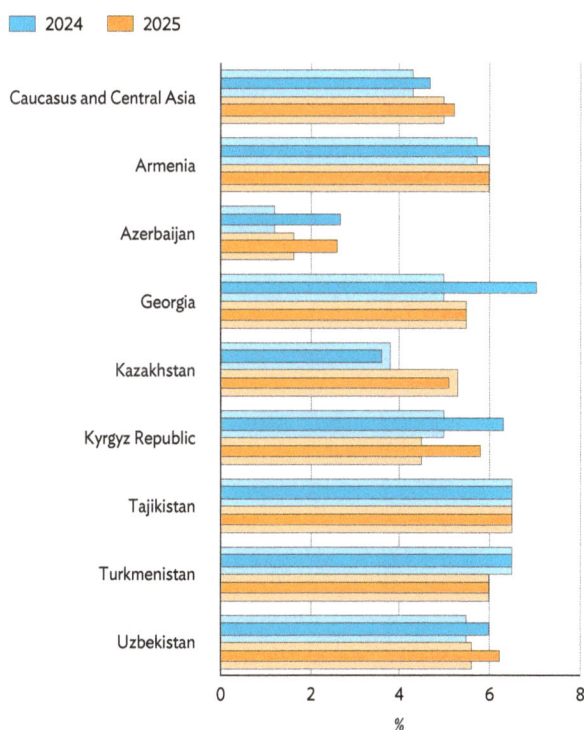

Note: Lighter-colored bars are forecasts in *Asian Development Outlook April 2024*.
Source: *Asian Development Outlook* database (accessed 5 September 2024).

The subregional assessment and prospects were written by Kenji Takamiya. Kazakhstan was written by Genadiy Rau, and the other economies by Begzod Djalilov, Grigor Gyurjyan, Jennet Hojanazarova, Elvin Imanov, Khagani Karimov, Gulnur Kerimkulova, George Luarsabishvili, and Shuhrat Mirzoev. All authors are in the Central and West Asia Department.

fueled by external inflows and credit growth. Armenia's economy expanded by 6.5% during the period, with a surge in industry, particularly jewelry and gold production. On the demand side, growth came from higher private consumption and massive expansion in gross fixed capital formation, particularly public investment. In Azerbaijan, growth accelerated to 4.3% due to expansion outside of the large hydrocarbon economy, supported by higher public spending and a substantial jump in investment.

Most Central Asian economies also expanded robustly during this period. Growth in the Kyrgyz Republic jumped to an estimated 8.1% in the first half of 2024, reflecting surges in services and construction. Demand-side data, available for only the first quarter of the year, show private consumption expanding rapidly on higher wages, inbound money transfers, and consumer lending. Tajikistan's economy grew by 8.2% in the first half of this year with expansion in all sectors, its high growth momentum sustained by strong remittances and higher public sector salaries, which boosted private consumption. The Government of Turkmenistan reported similarly broad-based growth, at 6.3%, driven by higher net exports and public investment. In Uzbekistan, growth at 6.4% reflected expansion in manufacturing and construction, with construction boosting investment and higher remittances stimulating consumption on the demand side. Growth in Kazakhstan slowed to 3.2% in the first 6 months of 2024 as oil production fell and floods undermined expansion in services. On the demand side, data from the first quarter show slowing consumption growth and declines in investment and net exports.

While several hydrocarbon exporters achieved current account surpluses in early 2024, each of the net importers of hydrocarbons recorded a current account deficit. Azerbaijan's current account surplus narrowed to equal 10.1% of GDP in the first quarter of 2024 from 18.9% in the same period of 2023 as its surplus in oil and gas trade shrank. Kazakhstan's current account is preliminarily estimated to have recorded a surplus equal to 0.4% of GDP in the first half of 2024 as profit repatriation declined and earnings received by the sovereign wealth fund increased. Armenia's current account deficit was little changed at 6.2% of GDP in the first quarter of 2024. Georgia's current account deficit widened to 5.0% of GDP in the same period as exports and inward money transfers

both declined. Reportedly, the current account deficit widened further for the Kyrgyz Republic to a massive 52.5% of GDP, reflecting both a rise in the recorded trade deficit and likely undervaluation of exports, as reexports are incompletely monitored. In the first 3 months of 2024, Tajikistan's current account deficit narrowed to 3.4% of GDP on higher inward remittances. In Uzbekistan, the current account deficit increased to 7.1% of GDP from 6.6% a year earlier, reflecting a rise in imports for industry. In Turkmenistan, gas exports are likely to expand over the medium term, and exports to rise faster than imports, probably widening the current account surplus in 2024 and 2025.

Inflation projections for the subregion are revised down amid a slowdown in global inflation, which has tended to lower prices for imports. Subregional inflation forecasts are lowered from 7.9% to 6.9% in 2024 and from 7.0% to 6.2% in 2025 (Figure 3.1.2). During the first 7 months of 2024, Armenia recorded deflation of 0.3% as food prices fell by 2.7%. In

Figure 3.1.2 Inflation in the Caucasus and Central Asia

Growth projections for most subregional economies are adjusted up following generally low or negative price increases so far in 2024.

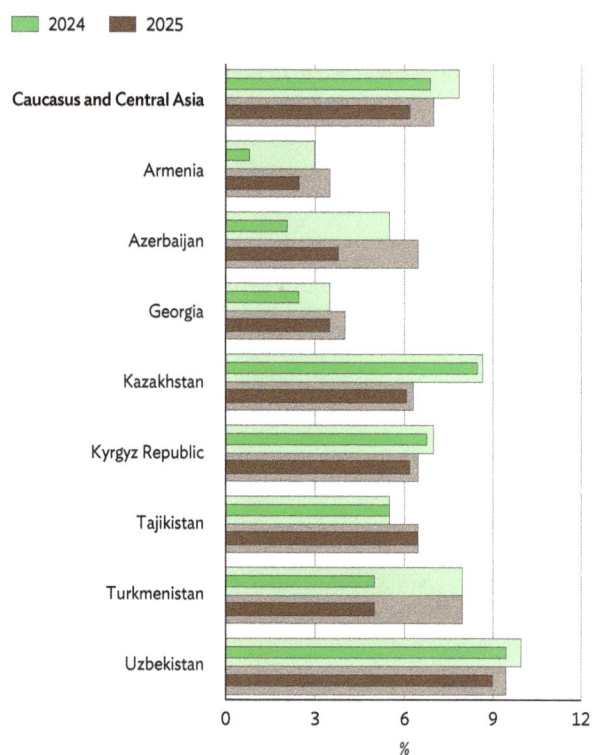

Note: Lighter-colored bars are forecasts in *Asian Development Outlook April 2024*.

Source: *Asian Development Outlook* database (accessed 5 September 2024).

Azerbaijan, inflation declined to 0.7% during the same period, also reflecting lower food prices. Helped by a stable exchange rate, Georgian inflation slowed to 1.1%. In Kazakhstan, inflation slowed to 8.9% during the first 7 months of 2024. However, inflation expectations for the next 12 months remain elevated because of price increases for state-regulated utilities. Inflation in the Kyrgyz Republic slowed to 5.1% in the first half of 2024, subdued partly by currency appreciation that helped reduce domestic prices for imported goods. In Tajikistan, inflation decelerated to 1.9% in the same period despite major tariff hikes and wage growth. Inflation in Uzbekistan, while still elevated, edged down to 9.5% in the first 7 months of 2024 as price increases diminished for food and imported goods. Modest inflation was observed in Turkmenistan. Many central banks in the subregion have relaxed their monetary policies in response to lower inflation or deflation.

Kazakhstan

Lower oil output and massive floods reduced growth in the first half of 2024. Restraint on oil production and lower-than-anticipated investment warrant marginal reductions to growth forecasts for both 2024 and 2025. Lower inflation projections for both years stem from slower inflation in the first half of 2024, relatively tight monetary policy, and a stable exchange rate. Rising exports will bring a current account surplus in 2025.

Updated Assessment

Lower oil production and massive floods slowed growth during the first half of 2024. Growth declined from 5.3% year on year in the first half of 2023 to 3.2% a year later as oil production fell by 1.6% and expansion in services decelerated from 5.5% to 3.3% (Figure 3.1.3). Slower growth in services reflected massive floods in the spring of 2024, the most devasting in decades, which slashed expansion in trade from 10.4% in the first half of 2023 to 3.9% and trimmed expansion in transport marginally to 7.3% from 7.4%. Growth in mining slowed from 3.7% in the first half of 2023 to 0.3% as a 5.8% rise in metal production barely offset the decline in oil output. Expansion in manufacturing accelerated from 3.4% in the first half of 2023 to 5.1%, including increases of 13.7% in ferrous metal production, 5.3% in chemical products, and 9.4%

Figure 3.1.3 Supply-Side Contributions to Growth

Growth in the first half of 2024 was lower than a year earlier.

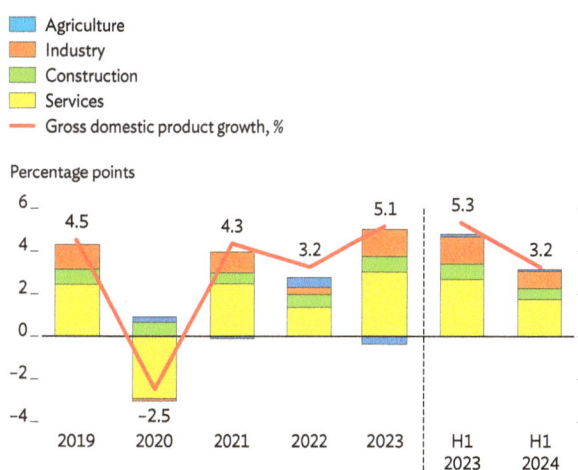

H = half.

Source: Republic of Kazakhstan. Agency for Strategic Planning and Reforms. Bureau of National Statistics.

in equipment. Growth in construction decelerated from 12.3% to 8.6% because of slowing demand for homes and high prices.

Consumption growth faltered while investment and net exports declined. Demand-side data, available for only the first quarter of 2024, show growth in consumption falling from 9.5% year on year in the first quarter of 2023 to 4.4% a year later, with private consumption expanding by 7.0% and public consumption contracting by 6.7%. Despite ongoing state programs for infrastructure and housing support, overall investment fell by 1.3%, reversing 29.8% expansion in the first quarter of 2023. Net exports declined marginally as a 1.7% drop in exports of goods and services was partly offset by a 6.3% decline in imports.

Inflation slowed, allowing some relaxation in monetary policy. Average inflation slowed from 17.2% in the first 7 months of 2023 to 8.9% in the comparable period this year, still above a 5% target set by the National Bank of Kazakhstan, the central bank (Figure 3.1.4). Prices rose by 13.4% for services, 7.9% for other goods, and 6.5% for food. With inflation declining, the central bank reduced its key policy rate in four steps from January to August 2024 by a cumulative 150 basis points to 14.25%. However, reported inflationary expectations for the next

Figure 3.1.4 Average Inflation

Inflation decelerated sharply in the first 7 months of 2024.

- Food, beverages, and tobacco
- Other goods
- Services
- All goods and services

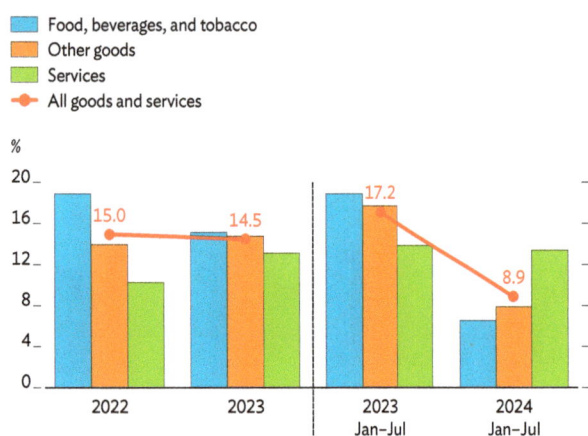

Source: Republic of Kazakhstan. Agency for Strategic Planning and Reforms. Bureau of National Statistics.

12 months remain elevated at 13.4%, reflecting in part price increases averaging 16.2% for state-regulated utilities. These include hikes of 33.6% for water, 32.0% for heat, and 27.2% for electricity, along with increases averaging 6.8% for gasoline and 4.8% for diesel fuel.

As bank deposits and credit grew, the percentage of nonperforming loans stirred from a low base. In the first half of 2024, deposits grew by 7.9% and credit by 6.9%, with loans rising by 3.2% for firms, 4.5% for mortgages, and 12.5% for consumer credit. Foreign currency deposits declined by 1.2%, to account for 20.9% of all deposits, while deposits in Kazakhstan tenge rose by 10.6%. Nonperforming loans increased from a historic low of 2.9% at the end of 2023 to 3.2% in June 2024, driven by nonperforming loans to households, which reached 3.8%. Broad money grew by a moderate 3.5% in the first half of 2024.

Total tax collection declined in the first half of 2024 as central government tax revenue fell by 13.9%. Tax revenue declined as a share of GDP from 12.8% in the first half of 2023 to 10.0%, with oil export duty down by 17.2% and value-added tax collection decreasing by 15.4%. Personal income tax receipts increased by 25.9% and social income tax by 27.5%, thus elevating revenue collection for provincial and local budgets, which was only marginally lower than in the same period of 2023. Increases in nontax receipts and the sale of assets partly offset the decline in tax collection. Transfers from the sovereign

wealth fund, the National Fund of the Republic of Kazakhstan (NFRK), helped keep the budget deficit and government borrowing in check. Transfers from the NFRK were 28.2% above those in the first half of 2023, with the government utilizing three-quarters of planned annual transfers in the period, compared with 53.6% in the same period of last year.

Fiscal expenditure was contained by lower spending on health care and defense. In the first half of 2024, while state budget expenditure was 6.5% above the same period of 2023, it declined as a share of GDP from 27.5% to 25.7%. Central government expenditure also declined as a share of GDP, from 22.1% to 20.2%. Expenditure decreased by 17.2% for health care and 21.8% for defense but rose by 15.4% for social services and 6.5% for education. However, lower health care and defense spending is temporary, as the government allocated only a third of the planned state budget for the year. Debt service expanded by 31.2% to exceed two-thirds of planned state budget allocations for the year. Driven by increased transfers from the NFRK, which are considered part of total receipts and reached 5.3% of GDP, state and central government fiscal budget deficits declined. At the same time, the central government's non-oil fiscal deficit grew by 1%.

External debt as a percentage of GDP reached a decade low. By the end of March 2024, external debt had declined to $162.5 billion, equal to 60.4% of GDP (Figure 3.1.5). Intercompany debt, primarily for oil and gas projects, declined to $91.6 billion, or 34.0% of GDP,

Figure 3.1.5 External Debt and Intercompany Debt

External and intercompany debt declined in tandem.

- External debt
- Intercompany debt

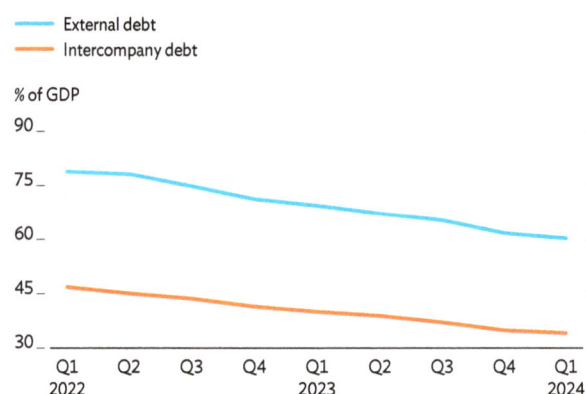

GDP = gross domestic product, Q = quarter.
Source: National Bank of the Republic of Kazakhstan.

with $15.2 billion coming due in 2024. Public sector external debt decreased to $28.8 billion, or 10.7% of GDP, with $2.7 billion due this year.

Lower profit repatriation and higher NFRK earnings lifted the current account into surplus. Preliminary estimates indicate a current account surplus of $0.8 billion in the first half of 2024, equal to 0.4% of GDP. Merchandise imports fell by 4.3% to $28.2 billion, while exports increased by 1.2% to $39.5 billion. The deficit in primary transfers narrowed by 27.7% to $9.4 billion, reflecting a 23.3% decrease in profit repatriation and a 79.0% rise in reported NFRK earnings to $1.5 billion.

Combined NFRK and central bank reserves surpassed $100 billion. Gross foreign exchange reserves increased in the first half of 2024 by 11.1% to $39.9 billion (Figure 3.1.6), of which 56.0% were monetary gold. Reserves provided cover for 6.7 months of imports of goods and services. Sovereign wealth fund receipts declined by 3.1% from the first half of 2023, hit by lower oil production and prices. However, NFRK assets increased to an estimated $61.5 billion at the end of June 2024 as asset values rose. The tenge fluctuated and appreciated against the US dollar during the first 5 months of 2024 before depreciating by an average of 4.0% in June and July (Figure 3.1.7). During these 7 months, the central bank converted to tenge $6.2 billion in foreign exchange receipts from the NFRK before transferring them to the state budget.

Figure 3.1.6 Foreign Currency Reserves and Sovereign Wealth Fund Assets

Gross reserves and sovereign wealth fund assets both increased.

Source: National Bank of the Republic of Kazakhstan.

Figure 3.1.7 Exchange Rate

The tenge fluctuated and appreciated against the US dollar during the first 5 months of 2024 before depreciating in June and July.

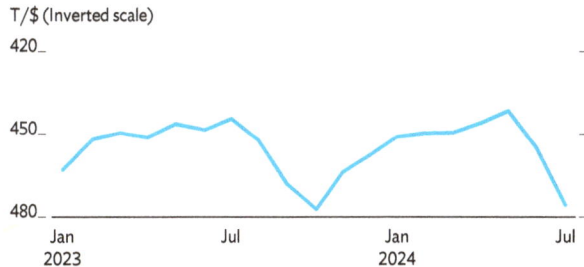

Source: National Bank of the Republic of Kazakhstan.

Prospects

Growth is projected to recover slightly in the rest of 2024 before accelerating in 2025. Restrictions on oil production agreed in June under the OPEC+ arrangement led by the Organization of the Petroleum Exporting Countries will cause mining to contract this year. However, the completion of a Tengiz oilfield expansion project in the second half of 2025 should boost oil production, assuming no additional restrictions under OPEC+. The subdued outlook for mining prompts a reduced forecast for growth in industry, though state and foreign direct investment is expected to raise manufacturing output by 4.8% this year and 4.2% in 2025, up from 3.9% and 3.7% projected in *ADO April 2024*. The forecast for growth in services in 2024 is cut to 4.4% from 4.7%, reflecting a decline in the consolidated business activity index for services. However, with anticipated expansion in trade, transport, and communications, growth should accelerate to 5.1% in 2025 (Figure 3.1.8). Government

Figure 3.1.8 Gross Domestic Product Growth

Growth is projected to recover slightly in the rest of 2024 before accelerating in 2025.

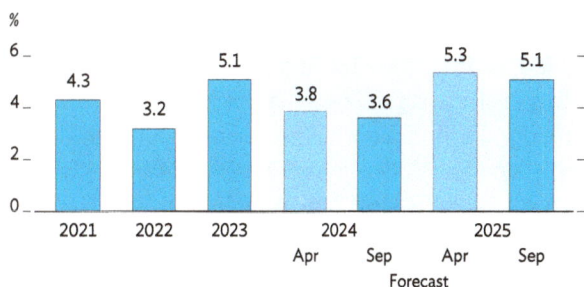

Source: *Asian Development Outlook* database (accessed 5 September 2024).

support for districts affected by flooding will raise 2024 construction growth to 9.8%. Further delays to oilfield expansion plans pose a downside risk to the outlook, as do issues with export routes.

Disappointing investment expansion explains slower growth on the demand side. Private investment slowed significantly despite government efforts to attract investment in manufacturing. Accordingly, forecast expansion in gross capital formation in 2024 is cut to 2.1% from 14.5%, accelerating in 2025 to 7.8%. Forecast growth in consumption remains unchanged at about 4% in both years, supported by moderate growth in real incomes. Higher exports and only a moderate increase in imports will further raise net exports in 2025. In view of these projections, the forecast for GDP growth is reduced for both 2024 and 2025 (Table 3.1.1).

Table 3.1.1 Selected Economic Indicators in Kazakhstan, %

Slow growth in the first half of 2024 prompts downward revision for 2024 and 2025 growth forecasts, while tight monetary policy and stable exchange support lower inflation projections for both years.

	2023	2024		2025	
		Apr	Sep	Apr	Sep
GDP growth	5.1	3.8	3.6	5.3	5.1
Inflation	14.5	8.7	8.5	6.3	6.1

GDP = gross domestic product.
Source: Asian Development Bank estimates.

Inflation is projected to slow somewhat more than earlier forecast because of lower prices for food and imported consumer goods. Relatively tight monetary policy and a stable exchange rate supported by the conversion of NFRK assets into local currency helped to moderate inflation for food and other goods. Accordingly, the inflation forecast for food is reduced from 9.4% to 7.2%, and for other goods from 6.7% to 6.4%. However, government-approved increases for utility tariffs and gasoline prices have raised the cost of producing and transporting goods, prompting a higher projection for inflation in services in 2024 from 9.8% in *ADO April 2024* to 12.6%. As substantial foreign reserves and commodity export earnings enable a stable exchange rate, this report lowers inflation projections marginally for both years (Figure 3.1.9).

Figure 3.1.9 Inflation

Inflation is projected to slow somewhat more than earlier forecast.

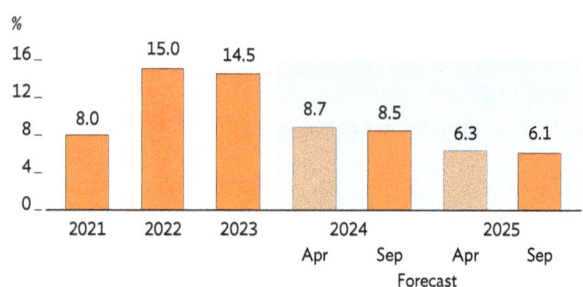

Source: *Asian Development Outlook* database (accessed 5 September 2024).

The state budget deficit is expected to widen in 2024. The 2024 state budget deficit is now projected to equal 3.0% of GDP, up from 2.6% projected in *ADO April 2024*. Budget expenditure is forecast to show little change, with no change for social outlays, which constitute more than half of state budget expenditure. However, the forecast for receipts is cut from 19.3% of GDP to 18.8% because of declining tax revenue. Tax revenue is projected to increase in 2025, reflecting both higher growth and the start of a universal requirement that property and income be declared. This forecast assumes that no additional sovereign wealth transfers will be allocated, ensuring compliance with fiscal rules.

A current account surplus is projected for 2025. Stable merchandise exports and declining imports will narrow the current account deficit in 2024, while increased exports from higher commodity prices and production volumes should bring about a current account surplus in 2025. The service deficit will ease gradually, supported by higher earnings from transportation, while a widening primary income deficit will reflect higher earnings for foreign investors from commodity exports.

Other Economies

Armenia

Growth moderated but remained strong because of gains in industry. Growth slowed to 6.5% in the first half of 2024 from a double-digit 10.5% a year earlier. On the supply side, a 33.7% decrease in net transfers from abroad halved expansion in services to 7.5% from 14.7% a year earlier as gains shrank across all subsectors. Growth in industry excluding construction surged to 7.5% from 2.5% in the first half of 2023. This largely reflected a 9.2% rise in manufacturing, particularly for jewelry production, and gains in utilities, offsetting a 10.7% drop in mining and quarrying. Construction grew by 15.9%, down from 19.4%, fueled by public investment in roads and social infrastructure and, to a lesser extent, private housing. Higher crop and livestock production doubled expansion in agriculture to 4.9% from 2.3% a year earlier.

On the demand side, private consumption and investment were the main growth drivers. Expansion in private consumption accelerated to 7.5% in the first half of 2024 from 6.8% the previous year, reflecting deflation and increased consumer lending. Public consumption fell by 14.9%, reversing growth in the previous year by 27.4% and reflecting a decline in budget outlays for operation and maintenance. Primarily supported by higher public investment, growth in gross fixed capital formation accelerated to 22.3% from 15.0% a year before despite somewhat weaker private investment. In line with developments in the first half of 2024, this report slightly raises the growth forecast for 2024, but it keeps unchanged the forecast for 2025 (Table 3.1.2).

Deflation persisted throughout the first 7 months of 2024. Domestically, lower public consumption curbed total domestic demand, and external inflationary pressure was contained by currency appreciation. Deflation by 0.3% was recorded in January–July 2024, with food prices dropping by 2.7%, more than offsetting a 2.8% increase in prices for services, while prices for other goods remained unchanged. Year-on-year inflation at 1.4% in July was below the Central Bank of Armenia's target range of 2.5%–5.5%. The central bank reduced its refinancing rate in several steps by a cumulative 150 basis points

Table 3.1.2 Selected Economic Indicators in Armenia, %

Developments in the first half of 2024 prompt a slightly higher growth projection for 2024, while deflation in early 2024 supports a lower inflation forecast for both 2024 and 2025.

	2023	2024		2025	
		Apr	Sep	Apr	Sep
GDP growth	8.3	5.7	6.0	6.0	6.0
Inflation	2.0	3.0	0.8	3.5	2.5

GDP = gross domestic product.
Source: Asian Development Bank estimates.

to 7.75% at the end of July 2024. Considering price developments in the first half of 2024, this report adjusts inflation forecasts downwards for 2024 and 2025.

Fiscal policy remained expansionary as spending growth outpaced revenue. Growth in revenue slowed to 7.1% in the first half of 2024 from 18.3% a year earlier as moderating economic growth slowed growth in value-added and excise tax collection. Higher social spending boosted growth in current expenditure to 18.2% from 12.1% a year earlier. Growth in capital outlays also accelerated, to 35.3% from 18.0% a year earlier, reflecting higher spending on road construction and outlays for infrastructure in regions damaged by floods in May 2024.

The current account deficit in the first quarter of 2024 was at 6.2% of GDP, little changed from 6.3% a year earlier. This reflected a decrease in the merchandise trade deficit that more than offset a decline in service exports and larger net outflow of private transfers. The merchandise trade deficit narrowed to 9.1% in the first quarter of 2024 from 13.6% a year earlier as exports, mainly reexports of gold and jewelry, grew by 160%, outpacing a 110% rise in imports. Exports and imports alike are projected to moderate in the rest of the year, slightly widening the deficits in both merchandise trade and the current account. A continued decline in money transfers will further deepen a deficit in net transfers. Offsetting these developments will be higher earnings from tourism, transportation, and information and communication technology services.

Azerbaijan

Strong performance outside of the large hydrocarbon economy boosted growth in the first half of 2024. Growth accelerated from 0.5% in the first half of 2023 to 4.3% in the first half of 2024 as the non-oil economy expanded by 6.9%, reflecting higher public spending. The hydrocarbon economy grew by 0.6% as a 3.4% rise in gas production more than offset a 4.9% decline in oil output. Industry expanded by 0.9% as gains in petrochemicals and food processing boosted manufacturing by 7.4%, reversing a 1.8% decrease of industry in the first half of 2023 caused by 3.7% contraction in mining. Notably higher investment doubled growth in construction from 9.2% in the first half of 2023 to 18.4% a year later. Expansion in services rose from 1.6% in the first half of 2023 to 6.1% this year, reflecting a rise of 15.4% in transportation. However, a decline in crop production cut expansion in agriculture from 3.4% in the first half of 2023 to 0.2% this year. As growth above earlier projections is expected to continue to the end of 2024, this report revises upward the *ADO April 2024* growth forecasts for 2024 and 2025 (Table 3.1.3).

Table 3.1.3 Selected Economic Indicators in Azerbaijan, %

Stronger-than-expected growth in the first half of 2024 supports higher growth projections for 2024 and 2025, and slow inflation in early 2024 prompts lower inflation forecasts for both years.

	2023	2024		2025	
		Apr	Sep	Apr	Sep
GDP growth	1.1	1.2	2.7	1.6	2.6
Inflation	8.8	5.5	2.1	6.5	3.8

GDP = gross domestic product.
Source: Asian Development Bank estimates.

The continuing effects of tight monetary policy helped ease inflation. Slowing global commodity price increases and declining inflation in Azerbaijan's main trading partners, along with high policy interest rates, slashed the average annual inflation rate from 12.7% in the first half of 2023 to 0.7% a year later. Prices declined by 0.6% for food but rose by 1.2% for other goods and 2.4% for services. With the decline in inflation, the Central Bank of Azerbaijan cut its policy interest rate in four steps from January to July 2024

from 7.75% to 7.25%. While higher administrative prices for fuel from the end of June are expected to raise inflation during the second half of 2024, the full-year inflation rate is expected to be less than earlier projected, given very low inflation during the first half. Accordingly, *ADO April 2024* inflation projections for 2024 and 2025 are revised down.

The fiscal surplus doubled as a percentage of GDP. It rose from 2.3% in the first half of 2023 to 4.7% this year as revenue grew notably. First-half revenue rose from 25.6% of GDP in 2023 to 31.7% this year, reflecting higher receipts from domestic taxes and customs duties. First-half expenditure rose from 23.3% of GDP in 2023 to an estimated 27.0% this year as higher public investment spending for reconstruction helped boost outlays by 14.1%.

Falling gas prices narrowed the current account surplus. The surplus dropped from 18.9% of GDP in the first quarter of 2023 to 10.1% in the first quarter of 2024. Relative to the first quarter of 2023, the surplus fell by 48.8% to $1.7 billion, as the surplus in oil and gas fell by 28.2% and the deficit in the rest of the current account expanded by 12.8%. The merchandise trade balance recorded a surplus of $2.7 billion as a $5.0 billion surplus in oil and gas dwarfed a $2.3 billion deficit in the rest of the trade account. Inward money transfers fell by 34.8% in the period. During the first half of 2024, sovereign wealth fund assets increased by 3.4% to $58.0 billion, and central bank gross official reserves reached $11.7 billion, covering 10 months of imports.

Georgia

Growth accelerated from 8.2% in the first half of 2023 to an estimated 9.0% in the first half of 2024. On the supply side, growth reflected rapid expansion in services by 11.3%, with increases of 9.7% in transport and storage, 8.5% in accommodation and food services, 12.2% in information and communication, and 9.6% in finance and insurance services. Industry grew by 1.8% as construction expanded by 10.3% but energy activities declined. On the demand side, domestic consumption was the main driver of growth, financed by external inflows, and by strong credit growth, which also helped expand domestic investment. Strong growth cut the unemployment rate by 4 percentage points to 14% in the first quarter of 2024. Growth is expected to moderate in line with slower expansion in major economies during the second half of 2024 and consequently diminished export prospects. Following strong growth during the first half of the year, this report raises the growth forecast for 2024, but it maintains the *ADO April 2024* forecast for 2025 (Table 3.1.4).

Table 3.1.4 Selected Economic Indicators in Georgia, %

Strong growth and lower inflation in the first half of 2024 prompt a higher growth projection for 2024 and lower forecasts for inflation in 2024 and 2025.

	2023	2024		2025	
		Apr	Sep	Apr	Sep
GDP growth	7.5	5.0	7.0	5.5	5.5
Inflation	2.5	3.5	2.5	4.0	3.5

GDP = gross domestic product.
Source: Asian Development Bank estimates.

Inflation slowed in the first half of 2024 but is edging up again. Average inflation decreased from 4.6% in the first half of 2023 to 1.1% in the first half of 2024, though inflation rose to 2.2% in June. Core inflation, which excludes food and nonalcoholic beverages, energy, regulated tariffs, and transportation, slowed to 1.4% from 2.0% at the end of 2023. Transport costs were the main driver of inflation, reflecting unstable oil prices, along with somewhat elevated prices for tobacco and alcoholic beverages. A relatively stable exchange rate and prudent fiscal policy helped keep prices from rising faster. With inflation slowing, the National Bank of Georgia, the central bank, cut its policy rate in three steps from 9.5% at the start of 2024 to 8.0% in May. Because of lower inflation during the first half of 2024, inflation forecasts for both years are reduced.

Prudent fiscal policy also helped keep public debt in check. An 18.5% increase in revenue erased the fiscal deficit during the first half of 2024. A balanced budget and a relatively stable lari also trimmed the ratio of public debt to GDP to 38.9% in mid-2024 from 39.2% a year earlier.

The current account deficit expanded as inward money transfers declined and exports shrank. Despite continued strong tourism, the current account

deficit rose to equal 5.0% of GDP in the first quarter of 2024 from 4.4% at the end of 2023, reflecting a larger merchandise trade deficit and declining inward money transfers. Money transfers fell by 30.3% as those from the Russian Federation plunged by 71.4% but were partly offset by higher inflows from the United States and Europe. Service exports rose on the strength of information and computer technology and accommodation and transportation as tourism revenue remained high, rising by 5.2% in the first half of 2024 to about 30% above the 2019 pre-pandemic level. However, merchandise exports declined by 6.7% as vehicle reexports moderated and global demand for ferroalloys remained weak.

Downside risks remain at the fore. Risks to the current account include domestic policy uncertainty and geopolitical risks, which may exacerbate exchange rate pressures. In addition, potential disruption to trade from the knock-on effects of Russia's war in Ukraine could hit supply chains, creating inflationary pressures from higher commodity prices. Higher growth in transit trade may surprise on the upside.

Kyrgyz Republic

Growth jumped to an estimated 8.1% in the first half of 2024 from 2.2% a year earlier. Expansion in services more than doubled, from 3.1% in the first half of 2023 to 7.7% this year, as wholesale and retail trade rose by 18.3%. Significantly higher foreign and domestic investment quadrupled growth in construction from 11.1% to 48.5%. Agriculture grew by 3.3% as both livestock and crop production increased. Industry reversed a 0.8% decline in the first half of 2023 to expand by 0.9%, mainly on gains in textiles, energy, and water supply, and despite continued decline in metal production, mainly gold. Demand-side data, available for only the first quarter, show growth in private consumption surging from 1.9% to 19.1%. This reflects a 22% increase in net money transfers including remittances from abroad, a 27% rise in consumer lending, and a 5% increase in real wages. In view of the robust expansion during the first half of 2024 and the expectation of sustained domestic demand, this report upgrades *ADO April 2024* growth forecasts for 2024 and 2025 (Table 3.1.5). Downside risks include weaker growth in key trade partners and spillover from sanctions on the Russian Federation.

Table 3.1.5 Selected Economic Indicators in the Kyrgyz Republic, %

Robust growth and a continued decline in inflation in the first half of 2024 prompt higher growth and lower inflation projections for 2024 and 2025.

	2023	2024		2025	
		Apr	Sep	Apr	Sep
GDP growth	6.2	5.0	6.3	4.5	5.8
Inflation	10.8	7.0	6.8	6.5	6.2

GDP = gross domestic product.
Sources: National Statistics Committee of the Kyrgyz Republic; Asian Development Bank estimates.

Inflation slowed across all major categories and especially for food. Average annual inflation fell from 12.7% in the first half of 2023 to 5.1% a year later, below expectations in April forecast and reaching 4.5% year on year in June 2024. Core inflation fell from 13.7% to 5.8%. Deceleration was broad-based, with food prices rising by only 1.0%. The slowdown reflected lower import prices and improved supplies of essential goods, local currency appreciation, and the lagged effects of earlier monetary tightening. As inflation fell within its target range of 5%–7%, the National Bank of the Kyrgyz Republic, the central bank, lowered its policy rate by a cumulative 400 basis points to 9.0% in two steps in April and May 2024, the first decreases since November 2022. Inflationary risks remain from volatile global food and energy prices, possible currency depreciation, persistently elevated inflation expectations, and strong demand pressure. With inflation slowing more than expected in the first half of 2024, this report marginally reduces inflation projections for 2024 and 2025.

Strong tax revenue and ongoing fiscal consolidation raised the budget surplus. Budget revenue grew by 24.7% in the first half of 2024, outpacing a 5.9% increase in public expenditure and widening the general government surplus to an estimated 6.9% of GDP from 1.1% a year earlier. The strong revenue performance reflected enhanced tax administration, accelerated economic growth, a surge in imports, and the early and increased transfer of central bank profits to the budget. Fiscal policy is expected to be more expansionary during the rest of this year, yielding a smaller full-year surplus.

The recorded current account deficit widened further, reflecting a larger trade deficit, while errors and omissions remained large. Already massive in 2023, the current account deficit widened to equal 52.5% of GDP in the first quarter of 2024 from 42.9% a year earlier. The large deficit reflects inability to fully count reexports to the Russian Federation because of incomplete monitoring of trade within the Eurasian Economic Union. Recorded merchandise exports increased by 12.7% on strong supplies of non-monetary gold, while imports rose by 33.2% on high imports of vehicles, machinery, and equipment. Gross official reserves rose from 2.3 months of cover for prospective imports of goods and services at the end of March 2023 to 3.2 months at the end of March 2024.

Tajikistan

Growth reached 8.2% in the first half of 2024, which exceeded the government's expectations. All sectors expanded, with services and agriculture contributing the most to growth. Growth in services jumped from 5.5% in the first half of 2023 to 16.6%, reflecting gains in transportation and catering, and despite slower growth in finance and other services. Favorable weather and early crop planting boosted growth in agriculture from 9.6% in the first half of 2023 to 11.5%. Expansion in industry excluding construction rose from 10.3% in the first half of 2023 to 11.5%. This reflected an 11.0% rise in manufacturing from gains in food production, fabricated metals, nonmetallic mineral products, and textiles, and a 21.4% jump in mining driven by gold, coal, and metallic ores. Growth in construction slowed to 9.5% from 11.6%.

On the demand side, strong remittances and a rise in public sector salaries boosted private consumption. Remittances are estimated to have risen by 56% in the first quarter of 2024 from the same period in 2023, with slower growth in the second quarter. In May 2024 salaries averaged 14.5% above those a year earlier, with a further 40% rise in public sector salaries on 1 July alongside higher minimum wages, stipends, and pensions. However, growth is expected to moderate in the second half of 2024 because tariff increases for electricity and irrigation water in January, and for broadband services in April, will slow business activity. More stringent regulation of migrants in the Russian Federation will lower

Table 3.1.6 Selected Economic Indicators in Tajikistan, %

Despite strong growth and lower-than-expected inflation in the first half of 2024, growth and inflation projections are maintained because growth is expected to slow during the second half of the year, and tariff hikes and wage increases are expected to raise inflation.

	2023	2024		2025	
		Apr	Sep	Apr	Sep
GDP growth	8.3	6.5	6.5	6.5	6.5
Inflation	3.8	5.5	5.5	6.5	6.5

GDP = gross domestic product.
Source: Asian Development Bank estimates.

remittances, constraining growth. For these reasons, full-year growth projections remain unchanged from those in *ADO April 2024* (Table 3.1.6).

Inflation decelerated despite major tariff hikes and wage growth. Average annual inflation slowed from 2.3% in the first half of 2023 to 1.9% this year. However, year-on-year inflation rose from 2.4% in June 2023 to 3.5% in June 2024, reflecting notable price increases for food at 2.4%, other goods at 5.4%, and services at 4.1%. With inflation below its 4%–8% target, the National Bank of Tajikistan, the central bank, lowered its key policy rate by 0.25 percentage points to 9.25% in February 2024. The Tajik somoni appreciated by 2.7% against the US dollar in the first half of 2024 but lost 2.4% of its value against the Russian ruble, the dominant currency of remittance inflows from labor migrants. With inflation expected to accelerate in the second half of 2024 from higher utility tariffs and salaries, inflation projections for 2024 and 2025 remain unchanged.

Higher revenue and constrained spending led to a budget surplus during the first half of 2024. Revenue totaled TJS21.2 billion, 5.3% above the same period in 2023. Tax revenue exceeded the government's projections by 5.7%, accounting for 65.8% of total revenue, up from 61.6% a year earlier due to a broadened tax base and improved collection. Expenditure was TJS20.0 billion, with social outlays accounting for 61.5%. Public debt equaled $3.6 billion or 27.5% of GDP.

Strong remittances narrowed the current account deficit to 3.4% of GDP during the first quarter of 2024 despite a larger trade deficit. The

merchandise trade deficit widened by 17.5% year on year to $2.4 billion, reflecting a 24.9% rise in imports and a 47.1% rise in exports. The sale of gold and other precious metals accounted for 30.0% of merchandise exports, followed by mineral products at 21.9% and nonprecious fabricated metal products at 21.5%. Gross international reserves rose from $2.4 billion at the end of March 2023 to $3.6 billion a year later, providing cover for 7.3 months of imports of goods and services.

Turkmenistan

The government reported growth at 6.3% in the first half of 2024, the same as in the first half of 2023, with expansion in all sectors. In the large hydrocarbon economy, it reflected higher production and exports of natural gas, crude oil, and oil products. Growth in the rest of the economy came from expansion in construction at 9.3%, wholesale and retail trade at 7.8%, transport and communications at 7.3%, and catering and other services at 7.9%. Industry expanded by 3.6%, reflecting stable output in electricity, chemicals, textiles, food processing, and other agro-industrial products. The government provided substantial financial support to private firms for the targeted production of goods for import substitution. Half-year reports showed agriculture expanding by an impressive 24% in the first half of 2024 over the same period in 2023, with a successful wheat harvest, cotton cultivation and livestock production in line with annual production targets, and the planting of a large variety of fruits and vegetables.

On the demand side, the government reported higher net exports and public investment in industrial and social infrastructure. Investment in the first half of 2024 was 20.8% higher than in the same period of 2023 and comprised 17.3% of GDP. Industrial infrastructure attracted 48.5% of investment, with the rest going for social projects. In view of these developments, this report maintains *ADO April 2024* growth projections for 2024 and 2025, in line with government forecasts (Table 3.1.7).

Disinflation in 2023 turned to low inflation in 2024. Prices for both imported and domestically produced goods were observed to have risen slightly during the first half of 2024, following disinflation observed in 2023 in line with lower world commodity prices.

Table 3.1.7 Selected Economic Indicators in Turkmenistan, %

Growth forecasts for 2024 and 2025 are maintained, while inflation projections are revised downward.

	2023	2024		2025	
		Apr	Sep	Apr	Sep
GDP growth	6.3	6.5	6.5	6.0	6.0
Inflation	5.9	8.0	5.0	8.0	5.0

GDP = gross domestic product.
Source: Asian Development Bank estimates.

Monetary policy remains focused on containing inflation by maintaining price controls and a fixed exchange rate to anchor prices for basic goods and services. The bulk of financial support in the form of concessional credits and official foreign exchange convertibility is provided to priority firms engaged in import substitution or oriented toward exports. Exchange market pressures continue as excess demand for foreign exchange at the official rate has induced foreign currency rationing. As inflation has been perceived lower than expected in *ADO April 2024*, this report slightly reduces inflation forecasts for 2024 and 2025.

The fiscal outlook is broadly consistent with the goal of containing inflation. The government aims to keep the state budget balanced in 2024 and 2025, benefiting from a positive outlook for energy exports and corresponding revenue. Fitch Ratings upgraded Turkmenistan's credit rating to BB– in August 2024 in line with strengthening fiscal and external buffers and a projected decline in public debt to 2.9% of GDP by the end of 2026. Fitch noted that, given high public investment, spending efficiency needs to be enhanced through improved fiscal reporting and transparency.

Growth in gas exports to the People's Republic of China in the first half of 2024 is estimated to have been stable. Recently concluded agreements on gas exports indicate strong demand for gas in that market and regionally in Azerbaijan, Iran, and Iraq, suggesting that gas exports may rise in the second half of 2024 and in 2025. Imports are projected to increase only slowly, constrained by government import-substitution programs and capital controls. With exports currently increasing faster than imports, the current account surplus is likely to rise in 2024 and 2025.

Uzbekistan

The government reported growth rising from 6.2% in the first half of 2023 to 6.4% this year, with gains in industry and construction. Growth in industry accelerated from 5.6% to 7.8%, driven by strong gains in manufacturing. Expansion in construction doubled from 5.2% to 10.1% with rapid growth in housing and infrastructure. Expansion in agriculture rose marginally, from 3.7% to 3.8%, with modest increases in crop and livestock production. Growth in services decreased from 7.9% to 6.4% as gains in trade were exceeded by slowdowns in transportation, storage, information and communication, and accommodation and food services.

A sharp rise in investment and steady growth in consumption boosted growth on the demand side. Expansion in gross capital formation soared from 19.7% in the first half of 2023 to 36.6% this year on robust infrastructure spending and the modernization of machinery and equipment. Growth in consumption increased from 4.3% to an estimated 5.5% as household expenditures rose due to higher wages and pensions and a 25% rise in remittance inflows, mainly from Germany, Poland, the Republic of Korea, and the United States. The government's programs to diversify the destinations of migrant workers from Uzbekistan helped reduce the share of remittances from the Russian Federation from about 87% in 2022 to 78% in 2023 and 77% in the first half of 2024. The deficit in net exports of goods and services widened by 8.0%, with the trade deficit expanding by 19.4% for goods, reflecting higher imports of petrochemicals, machinery, and transport equipment. In the second half of 2024, rising remittances, wages, and pensions should maintain growth in consumption. Continued growth is also anticipated for investment, on the expectation of high global prices for gold and copper, high domestic needs for industrial goods and housing, strong foreign direct investment, and structural reform to liberalize markets and regulated prices. With these projections, this report raises growth forecasts for 2024 and 2025 (Table 3.1.8).

Inflation decelerated in the first 7 months of 2024 despite higher domestic prices for energy. Inflation slowed from 10.7% in the 7 months of 2023 to 9.5% this year because of smaller price increases for food and imported goods. Food price inflation

Table 3.1.8 Selected Economic Indicators
in Uzbekistan, %

*Growth forecasts for 2024 and 2025 are raised after growth
accelerated in the first half of 2024. Less inflation during the first
half of 2024 prompts lower inflation forecasts for 2024 and 2025.*

	2023	2024		2025	
		Apr	Sep	Apr	Sep
GDP growth	6.0	5.5	6.0	5.6	6.2
Inflation	10.0	10.0	9.5	9.5	9.0

GDP = gross domestic product.
Source: Asian Development Bank estimates.

fell from 13.4% to 8.4% with higher domestic supplies
of fruit and vegetables and lower costs for imported
food. Inflation for other goods declined from 9.2% to
7.0% with smaller price increases for apparel, shoes,
and household items. Higher administered prices for
energy doubled inflation for services from 8.3% to
17.3%. Even though the inflation rate is still above the
target since inflation has been slowing, the monetary
authorities cut the policy interest rate from 14.0% to
13.5% in July 2024, the first reduction since March
2023. In view of price development thus far, inflation
projections for 2024 and 2025 are revised down
despite government plans for further energy price
increases in April 2025.

**The current account deficit expanded from the
equivalent of 6.6% of GDP in the first quarter of
2023 to 7.1% a year later.** The trade deficit widened
by 3.1% as imports of goods rose by 3.4% on higher
imports of machinery and equipment, ferrous metals,
and petrochemicals. Exports of goods, which are
smaller than imports, rose by 6.3%, with growth in
gold, textiles, foodstuffs, copper, and petrochemicals.
Service exports soared by 22.9% as demand for
transport and tourism services surged, while service
imports rose by 8.9% on higher demand for shipping,
business services, and support for foreign tourism.
Inward money transfers rose by 6.0%, and interest on
external debt increased, cutting the income surplus
by 13.3%. International reserves provided cover for
10.5 months of imports at the end of March 2024.

EAST ASIA

GDP growth in East Asia is now forecast slightly higher this year than projected in *ADO April 2024*, as growth in Mongolia; the Republic of Korea; and Taipei,China accelerates. Inflation in 2024 will edge up less than previously forecast, remaining below 1%. As projected in April, growth in the subregion will likely moderate in 2025 while inflation rises and the current account surplus narrows.

Subregional Assessment and Prospects

The East Asian economy grew by 4.8% year on year in the first half (H1) of 2024. In the People's Republic of China (PRC), growth moderated to 5.0% year on year in H1 2024 as softer domestic demand dampened growth in the second quarter (Q2) following higher exports than expected and continued policy support in Q1. Investment growth remained robust, but consumption was sluggish as confidence remained weak. Driven by exports, economic growth in the Republic of Korea (ROK) rose to 2.8% year on year in H1 as a 3.3% expansion in Q1 moderated to 2.3% in Q2. Similarly, in Taipei,China, robust growth in domestic demand and exports driven by the boom in artificial intelligence-related products pushed growth up to 5.8% in H1, contrasting sharply with the 1.0% contraction in H1 2023. In Hong Kong, China as well, growth accelerated to 3.0% in H1 driven by a sharp recovery in exports, even as consumption moderated and tourism growth softened. Rising demand in the PRC for coal imports raised mining and services output in Mongolia pushing growth up to 5.6% in H1 2024.

Subregional inflation remained low at 0.5% in H1 2024. Declining food and property prices in the PRC moderated consumer price inflation to 0.1% year on year from 0.7% in H1 2023. Core inflation (excluding food and energy prices) rose to 0.7%, but food prices declined by 2.7%. Property prices fell although mortgage rates and the "down payment" requirement for housing loans were lowered. Inflation also eased in the ROK to 2.8% year on year in H1, still above the central bank's target, with lower price increases across categories such as utilities and restaurants and hotels. Food price increases also drove inflation in Taipei,China, but with core inflation falling to 1.8% in Q2 2024, headline inflation moderated to 2.3% in H1 year on year. Inflation in Hong Kong, China averaged 1.6% in H1 2024 on moderate food and housing prices. The underlying inflation that excludes one-off measures also remained muted at 1.0% in June. In Mongolia, inflation remained much higher than elsewhere in the subregion, averaging 6.5% in H1, but substantially lower than H1 2023.

East Asia's current account surplus narrowed in H1 2024. In the PRC, the current account surplus equaled 1.1 % of GDP, slightly lower than in H1 2023. The merchandise trade surplus narrowed slightly to 3.3% of GDP and the services trade deficit widened to 1.4% of GDP from 1.1% in H1 2023. Surpluses rose in other economies of the subregion, except in Mongolia where the deficit widened as both the trade and services deficits increased. In the ROK, robust export growth, a decline in imports on weak domestic demand, and an increase in inbound tourism underpinned the

The section on the PRC was written by Akiko Terada-Hagiwara, Yothin Jinjarak, Wen Qi, and Yajing Wang. The part on other economies by David De Padua, Edward Faber, Jules Hugot, Henry Ma, Madhavi Pundit, Melanie Grace Quintos, Cara Tinio, and Michael Timbang, consultant. All authors are in the East Asia and Economic Research and Development Impact departments of ADB. Subregional assessment and prospects was written by Reza Vaez-Zadeh, consultant, Economic Research and Development Impact Department of ADB.

current account surplus. In Hong Kong, China, export growth helped widen the current account surplus in Q1 2024, and in Taipei,China, higher exports and rising remittances widened the surplus to 19.1% of GDP in H1 from 11.6% in the same period last year.

Subregional GDP growth is now forecast to edge down from 4.7% in 2023 to 4.6% in 2024—slightly better than in *ADO April 2024*—before moderating to 4.2% in 2025 as previously forecast (Figure 3.2.1). In the PRC, growth will likely be on a downward trend, falling to 4.8% in 2024 and 4.5% in 2025 as forecast in *ADO April 2024*, driven by a contraction in real estate investment and moderating services growth. Based on the strong Q1 performance and benefiting from the technology export momentum, this year's GDP growth in the ROK is forecast to be higher than projected in April, but the 2025 forecast remains unchanged. The April projections for growth in Hong Kong, China also remain unchanged, with export growth expected to weaken in H2 2024, while consumption and investment slated to pick up in 2025. In Taipei,China, 2024 growth is now forecast to be

higher than projected in April on stronger H1 export growth, then moderate next year to the level originally forecast. Strong mining expansion will push growth in Mongolia this year higher than previously forecast and lift growth further in 2025 to the level expected in April.

Inflation in East Asia is forecast at 0.8% in 2024 and 1.3% in 2025 (Figure 3.2.2). Inflation in the PRC is forecast to rise from 0.2% in 2023 to 0.5% in 2024, less than projected in April, due to persistent food price deflation and excess supply in some industries. However, improving domestic demand is expected to push inflation to 1.2% in 2025, slightly below the April forecast. As global price pressures dissipate and food prices ease in the ROK and Taipei,China, inflation in these economies should moderate this year and next to the levels forecast in April. In Hong Kong, China, inflation is expected to remain muted in H2 2024 and below that forecast in April, as growth slows, the local currency strengthens, and interest rates remain elevated. However, US monetary policy easing can lead to higher inflation in 2025 as projected in April.

Figure 3.2.1 Gross Domestic Product Growth in East Asia

Growth in East Asia will moderate slightly in 2024 and 2025, reflecting the trend in the PRC.

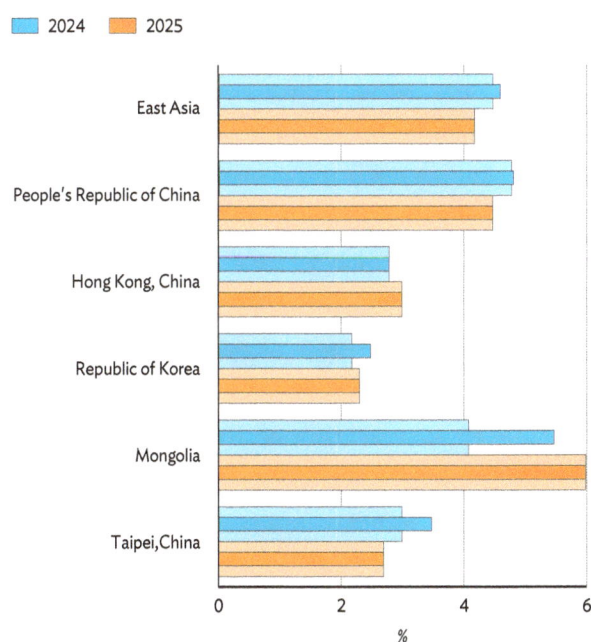

Note: Lighter-colored bars are *Asian Development Outlook April 2024* forecasts.
Source: *Asian Development Outlook* database (accessed 5 September 2024).

Figure 3.2.2 Inflation in East Asia

Inflation in East Asia will be lower in 2024 than the April forecast mainly on food price deflation in the PRC, edging up in 2025 on improved domestic demand as previously forecast.

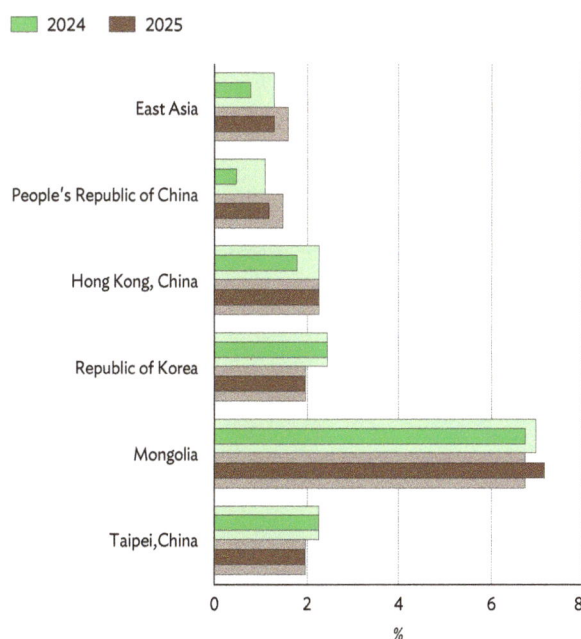

Note: Lighter-colored bars are *Asian Development Outlook April 2024* forecasts.
Source: *Asian Development Outlook* database (accessed 5 September 2024).

In Mongolia, inflation will remain higher than the rest of the subregion. It will be lower in 2024 than the April forecast on muted H1 price changes, but higher in 2025 than the earlier forecast on wage and tariff adjustments.

The subregional current account surplus is forecast to decline in 2024 and 2025 as rising domestic demand pushes up imports. In Mongolia, rising demand for imports will widen the deficit, but in other economies robust export growth will drive the surplus. In the PRC, exports should grow on robust global demand for electronics and the price competitiveness of PRC export products, but the trade deficit in services will widen as outward cross-border tourism continues to recover. In the ROK, the current account is expected to remain in surplus for the remainder of 2024, supported by solid exports, though the surplus may narrow in 2025 as domestic demand strengthens. The current account surplus of Hong Kong, China is unlikely to grow beyond its Q1 2024 level as export growth moderates, and the surplus in Taipei,China should narrow in 2025 as investment drives imports higher.

The risks to the East Asian economic outlook are tilted to the downside. Risks include further deterioration of the PRC property market, escalation of trade tensions stemming from uncertainty surrounding the US election, and global fragmentation due to geopolitical issues that could lower economic growth in the PRC and affect exports of the other economies in the subregion. On the upside, implementing policy measures announced by the PRC to support the property market and encourage consumption could boost consumer and investor confidence more than expected, pushing growth and inflation in the PRC above the forecast, with positive spillovers throughout East Asia.

People's Republic of China

Higher exports than forecast and continued policy support to manufacturing helped drive growth in the first half (H1) of 2024. Inflation remained subdued on declining food prices, and the current account surplus narrowed given the wider trade deficit in services. Nonetheless, projected GDP growth rates remain at 4.8% for 2024 and 4.5% for 2025. Inflation is revised down to 0.5% for 2024 and 1.2% for 2025 due to a slower recovery in domestic demand.

Updated Assessment

Growth averaged 5.0% year on year in H1 2024, down from 5.5% in H1 2023. Driven by a strong recovery in exports and robust industrial activities, GDP growth rebounded to 5.3% year on year in the first quarter (Q1), then moderated to 4.7% in Q2 due to softer domestic private demand (Figure 3.2.3). Growth slowed from 1.6% quarter on quarter in Q1 to 0.7% in Q2.

Figure 3.2.3 Economic Growth

After rising in Q1 2024, economic growth moderated in Q2 on softer domestic demand.

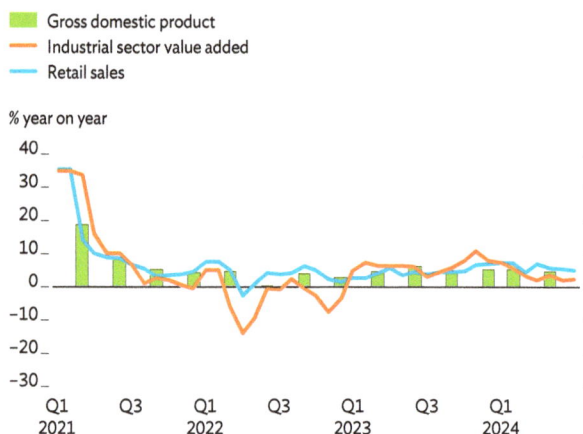

Q = quarter.
Sources: CEIC Data Company; Asian Development Bank estimates.

Consumption growth remained sluggish in H1 2024. Consumer confidence has yet to recover to pre-pandemic levels and is a significant headwind to economic recovery. Consumption's contribution to GDP growth fell to 3.0 percentage points from 4.3 points in H1 2023 (Figure 3.2.4). Lower demand for durable goods significantly dragged down retail

Figure 3.2.4 Demand-Side Contributions to Growth

Net exports boosted growth in H1, a reversal from last year, while contributions from investment and consumption decreased.

- ■ Consumption
- ■ Investment
- ■ Net exports
- — Gross domestic product growth, %

Percentage points

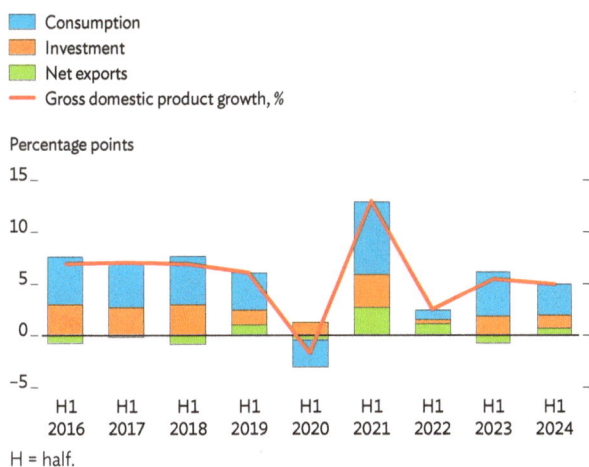

H = half.

Source: CEIC Data Company.

sales growth to 3.5% year on year in the first 7 months of 2024 from 7.3% during the same period in 2023. Slower real income growth and negative wealth effects from the weakened property market reduced household demand for big-ticket items such as automobiles and luxury goods. Yet consumer spending on services remained robust, with leisure and tourism activities such as catering, transportation, culture, and entertainment continuing to thrive, buoyed by the strong post-pandemic recovery in domestic travel. Since Q2 2023, consumption per capita growth has declined with real income growth (Figure 3.2.5).

Figure 3.2.5 Real Growth in Income and Consumption Expenditure per Capita

Income and consumption per capita growth have been trending down.

- — Real income per capita
- — Real consumption per capita

% year on year

Q = quarter.

Sources: CEIC Data Company; Asian Development Bank estimates.

The rise in manufacturing and infrastructure investment was offset by the decline in real estate investment (Figure 3.2.6). In the first 7 months of 2024, investment contributed 1.3 percentage points to growth, down 0.6 points from the previous year, largely due to the slowdown in real estate investment. Fixed asset investment increased by 3.6%, driven by growth in manufacturing and infrastructure investments. Manufacturing investment surged 9.3% supported by policies promoting equipment upgrades and strategic sectors. Infrastructure investment increased by 4.9%, backed by an additional CNY1 trillion government bond issuance at the end of 2023. However, real estate investment contracted by 10.2%, a sharper decline compared to last year's 8.5% fall due to poor market sentiment and continued low activity in the sector.

Figure 3.2.6 Growth in Fixed Asset Investment

Real estate investment continued declining in the first 7 months of 2024, but infrastructure and manufacturing investment remained steady.

- — All fixed assets
- — Manufacturing
- — Infrastructure
- — Real estate

% year on year, year to date

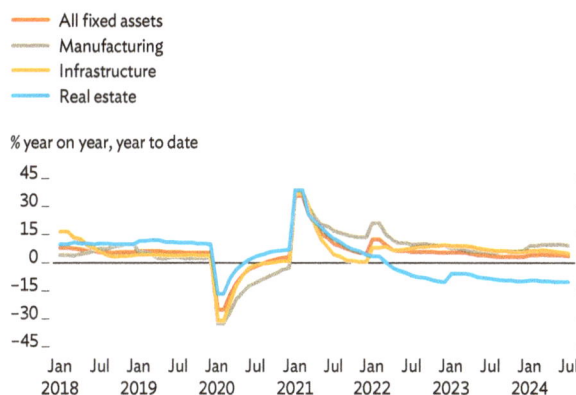

Source: CEIC Data Company.

Net exports rose on higher external demand, contributing 0.7 percentage points to growth in H1 2024, reversing the 0.7 point drag last year. Besides benefiting from a base effect, exports and imports recovered significantly. In H1 2024, exports grew by 3.5% in dollar terms, reversing the 3.5% decline in H1 2023. Imports increased by 2.0% from a 7.1% decline last year. Overseas demand for machinery, integrated circuits, passenger and cargo ships as well as household and home appliances led the export growth.

Supported by the growth in exports and policy support, industry value-added grew 6.0% in H1 2024. Industry's contribution to GDP growth rose to 2.2 percentage points from 1.6 points in H1 2023, in line with rapid growth in the secondary sector (Figure 3.2.7). Key drivers included equipment and high-tech manufacturing bolstered by government efforts to boost production capacities. Due to strong exports, new-energy automobiles and integrated circuit manufacturing grew by double digits. Construction, however, decelerated to 4.8% growth in H1 2024 from 7.7% a year ago amid the prolonged property market downturn.

Figure 3.2.7 Supply-Side Contributions to Growth

Strong export-led manufacturing helped industrial output growth.

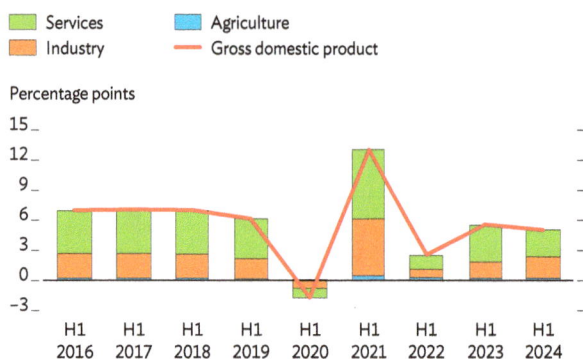

H1 = first half.
Source: CEIC Data Company.

Services continued to recover but at a slower pace. Services value-added increased by 4.6% year on year in H1 2024, down from 6.4% a year ago, decreasing its contribution to growth from 3.7 percentage points in H1 2023 to 2.6 percentage points in H1 2024. While high-tech sectors such as information and technology services grew rapidly, financial sector growth slowed to 4.8% from 7.3% a year ago largely because of methodological changes in calculating financial sector GDP. Real estate services contracted by 5.0%. Agriculture's contribution to GDP growth remained at 0.2 percentage points.

The labor market remains soft. Labor market indicators such as urban unemployment and the number of new jobs remained stable. The youth unemployment rate improved in H1 partly due to government financial incentives to employers hiring college graduates. The number of rural migrants working in urban areas has already exceeded pre-pandemic levels at the end of H1 due to the continued recovery in services, given

increased employment in wholesale and retail sales, accommodation and catering, transportation, and information technology. Nonetheless, the average wage income growth slowed from 6.8% in H1 2023 to 5.8% in H1 2024, as economic growth moderated and domestic demand weakened.

Declining food prices dampened consumer price inflation in the first 7 months of 2024 to 0.2% from 0.5% a year ago (Figure 3.2.8). Nonfood prices grew by 0.8%. But, despite a recovery in the price of pork, food prices overall declined by 2.3% due to lower prices for fresh fruit, beef, and eggs. Core inflation (excluding food and energy prices) remained stable averaging 0.6% for the first 7 months of 2024. The recovery in global commodity prices contributed to a moderation in producer price deflation to 1.9% from 3.2% a year ago. Prices for newly constructed homes in 70 major cities fell the most in July since 2015, with the most significant drops in lower-tier cities.

Figure 3.2.8 Supply-Side Contributions to Growth

Inflation remained low due to declining food prices, with less producer price deflation.

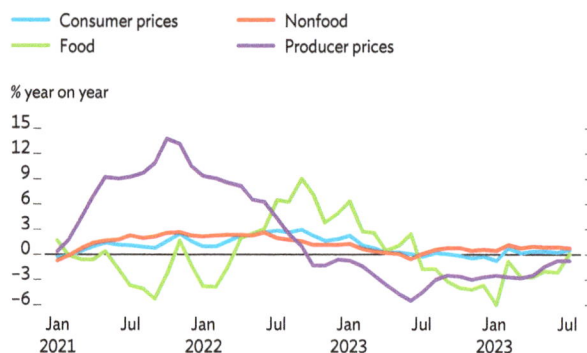

Source: CEIC Data Company.

Monetary policy gradually eased this year. The People's Bank of China (PBOC) lowered the reserve requirement ratio by 50 basis points in February 2024 and cut key policy rates in July—including the 7-day reverse repo rate, standing lending facility rate, and medium-term lending facility rate—to support credit growth and economic activity (Figure 3.2.9). It also reduced the 1-year loan prime rate from 3.45% to 3.35% and twice trimmed the 5-year loan prime rate, used to price mortgages, by a total of 35 basis points to 3.85%, to support the ailing real estate industry. The central bank also injected CNY350 billion into

Figure 3.2.9 Bank Lending and Policy Rates

Low inflation allowed some headroom for monetary easing and the central bank cut key policy rates for the first time this year in July.

- Lending rate, weighted average
- 1-year loan prime rate
- 1-year medium-term lending facility

Source: CEIC Data Company.

policy banks via the Pledged Supplementary Lending facility to provide low-cost funding to social housing and infrastructure.

Credit growth slowed on weak credit demand.
Outstanding total social financing—which includes bank loans, shadow bank financing, government and corporate bonds, and equity financing—was up by 8.2% year on year at the end of July 2024 but down from the 9.2% growth at end-July 2023 on weak credit demand (Figure 3.2.10). Outstanding loans grew by 8.1% year on year, down from 11.1% at the end of July 2023. Soft domestic demand and methodological

Figure 3.2.10 Growth in Broad Money, Credit Outstanding, and Government Bonds Outstanding

Despite an acceleration in the growth of government bonds, total social financing grew slowly as loan growth decelerated.

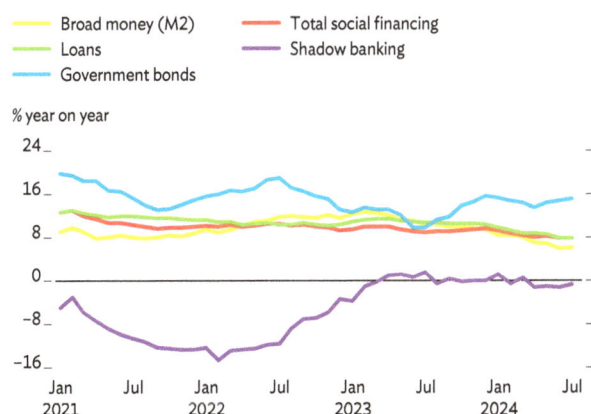

- Broad money (M2)
- Loans
- Government bonds
- Total social financing
- Shadow banking

Note: Shadow banking comprises entrust loans, trust loans, and banks' acceptance bills.
Sources: CEIC Data Company; Asian Development Bank estimates.

changes in calculating financial sector GDP contributed to the slowdown. At the same time, government bonds outstanding climbed by 15.4%, up from 10.1% a year ago, as government borrowing accelerated. Shadow bank financing outstanding decreased by 0.6% at the end of July from a year ago. Broad money growth slowed to 6.3% year on year at the end of July from 10.7% a year earlier.

The budget deficit widened from 2.5% of GDP in H1 2023 to 3.3% in H1 2024 as fiscal revenue declined (Figure 3.2.11). General government fiscal revenue decreased by 2.8% as tax revenue fell due to a high base last year and the impact of tax policies previously introduced for advanced manufacturing enterprises. Meanwhile, fiscal expenditure grew by 2.0%. New local government special bonds issued— not included in the general budget—amounted to CNY1.5 trillion by the end of June 2024, or 39.3% of the annual ceiling (Figure 3.2.12). The lower bond issuance in H1 was partly due to the high volume of bond issuance during the pandemic, restrictions on some high-risk regions from launching new projects, and the winding down of projects financed by the sovereign bonds issued in Q4 2023.

The current account surplus equaled 1.1% of GDP in H1 2024, slightly lower than the 1.6% in H1 2023, as the services trade deficit widened.
Driven by recovering cross-border tourism, the services

Figure 3.2.11 General Government Fiscal Revenue and Expenditure

The budget deficit widened as fiscal revenue declined despite slowing expenditure growth.

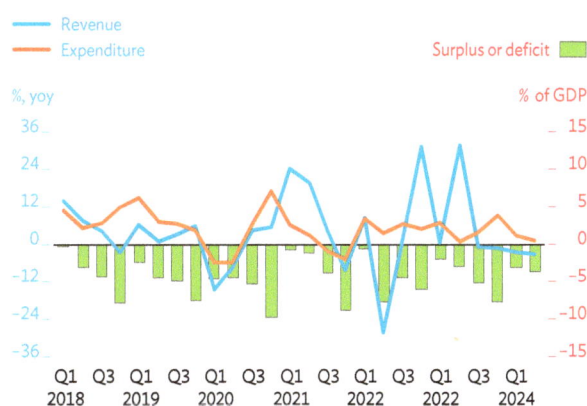

- Revenue
- Expenditure
- Surplus or deficit

GDP = gross domestic product, Q = quarter.
Note: Public finance budget only.
Sources: CEIC Data Company; Asian Development Bank estimates.

Figure 3.2.12 Local Government Special Bond Issues

Local government special bond issuance slowed in H1 2024 compared to previous years.

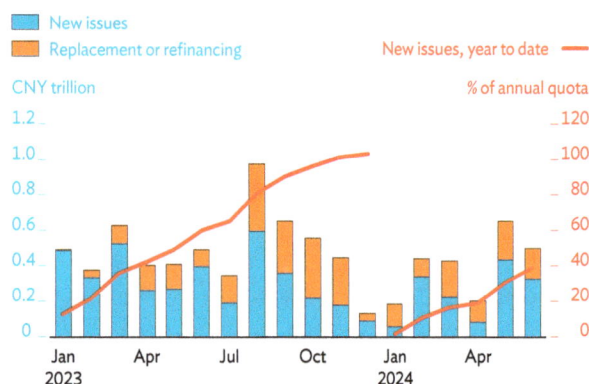

Sources: CEIC Data Company; Asian Development Bank estimates.

trade deficit widened from the equivalent of 1.1% of GDP in H1 2023 to 1.4% of GDP in H1 2024. The merchandise trade surplus was stable at 3.3% of GDP, slightly down from 3.4% in H1 2023 (Figure 3.2.13). In the first 7 months of 2024, merchandise exports surged by 4.0% in dollar terms and 5.5% by volume on increased overseas demand, especially from the US and Asia, and the global electronics cycle upturn. The expansion of machinery, integrated circuits, passenger and cargo ships, and household and home appliances led the export expansion. Geographically, the increase

Figure 3.2.13 Current Account Balance and Merchandise Trade

The merchandise trade surplus remained stable, while the trade deficit in services widened with the recovery in cross-border tourism.

GDP = gross domestic product, Q = quarter.
Note: January and February data are combined to exclude the Lunar New Year effect.
Sources: CEIC Data Company; Asian Development Bank estimates.

of exports to ASEAN countries and the US offset an export decline to the European Union (EU) and Japan. Imports grew by 2.8% in dollar terms and 5.1% by volume, driven by strong commodity imports and export processing.

Net foreign direct investment outflows increased from 0.6% of GDP in H1 2023 to 1.3 % in H1 2024. The increase reflected resilient outbound direct investment, which rose by 23% year on year in H1 2024, and lower foreign direct investment inflows. Geopolitical concerns added to the weak foreign investor sentiment. Net portfolio investment outflows slowed to $21.6 billion in H1 2024 from $56.5 billion in Q1 2023 on higher portfolio investment inflows ($32.2 billion). Official reserve assets reached $3.5 trillion at the end of July 2024, or $94.6 billion more than a year earlier. In the first 7 months, the renminbi depreciated by 0.73% against the US dollar and by 0.91% in real effective terms against a trade-weighted basket of currencies.

Prospects

GDP is forecast to grow by 4.8% in 2024, within the government's target of about 5.0%, and by 4.5% in 2025, as projected in ADO April 2024 (Table 3.2.1). The growth outlook remains balanced amid a prolonged correction in the property market and weak investor and consumer confidence. Continuing policy support for strategic industry and sustained and diversified export growth based on technology and cost advantage should mitigate some headwinds from the property market downturn and trade tensions with the US and EU. The government will likely accelerate bond issuance in the coming months to boost domestic investment as signaled during the Third

Table 3.2.1 Selected Economic Indicators in the People's Republic of China, %

The growth forecasts remain unchanged from ADO 2024, but the inflation forecast is revised downward for 2024 and 2025.

	2023	2024		2025	
		Apr	Sep	Apr	Sep
GDP growth	5.2	4.8	4.8	4.5	4.5
Inflation	0.2	1.1	0.5	1.5	1.2

GDP = gross domestic product.
Sources: CEIC Data Company; Asian Development Bank estimates.

Plenum's resolution and the Politburo meeting in July. Nevertheless, economic activity is expected to slow further in 2025 if the property market challenges and weak private consumption persist.

Investment should support domestic demand while the property market correction continues. On 13 March, the government released an action plan to promote the large-scale renewal of equipment and trade-in of consumer goods. In July, it backed the plan by allocating CNY300 billion in ultra-long bonds. The equipment upgrade policy, strong exports, and ongoing policy backing for high-tech manufacturing should boost investment this year and in 2025. Infrastructure investment should regain momentum with the expected acceleration of the local government special bond issuance in H2. However, the property sector recovery is expected to drag on the economy. The contraction in real estate investment will likely continue into 2025 with overall investment growth slowing further. Measures such as trade-in programs for consumer goods will not fundamentally prop up private consumption while weak consumer confidence, soft income growth, and adverse wealth effects from falling property prices persist.

On the supply side, export-led industrial growth will likely outpace growth in services this year. Within secondary industries, strong global demand and increased credit availability for certain industries—including semiconductors, high-tech equipment, artificial intelligence, and low-carbon technologies including electric vehicles (EVs), lithium-ion batteries, and renewables—will drive growth this year and next. Infrastructure investment and public projects will support construction. Growth in services will continue to normalize after the post-pandemic rebound in H2 2024 and 2025.

Global demand and the domestic cost advantage in manufacturing should bolster external trade amid foreign trade tensions. In May 2024, the US announced tariff hikes on $18 billion worth of its PRC imports, targeting strategic sectors such as EVs, batteries, steel, and critical minerals. In particular, the US quadrupled tariffs on PRC EVs to 100%. Later in June, the EU also announced additional duties of up to 38.1% on imported EVs from the PRC. The impact of these measures on exports should be limited. First, only a small volume of affected PRC exports (approximately 0.5% of PRC total exports in 2023) goes to the US.

Second, the EU duties will likely be offset by the significant cost advantage of EVs exported from the PRC over those produced in the EU. Third, given the robust demand for electronics and green technology products globally, price competitiveness should help carry the strong performance of PRC exports for the remainder of 2024 and into 2025. The services trade deficit is expected to rise as cross-border travel returns to pre-pandemic levels this year and next. On balance, the current account surplus will likely decline this year and next.

The labor market should benefit from manufacturing and government policy initiatives. The government aims to create 12 million new urban jobs and keep the unemployment rate below 5.5% in 2024. Strong growth in some services and manufacturing—such as high-end manufacturing, clean energy EVs, semiconductors, and robotics—are expected to boost employment. However, the challenge of youth unemployment will likely remain amid the increased supply of graduates. To address these challenges, the government announced several initiatives in June, including subsidies for companies hiring college graduates and a scheme to create at least 1 million internships annually for young people by the end of 2025.

Consumer price inflation is now forecast to be lower than the April projections. Average consumer price inflation was just 0.2% year on year in the first 7 months of this year amid weak domestic demand. But it should rise moderately in H2 from last year's low base. However, due to the persistent drop in food prices, price competition in industries such as EVs, solar photovoltaics, semiconductors, and steel, and the prolonged weak domestic demand, the consumer price inflation forecast has been revised down from 1.1% to 0.5% in 2024 and from 1.5% to 1.2% for 2025.

Expansionary fiscal policy will drive growth. Consolidated budget spending as a percentage of GDP will increase for the first time since 2020, according to the government's budget report. This will be supported by the issuance of CNY1 trillion in sovereign special bonds by November and accelerated bond issuance by local governments. Fiscal policy will support national strategic projects, high-end manufacturing, technology advancement, and small and medium-sized enterprises.

Monetary and credit policies will likely remain accommodative and complementary to fiscal policy. To bolster the property market, the PBOC will provide funds at low interest rates to 21 banking institutions that will use the funds to lend to state-owned enterprises for purchasing completed but unsold commercial homes. These will be converted into subsidized housing for low- and middle-income citizens. The PBOC will also provide low-interest funds to strategic sectors through its structural lending facilities. It has introduced a new re-lending facility to encourage equipment upgrades in manufacturing. However, banks' concerns over risk may temper the effectiveness of these policies.

The risks to the outlook are balanced. On the downside, potential threats include stronger-than-expected deterioration in the property market; escalation of trade tensions stemming from uncertainty around the US election outcome and associated trade policies, such as higher tariffs on PRC goods; and global fragmentation due to geopolitical issues. On the upside, acceleration and effective implementation of policy measures, including speedy implementation of policies announced in the Third Plenum, could raise consumer and investor confidence faster than expected, resulting in higher growth and inflation than forecast.

Other Economies

Hong Kong, China

The economy grew by 3.0% in the first half (H1) of 2024 from 2.2% in H1 2023, driven by a sharp recovery in exports. Mainly lifted by recovering external demand, GDP rose by 2.8% year on year in the first quarter (Q1), with larger investment growth pushing it up further to 3.3% in Q2. Goods exports grew by 6.8% in Q1 and by 7.5% in Q2, buoyed by sustained external demand. Exports to the People's Republic of China (PRC) continued to rise in Q2, while exports to the US and major Asian markets also improved. In tandem with higher growth, goods imports increased by 3.4% in H1 2024. Exports of services softened, however, from 9.4% growth year on year in Q1 to 1.4% in Q2 on slower growth in tourist arrivals, particularly from the PRC. In contrast, exports of transport and financial services expanded on

increased regional trade. Meanwhile, services imports grew by 15.2% in H1. In sum, net exports contributed 3.5 percentage points to growth in H1 2024. The robust export growth helped widen the current account surplus in Q1 2024, but the trend is not expected to continue through the rest of the year and in 2025.

Private consumption declined in H1 2024, while fixed investment increased. After growing by 1.2% in Q1, private consumption declined by 1.5% in Q2—the first contraction since Q3 2022 amid pandemic restrictions—as weaker demand for goods was only partly offset by stronger services consumption. Retail sales contracted by 13.5% year on year in Q2, despite a solid labor market and rising wages. This contraction was partly driven by a strong Hong Kong dollar, which reduced tourist spending and encouraged residents to increase overseas expenditure. In contrast, government consumption expenditure increased by 2.0% in Q2, after 4 consecutive quarters of contraction. Fixed investment rose by 3.1% in H1, adding 0.5 percentage points to growth. This was mostly due to a 16.0% expansion in buildings and construction in Q2, driven by public spending.

Growth forecasts for 2024 and 2025 remain unchanged from *April ADO 2024* projections (Table 3.2.2). The same growth drivers in H1 should provide a boost in H2 2024. A favorable labor market and government initiatives to boost sentiment should help private consumption recover, partially offsetting slowing export growth. Services exports may also pick up as tourism bounces back, especially should the US dollar—and thus the Hong Kong dollar—weaken. Public and private investment will rise as government projects are implemented and interest rates are cut in tandem with monetary policy easing in the US.

Table 3.2.2 Selected Economic Indicators in Hong Kong, China, %

Growth forecasts for 2024 and 2025 remain unchanged as rising net exports offset weaker domestic demand.

	2023	2024		2025	
		Apr	Sep	Apr	Sep
GDP growth	3.3	2.8	2.8	3.0	3.0
Inflation	2.1	2.3	1.8	2.3	2.3

GDP = gross domestic product.

Source: Asian Development Bank estimates.

Risks to this outlook include geopolitical tensions, especially given the upcoming US Presidential election, a continuing decrease in the attractiveness of Hong Kong, China as a PRC tourist destination, and rising outbound tourism.

The April inflation forecast is revised down for this year but maintained for 2025. Inflation averaged just 1.6% in H1 2024, although it rose to 2.5% in July due to the phase out of a housing subsidy in June. Inflation is expected to remain low in H2 2024 on slower growth, a strong Hong Kong dollar, and elevated interest rates. However, US monetary policy easing may still trigger slightly higher inflation in H2 2024 and in 2025.

Republic of Korea

Economic growth rose to 2.8% year on year in the first half (H1) of 2024 driven by exports. GDP grew by a higher-than-expected 3.3% in the first quarter (Q1) followed by 2.3% in Q2. After rising steadily since H2 2023, exports grew by 9.1% in H1 2024 on strong global demand for semiconductors (particularly memory chips) and automobiles. With lower imports, net exports added 3.4 percentage points to growth. However, weak domestic demand limited growth, with consumption adding just 0.7 points and investment subtracting 1.3 points. Private consumption moderated to 1.0% amid high borrowing costs and household debt, while public consumption growth remained small at 0.9% due to tightened fiscal policy. Lower investment in facilities and construction and a drawdown in inventories pulled down investment by 3.9%. On the supply side, manufacturing rebounded by 5.5% on robust exports and was the primary driver of growth in H1 2024. Services expanded by a tepid 1.8% reflecting subdued consumer spending, while agriculture contracted by 2.4%.

In August 2024, inflation significantly eased to the central bank's target of 2.0%, the lowest rate since March 2021. The decline was primarily driven by a drop in global oil prices and slower price increases in agricultural products. Consumer prices rose by 2.7% in the first 8 months of the year, with lower price increases across categories such as utilities and restaurants and hotels. Core inflation, which excludes volatile food and energy prices, has trended down averaging 2.3% year on year from January through August 2024 on the modest growth in domestic demand. Compared to the start of the year, the Korean won depreciated by 3.6%

against the US dollar as of end-August. The central bank has kept its policy rate at 3.50% since January 2023, while continuing to monitor domestic demand, inflation, currency depreciation and financial stability to determine the timing of a rate change.

The current account surplus increased from $35.5 billion in 2023 to $37.7 billion in H1 2024, equivalent to 4.1% of GDP. Robust export growth, particularly in semiconductors, and a decline in import on weak domestic demand led to a significant rise in the merchandise trade surplus. The services deficit also shrank to less than one half of the 2023 level, as inbound tourism increased. The current account is expected to remain in surplus for the remainder of 2024, supported by solid exports, though the surplus may narrow in 2025 as domestic demand strengthens.

The growth forecast for 2024 is more upbeat than in April following the strong Q1 performance, despite lingering headwinds (Table 3.2.3). Exports and manufacturing will continue to benefit from the technology export momentum this year and in 2025. The seasonally adjusted manufacturing purchasing managers' index remained expansionary for the fourth consecutive month in August, although a slowdown in new export orders compared to the previous month and softer business sentiment suggests some moderation can be expected. Weak retail sales and property sector data show lackluster domestic demand, but the further easing of price pressures and supportive government policies, particularly toward small businesses, could boost spending in H2 this year. The GDP forecast is thus revised upwards for 2024 and maintained for 2025. The growth outlook still faces risks of renewed global trade and geopolitical tensions, with the fragile property market a domestic risk.

Table 3.2.3 Selected Economic Indicators in the Republic of Korea, %

Growth is revised up for 2024 and maintained for 2025, with inflation forecasts retained for both years.

	2023	2024		2025	
		Apr	Sep	Apr	Sep
GDP growth	1.4	2.2	2.5	2.3	2.3
Inflation	3.6	2.5	2.5	2.0	2.0

GDP = gross domestic product.

Source: Asian Development Bank estimates.

April's inflation forecasts are maintained for both 2024 and 2025. The central bank expects inflation to stabilize around its 2% target level in H2 2024 as global price pressures dissipate. However, adverse weather and geopolitical events that could affect global commodity and freight prices remain key risks.

Mongolia

GDP grew by 5.6% year on year in the first half (H1) of 2024, fueled by mining and services. Mining output rose by 15.4%, contributing 1.8 percentage points to GDP growth as coal export volumes increased by 37.6% year on year on higher than projected demand from the People's Republic of China (PRC). This helped services—notably goods transport—to grow by 9.3% during the period, which added a further 4.4 points to growth. Net taxes and non-mining industry added another 2.3 points to growth. Agriculture dropped by 26.7% due to massive livestock losses during the harsh first quarter winter, deducting 3.9 points from growth. On the demand side, consumption was the largest driver of growth, boosted by moderating inflation. Domestic demand increased markedly, with household consumption contributing 12.1 points to growth, government consumption 9.3 points, and gross capital formation 6.2 points. However, net exports of goods and services deducted 21.9 points as exports declined in real terms while imports rose significantly.

The budget surplus was equivalent to 5.5% of GDP in H1 2024, compared to 6.6% during H1 2023. Revenues were 35.2% higher year on year as tax receipts, particularly from income and value-added taxes, as well as mineral royalties, rose significantly on continued growth in overall economic activity. Expenditure rose by 42.9% year on year, with substantial increases in both current and capital outlays. Fiscal spending—including higher public sector wages, which rose 171.8% year on year in H1 2024— is expected to increase further alongside sustained economic momentum.

The strong H1 2024 economic performance led to an upward adjustment to the growth forecast for the year (Table 3.2.4). Mining output is expected to remain robust for the rest of 2024, driven by sustained demand from the PRC for Mongolia's coking coal. Consumption, particularly government consumption, will also remain strong, supported by a recent budget

Table 3.2.4 Selected Economic Indicators in Mongolia, %

Growth should be higher than the April forecast this year, with inflation lower than earlier forecast in 2024 and higher in 2025.

	2023	2024		2025	
		Apr	Sep	Apr	Sep
GDP growth	7.4	4.1	5.5	6.0	6.0
Inflation	10.4	7.0	6.8	6.8	7.2

GDP = gross domestic product.
Sources: National Statistics Office of Mongolia. Statistical Information Services; Asian Development Bank estimates.

amendment that increased expenditures by 11.4% compared to the original budget. Robust growth should continue into 2025, fueled by continued expansion in mining, led by the Oyu Tolgoi mine. A recovery in agriculture and growth in services and non-mining industries will also contribute to GDP growth, bolstered by an expected increase in government expenditure.

The inflation forecast is revised down for 2024 and up for 2025. Average consumer price inflation was 6.5% year on year in H1 2024, down from 11.6% in H1 2023 and within the central bank's 6.0%–8.0% target. In May 2024, the central bank reduced the policy rate to 11%. Nevertheless, inflation dropped to 5.1% year on year in June, down from 5.7% in May. Price increases were muted across most of the consumer price basket in H1 2024. Transport prices were 0.3% lower than in H1 2023. However, higher public sector wages and energy tariff adjustments, if implemented, will likely increase price pressures during H2 2024 and into 2025. Domestic demand will likely remain high in 2025 on faster growth and increased government spending.

The current account deficit widened to 5.3% of GDP in H1 2024. Merchandise imports grew by 29.8% year on year, narrowing the merchandise trade surplus. Deficits in services trade and the primary income balance also widened during the period. The current account is expected to remain in deficit in 2024 and 2025 due to sustained demand for imports. Foreign exchange reserves averaged $5.0 billion in H1 2024, equivalent to 4.2 months of goods and services imports—up from $3.6 billion (3.4 months) during H1 2023.

There are a number of risks to the outlook. Lower growth in the PRC can reduce the country's demand for Mongolia's commodity exports. And any delays in boosting output from the Oyu Tolgoi mine can reduce mining's positive impact on economic growth, government revenues, and the external position. Disruptions from geopolitical tensions can constrain access to imported goods and production inputs, push up prices, and dampen investor confidence. Finally, any further climate-related shocks may require unanticipated government expenditure and hamper the recovery in agriculture.

Taipei,China

GDP expanded by 5.8% in the first half (H1) of 2024, contrasting sharply with the 1.0% contraction in H1 2023. After an export-driven 6.6% rise in the first quarter (Q1), growth slowed to 5.1% in Q2 as private consumption moderated and net exports contracted as robust investments spurred imports to grow faster than exports. Overall, however, exports remained the key driver of growth in H1, with net exports growing by 19.7% and contributing 2.5 percentage points to growth. Private consumption grew by 3.6% in H1 2024, contributing 1.8 points. Government consumption rose modestly (1.6%), contributing 0.2 points. The government's 2024 budget shows the fiscal deficit widening to 1.9% of GDP from 0.9% in 2023 largely due to lower revenues. However, tax revenue increased in H1 while expenditure was lower than expected, narrowing the deficit in H1 below what was initially programmed. Strong exports led firms to raise planned investment, spurring gross fixed capital formation to grow by 5.1%, reversing the 9.4% contraction in H1 2023, contributing 1.3 points to GDP growth.

Strong demand for artificial intelligence (AI)-related goods is driving exports. Although exports of certain electronic products, including electronic integrated circuits, fell by 5.6%, exports of AI-related products including central processing units, computer peripherals and data storage jumped by 109%. Exports to the US grew by 61% followed by ASEAN at 22.6%. Exports to the People's Republic of China (PRC), however, fell by 2.2%. The strong export demand for goods along with higher remittances widened the current account surplus to 19.1% of GDP in H1 from 11.6% in the same period last year. The surplus is expected to narrow in 2025 as investment will drive imports higher.

Growth in 2024 is now expected to be higher than that projected in April, moderating next year. The stronger H1 export growth has put the economy on a higher growth trajectory. However, export orders, a leading indicator of export performance, declined by 5.5% in June. This suggests export growth could slow somewhat in H2, although it will likely remain robust. Export growth is expected to fuel more investment, which increases imports and limits the contribution of net exports to growth. For 2025, export growth is projected to continue moderating from its strong 2024 base and private consumption should ease due to weak growth in real earnings. This should lower GDP growth next year back to the level projected in April (Table 3.2.5).

Table 3.2.5 Selected Economic Indicators in Taipei,China, %

The growth forecast is raised for 2024 and maintained for 2025, while inflation projections remain unchanged.

	2023	2024		2025	
		Apr	Sep	Apr	Sep
GDP growth	1.3	3.0	3.5	2.7	2.7
Inflation	2.5	2.3	2.3	2.0	2.0

GDP = gross domestic product.
Source: Asian Development Bank estimates.

Inflation slowed gradually to average 2.3% year on year in H1 2024. While January inflation was 1.8%, June inflation was considerably higher at 2.4%, with much volatility in the intervening months. Nevertheless, core inflation has fallen and remained flat at 1.8% year on year in Q2, suggesting that broader underlying price pressures are fading. Food prices were the key driver of inflation, averaging 3.6% year on year for H1 2024 while services inflation averaged 2.6% year on year, spurred by robust private consumption. Looking ahead, oil prices are expected to remain mostly subdued, there are signs of food prices easing, and the effects of a hike in the central bank's policy rate in March is expected to take hold in the coming months. On balance, the *ADO April 2024* forecasts for 2024 and 2025 should stand.

The concentration of growth in AI-related goods exports coupled with geopolitical risks poses a downside risk to growth. Although the AI boom is fueling growth, other electronics that make up the bulk of exports are lagging. The export boom, therefore, is at risk should exports to the PRC remain weak due to its subdued growth and the ongoing reconfiguration of supply chains, geopolitical tensions lead to global trade disruptions, or wider conflict in the Middle East raise oil prices and inflation.

SOUTH ASIA

The subregional economic growth forecast is unchanged from *ADO April 2024* for 2024 and slightly lower for 2025. The growth outlook for most countries in the subregion is either unchanged or improved since April. The exceptions are Bangladesh and Maldives, where lower growth is forecast in both 2024 and 2025. Most inflation forecasts are little changed. Risks to the outlook are balanced in India but on the downside in other South Asian economies.

Subregional Assessment and Prospects

Aggregate subregional GDP is forecast to expand by 6.3% in 2024 and 6.5% in 2025 (Figure 3.3.1). The projection for 2024 is unchanged from *ADO April 2024*, but the projection for 2025 is slightly lower than in April. Subregional forecasts for growth in South Asia reflect in large part growth in India, as its economy is weighted at almost 80% of the subregional economy.

India's growth prospects remain robust. GDP growth is expected at 7.0% in fiscal year 2024 (FY2024, ending 31 March 2025) and 7.2% in FY2025, both as forecast in *ADO April 2024*. While GDP growth slowed to 6.7% year on year in the first quarter of FY2024, it is expected to accelerate in the coming quarters with improvement in agriculture and a largely robust outlook for industry and services. Exports in FY2024 will be higher than earlier projected, led by larger services exports, particularly in IT and professional services. Growth in merchandise exports will be relatively muted in FY2024 and FY2025, though some segments, notably electronics, may experience faster growth. Private consumption is expected to improve, driven by rural consumption fueled by stronger agriculture and by already robust urban consumption. The outlook for private investment is upbeat, but growth in public

Figure 3.3.1 Gross Domestic Product Growth in South Asia

The forecast for 2024 remains as in ADO April 2024, but slightly revised down for 2025.

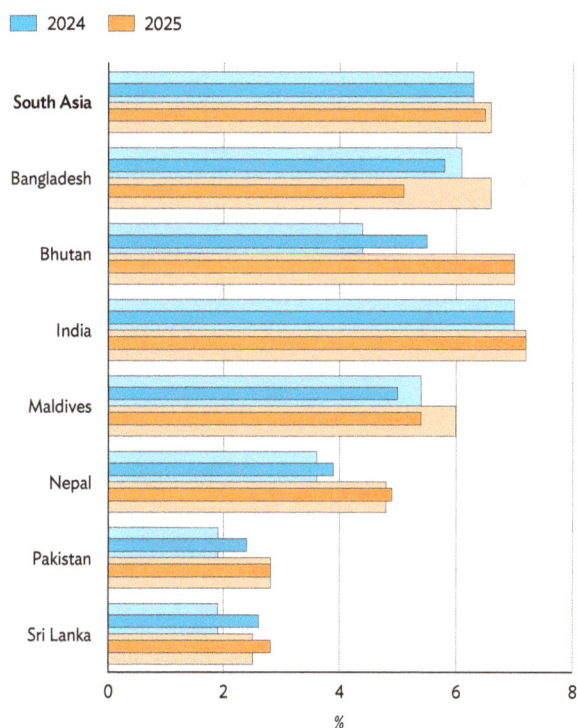

Note: Lighter-colored bars are *Asian Development Outlook April 2024* forecasts.
Source: *Asian Development Outlook* database (accessed 5 September 2024).

The subregional assessment and prospects was written by Rana Hasan, Kiyoshi Taniguchi, and Mia Andrea Soriano, consultant. The section on Bangladesh was written by Barun K. Dey and Chandan Sapkota; Bhutan by Sonam Lhendup; India by Chinmaya Goyal and consultant Simran Uppal; Maldives by Elisabetta Gentile and consultants Macrina Mallari and Nasheeda Rasheed; Nepal by Manbar Singh Khadka and Neelina Nakarmi; Pakistan by Marcel Schroder, Khadija Ali, and Maleeha Rizwan; Sri Lanka by Lakshini Fernando, Nirukthi Kariyawasam, and Dinuk de Silva. ADB placed on hold its regular assistance in Afghanistan effective 15 August 2021.

capital expenditure, heretofore high, will moderate in FY2025. Efforts toward fiscal consolidation are expected to drive down the fiscal deficit to a level last seen before COVID-19, reflecting robust revenue collection and restrained current expenditure. A recent policy announcement offering workers and firms employment-linked incentives could boost labor demand and bolster job creation starting in FY2025.

Afghanistan's economy is likely to have grown modestly in FY2024 (ended 20 March 2024). Growth is thought to have resulted from expanded production in mining and quarrying, retail, and transport. However, the country's economic outlook remains highly uncertain and at risk of stagnation in the short and medium term for the lack of adequate productive capacity.

Bangladesh recorded GDP growth in FY2024 (ended 30 June 2024) lower than earlier expected. This result came as reduced export demand and domestic energy shortages took their toll on industrial growth, and as adverse weather constrained agriculture. GDP is now expected to grow by 5.1% in FY2025, which is lower than projected in *ADO April 2024* to take into account adverse effects from political unrest in July and August and from recent floods. Further, fiscal and monetary policies are expected to be tight, subduing consumption and investment demand. The forecast is highly uncertain as significant downside risks muddy the macroeconomic outlook. These risks arise mostly from continuing political uncertainty, an insecure law-and-order situation, and financial sector vulnerabilities.

Bhutan's growth prospects in 2024 are revised up by a little over 1 percentage point to 5.5%. The growth forecast for 2025 is maintained at 7.0%. In addition to enhanced electricity output from the commissioning of the Punatsangchhu II hydropower plant, contributors to growth in 2024 and 2025 will include a sharp rise in government expenditure, higher tourist arrivals, and the lifting of a credit moratorium on construction in July 2024.

In Maldives, growth forecasts for this year and the next are lowered. Robust growth in tourism is outweighed by lower output from fisheries and dampened construction activity due to a planned reduction in public sector investment as the government attempts to contain overall and primary fiscal deficits. Downside risk to the outlook arises from Maldives' soaring public debt and thin foreign exchange buffers.

Nepal's economy grew at 3.9% in FY2024 (ended mid-July 2024), higher than expected. This reflects improved agricultural production, higher electricity generation, and increased tourist arrivals. Growth is expected to accelerate further in FY2025, fueled by an increase in planned infrastructure projects and their accelerated implementation, continued monetary easing, ongoing finance sector reform, and the revitalization of tourism and related services.

Growth in Pakistan rebounded to 2.4% in FY2024 (ended 30 June 2024). Economic activity was boosted by fiscal discipline, a market-determined exchange rate, energy sector efficiency, climate resilience, and an improved business environment. Growth is likely to accelerate in FY2025 on the implementation of a comprehensive economic reform program agreed with the International Monetary Fund.

The Sri Lankan GDP growth forecast for 2024 is revised up to 2.6%. In the first quarter, industry expanded faster than anticipated alongside modest growth in services and agriculture. Forward-looking indicators suggest continued robust growth in 2024 and beyond, supported by looser monetary policy, better public financial management, and progress in debt restructuring. Downside risks include a loss in reform momentum and delay in finalizing debt-relief agreements.

The forecast for subregional inflation in 2024 is retained at 7.0% and increased slightly to 6.1% in 2025 (Figure 3.3.2). The upward revision for 2025 reflects mainly higher projected inflation in Bangladesh, which rose to an average of 9.7% in FY2024 because agricultural production weakened, electricity prices were adjusted up, domestic fuel prices underwent periodic adjustment under an automated fuel-pricing mechanism, and the currency depreciated. Inflation is expected to accelerate further to 10.1% in FY2025 with supply-side disruption and higher import costs. In India, the FY2024 inflation forecast is revised up slightly to accommodate higher food prices, while the forecast for FY2025 is maintained in the expectation that core inflation will rise as food inflation moderates.

Figure 3.3.2 Inflation in South Asia

The subregional forecast is unchanged for 2024 but revised up for 2025, reflecting mainly higher projected inflation in Bangladesh.

■ 2024   ■ 2025

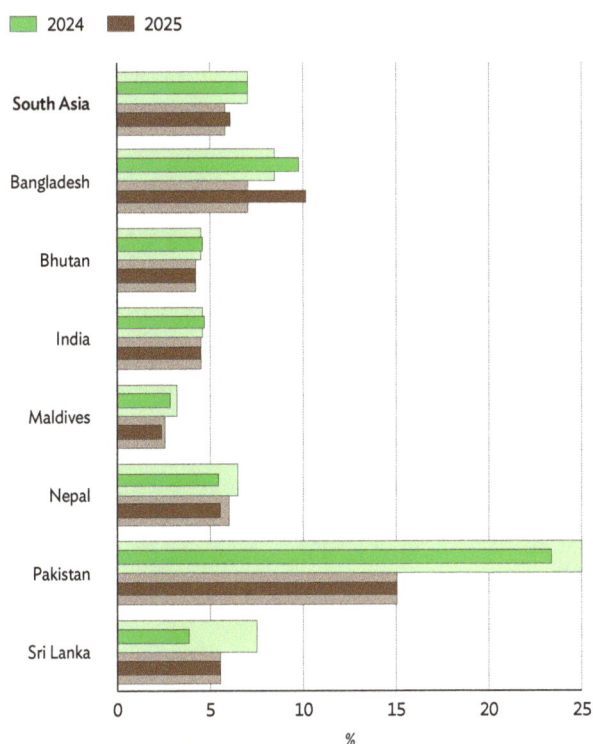

Note: Lighter-colored bars are *Asian Development Outlook April 2024* forecasts.
Source: *Asian Development Outlook* database (accessed 5 September 2024).

The outlook for inflation elsewhere in South Asia is mixed. The inflation forecast for Bhutan is revised slightly up for 2024 due to higher-than-expected food prices; the April forecast for 2025 is retained. Inflation in Maldives is expected to decline in 2024, reflecting discounts on water and electricity granted by utility companies and delays in the move from price subsidies to targeted subsidies; the inflation forecast for 2025 is lowered on easing of global commodity prices. In Nepal, the inflation forecast is revised down for FY2024 as the increase in food prices is offset by moderating prices for fuel and other nonfood items; the FY2025 inflation forecast is also revised down on the assumption of a normal harvest and a modest decline in inflation in India, the country's largest trade partner. Inflation in Sri Lanka was muted in the first half of 2024 owing to substantial reductions in utility prices, Sri Lankan rupee appreciation, and weak consumption demand; the inflation forecast for FY2025 is maintained, however, on the expectation of higher economic growth.

In Afghanistan, the consumer price index dropped by 7.7% in FY2024. Contributors to deflation were the appreciation of the afghani against the currencies of the country's major trade partners, notably Pakistan and Iran, and falling foreign currency prices for imported products.

In Pakistan, average inflation eased to 23.4% in FY2024 from 29.2% in FY2023. Inflation improved thanks to a tight monetary policy and a decline in food price inflation owing to increased agricultural production.

Risks to the outlook are balanced in India but on the downside in other South Asian economies. Significant risks include high public debt, weak external reserves positions, geopolitical tensions, and political uncertainties.

Bangladesh

GDP growth was steady in fiscal year 2024 (FY2024, ended 30 June 2024) but lower than expected. Demand continued to be held down by elevated inflation, tight global monetary conditions, and other macroeconomic challenges. Inflation remained elevated due to high commodity and energy prices and currency depreciation. The current account deficit narrowed following a drop in both exports and imports. Following political unrest and supply disruption, growth in FY2025 is expected to moderate, but inflation is projected to edge up into the double digits. Restoring and sustaining macroeconomic stability depends on accelerated reforms to raise revenue for a better fiscal balance, stabilize the finance sector through better interest and exchange rate regimes, and diversify the economy.

Updated Assessment

GDP growth is estimated at 5.8% in FY2024, lower than 6.1% projected in *ADO April 2024* but the same as in FY2023 (Figure 3.3.3). Reflecting reduced export demand and domestic energy shortages, industry growth moderated by 1.7 percentage points to 6.7% in FY2024 as growth in large-scale manufacturing fell from 8.4% in FY2023 to 6.6% in FY2024. Growth also moderated in agriculture, to 3.2% from 3.4% in the previous fiscal year, due to inclement weather

Figure 3.3.3 Supply-Side Contributions to Growth

Growth stagnated because of weak external demand in FY2024 and is forecast to drop in FY2025 following political unrest and floods.

- Agriculture
- Industry
- Services
- Gross domestic product growth, %

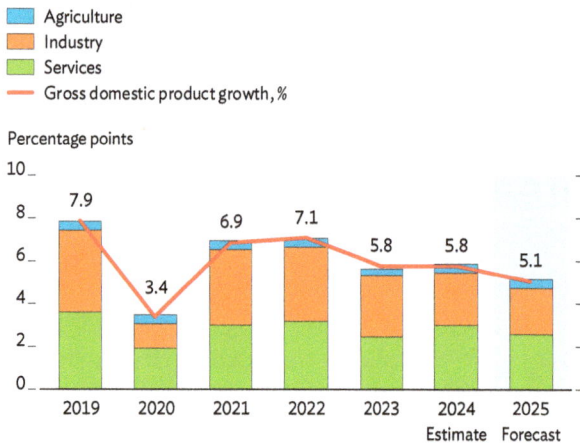

Note: Years are fiscal years ending on 30 June of that year.
Sources: Bangladesh Bureau of Statistics; Asian Development Bank estimates.

including floods and cyclones. Service growth, however, accelerated to 5.8% from 5.4% with better performances in financial, public administration, education, and health services.

On the demand side, domestic demand increased marginally in FY2024 and growth in net exports slowed (Figure 3.3.4). Despite high inflation, growth in private consumption edged up, aided by higher remittances, while government austerity

Figure 3.3.4 Demand-Side Contributions to Growth

A lower contribution from net exports moderated growth.

- Consumption
- Investment
- Net exports
- Statistical discrepancy
- Gross domestic product growth, %

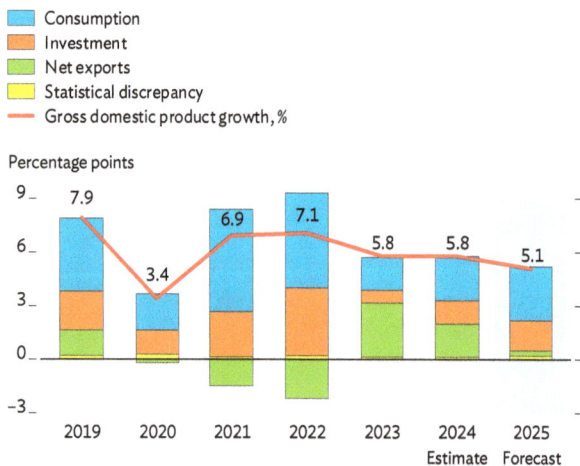

Note: Years are fiscal years ending on 30 June of that year.
Sources: Bangladesh Bureau of Statistics; Asian Development Bank estimates.

measures slowed public consumption growth. Private investment increased, reflecting steady but moderating growth in credit to the private sector. Owing to implementation bottlenecks and foreign exchange shortages, expenditure achieved in the government's annual development program was just 80.9% of the budgeted amount in FY2024, down from 85.2% in FY2023.

Inflation accelerated to an average of 9.7% in FY2024 from 9.0% in FY2023 (Figure 3.3.5). Food inflation increased to 10.7% in FY2024 from 8.7% in FY2023, but nonfood inflation decreased to 8.9% from 9.4%. The main causes of worsening inflation were weaker agricultural production, upward adjustment to electricity prices, periodic adjustments to domestic fuel prices under an automated fuel pricing mechanism, and marked depreciation of the Bangladesh taka against the US dollar. Inflation increased to 11.7% in July 2024 from 9.7% in July 2023 owing to a 14.1% increase in food prices.

Figure 3.3.5 Monthly Inflation

Price pressure accelerated in FY2024.

- Food
- Nonfood
- Overall

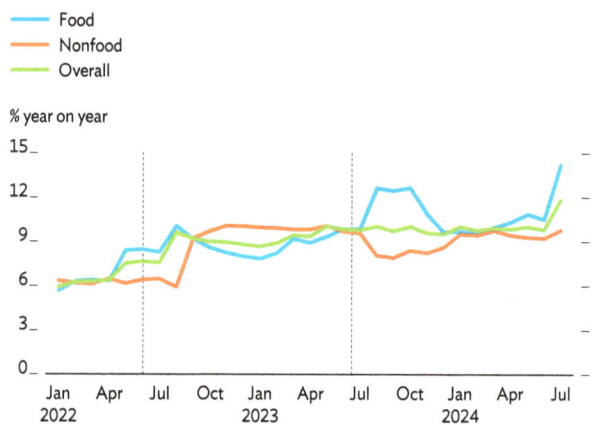

FY = fiscal year.
Source: Bangladesh Bank. 2024. *Monthly Economic Trends.* August.

Money supply growth dropped to 7.7% in FY2024 from 10.5% in FY2023. Growth in credit to the public sector plummeted to 9.6% from 35.0% in FY2023 as the government and other public sector organizations contained expenditure as an austerity measure, favoring priority projects (Figure 3.3.6). Private sector credit in the same period grew by 9.8%, slowing from 10.6% in FY2023 because of higher interest rates and import restrictions. To rein in credit growth and

Figure 3.3.6 Monetary Indicators

Credit growth moderated in 2024 as contractionary monetary policy came into effect.

- Broad money
- Net credit to the government
- Credit to the private sector
- Net foreign assets
- Domestic credit

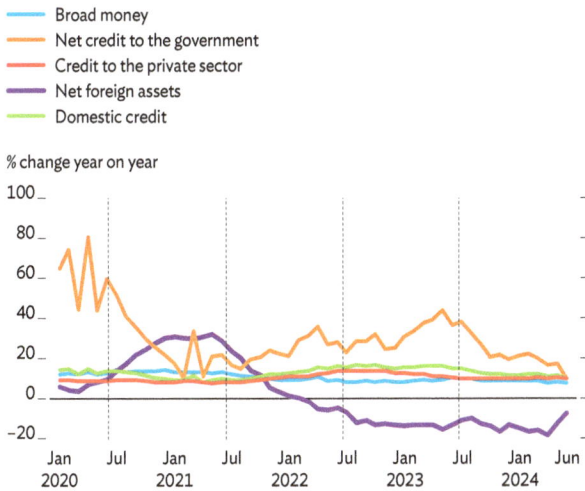

Source: Bangladesh Bank. 2024. *Major Economic Indicators: Monthly Update.* July.

inflation, Bangladesh Bank, the central bank, withdrew caps on lending and deposit rates in July 2023 and linked bank lending rates to the 6-month moving average treasury bill rate (SMART), which allowed banks' lending rates to move upward. However, the central bank abolished the SMART in May 2024, considering it inadequate to control inflation, and left interest rates fully market based. It also raised its policy repo rate to 8.5% to minimize the impact of currency devaluation. Consequently, the weighted average deposit and lending rates of banks and nonbank financial institutions increased. The call money rate also increased, to 9.1% in FY2024 from 6.1% in FY2023.

The fiscal deficit is estimated at 4.6% of GDP in FY2024, as in FY2023. The government's ambitious fiscal targets in the FY2024 revised budget were not achieved. Revenue collection by the National Board of Revenue (which accounts for 90% of all collections) increased by 15.3% in FY2024, compared to 30.4% growth set in the FY2024 revised budget, and came mainly from higher receipts from value-added tax and income tax. Public spending also rose more slowly than the programmed rate of 24.5%. It grew by only 14.6% in the first 9 months, constrained by expenditure rationalization that aimed to tame twin inflationary and foreign exchange pressures.

Revised data show the current account deficit narrowing sharply in FY2024. It fell to $6.5 billion, equal to 1.4% of GDP, from $11.6 billion in FY2023, or 2.6% of GDP (Figure 3.3.7). Both exports and imports declined, but remittances grew. Exports decreased by 5.9% to $40.8 billion as global demand remained weak (Figure 3.3.8). Specifically, exports of knitwear, frozen food, leather, jute goods, and engineering products declined. Imports declined by 10.6% to $63.2 billion on import restrictions aimed to stem a marked decline

Figure 3.3.7 Current Account Components

The current account deficit narrowed in FY2024 on lower imports and higher remittance inflows.

- Exports
- Imports
- Net services
- Net income
- Remittances
- Other net transfers
- Current account balance

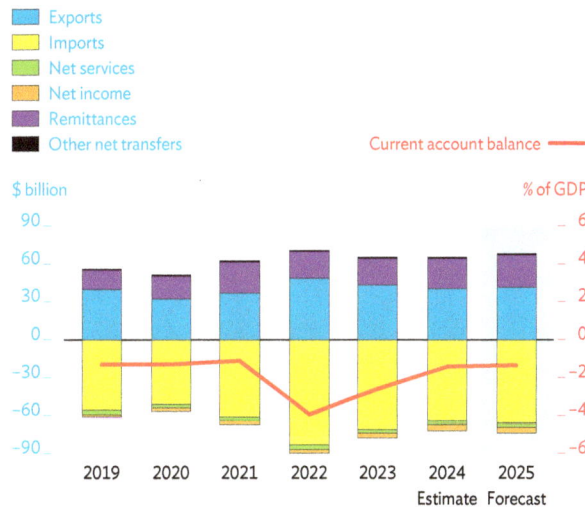

FY = fiscal year, GDP = gross domestic product.
Note: Years are fiscal years ending on 30 June of that year.
Source: Bangladesh Bank.

Figure 3.3.8 Monthly Exports and Imports

The trade deficit narrowed as imports declined.

- Exports
- Imports

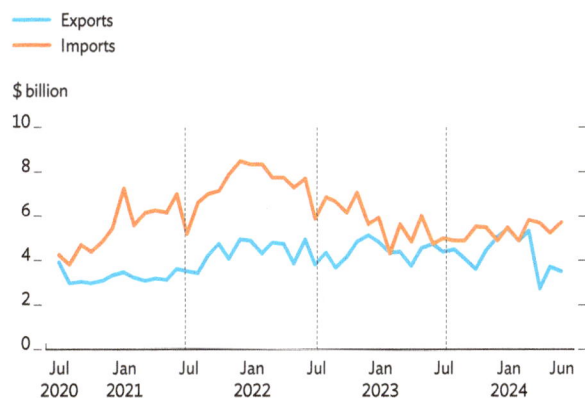

Source: Bangladesh Bank. 2024. *Major Economic Indicators: Monthly Update.* July.

in foreign exchange reserves. Imports of intermediate goods decreased by 9.1%, reflecting lower imports for garments and other manufactures. Imports of capital goods decreased by 21.9%. Remittances picked up to $23.9 billion, aided by sharp taka depreciation, a 2.5% cash incentive on remittances transferred through formal channels, and ease of transfers through mobile financial services. Based on the latest export data, the financial account recorded a surplus of $4.5 billion in FY2024, down from $6.9 billion the previous year and gross foreign exchange reserves shrank by $4.4 billion to $26.8 billion, or cover for 4.4 months of imports of goods and services (Figure 3.3.9).

The taka depreciated by 10.2% against the US dollar in FY2024 (Figure 3.3.10). On 8 May 2024, the central bank adopted a unified exchange rate regime

that allowed banks to determine the rate based on the market and raised the crawling peg reference exchange rate to Tk117 per dollar from Tk110 per dollar.

Prospects

GDP is expected to grow by 5.1% in FY2025, lower than the projection in *ADO April 2024* (Table 3.3.1). The forecast is highly uncertain because the economic impact from political unrest in July and August and from recent floods has yet to be adequately assessed. Economic activity was already slowing prior to July as industry had weakened. Manufacturing output, notably readymade garments, will lag further following disruption at factories and at ports, backlogging shipments. Service output was also hindered by the political unrest and flooding and will be further affected if nonperforming loans worsen and other banking vulnerabilities persist. Tight monetary and fiscal policies will continue to subdue consumption and investment demand. Port disruption and weak external demand will slow export growth.

Figure 3.3.9 Gross Foreign Exchange Reserves

Central bank reserves stabilized.

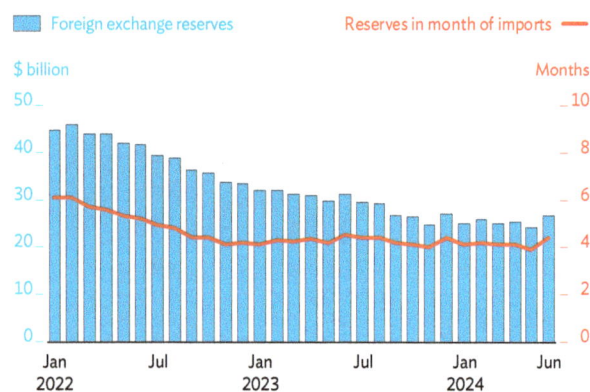

Source: Bangladesh Bank.

Figure 3.3.10 Exchange Rates

The taka depreciated markedly against the dollar.

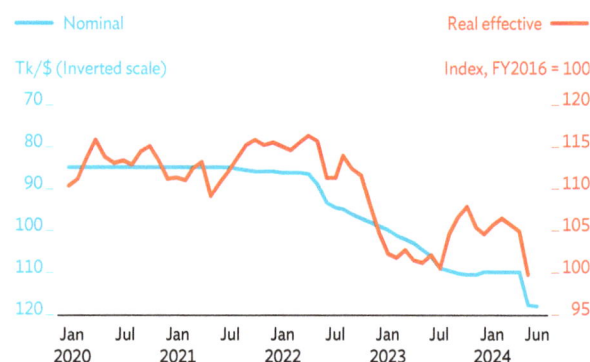

FY = fiscal year.
Source: Bangladesh Bank.

Table 3.3.1 Selected Economic Indicators in Bangladesh, %

Growth forecasts are revised down because of weak global demand and political unrest, while inflation forecasts are revised up on elevated prices in the first half of 2024.

	2023	2024		2025	
		Apr	Sep	Apr	Sep
GDP growth	5.8	6.1	5.8	6.6	5.1
Inflation	9.0	8.4	9.7	7.0	10.1

GDP = gross domestic product.
Note: Years are fiscal years ending on 30 June of that year.
Sources: Bangladesh Bureau of Statistics; Asian Development Bank estimates.

Inflation is projected to increase to 10.1% in FY2025, higher than the April forecast. Elevated food and nonfood prices in the first half of the fiscal year reflect supply-side disruption and higher import costs due to currency depreciation, pushing up inflation forecasts. However, inflationary pressures are expected to moderate in the second half of the fiscal year as tight monetary and fiscal policies lower domestic demand.

The central bank's monetary policy statement indicates tight monetary policy continuing in FY2025. In a statement presented before the political unrest, the central bank had committed to maintaining a contractionary monetary policy, adjusting the policy repo rate upward to 8.5%, the standing deposit facility rate to 7.0%, and the standing lending facility rate to 10.0%. It had also planned to streamline open market operations, cease currency swaps with and among banks, and refrain from lending to finance the budget deficit. In line with its statement, the central bank again increased its repo rate by 50 basis point to 9.0% on 25 August, the standing deposit facility rate to 7.5%, and the standing lending facility rate to 10.5%. It will likely raise the policy rate further as needed to manage inflationary expectations.

The FY2025 budget plans a deficit equal to 4.6% of GDP, narrower than the 4.7% target in the revised FY2024 budget. Fiscal revenue is slated to grow to 9.6% of GDP while expenditure is contained at 14.2% of GDP. Current expenditure is projected to increase by 8.0% and capital expenditure by 8.2%. About 63.0% of the fiscal deficit will be financed domestically, 85.5% from banks and 14.5% from other sources, mostly the sale of national saving certificates. However, given the state of public finance following the political unrest, these revenue and expenditure targets may be somewhat ambitious. The interim government expects to revise its budget estimates according to realistic projections for revenue mobilization and expenditure consolidation. The revised budget will include a number of measures to expand the tax base and will recognize that higher interest payments on outstanding public debt accumulated in recent years will constrain public capital spending.

The external position is expected to remain weak in FY2025. The current account deficit is forecast to equal to 1.3% of GDP, little changed from FY2024. Imports will likely grow at a slightly faster pace than in FY2024 while export growth continues to slow, but high remittance inflows should narrow the current account deficit marginally in FY2025. Tighter policies and low foreign exchange reserves will limit import growth, and supply disruption in the first quarter will constrain export growth. Growth in workers' remittances will be aided by a weakened currency and improved ease of transfer through formal banking channels. Pressure on foreign exchange reserves is likely to remain in the near term. However, continued alignment of the exchange rate through further widening of the currency band, monetary policy

tightening, import compression measures, robust remittance inflows, and foreign investment, should lead to a build up of reserves over the medium term.

Significant downside risks muddy the macroeconomic outlook. These risks arise from evolving political uncertainties, the law-and-order situation, data gaps and integrity, the challenge to achieve fiscal objectives, finance sector vulnerabilities, and weak external demand. In the face of these risks, the interim government has formed a committee to prepare a white paper that transparently lays out the state of the economy and recommends reforms for macroeconomic stability, achieving the Sustainable Development Goals, and mitigating challenges that will arise after Bangladesh graduates from the least-developed country category in 2026. The government also plans to form three task forces to lay out a road map for banking sector reform.

India

GDP growth in fiscal year 2024 (FY2024, ending 31 March 2025) and FY2025 is forecast at 7% and 7.2%, respectively, the same as in ADO April 2024. Growth slowed year on year (yoy) in the first quarter (Q1) of FY2024 but is expected to rise in the coming months on improved agricultural performance and higher government spending. Industry and services are expected to continue performing robustly. The current account deficit will remain moderate, helped by strong service exports and remittances. Elevated food prices will likely mean higher inflation in FY2024 than previously forecast, but inflation should moderate in FY2025 to the earlier forecast for that year.

Updated Assessment

GDP growth slowed to 6.7% yoy in Q1 FY2024 as net taxes rose less than in Q4 FY2023 (Figure 3.3.11). Growth in agriculture improved from 0.6% yoy in Q4 FY2023 to 2.0%, and in services from 6.7% to 7.2%, while industry growth remained stable at 8.3%. Industry growth was led by construction and utilities, as strong demand fueled growth above 10%, while manufacturing expansion slowed to 7.1% mainly because of higher input costs. Financial, real estate, and professional services grew by 7.1%, reflecting robust demand, while public administration, defense, and other services grew by 9.5%. Net taxes rose by only 4.1% in Q1 FY2024, down from 22.2% in Q4 FY2023 when government subsidies had declined from higher payouts in response to COVID-19, especially for fertilizer.

Strong private consumption and investment raised domestic demand in Q1 FY2024 even as public spending moderated (Figure 3.3.12). Improved

Figure 3.3.11 Supply-Side Contributions to Growth

Expansion in industry and services drove growth in Q1 FY2024.

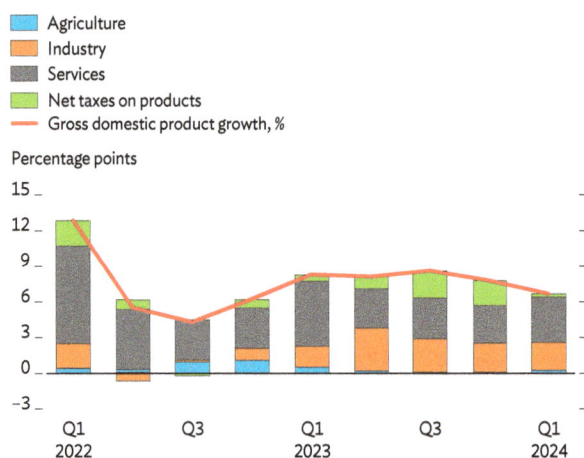

Q = quarter.
Notes: Years are fiscal years ending on 31 March of the next year. Growth rates are year on year. Net taxes on products are tax receipts minus subsidies.
Source: CEIC Data Company.

Figure 3.3.12 Demand-Side Contributions to Growth

Recovery in private consumption and strong exports drove growth in Q1 FY2024.

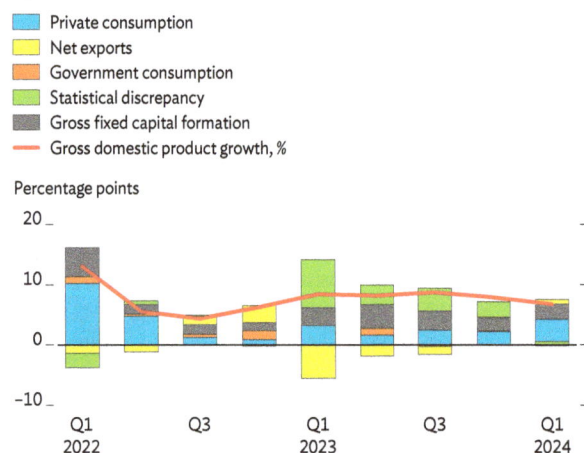

Q = quarter.
Note: Years are fiscal years ending on 31 March of the next year.
Source: CEIC Data Company.

rural consumption raised private consumption growth to 7.5% in Q1 FY2024 yoy from 4.0% in the previous quarter. Public consumption contracted, however, by 0.2%, as a general election held in the quarter impacted government works. Gross fixed capital formation grew by 7.5% despite sharp contraction in government capital expenditure, implying strong growth in investment by private corporations and households. Export growth in real terms was strong at 8.7%, led by services, while import growth fell to 4.4%, reducing net exports' drag on GDP growth.

Consumer prices rose by 5.0% yoy during the first half (H1) of 2024, above the monetary policy target of 4.0%. The main cause was rising prices for food, which is weighted at more than 45% in the consumer price index basket. Food prices have remained elevated in 2024, as prices for vegetables, pulses, cereals, and other staples rose with adverse weather, notably heatwaves, that caused supply shortages. On the other hand, core inflation, which excludes food and energy prices, declined to 3.3%, and fuel prices dropped steeply after the government reduced household gas prices in March 2024 (Figure 3.3.13). In July 2024, inflation dropped to 3.5% yoy from a high 7.4% in July 2023, while food inflation moderated to 5.1%.

Monetary policy has remained focused on bringing inflation closer to the 4% target and keeping it there. The policy rate of the Reserve Bank of India, the central bank, has remained stable since February

Figure 3.3.13 Inflation

Inflation remained close to 5% in the first half of 2024 due to elevated food inflation but moderated in July.

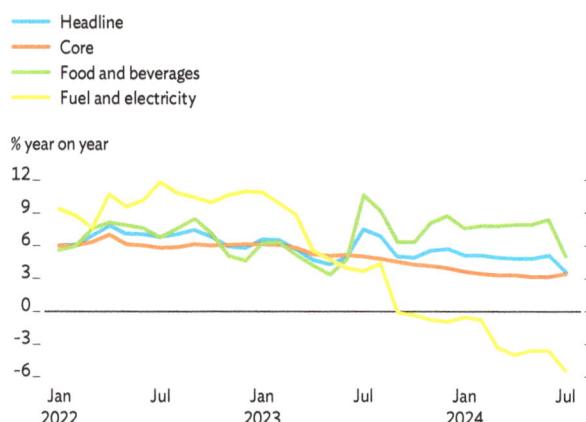

Source: CEIC Data Company.

Figure 3.3.14 Interest Rates

The central bank policy rate has remained stable, aiming to hold inflation to the 4% target.

— Policy repo rate, month end
— Weighted average lending rates for fresh commercial bank rupee loans
— Yield on 10-year government securities

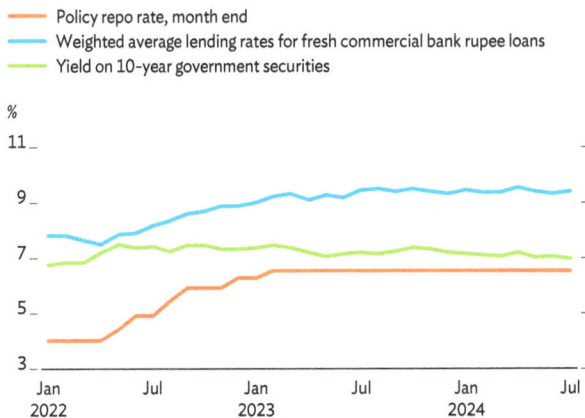

Source: CEIC Data Company .

Figure 3.3.15 Growth in Bank Credit

Demand for credit remains steady despite moderation in the second quarter of 2024.

— Industry   — Agriculture
— Services   — Nonfood credit
— Personal

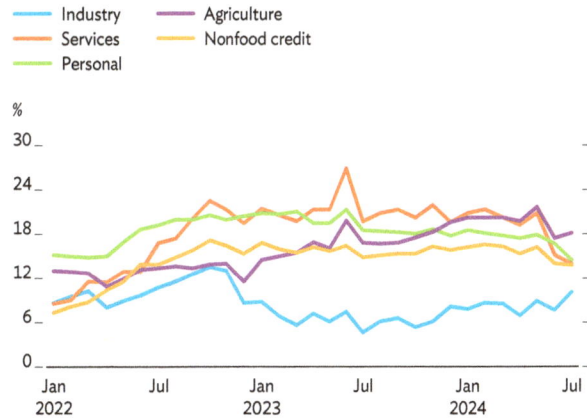

Notes: Excludes public loans to buy crops from farmers and the impact of a merger combining HDFC, a large bank, with a nonbank financial corporation, which drove up outstanding bank credit from July 2023 to June 2024.
Sources: CEIC Data Company; Reserve Bank of India.

2023 at 6.5%, after increasing by 250 basis points from May 2022 to February 2023 (Figure 3.3.14). Monetary policy transmission has been broadly effective, as lending rates for new loans have gradually increased by 189 basis points since May 2022.

Bank credit growth moderated in the wake of tighter prudential regulation and increased real interest rates. Outstanding bank credit expanded by 13.7% yoy as of the end of July 2024, with all sectors showing robust demand for credit, albeit with a slowdown in the first 4 months of FY2024 (Figure 3.3.15). This moderation, particularly in services and personal loans, reflects both higher real interest rates and changes in prudential regulations in November 2023 requiring banks to set aside more reserves against certain forms of consumer credit such as credit cards and personal loans.

Banks remain healthy, with improved asset quality and earnings. Higher interest rates have supported increased bank earnings and profitability. Gross nonperforming loans declined across all sectors to a decade low of 2.8% of all loans at the end of March 2024, down from 3.9% in March 2023. In the case of nonbank financial institutions, they dropped to 4.0%. However, further monitoring is required to track financial risks to banks and nonbank financial corporations, including new fintech startups, from elevated unsecured lending to retail borrowers, despite recent moderation in the share of unsecured lending.

Robust central government revenue and muted expenditure sharply curtailed the fiscal deficit in the first 4 months of FY2024. Central government revenue grew by 33.5% yoy, driven by a 21.2% increase in gross tax collection and a greater-than-expected dividend from the central bank. Meanwhile, central government current expenditure contracted by 2.3% in the same period, and capital expenditure fell by 17.6%, tamped down by the general election.

The merchandise trade deficit widened in the first 4 months of FY2024 by nearly 14%. Merchandise exports grew by 4.1% yoy, driven by electronics, chemicals, and garments. After contracting by 5.7% in FY2023 due to weak global prices, goods imports expanded by 7.6% in the first 4 months of FY2024, driven by imports of petroleum and crude products, electronics items, and agricultural products. With the extension of duty-free imports of certain pulses until March 2025, and curbs on exports of wheat, rice, sugar, and onions to stabilize domestic prices for these key food commodities, India's imports of pulses more than doubled in FY2023 and rose by 104% yoy in first 4 months of FY2024. Meanwhile, exports of services increased by 11.9% yoy, up from 4.8% in the whole of FY2023, and imports increased by 8.6%, reversing a 2.1% contraction in FY2023.

Foreign exchange reserves rose by $21 billion in the first 4 months of FY2024 to reach $667 billion. This provides cover for 11.6 months of imports. In Q1 FY2024, net foreign direct investment increased to $6.9 billion, following a decline in flows to only $9.7 billion in the whole of FY2023, while portfolio investment registered net inflow of $1.1 billion in Q1 FY2024, compared with $44.1 billion in the whole of FY2023 (Figure 3.3.16). The exchange rate vis-à-vis the US dollar remained largely stable, with an average rate of ₹83.6 per dollar from April to August 2024 little changed from ₹82.8 in FY2023.

Figure 3.3.16 Foreign Direct and Portfolio Investment

Net foreign direct investment picked up in Q1 FY2024, while net foreign portfolio investment was muted.

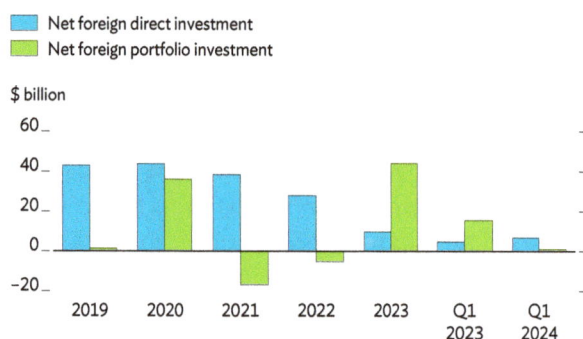

Q = quarter.
Note: Years are fiscal years ending on 31 March of the next year.
Sources: Haver Data Analytics; Asian Development Bank estimates.

Prospects

Overall growth prospects remain robust. GDP growth in FY2024 is expected at 7.0%, as forecast in *ADO April 2024* (Table 3.3.2). It is expected to accelerate in the coming quarters with improvement in agriculture and the ramping up of government spending. The FY2025 growth forecast also remains unchanged, at 7.2%, as consumption and export demand improve.

Faster agriculture growth is forecast in FY2024 with rice and pulse production improved in the summer season. Monsoon rainfall has sustained a trajectory higher than average, but with uneven regional distribution. As of 2 September, the sowing of summer rice was 3.8% higher than in the previous year, and of summer pulses by 7.3%.

Table 3.3.2 Selected Economic Indicators in India, %

Growth forecast is unchanged for FY2024 and FY2025 from ADO April 2024 projections, while the inflation forecast is raised for FY2024 and maintained for FY2025.

	2023	2024		2025	
		Apr	Sep	Apr	Sep
GDP growth	8.2	7.0	7.0	7.2	7.2
Inflation	5.4	4.6	4.7	4.5	4.5

GDP = gross domestic product.
Note: Years are fiscal years ending on 31 March of the next year.
Sources: Ministry of Statistics and Programme Implementation, Government of India; Reserve Bank of India; Asian Development Bank estimates.

The outlook for industry and services remains robust in FY2024 and FY2025. The manufacturing purchasing managers' index averaged 58.0 in the first 5 months of FY2024, which was higher than the long-term average and strongly indicative of expansion (Figure 3.3.17). A central bank industrial outlook survey showed moderation in manufacturers' expectations of sales and profit growth in Q2 FY2024 as the business expectations index fell from 127 in Q1 FY2024 to a still robust 119 in Q2, a reading above 100 signaling expansion. The services purchasing managers' index averaged 60.5 in the first 5 months of FY2024, also indicating strong future growth. Service export growth is expected to be higher than earlier forecast, driven by professional services. Expectations for expansion in construction in the remaining quarters of FY2024 and in FY2025 have moderated somewhat with slower-expected-growth in the housing segment.

Figure 3.3.17 Purchasing Managers' Indexes

Manufacturing and services indexes moderated in the first half of 2024 but remained robust.

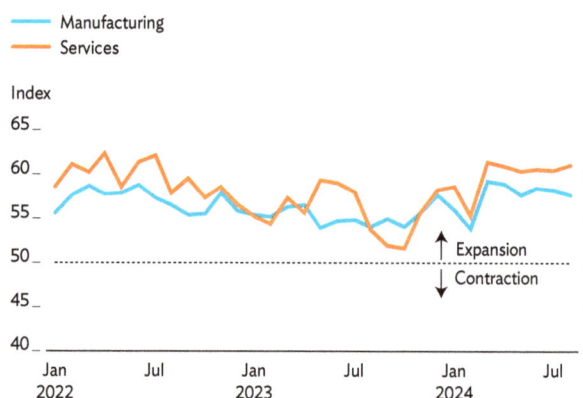

Source: CEIC Data Company.

Net exports will subtract from growth in FY2024 but by less than was expected in April. Export growth is now projected to be higher than previously forecast in FY2024 but lower in FY2025. Higher export growth in FY2024 will be led by services, in particular professional services and those enabled by information technology. Merchandise exports will be relatively muted in FY2024, though some segments, notably electronics, will experience faster growth. Export growth in FY2025 will be lower, coming off a high base in FY2024, due to relatively muted global demand. Import growth will be robust, though lower than projected in *ADO April 2024*.

Consumption growth will be robust this fiscal year and next, as earlier forecast. Rural consumption has shown signs of improvement as agriculture strengthens, but the sustainability of the growth recovery seen in Q1 FY2024 is uncertain. There are signs of a more robust rural economy, as demand for workfare under the Mahatma Gandhi National Rural Employment Guarantee Act fell in the period from April to August 2024 by 10.8% yoy (Figure 3.3.18). Prospects for urban consumption remain strong but with signs of moderation. The proportion of workers in the urban population decreased by 10 basis points in Q1 FY2024 to 46.8%, but the unemployment rate fell marginally to 6.6%. Urban consumers remained optimistic even as the future expectation index dropped from 124.8 in May to 120.7 in July 2024, likely reflecting elevated consumer prices (Figure 3.3.19). A recent policy announcement

offering workers and firms employment-linked incentives could boost labor demand and support the creation of jobs starting in FY2025. Government consumption is likely to be moderately higher, supported by strong government revenue.

The outlook for private investment is upbeat, but public capital expenditure growth, heretofore high, will moderate in FY2025. Private projects under implementation and project completion by the private sector dropped in Q1 FY2024 (Figure 3.3.20). However, prospects for private investment are helped by increased capacity utilization, significant deleveraging of corporate balance sheets, and a strong project pipeline. In FY2023, financial institutions approved 46.7% more in large private sector projects,

Figure 3.3.19 Consumer Confidence

Consumers remain optimistic about the future but with moderating expectations.

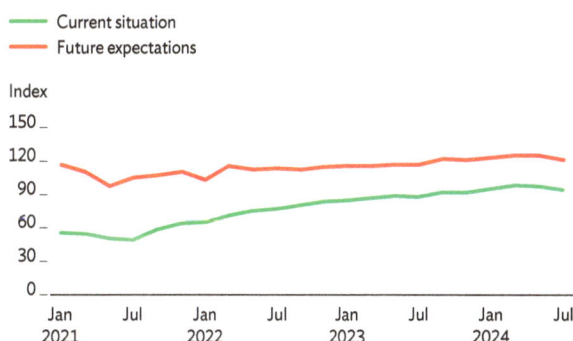

Note: Years are fiscal years ending on 31 March of the next year.
Source: Reserve Bank of India.

Figure 3.3.18 Work Applications Under the Mahatma Gandhi National Rural Employment Guarantee Act

Lower demand for employment under the government's job program in FY2024 indicates stronger rural employment.

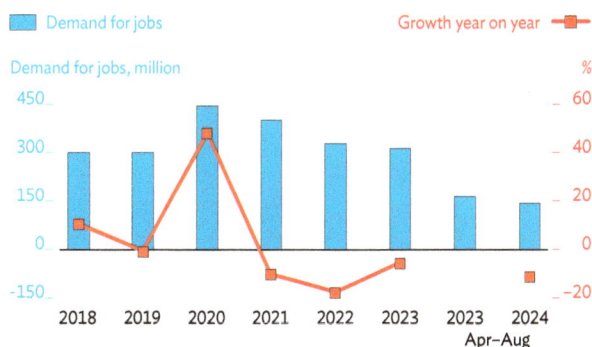

Notes: Years are fiscal years ending on 31 March of the next year; 2024 is until August 2024.
Source: CEIC Data Company.

Figure 3.3.20 Private Sector Investment Projects

Projects under implementation and completed by the private sector dropped in Q1 FY2024.

Q = quarter.
Note: Years are fiscal years ending on 31 March of the next year.
Source: Centre for Monitoring of Indian Economy.

defined as those valued above ₹100 million, than in FY2022. This will have spillover impact on private investment expenditure in this fiscal year and next.

Fiscal policy aims for fiscal consolidation through robust revenue collection. The full budget announced in July lowered the FY2024 fiscal deficit target to the equivalent of 4.9% of GDP, down from 5.6% in FY2023, in anticipation of higher revenue owing primarily to an expected increase in dividend payments from the central bank (Figure 3.3.21). The fiscal deficit estimate for FY2023 and the target for FY2024 are both lower by 0.2% of GDP relative to the interim budget. Current expenditure is increased marginally to ₹37.1 trillion, or 1.5% over the interim budget. Capital expenditure is programmed at 3.4% of GDP in FY2024, unchanged from the interim budget. As a result of fiscal consolidation, central government debt is expected to decline from 58.2% of GDP in FY2023 to 56.8% in FY2024. The general government deficit, which includes state governments, is expected to decline to below 8.0% of GDP in FY2024.

The inflation forecast for FY2024 is raised to 4.7% on higher food inflation. Food prices have continued to be elevated despite expectations of higher output and increased imports of key commodities. While food inflation is expected to moderate gradually over the fiscal year, it will likely push consumer inflation above

the *ADO April 2024* projection of 4.6%. The forecast for inflation in FY2025 is maintained at 4.5% as higher core inflation will be countered by moderating food inflation.

Monetary policy is expected to become less restrictive but not as soon as expected earlier. Elevated food price inflation and the concern that it may spill over into the prices of other goods and services has delayed the adoption of a more accommodative monetary policy. However, if improved supply succeeds in moderating food price increases, the central bank will likely start lowering its policy rates in FY2024, which will improve prospects for bank credit expansion.

The current account deficit is expected to widen in FY2024 and FY2025, but less than expected previously. This reflects better exports and lower imports than expected in April, as well as continued strong inflow of remittances. The deficit is now projected to equal 1.0% of GDP in FY2024 and 1.2% in FY2025, down from previous forecasts of 1.7% for both years (Figure 3.3.22). India's balance-of-payments position will remain robust, especially if foreign direct investment inflows continue to recover and foreign portfolio inflows remain strong. Foreign exchange reserves are expected to trend up.

Figure 3.3.21 Central Government Fiscal Deficit

The central government fiscal deficit is expected to approximate levels last seen before COVID-19, helped by improving revenue and restrained current expenditure.

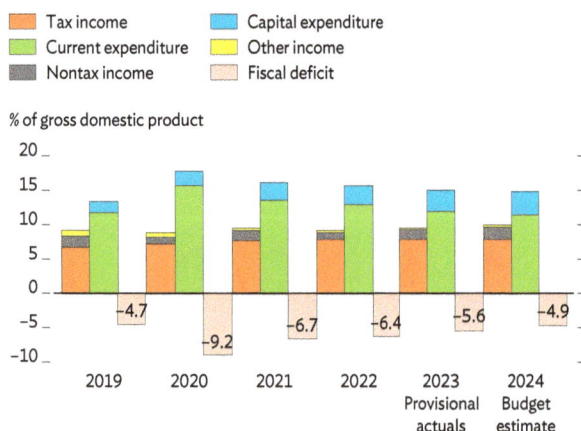

Notes: Years are fiscal years ending on 31 March of the next year.
Source: Ministry of Finance Union Budget.

Figure 3.3.22 Current Account Balance Projections

The current account deficit as a percentage of GDP is expected to widen in FY2024 and FY2025.

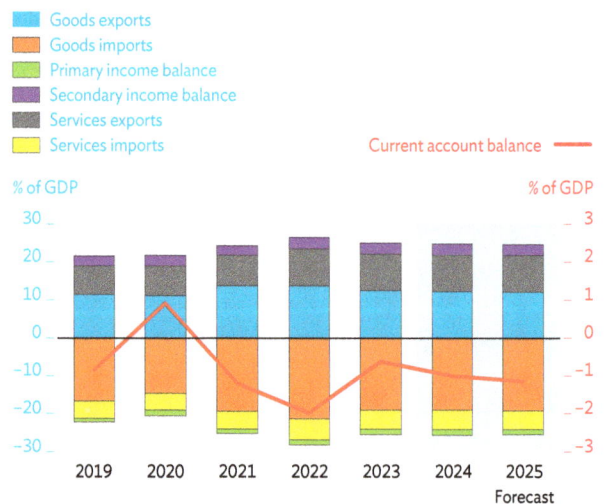

FY = fiscal year, GDP = gross domestic product.
Note: Years are fiscal years ending on 31 March of the next year.
Sources: CEIC Data Company; Asian Development Bank estimates.

Near-term risks to growth are balanced.
Geopolitical shocks may affect global supply chains and commodity prices, while weather shocks may pose risks to agricultural output. Another downside risk in FY2024 is the failure of government to meet its capital expenditure target. Slow expenditure implementation in Q1 FY2024 means that, to achieve the planned capital expenditure target, central government capital spending needs to grow by 39% yoy in the remaining 9 months, which may be difficult. On the upside is potential for higher foreign direct investment, which could support growth and investment, especially in manufacturing. It is also possible that the supply of agricultural products will improve beyond expectations, pushing down food prices and taking consumer inflation lower than forecast.

Pakistan

Growth rebounded and inflation proved lower than expected in fiscal year 2024 (FY2024, ended 30 June 2024). Higher income from agriculture and increased remittances bolstered private consumption, while improved crop production curbed a rise in food prices. A comprehensive economic reform program supported by the International Monetary Fund (IMF) is projected to increase growth and reduce inflation in FY2025.

Updated Assessment

Following a 0.2% downturn in FY2023, a series of policy reforms stabilized the economy in FY2024. Growth rebounded to an estimated 2.4% (Figure 3.3.23). Reforms aimed to tighten fiscal discipline, move toward a market-determined exchange rate to absorb external pressures, enhance efficiency in the energy sector, strengthen climate resilience, and improve the business environment to boost growth. A 9-month program under the IMF Stand-By Arrangement that concluded in April 2024 furthered economic stabilization by improving foreign exchange reserves and restoring bilateral and multilateral finance inflows. Administrative restrictions on imports eased during FY2024. Pakistan made progress in reestablishing a market-determined exchange rate. General elections in February 2024 brought in a new coalition government in March 2024, alleviating political uncertainty that had prevailed since the start of the fiscal year.

Figure 3.3.23 Supply-Side Contributions to Growth

Growth rebounded in 2024, driven by robust agriculture performance.

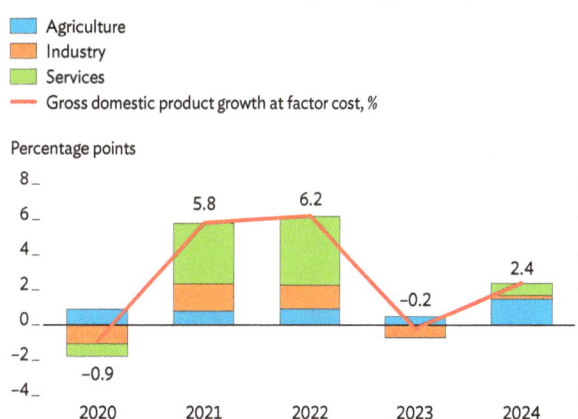

Notes: Years are fiscal years ending on 30 June of that year. GDP at factor prices excludes indirect taxes less subsidies.
Source: Pakistan Bureau of Statistics. National Accounts Tables Base FY2016: Table 6 and 7a.

Modest recovery came from higher consumption supported by increased income from agriculture and workers' remittances. Private consumption expanded by 5.5% in FY2024 (Figure 3.3.24), up from 2.6% growth in FY2023 as agriculture surged by 6.3% following losses from devastating floods in FY2023. Production of key crops increased significantly, with cotton output more than doubling, rice up by 34.8%, and wheat by 12.0%. Livestock grew by 3.9%. Remittances increased by $3 billion to $30.3 billion in FY2024, equal to 8.1% of GDP (Figure 3.3.25). Regarding the Pakistan rupee exchange rate, the

Figure 3.3.24 Demand-Side Contributions to Growth

Private consumption boosted growth in 2024, supported by higher agricultural income and remittances.

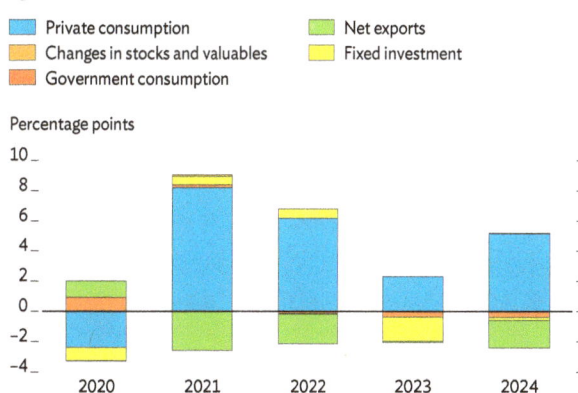

Notes: Years are fiscal years ending on 30 June of that year.
Source: Pakistan Bureau of Statistics. National Accounts Tables Base FY2016: Table 9.

Figure 3.3.25 Remittances

Remittances increased in 2024 with a return to a market-determined exchange rate.

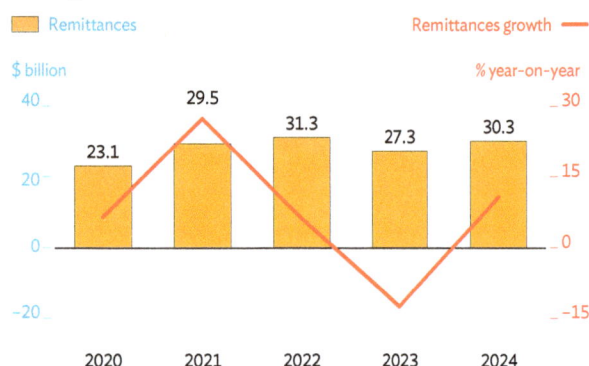

Note: Years are fiscal years ending on 30 June of that year.
Source: State Bank of Pakistan. Economic Data: External Sector. Worker's Remittances.

spread between official interbank and open market rates significantly narrowed thanks to external stability, a return to a market-determined exchange rate, stricter enforcement of laws against speculative and illegal currency trading by government agencies, and enhanced regulatory oversight of foreign exchange bureaus.

Growth was constrained by a decline in investment and lackluster expansion in industry and services. Gross fixed capital formation fell by 2.4% as macroeconomic uncertainty reduced both private and public investment. As a result, the share of private consumption in GDP rose to 93.5% in FY2024 from 91.0% in FY2023. While the performance of industry and services improved, growth in both sectors was slow at 1.2%. Notable contributions to recovery in services came from transport and storage, education, real estate services, and wholesale and retail trade.

Inflation eased slightly as the State Bank of Pakistan, the central bank, maintained a relatively tight monetary policy. Average inflation in FY2024 slowed to 23.4% from 29.2% in FY2023. Inflation remained elevated in the first half of FY2024 but subsided afterward, particularly during the fourth quarter. A decline in food price inflation from increased agricultural production helped reduce overall inflation. From May to June 2024, food prices, which account for more than half of the consumer price index, increased by 2.4% in urban areas and 0.6% in rural areas, down from about 40% at the start of the fiscal year. Monthly

inflation, which hovered at around 29.0% from July 2023 to January 2024, fell to 12.6% in June and further to 11.1% in July (Figure 3.3.26). The central bank kept its policy rate at 22.0% after a cumulative increase of 1,500 basis points from FY2022 to FY2023, given high inflation and considerable risks to the outlook. Following rapid deceleration in headline inflation in the fourth quarter of FY2024, the central bank reduced the policy rate to 20.5% in June 2024 and further to 19.5% in July (Figure 3.3.27). Private sector lending strengthened as economic activity and confidence

Figure 3.3.26 Monthly Inflation

Inflation declined significantly starting in January 2024 as food price inflation moderated.

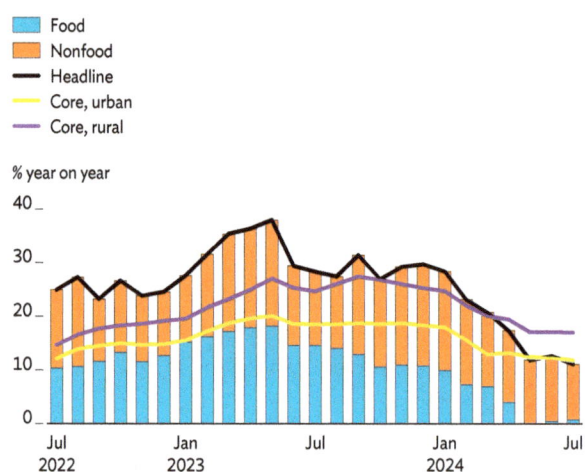

Source: Pakistan Bureau of Statistics. Monthly Review on Price Indices: July 2024.

Figure 3.3.27 Interest Rates and Inflation

The central bank maintained an elevated policy rate throughout FY2024 to counter inflationary pressure.

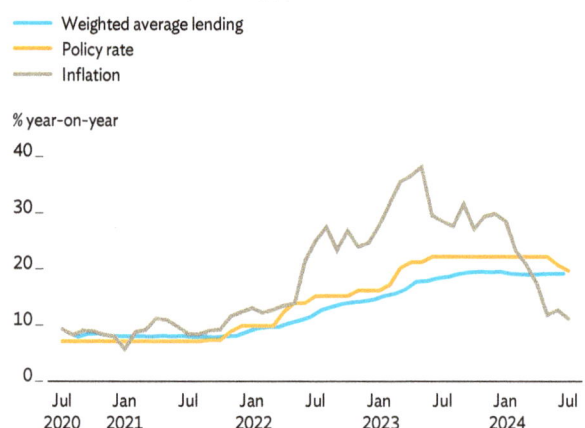

Source: State Bank of Pakistan. Economic Data.

recovered. In FY2024, loans to private firms rose by 6.6%, up from 0.4% growth in the previous fiscal year. Lending for fixed investment expanded by 3.3%, while lending for working capital increased by 8.9%.

A smaller trade deficit and higher remittances narrowed the current account deficit to 0.2% of GDP in FY2024 from 1.0% in FY2023 (Figure 3.3.28). In absolute terms, it fell from $3.3 billion to $0.7 billion. As exports are largely agricultural goods, recovery in agriculture helped raise exports of all goods and services by 9.7%. Imports of goods and services rose by 3.2% as the high cost of living and currency depreciation eroded purchasing power and weakened demand for imports. A good harvest and high international prices caused rice exports to nearly double to $3.9 billion in FY2024. Greater availability of domestic raw cotton boosted the volume of major textile exports, including readymade garments, bedwear, and knitwear. However, the value of textile exports, which represent 54% of total exports, rose by only 0.9% because of low international textile prices. The overall trade deficit declined by 5.7% to $24.4 billion, equal to 6.5% of GDP.

Figure 3.3.28 Current Account Components

The current account deficit narrowed in 2024 because of a smaller trade deficit and higher remittances.

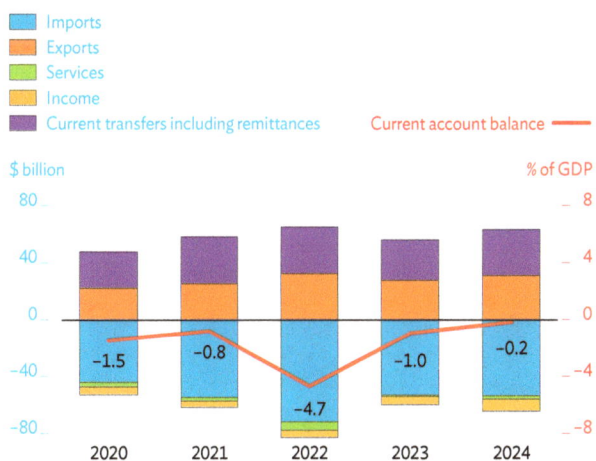

GDP = gross domestic product.
Note: Years are fiscal years ending on 30 June of that year.
Source: State Bank of Pakistan. Economic Data: External Sector. Summary Balance of Payments as per BPM6 - July 2024.

Figure 3.3.29 Gross Official Reserves and the Exchange Rate

International reserves more than doubled, and the exchange rate stabilized during FY2024.

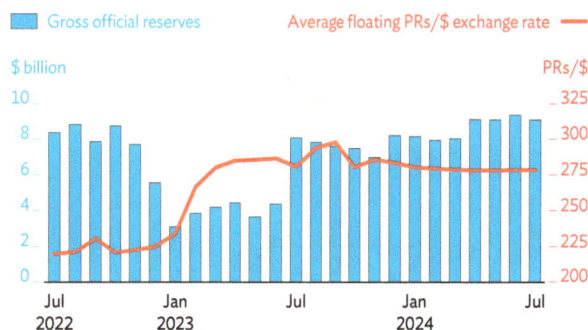

Source: State Bank of Pakistan. Economic Data.

Foreign exchange reserves more than doubled to $9.4 billion at the end of June 2024 from $4.4 billion a year earlier (Figure 3.3.29). Import cover tripled from 0.6 months to 1.8 months. The increase in reserves came mainly from central bank purchases of foreign exchange and recovery in external financing inflows under the IMF Stand-By Arrangement. The return to a market-determined exchange rate and higher remittances also boosted reserves. In addition, market sentiment improved as external vulnerabilities eased.

Government efforts advanced fiscal consolidation during FY2024. The budget achieved a primary surplus equal to 0.9% of GDP in FY2024, exceeding the 0.4% target and reversing a deficit of 1.0% in FY2023. The overall fiscal deficit including interest payments declined from 7.8% of GDP in FY2023 to 6.8% (Figure 3.3.30), slightly above the 6.5% target, largely because of higher interest payments. Tax revenue increased to 9.5% of GDP in FY2024 from 9.3% a year earlier as new tax measures introduced in a supplementary budget in February 2023 boosted direct taxes and excise duties. The measures revised income tax rates, imposed surtaxes on banks and other firms, rationalized withholding taxes for services and commercial importers, and levied higher property taxes. Nontax revenue rose to 3.0% of GDP from 2.2% a year earlier, boosted by higher profit transfers from the central bank and increased receipts from the petroleum development levy after rates were raised to the statutory upper limit.

Figure 3.3.30 Fiscal Indicators

The fiscal deficit declined in 2024 as the government reduced noninterest spending.

■ Tax revenue
■ Nontax revenue
■ Expenditure
■ Fiscal balance

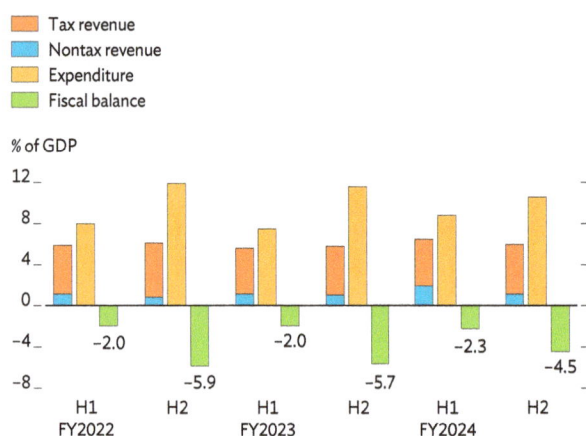

GDP = gross domestic product, H = half.

Note: Years are fiscal years ending on 30 June of that year. Data refer to consolidated federal and provincial governments.

Source: Ministry of Finance. Pakistan Summary of Consolidated Federal and Provincial Fiscal Operations 2022-23 and 2023-24.

Record interest payments on public debt kept spending high in FY2024. Interest payments increased to 7.7% of GDP in FY2024 from 6.8% in FY2023, absorbing 81% of tax revenue. The rise in interest payments came from elevated debt levels, high interest rates, and 3.2% rupee depreciation during FY2024. To contain the deficit, the government cut development and current spending, reducing noninterest expenditure from 12.5% of GDP in FY2023 to 11.6% in FY2024. However, higher interest payments kept total expenditure at 19.3% of GDP.

Prospects

Pakistan's outlook hinges on continued and effective economic reform. In July 2024, the IMF and Pakistan reached a staff-level agreement on a 37-month Extended Fund Facility (EFF) arrangement worth about $7 billion that should catalyze significant international financial support for the underlying economic stabilization and reform program. Once approved by the IMF Executive Board, the arrangement should enhance macroeconomic stability. The program aims to consolidate public finances, expand social spending and protection, rebuild foreign exchange reserves, reduce fiscal risks from state-owned enterprises, and improve the business environment to encourage growth led by the private sector.

The economy is expected to grow by a moderate 2.8% in FY2025 (Figure 3.3.31 and Table 3.3.3). The reform program is expected to support economic activity by providing a more stable macroeconomic environment. Private investment should rebound on more favorable macroeconomic conditions, including easier access to foreign exchange. This will also benefit manufacturing and services. However, higher personal income tax rates in the FY2025 budget and the government's efforts to limit spending will constrain private and public consumption. In addition, growth in agriculture is projected to slow in FY2025 as higher administered prices for gas and lower subsidies raise the cost of fertilizer.

Figure 3.3.31 Growth Outlook

Growth is projected at 2.8% in 2025 as economic reform boosts economic activity.

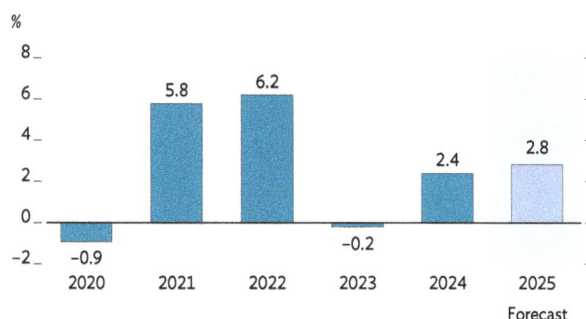

Note: Years are fiscal years ending on 30 June of that year.

Sources: Pakistan Bureau of Statistics. National Accounts Tables Base FY2016: Table 5; Asian Development Bank estimates.

Table 3.3.3 Selected Economic Indicators in Pakistan, %

Growth proved higher, and inflation lower, in FY2024 than earlier forecast. Projections for FY2025 remain unchanged.

	2023	2024		2025	
		Apr	Sep	Apr	Sep
GDP growth	−0.2	1.9	2.4	2.8	2.8
Inflation	29.2	25.0	23.4	15.0	15.0

GDP = gross domestic product.

Sources: Pakistan Bureau of Statistics, National Accounts Tables Base 2015–16, Table 6; State Bank of Pakistan, Monetary Policy Information Compendium, July 2024; Asian Development Bank estimates.

The government's medium-term fiscal consolidation effort envisages a multiyear strategy for revenue mobilization. The program aspires to create a more equitable tax system with reform to broaden the tax base and remove exemptions. The medium-term revenue mobilization program aims to bring the retail and export sectors under the regular tax regime and to align provincial agriculture income taxes with the federal personal and corporate income tax regime through legislative changes. Fiscal consolidation targets tax measures equal to 3.0% of GDP over the EFF program period. With tax revenue measures equal to 1.5% of GDP already implemented through the FY2025 budget, tax revenue is projected to rise to 11.2% of GDP in FY2025. With nontax revenue forecast at 3.1% of GDP, total revenue is expected to increase to 14.3% of GDP by the end of this fiscal year.

The government plans to achieve primary surpluses over the medium term to reduce public debt to a sustainable level. The EFF program targets a primary surplus equal to 1.0% of GDP in FY2025 and about 3.2% over the next 2 years to put the debt-to-GDP ratio on a sustainable declining path. The budget deficit in FY2025 is expected to equal 6.9% of GDP. Interest payments in FY2025 are projected to remain elevated at 7.9% of GDP, comprising about 57% of federal current expenditure and absorbing about 75% of federal taxes. Nevertheless, a disciplined fiscal stance is anticipated to significantly reduce these payments in the medium term. A robust revenue mobilization effort and some reduction in interest outlays will create the necessary fiscal space for much-needed social and development spending. Provincial spending will be restrained to achieve a cumulative provincial surplus equal to 1.0% of GDP in FY2025, and spending on defense and subsidies will be maintained at the FY2024 level in terms of GDP.

The central bank has committed to maintaining an adequately tight monetary policy to meet its medium-term inflation target. The central bank has adopted a data-driven, forward-looking monetary policy framework and aims to keep real interest rates positive to bring inflation down to its target of 5%–7% over the medium term. Inflation is expected to rise from its recent lows due to the impact of fiscal measures in the FY2025 budget, including higher sales taxes on some items, and energy tariff adjustment required to ensure cost recovery in the energy sector.

However, with an appropriately tight monetary policy, reduced exchange rate volatility, and a stable outlook for international food prices, inflation expectations are anticipated to moderate later in the year. Therefore, average inflation is projected at 15.0% in FY2025 (Figure 3.3.32).

Figure 3.3.32 Inflation Outlook

Inflation is projected to decline in 2025 under a stable outlook for international commodity prices.

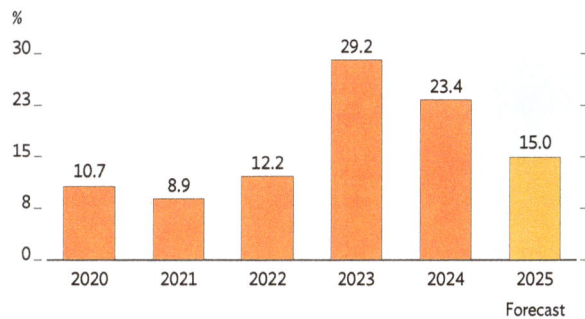

Note: Years are fiscal years ending on 30 June of that year.
Source: Pakistan Bureau of Statistics. Price Statistics: Monthly Review on Price Indices—June 2024; Asian Development Bank estimates.

The current account deficit is expected to remain moderate but rise to 1.0% of GDP in FY2025. The trade deficit is expected to widen as imports grow more rapidly than exports, driven by ongoing recovery in domestic economic activity and the improved availability of imported inputs. The rise in the trade deficit will be partly offset by higher worker remittance inflows. In addition, the new IMF program has improved prospects for multilateral and bilateral financing. Investment is also expected to revive as investor confidence is restored with the implementation of the program. Thus, despite a larger current account deficit, international reserves are expected to increase from 1.8 months of import cover in FY2024 to about 2.1 months in FY2025.

High downside risks cloud the economic outlook. With Pakistan's sizeable external financing requirements, its economic outlook is vulnerable to any shortfall in external inflows, making timely disbursements from multilateral and bilateral partners crucial. Lapses in policy implementation could jeopardize these inflows, increasing pressure on the exchange rate and worsening sovereign debt vulnerabilities. The new government has committed to the necessary stabilization and structural reforms but faces challenges owing to elevated political and institutional tensions and the prospects of social unrest from a steep drop in real incomes. Devastating floods in 2022 demonstrated Pakistan's vulnerability to climate-induced natural disasters, further complicating the economic outlook. Externally, the main risks to macroeconomic stability stem from the economic impacts of adverse geopolitical developments, including higher food and oil prices and tighter global financial conditions. On the upside, improved global financing conditions and lower international food and fuel prices would reduce fiscal and external vulnerability, lower inflation, and allow for a faster buildup of external buffers.

Other Economies

Afghanistan

Growth was modest during fiscal year 2024 (FY2024, ending 20 March 2024). Continued international assistance for humanitarian and basic needs supported growth, as did some improvement in governance. However, a poor investment climate, political and economic challenges, dwindling exports, stubborn deflation, and declining productivity kept growth sluggish. The private sector continued to operate well below 2019 levels, before COVID-19, despite an increase in the number of small businesses. Protracted weak demand, poor access to finance, a lack of liquidity, a banking system with little coverage or functionality, and policy gaps continue to be the primary constraints on private sector expansion.

Growth reflected robust expansion in mining and quarrying, retail, and transport, while agriculture, manufacturing, and other services remained subdued. Agriculture, which provides a third of gross domestic product and is the primary source of income for 76% of households, faces many challenges, including inadequate water supply, a lack of high-quality seeds and fertilizer, persistent pest and disease outbreaks, and poor market access. Moreover, a ban on opium cultivation without strategic guidance on alternative crops hurt the rural economy, and the forced repatriation of Afghan refugees from Pakistan weakened an already slack labor market.

Deflation continued through May 2024. In FY2024, deflation averaged 7.7%, reflecting year-on-year declines of 11.8% in food prices and 3.0% for other items. Deflation eased slightly to 7.4% in May 2024. Contributors to deflation were a strong afghani, low import prices for essential items, subdued domestic demand, and an easing of domestic and international supply chain disruption. In the first half of 2024, the afghani appreciated in real terms against the currencies of Pakistan and Iran, Afghanistan's major trade partners. Given Afghanistan's heavy reliance on imports, the impact of the exchange rate on inflation is significant, with domestic prices significantly reflecting exchange rate movements.

In FY2024, the fiscal revenue target was achieved through robust collection of nontax revenue and increased import tax receipts. Total domestic revenue collection increased by 9.0% to reach AF210.7 billion. Inland revenue collection surged by 13.0% on enhanced compliance and a broader tax base in FY2024. Customs receipts grew by 5.0%, driven primarily by a 26.0% increase in trade volume.

The trade deficit widened to $3.1 billion during the first 5 months of 2024. Imports surged by 22.0% over the same period in 2023 to $3.8 billion, driven mainly by a 63.0% rise in imports of machinery, transportation equipment, and chemicals. Exports declined by 16.0% to $0.63 billion as exports of coal plunged by 78.0% because demand for imported coal in Pakistan fell. Meanwhile, textile exports increased to $138.0 million during January–May 2024, which partly offset the decline in coal exports. Iran and Pakistan remain Afghanistan's biggest trade partners.

The economic outlook is challenged by stagnation in the short and medium term, as the economy lacks indigenous growth drivers. Sluggish macroeconomic performance may persist without concentrated policy effort to revive investment and foster productivity. This stagnation could significantly impede progress toward achieving Afghanistan's Sustainable Development Goals. Although inflation is expected to be near zero in FY2025, economic woes and international isolation pose significant risks of high inflation in the medium term. Inflation could rise as well with any decline in international assistance for humanitarian and basic needs or with decreased inflow of US dollars for such assistance, which could significantly depreciate the afghani and consequently push up prices.

Bhutan

Growth prospects for 2024 have improved on rising government expenditure, electricity output, and tourist arrivals. A 17% increase in the government budget for fiscal year 2025 (FY2025, ending 30 June 2025) will enhance industry growth and boost domestic demand this year and next. The commencement of the testing and commissioning process for the Punatsangchhu II hydropower plant in mid-August 2024—5 months ahead of schedule—will raise GDP growth by an estimated 1 percentage point. These developments will boost electricity generation and construction, with the latter also benefiting from the lifting in July 2024 of a credit moratorium on the sector. Following a marked uptick in tourist arrivals year on year in the first quarter of 2024, services will benefit from increased tourism promotion. The growth forecast for 2024 is thus upgraded (Table 3.3.4).

Table 3.3.4 Selected Economic Indicators in Bhutan, %

Half year indicators point to 2024 growth higher than projected 2024 growth, with inflation edging up.

	2023	2024		2025	
		Apr	Sep	Apr	Sep
GDP growth	4.0	4.4	5.5	7.0	7.0
Inflation	4.2	4.5	4.6	4.2	4.2

GDP = gross domestic product.
Source: Royal Government of Bhutan, Ministry of Finance; Royal Monetary Authority, Bhutan; Asian Development Bank estimates.

The growth forecast is maintained for 2025. The main drivers of growth will include higher industry output with the full operation of the Punatsangchhu II hydropower plant, the commissioning of three small hydropower plants, the implementation of a $318 million government economic stimulus program, increased construction output, and rising tourist arrivals.

Inflation forecasts are raised slightly from *ADO April 2024* projections. Headline inflation in the first 4 months of 2024 averaged 4.7% year on year, slightly higher than projected. High food price inflation, averaging 6.1% in the period, was the main driver. As Bhutan's harvest season begins, food prices are expected to edge down in the coming months

but remain slightly more elevated than previously forecast, reflecting a similar trend in food prices in India. Nonfood price inflation averaged 3.5% in the first 4 months of the year, driven mainly by increased prices for housing and utilities, health services, and communication. They are expected to rise slightly during the rest of the year.

Risks to the outlook arise from domestic and external sources and tilt to the downside. Prospects for growth and inflation in Bhutan are threatened by a wide fiscal deficit and continued weakness in the country's external reserves position, which has deteriorated from cover for 14.7 months of imports in December 2019 to about 4.5 months in May 2024. During that period, gross international reserves steadily declined, sinking below the constitutionally mandated reserve requirement of about $670 million as the current account deteriorated, mainly because of higher food and fuel prices and a considerable increase in imports of equipment for bitcoin mining. As Bhutan depends heavily on imports, further deterioration in reserves that trigger restrictive countermeasures to contain domestic demand would dampen growth. Energy output could be hit by delay in commissioning Punatsangchhu II, geological surprises that delay other hydropower projects, or low hydrological flows. Other risks include volatile commodity prices, geopolitical tensions, and a global slowdown, which would hit services and exports.

Maldives

GDP growth is projected to be lower in 2024 and 2025 than forecast in *ADO April 2024*. Robust growth in tourism will be outweighed by lackluster performance in construction and fisheries (Table 3.3.5). Tourist arrivals increased by 9.2% year on year (yoy) in the first half (H1) of 2024 to reach 1.02 million. The surge was driven mainly by arrivals from Europe, which grew by 12.8%, and the People's Republic of China, which grew by 90.3%, compensating for declines from India and the Russian Federation. Robust tourist arrivals pushed travel receipts in January–May 2024 up by 24.0% yoy. Conversely, construction declined as public sector investment fell by 41.9% yoy in H1 2024. Similarly, the volume and value of fish exports decreased substantially in H1 2024 as supply was disrupted. Ensis, a major tuna exporter, stopped cannery operations at the end of

Table 3.3.5 Selected Economic Indicators in Maldives, %

ADO April 2024 growth and inflation forecasts are revised down.

	2023	2024		2025	
		Apr	Sep	Apr	Sep
GDP growth	4.1	5.4	5.0	6.0	5.4
Inflation	2.9	3.2	2.8	2.5	2.3

GDP = gross domestic product.
Source: Maldives Monetary Authority. *Monthly Statistics. July 2024*; Asian Development Bank estimates.

2023 as the government raised the fish price by 47%, and operations at Koodoo fish plant were disrupted by protests in February 2024 after the Maldives Industrial Fisheries Company delayed payments to fishers. Tourist arrivals are expected to increase during the fourth quarter peak season, and the opening of a new airport terminal later this year should boost 2025 tourist arrivals to 2 million. However, growth will be dampened by an anticipated further fall in construction this year and next under a planned reduction in public sector investment.

Inflation is forecast to be lower than projected in April. In H1 2024, inflation remained muted at 0.5% yoy, reflecting a high base effect and electricity and water rate discounts granted by utility companies in March and April 2024. In addition, targeted subsidies were expected to replace price subsidies beginning in Q3 2024. However, this policy change is now postponed to Q4, implying that price increases this year will be further muted compared to the April forecast. Meanwhile, sustained easing of global commodity prices, as forecast, should temper any upward price movements in 2025. Monetary policy is expected to remain accommodative, given low inflationary pressure.

Both the overall fiscal deficit and the primary deficit declined substantially in H1 2024. With reduced public sector investment, the H1 2024 fiscal gap narrowed to equal 2.2% of GDP, from 5.8% in H1 2023. Likewise, the primary deficit fell by 82.2% yoy in H1 2024 to equal 0.6% of GDP, from an average of 12.6% from 2020 to 2023. Nevertheless, public debt at the end of March 2024 remained high at 116.7% of GDP.

The current account deficit is forecast to be higher at 18.5% of GDP in 2024 and 17.5% in 2025. With higher imports and contracting export growth, the merchandise trade gap widened in the first 6 months of 2024 compared to the same period in 2023 and is expected to stay elevated this year and next, owing to rising imports. However, the services balance recovered during January–May 2024 on the expansion in travel receipts, and the trend is expected to continue, moderating the rise in the current account deficit. Reflecting mainly a higher current account deficit, official foreign exchange reserves fell by 27.5% yoy to the end of June 2024, covering 1.2 months of imports.

Downside risk to the outlook arises from Maldives' soaring public debt and thin foreign exchange buffers. This situation necessitates comprehensive fiscal reform. Any slackening in the implementation of reform to reduce the burden on the budget from state-owned enterprises and subsidies would worsen the macroeconomic outlook.

Nepal

GDP growth almost doubled in fiscal year 2024 (FY2024, ended mid-July 2024). Improved agricultural production, higher electricity generation capacity, and buoyant tourist arrivals supported growth. Agriculture expanded on increased paddy output, while industry growth slowed slightly, as contraction in manufacturing and construction tamped down the growth impact from expansion in electricity and in mining and quarrying. Service growth accelerated on significant expansion in accommodation and food services and in storage and communications. On the demand side, investment was the main driver of GDP growth in FY2024. Public investment, mainly in new electricity generation projects, increased by 17.7%. Private investment also rose, by 16.6%, buoyed by relaxed monetary policy and gradual improvement in investor confidence. Private consumption grew modestly in real terms as remittance inflow strengthened and prices moderated. Even as imports fell and exports grew robustly in FY2024, the contribution to GDP growth from net exports of goods and services was substantially lower than in FY2023.

Table 3.3.6 Selected Economic Indicators in Nepal, %

Growth in 2024 will be higher than the ADO April 2024 forecast, benefiting from budget reform and easier monetary policy, but inflation will be lower in both 2024 and 2025.

	2023	2024		2025	
		Apr	Sep	Apr	Sep
GDP growth	2.0	3.6	3.9	4.8	4.9
Inflation	7.7	6.5	5.4	6.0	5.5

GDP = gross domestic product.

Note: Years are fiscal years ending in mid-July of that year.

Source: Asian Development Bank estimates.

GDP growth in FY2025 is expected to be above the forecast in *ADO April 2024* (Table 3.3.6). Domestic demand will be revitalized by an increase in planned infrastructure projects, their accelerated implementation, a cut in the central bank's policy rate by 50 basis points to 5%, further monetary easing, and ongoing finance sector reform. Public investment will ramp up as the government is committed to project implementation reform and settling arrears with contractors. Consumption will grow as remittances rise and government expenditure expands. Investment will grow as the implementation of government projects ramps up, pushing up imports substantially. Although exports of electricity to India will rise significantly under a 2024 trade agreement, net exports will be a drag on growth in 2025. Higher growth is expected in all production sectors. Agriculture will benefit from timely paddy plantation with normal monsoon and a recently announced raise in the minimum support price for paddy that has removed price uncertainty for farmers. Industry growth will be supported primarily by increased electricity generation capacity. Construction, heretofore stalled, will expand following the rollout by Nepal Rastra Bank, the central bank, of a series of initiatives that extend bank guarantees and loan repayment periods for construction businesses. Manufacturing will also gain momentum as interest rates soften, and services will benefit from higher tourist arrivals supported by construction of several five-star hotels and increased bank and financial institutional lending to hotel and tourism related industries.

Inflation forecasts are revised down for FY2024 and FY2025. Based on the latest official estimates, average inflation moderated to 5.4% in FY2024 from 7.7% a year earlier, as rising food prices were more than balanced by moderation in nonfood prices and falling oil prices. The inflation forecast for FY2025 is lowered from the *ADO April 2024* forecast, assuming a normal harvest; an expected modest decline in inflation in India, Nepal's main source of imports; and continued prudent monetary policy and fiscal discipline.

A declining trade deficit and strongly growing remittances fueled a current account surplus equal to 3.9% of GDP in FY2024. This outcome and broadly stable net financial inflows increased foreign exchange reserves to 13.0 months of imports. However, as imports are expected to rebound and remittance inflows to moderate, the current account will likely return to a deficit in FY2025.

Risks to the outlook tilt to the downside. Any intensified geopolitical tensions from wider conflict in the Middle East could hurt Nepal's remittance income. A global economic downturn could affect its tourism receipts. A perennial risk to economic growth in Nepal is high vulnerability to disasters including those caused by extreme weather events.

Sri Lanka

The economy outperformed expectations in the first quarter (Q1) of 2024 as headwinds diminished. GDP grew by 5.3% year on year (yoy). Industry expanded at a faster-than-anticipated 11.8% on a low base effect, decelerating inflation, and better supply of raw materials. Services posted modest growth at 2.6%, and agriculture at 1.1%. Growth was driven by 17.6% expansion in investments, while consumption growth remained muted at 0.5% under strong fiscal austerity measures, including hikes to value-added and income taxes. Net exports continued to contribute positively to growth as imports remained constrained, though recovering under easing import controls and better forex liquidity.

Leading indicators signal a strong recovery in the first half (H1) of 2024 and beyond. Forward-looking indicators show steady improvement thanks to loosening monetary policy, better public financial management, and negotiations to restructure external debt. Purchasing managers' indexes for manufacturing, services, and construction remained in expansionary territory through most of H1 2024. The index of industrial production rose by 7.3% in Q1 and 8.4% in April and May, though the index remains below 100, indicating decline from 2015. Based on these trends, growth projections for 2024 and 2025 are revised up from *ADO April 2024* (Table 3.3.7). However, following 2 consecutive years of contraction, the projected real GDP for 2025 remains below its 2019 value.

Table 3.3.7 Selected Economic Indicators in Sri Lanka, %

Growth forecasts are revised up for this year and next, and the inflation forecast for 2024 is revised down.

	2023	2024		2025	
		Apr	Sep	Apr	Sep
GDP growth	−2.3	1.9	2.6	2.5	2.8
Inflation	17.4	7.5	3.8	5.5	5.5

GDP = gross domestic product.
Sources: Department of Census and Statistics; Asian Development Bank estimates.

Inflation remained muted in H1 2024 and is now forecast to be lower this year than projected in April. Following the value-added tax rate hike, the Colombo consumer price index edged up to 6.4% yoy in January before easing to 5.9% in February. Monthly inflation has since remained at about 2.0% yoy, owing to substantially reduced utility prices following better hydropower generation, Sri Lankan rupee appreciation by 6.0% against the US dollar in H1 2024, and weak consumption demand despite cuts to the two policy rates of the Central Bank of Sri Lanka by 75 basis points each during January–July 2024. The inflation forecast for 2025 remains unchanged, however, on the expectation of faster growth.

The current account continues to improve in 2024. Relaxed import restrictions since mid-2023 and rupee appreciation fueled 6.4% growth in imports in H1 2024, outpacing 4.7% growth in export earnings. However, the resulting widening of the trade deficit was offset by expansion in net service exports as tourism earnings grew by 77.9% yoy in H1 2024, led by higher arrivals and spending per tourist, and expansion by 11.4% yoy in remittance inflows. Gross official reserves grew by $1.2 billion to equal 3.9 months of imports, from 3.1 months at the end of 2023, owing to the current account surplus, disbursement by the International

Monetary Fund (IMF), a $1.4 billion swap with the Peoples' Bank of China, and the central bank's net purchase of dollars.

Sri Lanka reached agreement with the Official Creditor Committee and the Exim Bank of China to restructure its bilateral debt. In addition to these memoranda of understanding, signed on 26 June 2024, a steering committee of major bondholders agreed on core financial terms for restructuring international sovereign bonds, including a 28% principal haircut, under a joint working framework. Next steps are IMF confirmation that restructuring terms meet debt sustainability objectives and confirmation of comparable debt treatment by the Official Creditor Committee. Any delay in ongoing negotiations with other commercial lenders will delay the finalization of the overall debt restructuring exercise. Earlier, the IMF completed its Article IV Consultation and Second Review under a 48-month External Fund Facility, and it has so far released approximately $1 billion. Sri Lanka has met several key benchmarks, notably the submission of the new public financial management bill to Parliament that aims to enhance fiscal discipline with a primary spending limit equal to 13% of GDP. It achieved a primary surplus of 0.6% of GDP in 2023.

Lost reform momentum ahead of elections is a major risk to the outlook. Presidential elections are to be held on 21 September, likely to be followed by parliamentary elections in Q1 2025. The impact of the election cycle is visible in delays to critical reform of state-owned enterprises and the submission of new tax measures to Parliament. Prolonged delays in the reform agenda could stifle growth, delay IMF disbursement, and hit investor sentiment. Other downside risks are delay in finalizing debt-relief agreements, unpredictable weather, and spillover from geopolitical tensions.

SOUTHEAST ASIA

Growth in Southeast Asia is now forecast slightly lower than *ADO April 2024* projections. Nonetheless, robust consumption, increased investment, the continued tourism recovery, and a rebound in electronic exports will support growth this year and next. In most economies, growth has been helped as inflation moderated to within central bank target ranges. Scope for monetary policy easing given the Fed's rate cut in September will further benefit consumers and businesses. Still, heightened geopolitical tensions could stall global trade once more. Severe weather disturbances could also disrupt growth momentum across the subregion.

Subregional Assessment and Prospects

Weaker growth in Myanmar, Thailand, and Timor-Leste drags growth forecast in 2024 but 2025 maintained supported by both domestic and external demand. The Singapore economy should benefit from strong services aided by an upturn in global electronics in 2024. Brunei Darussalam, Cambodia, Indonesia, Malaysia, the Philippines, and Viet Nam remain on track to meet their growth forecasts this year and next, supported by robust domestic and external demand. Compared to April, growth projections are easing in Thailand, Myanmar, and Timor-Leste in 2024, including the Lao People's Democratic Republic (Lao PDR) in 2025—amid political and economic uncertainties. The Southeast Asia GDP forecast for 2024 is slightly down to 4.5% from 4.6% in April and remains at 4.7% for 2025 (Figure 3.4.1).

Domestic demand continued to drive economic growth in the first half (H1) of 2024. Consumption remained robust in many economies, aided by positive labor market conditions and continuing policy support. The tourism rebound also helped private consumption

Figure 3.4.1 Gross Domestic Product Growth in Southeast Asia

Steady growth is forecast for most economies in 2024 and 2025.

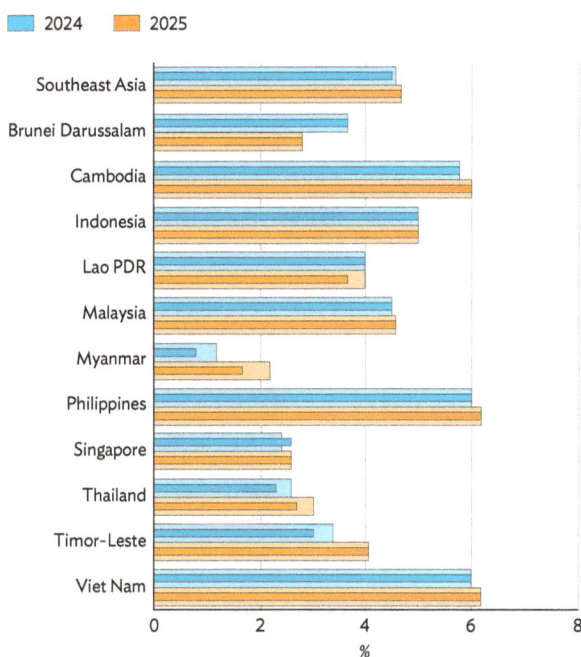

Lao PDR = Lao People's Democratic Republic.
Note: Lighter colored bars are *Asian Development Outlook April 2024* forecasts.
Source: *Asian Development Outlook* database (accessed 5 September 2024).

The subregional assessment and prospects was written by James Villafuerte and Dulce Zara. The section on Indonesia was written by Priasto Aji and Arief Ramayandi; Malaysia by Mae Hyacinth C. Kiocho, consultant, and James Villafuertes; the Philippines by Cristina Lozano, Teresa Mendoza and Sopanha Sa; Thailand by Chitchanok Annonjarn; Viet Nam by Chu Hong Minh, Nguyen Ba Hung, and Nguyen Luu Thuc Phuong. The other economies by Emma Allen, Poullang Doung, Kavita Iyengar, Pathoumthip Khounthalyvong, Soulinthone Leuangkhamsing, Eve Cherry Lynn, Nedelyn Magtibay-Ramos, Joel Mangahas, Duong Nguyen, Bold Sandagdorj, Shu Tian, Milan Thomas, and Mai Lin Villaruel. The authors are in the Southeast Asia and Economic Research and Development Impact departments, ADB and ADB Institute. Effective 1 February 2021, ADB placed a temporary hold on sovereign project disbursements and new contracts in Myanmar.

given its contribution to growth in transportation and hospitality. However, consumer sentiment fell in several economies. In Malaysia, it was tempered by increased worries over inflation and job prospects. It was dampened by tight monetary conditions in Thailand and high food inflation in the Philippines. Financial institutions tightened loan conditions due to rising defaults on auto and mortgage loans among low-income earners in Thailand.

Public spending is spurring growth in the bigger economies. In Indonesia, election-related spending and increased public investment contributed to robust growth in H1 2024. The budget deficit will likely exceed the target of 2.3% of GDP as the government extends social assistance and accelerates public infrastructure projects this year. Higher public investment is boosting the Philippine economy with large infrastructure projects underway. Malaysia benefited as well from ongoing and upcoming public mega infrastructure and data center building projects. Domestic demand in Viet Nam revived slowly in Q2 2024 with continued fiscal support, including an extension of the 2 percentage points value-added tax cut. Likewise, higher public spending increased consumption in Singapore.

Growth in several economies is weakening. A decline in public investment is dampening growth prospects for the Lao PDR, Thailand, and Timor-Leste. Multiple challenges in Myanmar led to a downgrade in growth forecasts for 2024 and 2025. Disrupted trade due to escalating conflict at major border trade zones, a volatile exchange rate, skyrocketing inflation, weaker investment and production, and macroeconomic instability impede recovery. Economic growth in Timor-Leste is being affected by lower public capital spending from delays in approvals and procurement. Delays in public disbursements coupled with a cabinet reshuffle in Thailand could slow growth. Political uncertainty could also delay the government's infrastructure investment plan and foreign direct investment. Debt servicing is also crowding out other important public spending in the Lao PDR, given its tight fiscal space. Total public and publicly guaranteed debt as a share of GDP declined from 112% in 2022 to 108% in 2023, but the ratio of external debt service to total government revenue jumped from 27% to 43%. To address liquidity challenges, the Lao PDR government continued to seek deferrals in scheduled loan service payments. External public debt service deferrals amounted to $1.9 billion between 2020 and 2023.

The continued recovery in tourism and expansion in other services support growth. Tourist arrivals to Southeast Asia reached 61.4 million in H1 2024, 32% more than H1 2023. Viet Nam already exceeded its pre-pandemic international tourist arrivals by July 2023. Various programs to boost tourism further were initiated across the region. Services in Singapore gained from a concert-driven boost in Q1 2024. Indonesia officially launched a golden visa program in August 2024 to offer long-term residency to foreign nationals who make substantial investments in the country. The program has issued 300 permits and attracted $123 million since its pilot in August 2023, and it targets 1,000 golden visas by year-end. Thailand announced the doubling of the visa exemption period to 60 days for visitors from 93 economies in July 2024. Malaysia benefits from increased flight capacities and increased tourist arrivals from the People's Republic of China (PRC) and India, who are now given visa exemptions. Visit Laos Year 2024, the ASEAN Chairmanship, and the railway service between the Lao PDR and the PRC significantly boosted tourism in the Lao PDR, which posted a 26% increase in H1 2024 over the same period last year.

Recoveries in exports are contributing to growth. Export growth by end-July 2024 turned positive for most Southeast Asian economies, with many benefiting from improved external demand in the US and ASEAN along with soaring global demand for semiconductors. Manufacturing in Viet Nam expanded in H1 2024 due to a resurgence in manufactured rubber, metal products, electrical equipment, electronics, and computers. Malaysia's exports to the US; Taipei,China; and Viet Nam increased significantly in H1 2024. Philippine merchandise exports, mainly electronic products, recovered as well. The ASEAN manufacturing purchasing managers' index stabilized above 50 in H1 2024, signifying expansion. The increase in production and purchasing reflected a continuing increase in both domestic and external demand.

Bullish foreign direct investment (FDI) inflows are sustaining the manufacturing recovery. FDI continued to rise in 2024 driven by global supply chain relocation and restructuring. Inflows to Indonesia, Malaysia, the Philippines, Singapore, Thailand, and Viet Nam reached $222 billion in 2023 compared to the $43 billion entering the PRC. The total FDI inflow remained steady at $144 billion in Q1 2024,

2% more than the Q1 2023 level, while the PRC saw FDI contract by 112% during the same period. Electric vehicle manufacturing and semiconductor chips captured the bulk of FDI inflows. Malaysia formally opened its first semiconductor integrated circuit design hub in August, the latest step in its attempt to move up the value chain. In the Philippines and Viet Nam, about 77% of newly registered foreign investment in H1 2024 was in manufacturing, including electronics. Other FDI went to financial services, information and communications (Singapore), and real estate (the Philippines and Viet Nam).

Inflation forecasts for Southeast Asia have been revised up for 2024 and 2025 (Figure 3.4.2). Significant price increases in the Lao PDR and Myanmar drove overall 2024 inflation for Southeast Asia up to 3.3% from April's 3.2%. Inflation in most economies fell as global food prices eased despite oil price volatility. Inflation estimates for Indonesia and Viet Nam for 2024 remain unchanged. But forecasts for Brunei Darussalam, Cambodia, Malaysia, the

Philippines, Singapore, Thailand, and Timor-Leste were revised down for the year, as H1 results were below *ADO April 2024* projections. For 2025, it is adjusted up from 3.0% to 3.2% mainly from higher estimates for Cambodia, the Lao PDR, and Myanmar. The impact of a weakening kip and ringgit against the US dollar will likely offset the inflation decrease in the Philippines and Thailand. To lessen the financial pressure on businesses and consumers, Thailand decided not to increase electricity tariffs in Q4 2024 as planned, and will maintain the current cap on electricity prices until the end of the year. Moderating inflation will likely lead to further monetary easing in the Philippines through 2025.

Monetary authorities adopted measures to stimulate growth. The Philippine central bank announced a 25 basis point cut in its policy rate in August to prop up consumer spending and investment. The State Bank of Vietnam continued to pursue its flexible monetary policy to facilitate low-cost financing to support growth. It has extended the deadline for adopting regulatory forbearance toward clients in difficulty until end-December 2024. The Lao PDR kip weakened amid economic uncertainty while the Indonesian rupiah, the Philippine peso and Thai baht stabilized in August on expectations of US interest rate cuts. Bank Indonesia kept its policy rate steady after a surprise hike in April to defend the rupiah's competitiveness.

Figure 3.4.2 Inflation in Southeast Asia

Most economies will benefit from moderating inflation.

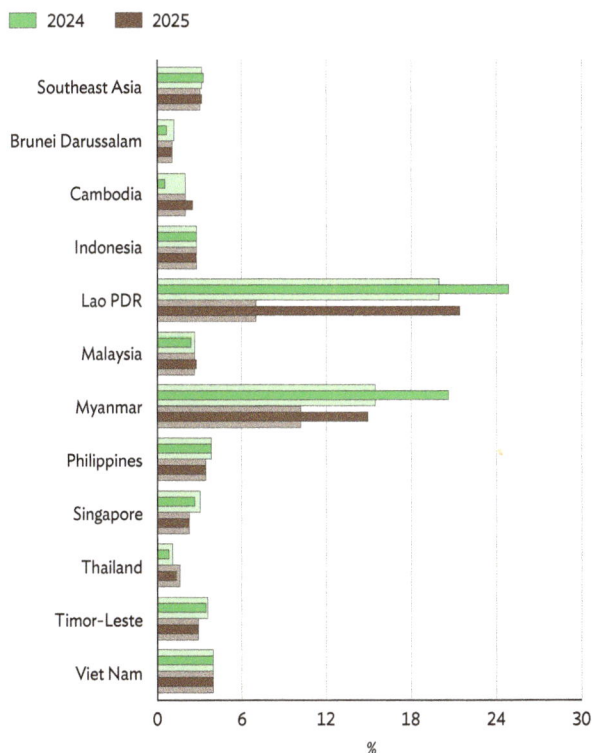

Note: Lighter colored bars are *Asian Development Outlook April 2024* forecasts.

Source: *Asian Development Outlook* database (accessed 5 September 2024).

Indonesia

The economy has performed in line with *ADO April 2024* forecasts for 2024 and 2025. Domestic demand will continue to cover the lower contribution from net exports to drive GDP growth up by 5.0% each year. As expected, inflation slowed and the current account deficit gradually expanded. Well-anchored inflation expectations, improved supply-side management, and the relatively stable exchange rate should keep inflation within Bank Indonesia's target range.

Updated Assessment

Domestic demand remained the main driver of growth this year, while net external demand provided little impetus. GDP growth eased to 5.0% year on year in the second quarter (Q2) of 2024, down from 5.1% in Q1. This led to a 5.1% expansion in the first half (H1) of the year, matching the H1 2023 growth rate (Figure 3.4.3). Growth slowed in Q2 in the aftermath of the national elections in mid-February. Growth was driven by robust private consumption and increased public investment.

Figure 3.4.3 Demand-Side Contributions to Growth

Domestic demand remained the principal growth driver, with net external demand providing little impetus.

- Domestic demand
- Exports of goods and services
- Imports of goods and services
- Statistical discrepancy
- Gross domestic product growth, %

Percentage points

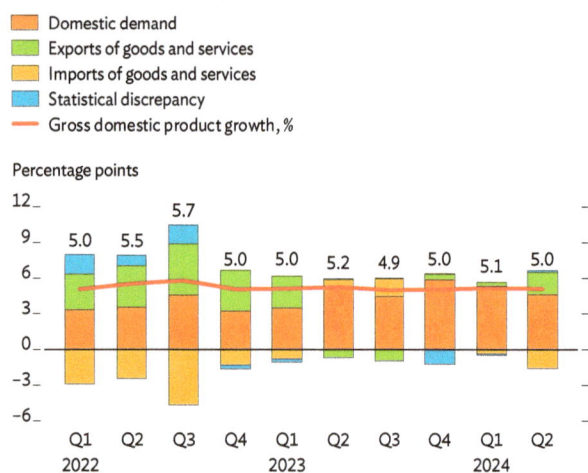

Q = quarter.
Source: Haver Analytics.

Figure 3.4.4 Contributions of Investment Components to Growth

Increased public infrastructure spending spurred investment.

- Buildings
- Changes in inventories
- Machinery
- Others
- Investment growth, %

Percentage points

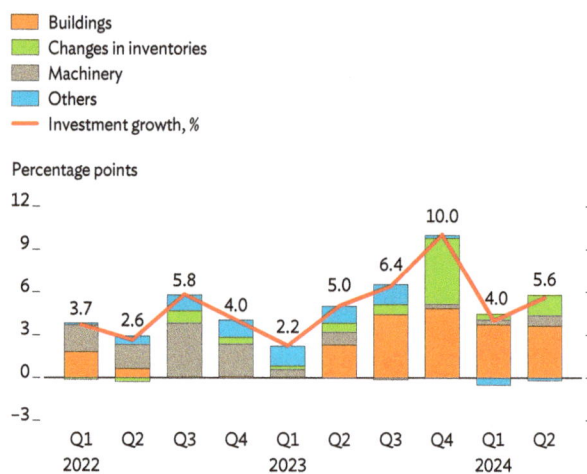

Q = quarter.
Source: Haver Analytics.

The national elections and a decline in nonfood inflation bolstered consumption. The February election, lower nonfood inflation, and an increase in public wages boosted private consumption spending—which accounts for 56% of GDP—by 5.2% in H1 2024, up from 4.9% in H1 2023. Government consumption surged by 9.1%, on the account of spending on the elections and personnel and social programs.

Increased public infrastructure spending fueled a rise in investment. Fixed capital formation increased by 4.1% in H1 2024, up from 3.3% in H1 2023. The increase was due to construction as the current administration accelerated priority infrastructure projects and the New Capital City development to meet targets set before its term ends in October 2024 (Figure 3.4.4). Investment in machinery also picked up in Q2 driven by investments in metal and chemical industries.

Although real imports grew faster than exports, net exports still contributed modestly to GDP growth. Goods and services exports grew by 4.7% in H1 2024, much lower than the double-digit growth rates in 2021–2022, then driven by the resumption of post-pandemic global trade and the commodity boom. After rising domestic demand and a low base last year, real imports grew by 5.2%. Overall, net exports contributed marginally to GDP growth by 0.1 percentage points.

A dwindling surplus in merchandise trade widened the current account deficit. Weak global demand and falling commodity prices in H1 2024 reduced merchandise exports in US dollar terms, offsetting gains in export volumes (Figure 3.4.5). Overall, exports by value fell by 3.6%. In contrast, merchandise imports edged up by 0.8%, driven by a stronger US dollar and increased imports of intermediate goods aligned with growth in export volume (Figure 3.4.6). As a result, the trade surplus decreased by 22.3% to $19.2 billion. Combined with larger deficits in services and income accounts, the drop led to a current account deficit of $5.4 billion, equal to 0.8% of GDP, reversing the $2.5 billion surplus in H2 2023.

Figure 3.4.5 Contributions to Merchandise Export Growth

Weak global demand lowered global commodity prices and offset growth in export volume.

- Palm oil
- Mineral products
- Others
- Growth in total value, %
- Growth in total volume, %

Percentage points

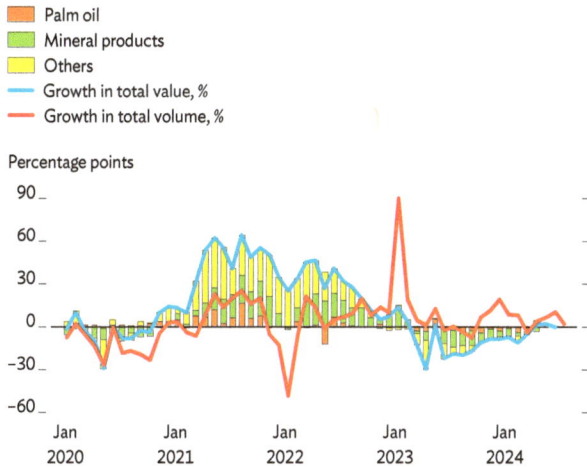

Source: Haver Analytics.

Figure 3.4.6 Contributions to Growth of Merchandise Imports

Merchandise imports grew in line with export volume growth.

- Consumption goods
- Raw materials
- Capital goods
- Total value growth, %
- Total volume growth, %

Percentage points

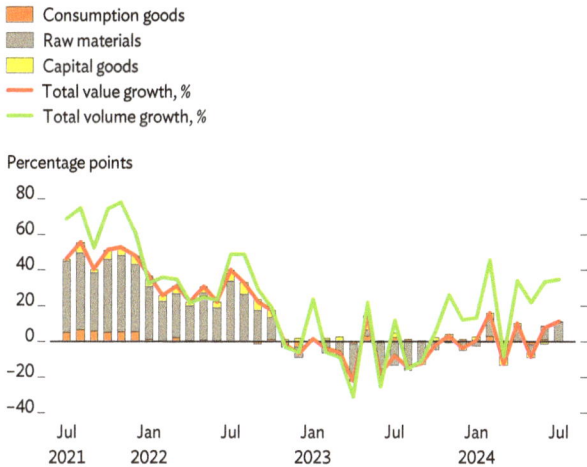

Source: Haver Analytics.

Prompt action by Bank Indonesia to manage capital outflows led to an improved capital and financial account. The capital and financial account recorded a $2.7 billion surplus in Q2, reversing the $1.6 billion deficit in Q1, as net portfolio investment recovered and the deficit in other investments declined (Figure 3.4.7). Bank Indonesia raised its policy rate by 25 basis points to 6.25% in April, the highest rate since 2016, to mitigate capital outflows, reduce pressure on foreign exchange reserves, and stabilize the weakening

Figure 3.4.7 Balance of Payments

In the first half of 2024, the overall capital and financial account surplus was unable to offset the current account deficit.

- Current account
- Financial and capital accounts
- International reserves

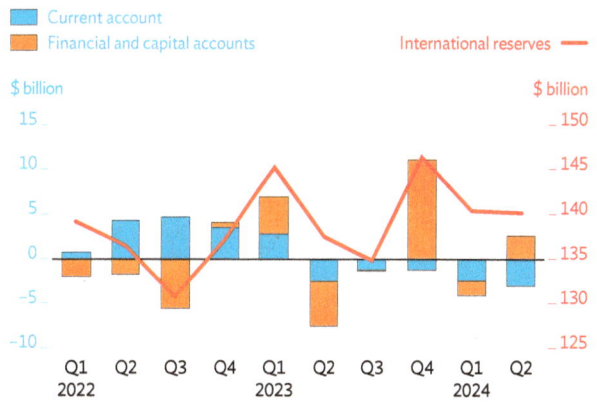

Q = quarter.
Source: Haver Analytics.

rupiah. The rate hike comes after the introduction of new foreign exchange-denominated securities in September 2023 to attract domestic and nonresident investors. The higher interest rate increased the appeal of these securities and led to a reversal of portfolio outflows. As a result, monetary authority liabilities increased by $5.5 billion in Q2 over Q1, and foreign capital flows into government bonds increased by $1.9 billion.

The balance of payments remained in deficit in H1 2024. The $1 billion surplus in the capital and financial account could not offset the current account deficit, resulting in an overall balance of payments deficit of $6.5 billion. Gross international reserves fell by $10.2 billion between December 2023 and April 2024 primarily due to foreign debt repayments and the central bank's support of the rupiah. However, reserves have increased since May following the interest rate hike in April and increased expectations of possible cuts in the US rate. International reserves stood at $147 billion in July 2024, $1.0 billion higher than in January, equivalent to about 6.5 months of imports (Figure 3.4.8). The rupiah depreciated by 0.4% through end-August 2024.

Fiscal policy continued to support growth in H1 2024. Central government expenditure and transfers to regions grew by 11.3%. Personnel and material spending increased significantly with an 8% increase in civil service wages and election spending,

Figure 3.4.8 Reserves and the Exchange Rate

The rupiah depreciated slightly in the first half, while gross international reserves rebounded.

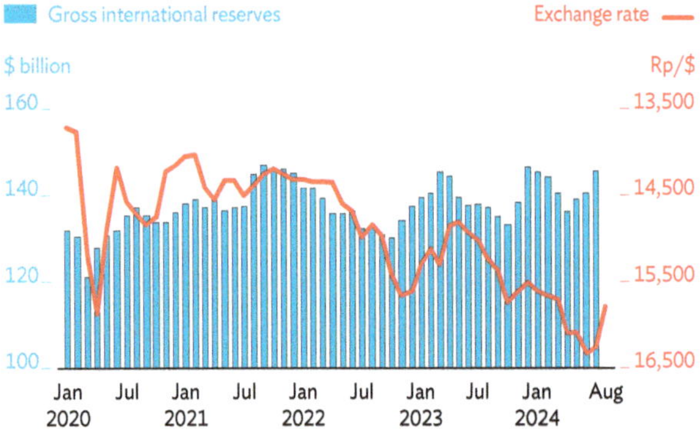

Source: Haver Analytics.

Figure 3.4.9 Monthly Inflation

Effective supply management by the government drove volatile food prices down.

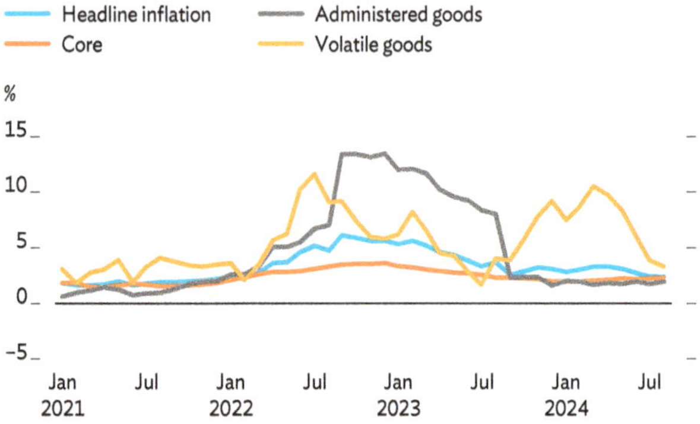

Source: Haver Analytics.

as did social spending with cash transfers and rice aid programs to mitigate the impact of increasing food prices. Capital spending grew by 31.3% in line with the New Capital City development target. Meanwhile, central government revenue and grants contracted by 6.2% due to subsiding commodity windfalls and lower tax revenues. The budget deficit was 0.3% of GDP in H1 2024, compared to a 0.7% surplus a year earlier. Total central government debt as a share of GDP was 39.0% in June 2024, slightly down from 39.2% in 2023 after peaking at 40.7% in 2021.

Agriculture and manufacturing grew more slowly, while other industries and services expanded faster. El Niño-induced drought reduced agriculture growth from 1.3% in H1 2023 to 0.1% in H1 2024. Within the same period, lackluster external demand also reduced manufacturing growth from 4.7% to 4.0%. Increased domestic consumption and political party election spending pushed services growth up from 6.6% to 6.8%. Public administration, social security, and social work expanded significantly. Construction increased from 2.7% to 7.4% due to public infrastructure projects, while mining increased modestly.

Inflation has remained within Bank Indonesia's target range since June. Inflation declined from 2.6% in January to 2.1% in August, averaging 2.6% in the first 8 months of 2024, close to the lower end of Bank Indonesia's 2.5%–3.5% target range (Figure 3.4.9). Despite weather-related damage to food production, the government's effective supply management drove

food prices down. Core inflation remained below 2.0% for the past 12 months, suggesting inflation expectations were well-anchored.

Prospects

The GDP growth forecasts for 2024 and 2025 remain unchanged at 5.0% (Table 3.4.1). Overall, the economy has performed in line with *ADO April 2024* projections. Domestic demand will continue to stimulate growth and offset the weaker contribution from net exports. Robust private consumption, public infrastructure spending, and gradually improving investment should sustain GDP growth during the forecast horizon.

Consumption will remain robust. Private consumption will likely hold up in the near term. November's regional elections, to be conducted

Table 3.4.1 Selected Economic Indicators in Indonesia, %

Domestic demand will drive GDP growth to 5.0% in 2024 and 2025.

	2023	2024		2025	
		Apr	Sep	Apr	Sep
GDP growth	5.0	5.0	5.0	5.0	5.0
Inflation	3.7	2.8	2.8	2.8	2.8

GDP = gross domestic product.

Sources: Central Bureau of Statistics; Asian Development Bank estimates.

simultaneously in 37 provinces, 415 districts, and 93 cities, should boost consumption further this year. Low and stable inflation, along with another increase in civil servant salaries and new social spending programs from the incoming administration, should underpin consumer spending growth in 2025. Consumer confidence and retail sales trends are broadly in line with pre-pandemic levels (Figure 3.4.10).

Figure 3.4.10 Consumer Demand Indicators

Consumer demand indicators are broadly at pre-pandemic levels.

Source: Haver Analytics.

Investment is expected to gradually improve.

The current administration is speeding up priority infrastructure and New Capital City projects until the new government takes office in October. Public investment should remain buoyant, with planned infrastructure spending remaining strong into next year. Private investment will likely improve over the forecast period, benefiting from the positive sentiment after successful election cycles and earlier reforms. The gradual adoption of the Omnibus Job Creation Law should also help to boost investment in 2025. However, boosting competitiveness remains a challenge in promoting further private investment. Factory activity fell for the second consecutive month in August 2024, with output and new orders falling to their lowest levels in 3 years. Foreign orders are falling at the fastest rate since January 2023, causing the S&P global manufacturing purchasing managers' index (PMI) to decline to 48.9 from 49.3 (Figure 3.4.11). The weakening index is likely attributable to a recent decrease in nickel demand from the People's Republic of China and continuing challenges in domestic labor-intensive industries such as textiles and footwear in the face of weak global demand and the lingering problems with competitiveness (Figure 3.4.12).

Figure 3.4.11 Purchasing Managers' Index, by Component and Distance from Threshold

Factory activity contracted for the second straight month in August 2024 as foreign orders decreased at the fastest rate since January 2023.

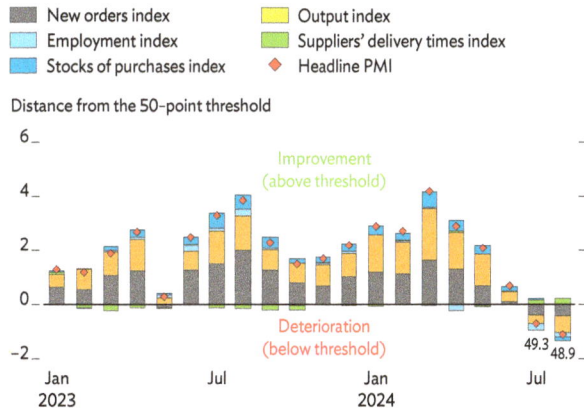

PMI = purchasing managers' index.

Note: Numbers below red marker refers to actual PMI readings. Distance from threshold is calculated as the PMI Index or Subindex minus 50, while the contributions are the distance multiplied by weight. Positive distance or readings above 50 indicate improvement, while negative distance or readings below 50 indicate deterioration.

Sources: Staff calculations using data from CEIC Database, and S&P.

Figure 3.4.12 Manufacturing Growth, Selected Industries

Labor-intensive industries face ongoing challenges of weak global demand and a lingering problem with competitiveness.

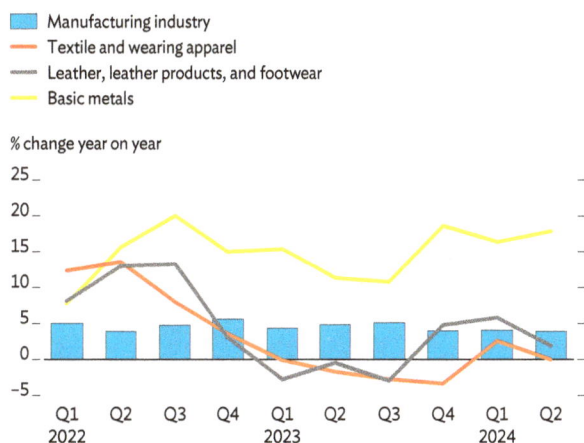

Q = quarter.
Source: CEIC Data Company.

Fiscal policy will likely continue to support growth.

Extending existing social assistance programs and accelerating public infrastructure projects should result in a higher 2024 budget deficit than the government's original target of 2.3% of GDP. However, the proposed 2025 budget remains prudent, keeping the deficit equivalent to 2.5% of GDP with 5.9% growth in spending lower than the 6.9% growth in revenue. To stimulate growth, the incoming government appears to be focusing on programs aimed at increasing purchasing power. The government plans to increase public service expenses by 8.2% in 2025, which suggests a rise in civil servant pay. Social protection spending is expected to increase by 4.0%, healthcare by 5.4%, and education, including the flagship free school meal program, by 24.3%. Infrastructure spending is expected to remain high, albeit declining by 5.5%. Tax income is projected to increase by 12.3%, with the tax to GDP ratio rising from 9.8% in 2024 to 10.2%.

Bank Indonesia will continue to manage capital flows and exchange rate fluctuations. The policy interest rate within the forecast horizon will be influenced by US interest rate movements. To mitigate the impact of high interest rates on domestic economic activity, the reserve requirement ratio for bank lending to strategic sectors will remain low. Credit growth to the private sector increased from 9.0% in October 2023 to 10.5% in April, then fell to 8.4% in July following the April rate hike. The current account deficit should widen due to weak commodity prices and global demand affecting exports, while imports will likely expand with more robust investment prospects. Overall, the exchange rate should remain stable as the effects of a wider current account deficit are compensated for by the return of capital inflows, driven by expected lower interest rates globally.

Inflation should remain within Bank Indonesia's target range. Headline inflation is expected to remain relatively stable, averaging 2.8% in 2024 and 2025. Core inflation will likely remain subdued, reflecting well-anchored inflation expectations. Food inflation will remain manageable, thanks to inflation control measures implemented by the country's official regional inflation task force. There are concerns over the potential weakening of economic momentum due to consecutive month-on-month deflation since May this year. However, this outlook does not reflect those concerns, as the month-on-month deflation so far has been driven mainly by a fall in prices in volatile food components from improved harvests.

Risks to the forecast are evenly balanced. Smooth elections this year may improve business confidence, potentially leading to stronger and faster investment growth. The US has started easing, thus improving

stability in global demand, potentially reducing borrowing costs, and easing access to external financing. On the downside, risks are primarily external. The possibility that US interest rates will remain higher for longer than expected, continuing geopolitical uncertainty, and further climate change-related shocks may disrupt global value chains and induce sharper declines in the terms of trade. Demand from the People's Republic of China, Indonesia's largest trading partner, could fall further if the economy weakens more than anticipated.

Malaysia

Economic growth accelerated in the first half (H1) of 2024 but is expected to moderate in the year's second half (H2). The growth forecast from *ADO April 2024* remains at 4.5% for 2024 and 4.6% for 2025. The headline inflation rate forecast is lowered from 2.6% to 2.4% for 2024, with the forecast for 2025 increased from 2.6% to 2.7%, mainly because the rationalization of fuel subsidies is being pushed to the latter part of the year (Table 3.4.2).

Table 3.4.2 Selected Economic Indicators in Malaysia, %

Growth projections for 2024 and 2025 remain unchanged while inflation is now expected to be lower for 2024 and higher for 2025.

	2023	2024		2025	
		Apr	Sep	Apr	Sep
GDP growth	3.6	4.5	4.5	4.6	4.6
Inflation	2.5	2.6	2.4	2.6	2.7

GDP = gross domestic product.
Sources: Department of Statistics Malaysia; Asian Development Bank estimates.

Updated Assessment

GDP grew 5.9% in the second quarter (Q2) of 2024, resulting in 5.1% growth for H1 2024, compared to 4.1% in H1 2023. Growth was driven by robust consumption, strong public and private investment growth, and a recovery in external trade (Figure 3.4.13). All sectors expanded, led by construction, which grew in double digits.

Figure 3.4.13 Demand-Side Contributions to Growth

Consumption continued to be robust, along with solid public and private investment growth.

- ■ Private consumption
- ■ Government consumption
- ■ Public fixed investment
- ■ Private fixed investment
- ■ Change in stocks
- ■ Exports of goods and services
- ■ Imports of goods and services
- — Gross domestic product growth, %

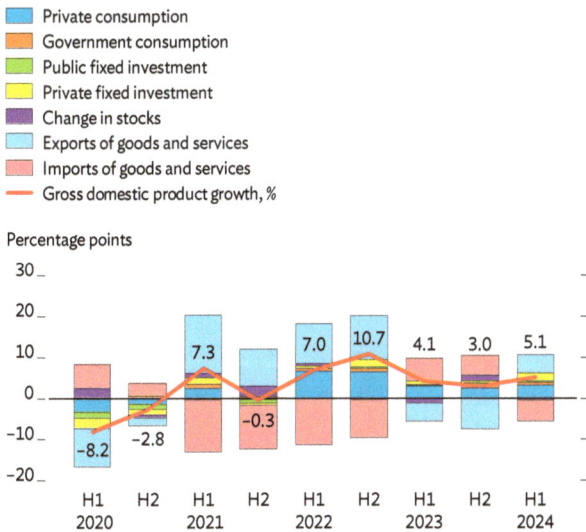

H = half.

Sources: Department of Statistics Malaysia Official Portal; Haver Analytics.

Private consumption continued strong as favorable labor market conditions and government policy support lifted private spending. Private consumption expanded 5.3% in H1 2024. With rising worker demand, labor market conditions remained robust. Labor force participation rose to 70.4% in June 2024 compared to 70.0% in June 2023 and those employed increased to 16.6 million, up by 1.8% from June 2023. The unemployment rate has been 3.3% over the past 8 months. To further support private spending amid subsidy rationalization, the government allowed the Employees Provident Fund to be flexible in making it more accessible to contributors.

Public consumption increased by 5.5% in H1 2024 compared to just 0.6% in H1 2023. Although rationalization will reduce the cost of subsidies, government spending grew with significant increases in expenditures for emoluments, pensions and gratuities, supplies and services, grants, and transfers to state governments and public entities. Given the changes in the Employees Provident Fund, as of early June RM7.81 billion ($1.78 billion) of retirement savings had been withdrawn from the national pension fund.

A substantial increase in investment spurred growth. Private investment rose by 10.6% in H1 2024 while public investment grew by 10.3%. Ongoing and expected public

mega infrastructure and data center projects boosted investment in structures by 12.7% and machinery and equipment by 12.1%. These included spillovers from the current construction of Pan Borneo Sarawak Phase 1, Pan Borneo Sabah Phase 1, and Sarawak Link Road.

External trade recovered with growth in exports and imports. Exports rebounded in H1 2024, expanding by 6.8% after a decline of 6.0% in H1 2023 (Figure 3.4.14). This was due to greater exports to the US, which increased by 12.1%, and regional markets such as Taipei,China and Viet Nam, where exports grew by 44.3% and 32.4%, respectively. Manufactured exports, which account for 85.3% of total exports, rose by 3.9% in H1 2024, led by machinery, equipment and parts. Other exports, such as agriculture, increased by 3.8% and mining by 3.5%. Imports grew by 8.4% in H1 2024. Capital goods expanded by 35.0% with intermediate goods rising by 21.2%, while consumption goods increased by 15.2%. As import growth outpaced export growth, the trade balance decreased by $1.0 billion.

Figure 3.4.14 Export Growth

External trade recovered with exports rebounding in the first half of 2024.

- ···· Exports
- — Manufactured goods
- — Machinery and transport equipment
- — Mineral fuels, lubricants, etc.

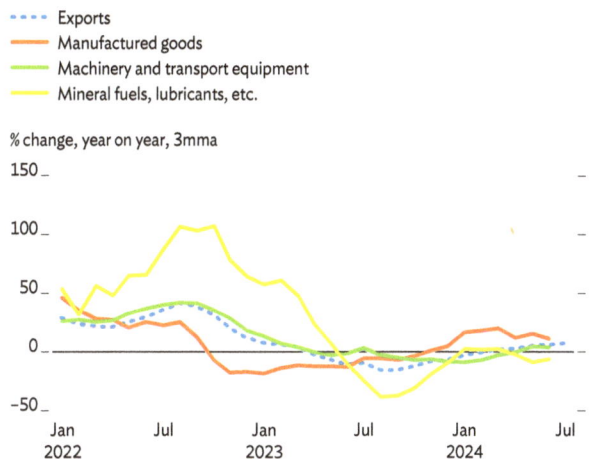

Source: Haver Analytics.

On the supply side, all sectors expanded, led by construction and services. Construction grew by 14.6% in H1 2024, almost twice the rate of H1 2023 (Figure 3.4.15). Services expanded by 5.4% in H1 2024, lower than the 5.8% growth in H1 2023. Nonetheless, tourism-related services, including accommodations and transport and storage services, remained robust. There were also substantial increases in real estate,

Figure 3.4.15 Supply-Side Contributions to Growth

All sectors expanded, led by construction.

- Agriculture
- Industry
- Services
- ─── Gross domestic product growth, %

Percentage points

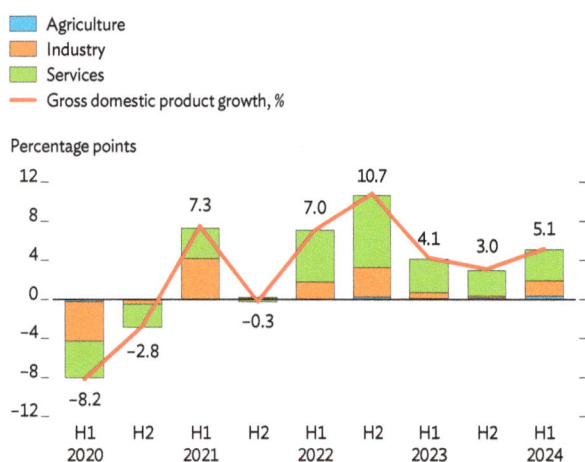

H = half.

Sources: Department of Statistics Malaysia Official Portal; Haver Analytics.

finance, insurance, and business services, with each growing by 8.0%–10.0%. Consumer-related services such as retail and food and beverage continued to increase, albeit at a slower pace of 4.3% and 3.6%, respectively.

Manufacturing expanded nearly double the rate a year ago. Manufacturing grew by 3.3% in H1 2024 compared to 1.7% in H1 2023 (Figure 3.4.16). Electrical products, accounting for 32.8% of the sector, grew by 1.8% in H1 2024 compared to 1.2% in H1 2023. There were also substantial improvements in other subsectors, such as non-metallic mineral product manufacturing, basic metals, and fabricated metal products, which accelerated to 8.3% in H1 2024

Figure 3.4.16 Manufacturing

Manufacturing rebounded with substantial improvements across sub-sectors.

% change year on year

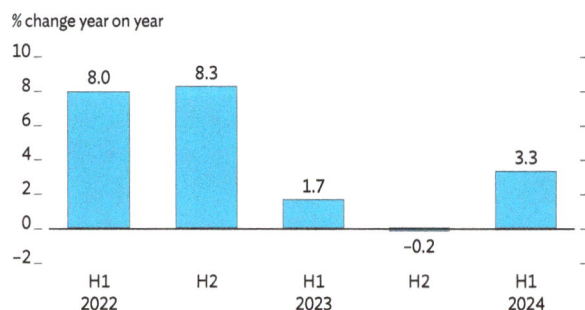

H = half.

Source: Haver Analytics.

from 4.5% in H1 2023. Similarly, manufacturing of petroleum, chemical, rubber, and plastic products rose by 2.6% in H1 2024 compared to 0.1% in H1 2023.

Agriculture and mining also improved. Agriculture rose by 4.5% in H1 2024, up from a minimal 0.3% growth in H1 2023. Except for aquaculture, forestry, and logging, all subsectors recovered after contracting in H1 2023. Palm oil grew by 10.7%, marine fishing by 7.6%, and livestock by 5.2%. Mining and quarrying recovered from a 0.2% decline in H1 2023, growing by 4.3% in H1 2024. The expansion was largely due to increased production in the natural gas subsector.

Inflation remained manageable. Inflation moderated to an average of 1.8% in H1 2024 from 3.2% in H1 2023. Inflation in food and beverages fell from 6.2% in H1 2023 to 1.9% in H1 2024. From 3.6% in H1 2023, core inflation decreased to 1.8% in H1 2024 (Figure 3.4.17). Given robust growth and low inflation, Bank Negara Malaysia (BNM) kept its monetary policy rate at 3.0% to continue supporting growth.

Coordinated efforts by the government and BNM led to a slight pause in the depreciation of the Malaysian ringgit against the US dollar. The weakening of the ringgit, which began late last year, was mainly attributed to external factors such as the slower-than-expected recovery in the PRC and continued elevated monetary policy rate in the US. The exchange rate was RM4.60 per US dollar in July 2024, a depreciation of 0.32% from RM4.59

Figure 3.4.17 Monthly Inflation

Inflation moderated to an average of 1.8%.

- Overall
- Food
- Nonfood

%

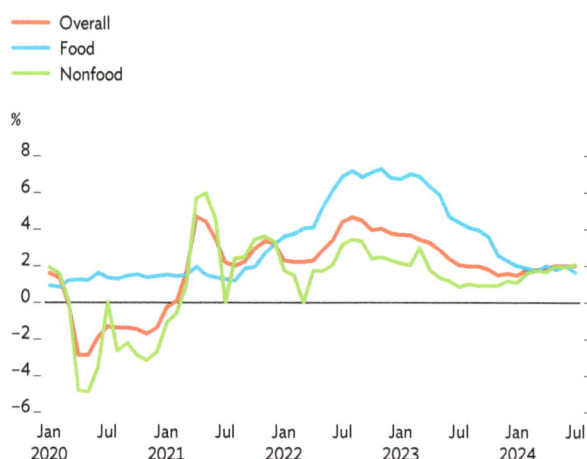

Source: Haver Analytics.

per US dollar in end-December 2023. July 2024 showed slight improvement compared to the previous months of 2024, when the exchange rate was higher than RM4.70 per US dollar (Figure 3.4.18). To strengthen the currency, the government and central bank undertook initiatives such as repatriating foreign income from government-linked investment companies, converting foreign income to ringgit, and encouraging export companies to convert export earnings and conduct export settlements in the local currency.

Figure 3.4.18 Exchange Rate

The ringgit slightly strengthened against the dollar in July.

RM/$ (inverted scale)

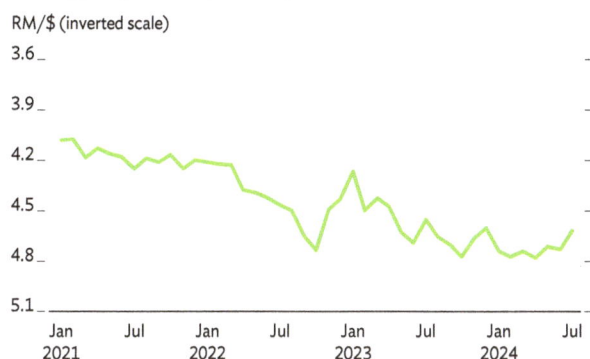

RM = Malaysian ringgit.
Source: CEIC Data Company.

The fiscal deficit and external debt inched higher, although international reserves strengthened.
The fiscal deficit was higher at 5.5% in H1 2024 from 4.5% in H1 2023. Revenues declined by 6.3%, led by a 19.2% decrease in tax revenue collections in Q1 2024. Expenditures increased by 1.3%, with operating expenditures rising by 9.2%. External debt rose to 70.8% of GDP in June 2024 from 67.3% in June 2023 due to increased interbank borrowings and other debt liabilities from trade credits. However, the import cover ratio improved to 5.5 months in July 2024 from 5.1 months in July 2023, with international reserves rising from $114.7 billion to $112.9 billion.

Prospects

Economic growth is projected to remain strong.
Although the high-frequency drivers of private spending seem to have slowed, private consumption will be lifted by future job opportunities from expected investment projects and income support measures (Figure 3.4.19).

Figure 3.4.19 Gross Domestic Product Growth

Growth is projected to remain strong.

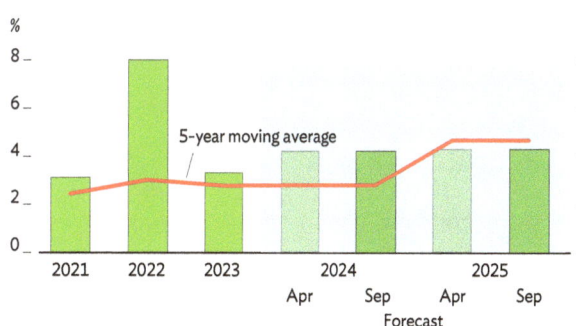

Source: *Asian Development Outlook* database (accessed 5 September 2024).

Investment and construction momentum will continue, given the government's drive to fast track infrastructure projects and its goal to become a regional digital hub. There has been substantial growth in tourist arrivals, and they are expected to surpass pre-pandemic levels starting this year. Demand for commodities and export goods has recovered, although demand from major trading partners remains tempered.

Private consumption will continue to drive growth, although some indicators show signs of a possible slowdown. The consumer sentiment index dropped to 87.1 in Q1 2024 from 89.4 the previous quarter, with a less vibrant outlook for the labor market, a drop in expected financing and increasing worries about inflation. Nonetheless, policy support such as restructuring the Employees Provident Fund and plans to increase civil servant wages by more than 13.0% at the end of 2024 will boost spending. In addition, robust investment and construction activities should provide more job opportunities.

Vibrant tourism will continue to boost private spending. In H1 2024, tourism arrivals reached 11.8 million, up by 28.9% compared to last year. The government targets 27.3 million tourist arrivals in 2024, up by 35.5% from 2023 and 4.6% from pre-pandemic 2019. This will bring robust growth to tourism and related services.

Positive expectations on the business environment bode well. The business conditions index increased to 94.3 in Q1 2024 from 89.0 in Q4 2023 on rising sales and domestic orders (Figure 3.4.20). From the Q2 2024 Business Tendency survey, firms' business

Figure 3.4.20 Consumer and Business Confidence

Positive expectations bode well for business.

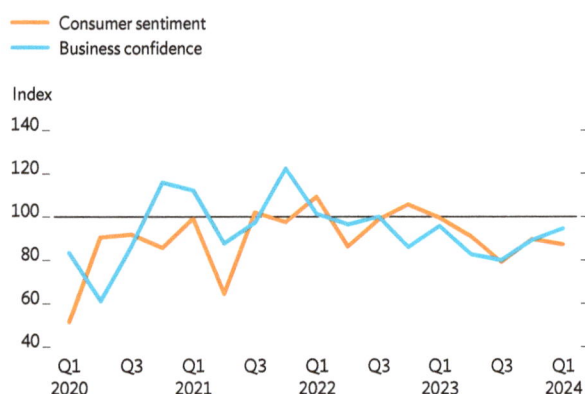

Q = quarter.
Sources: CEIC Data Company; Haver Analytics.

Figure 3.4.21 Investment

The digital transformation will boost investment.

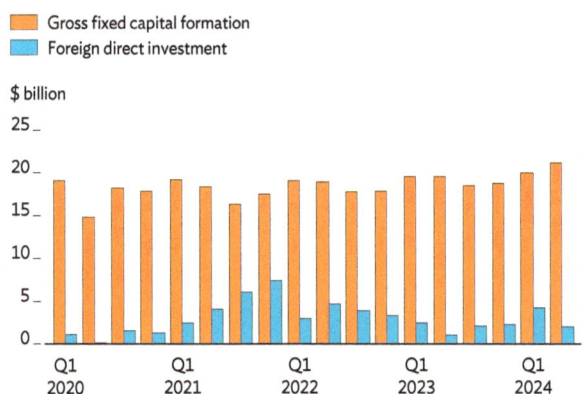

Q = quarter.
Source: CEIC Data Company.

outlook from April to September 2024 is positive, driven by optimism across sectors except wholesale and retail trade.

Manufacturing and exports should continue to recover this year, although uncertainties in external demand could become a constraint. The growth of manufactured goods and exports will continue with the technology upcycle as the global market for semiconductors is forecast to grow by 16.0% this year. Since January 2024, growth in manufacturing sales of electrical products has been positive after contracting in Q4 2023. The growth of manufactured goods and exports may be tempered however by reduced external demand mainly due to the slower-than-expected recovery in the PRC. Exports to Malaysia's top two trading partners—the PRC and Singapore—have yet to recover, although demand from other markets has picked up.

The economy's digital transformation will boost investment alongside government reforms to ease the entry of foreign direct investment. In Q1 2024, approved investments were driven by a 19.2% increase in foreign investment compared to Q1 2023 (Figure 3.4.21). The *2024 Global Data Centre Index* identifies the state of Johor as Southeast Asia's fastest-growing data center. Thus, tech companies such as Google, Microsoft, and Nvidia have committed investments and developed plans to establish data centers and artificial intelligence infrastructure in the country. Government initiatives to support these

investments include creating the Digital Investment Office, a platform to coordinate and facilitate both local and foreign investments, and Malaysian Digital, which provides incentives and privileges for eligible companies undertaking digital activities defined under the program. With data centers consuming a large amount of energy and water, the Energy Transition and Water Transformation Ministry plans to implement a framework for the data center industry alongside its commitment to ensure effective resource use.

Construction will continue to benefit from spillovers from the government push for mega infrastructure projects and the digital expansion. The number of construction projects in H1 2024 increased by 15.5%, driven mainly by building new data centers (Figure 3.4.22). These projects will continue for the rest of the year, along with the rollout of government development projects. Near-term projects include the Pan Borneo Highway Phase 1B, the Penang Light Rail Transit, and the Sarawak-Sabah Link Road Phase 2.

Inflation is forecast to trend upward over the next 2 years. The government has lifted some of its blanket subsidies. The rationalization of diesel subsidies starting June 2024 substantially affected inflation, which increased from 1.7% in Q1 2024 to 1.9% in Q2 2024. The price cap on diesel was lifted only for Peninsular Malaysia, while diesel prices remain low for Sabah, Sarawak, and Labuan. In addition, the government has postponed rationalization of the RON95 petrol

Figure 3.4.22 Construction

Construction will benefit from spillovers from mega infrastructure projects.

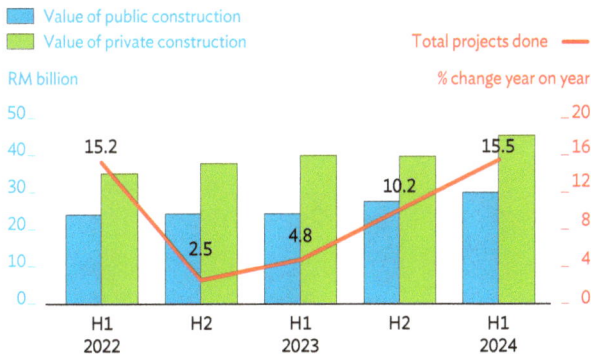

■ Value of public construction
■ Value of private construction
Total projects done —

H = half.
Source: Haver Analytics.

subsidies. Headline inflation for 2024 is projected to be 2.4%, slightly down from the 2.6% projected in April. Further rationalization of fuel subsidies will likely be pushed toward the latter part of 2025. Thus, the inflation forecast for 2025 is increased to 2.7% from 2.6%.

The monetary policy rate is expected to remain at 3.0%. The upside risk to inflation has been delayed due to the postponement of the reduction in RON95 subsidies. Even with the diesel subsidy rationalization in June 2024, inflation is still under control, averaging below BNM's target of 2.0%–3.5% for 2024. BNM is unlikely to use monetary policy to bolster the ringgit. Coordinated efforts of the government and BNM, such as the repatriation of foreign income by government-linked companies and investment companies, have strengthened the ringgit. The ringgit dropped to RM4.31 at the end of August after floating above RM4.70 since the start of 2024.

Downside risks to the forecast primarily come from uncertainties in the external environment. Slower-than-expected growth among major trading partners could weaken export performance. Other downside risks include increased geopolitical tensions and shocks to commodity prices and production. Upsides to growth could come from more significant spillovers from the technology upcycle and greater realization of investments.

Philippines

Growth forecasts remain unchanged from *ADO April 2024* while the inflation outlook is improved. Real GDP growth remained strong in the first half (H1) of the year driven by domestic demand and a recovery in goods exports. Moderating inflation and monetary easing should continue to support growth.

Updated Assessment

Domestic demand lifted growth to 6.3% year on year in the second quarter (Q2), bringing H1 2024 growth to 6.0% compared to 5.3% in the same period last year. A sustained expansion in household spending and investment, and a rebound in government consumption lifted growth. Household consumption moderated to 4.6% year-on-year growth in H1 2024 from 5.9% in H1 2023, though it remained the largest contributor to GDP, accounting for over 50% of the expansion (Figure 3.4.23). Stronger employment, higher overseas workers' remittances, and rapid consumer loan growth continued to support household spending. The unemployment rate has declined from a year earlier to 4.7% in July 2024 from 4.9% in July 2023. Remittances from overseas workers rose 2.9% to $18.1 billion in H1 2024, equal to 8.2% of GDP. Consumer lending grew briskly and was 24.3% higher in July 2024 compared to a year ago, driven by credit card debt. Public consumption rebounded from a 2023 contraction, growing 6.6% in part on measures to improve budget execution.

Figure 3.4.23 Demand-Side Contributions to Growth

Household consumption and investment continued to drive growth.

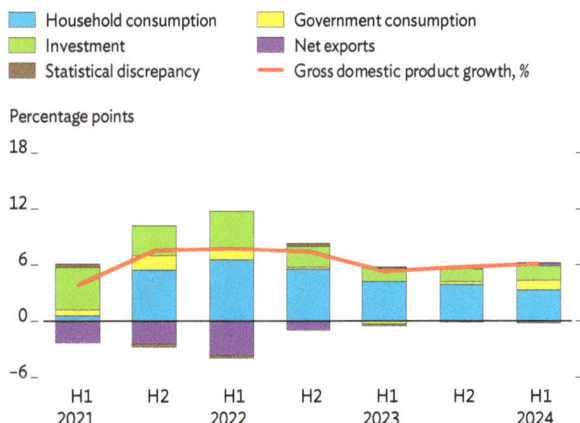

■ Household consumption   ■ Government consumption
■ Investment   ■ Net exports
■ Statistical discrepancy — Gross domestic product growth, %

H = half.
Sources: Philippine Statistics Authority; CEIC Data Company.

Investment was fueled by brisk public construction.
Investment grew by a strong 6.5% year on year in
H1 2024 from 5.9% in H1 2023, accounting for
one-fourth of the GDP expansion. Public construction
rose by 19.5% on several ongoing infrastructure
projects, including railways, ports, and expressways.
Private construction expanded by 7.5%. Investment in
durable equipment fell with lower outlays for transport
equipment from last year's high base, partly tempered
by an increase in general industrial machinery.

**Net exports added to GDP growth on a rebound in
merchandise exports.** Exports of goods and services
rose faster (6.3% year on year, constant terms) than
imports (3.7%). Merchandise exports recovered with
the rise in global merchandise trade, while services
exports, mainly tourism and business processing
outsourcing, remained buoyant.

**On the supply side, services largely drove GDP
growth, led by retail trade and tourism.** Robust
services growth (6.8% year on year in H1 2024 from
7.1% in H1 2023) contributed nearly three-fourths
of the GDP expansion (Figure 3.4.24). Finance,
professional, and business services also posted strong
gains. Industry grew by an accelerated 6.4% year on
year, more than double last year. Manufacturing grew
by 4.0% while construction sustained its double-
digit growth at 12.4% propelling industry forward
(Figure 3.4.25). Agriculture declined by 0.9% as major
crops, including rice and corn, fell due to the drier
effects of El Niño.

Figure 3.4.24 Supply-Side Contributions to Growth

Robust services and a pickup in industry lifted growth.

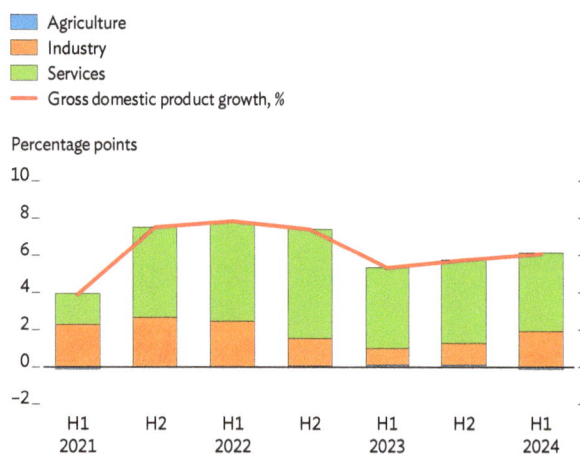

Legend:
- Agriculture
- Industry
- Services
- Gross domestic product growth, %

Percentage points

H = half.
Sources: Philippine Statistics Authority; CEIC Data Company.

Figure 3.4.25 Contributions to Industry Growth

*Brisk construction and stronger manufacturing boosted industrial
production.*

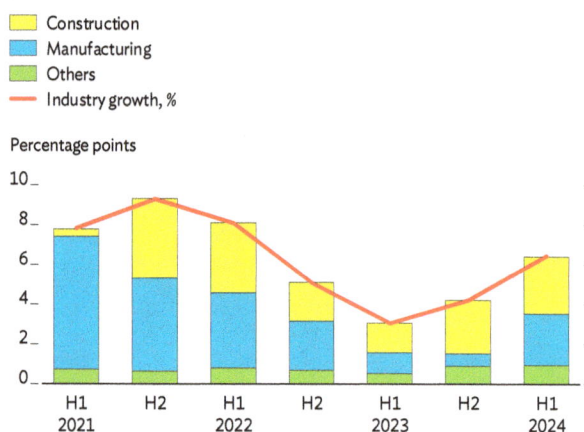

Legend:
- Construction
- Manufacturing
- Others
- Industry growth, %

Percentage points

H = half.
Sources: Philippine Statistics Authority; CEIC Data Company.

**Inflation eased on a moderation in food and
transport prices.** Headline inflation slowed to 3.3% in
August averaging 3.6% in the first 8 months compared
to 6.6% in the same period in 2023 with food inflation
contributing about half (Figure 3.4.26). Food inflation
decelerated to 4.2% from 6.7% in July with a slowdown
in price increases of rice and meat, while fish and
vegetable prices declined. Rice inflation has eased
since March to 14.7% in August, and fell by 0.5% month
on month on continued imports levied with lower
tariff. Transport inflation declined on lower domestic
petroleum prices. Core inflation has been down this
year, to 2.6% in August from 2.9% in July, on the

Figure 3.4.26 Contributions to Inflation, 2018 = 100

Inflation slowed on a moderation in food and transport prices.

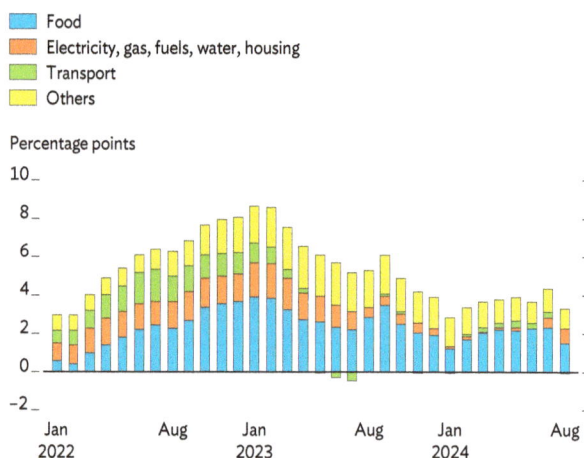

Legend:
- Food
- Electricity, gas, fuels, water, housing
- Transport
- Others

Percentage points

Sources: Philippine Statistics Authority; CEIC Data Company.

lagged effects of tight monetary policy. Core inflation averaged 3.2% in the first 8 months, below headline inflation (Figure 3.4.27). Domestic liquidity continued to rise in July by 7.2% year on year with brisk bank lending. The banking system's nonperforming loan ratio was 3.2% as of end-June 2024, about the same as the 3.1% at end-June 2023.

Figure 3.4.27 Headline and Core Inflation, 2018 = 100

The lagged effects of tight monetary policy reined in core inflation.

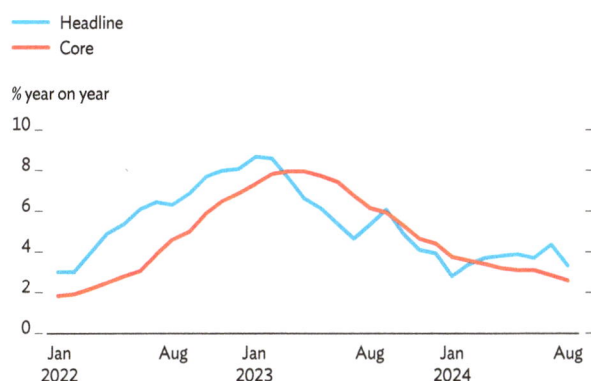

Sources: Philippine Statistics Authority; CEIC Data Company.

The fiscal deficit equaled 4.9% of GDP in H1 2024 and will likely stay within the 5.6% of GDP target for the full year. Higher revenues contained the deficit, rising 15.6% year on year in H1 2024 from 7.7% in H1 2023, 3.7% higher than programmed. Tax collection comprises 85% of revenues and rose by 10% year on year, while non-tax revenue increased by a substantial 63.3% as the government hiked dividend rates of government-owned and -controlled corporations to 75% of their net earnings from 50%. Government measures to boost digitalization to enhance tax administration also lifted revenue collection. Expenditures excluding interest payments rose by 12.1% year on year in H1 2024, with higher spending for infrastructure and social services.

The current account deficit narrowed to 3.2% of GDP in H1 2024 from 4.1% in H1 2023 on a lower merchandise trade deficit. The merchandise trade deficit fell to 14.2% of GDP from 16.0% as exports, mainly electronic products, rebounded in line with improved external demand. Imports fell as global commodity prices moderated. Higher remittances from overseas workers and earnings from services exports also supported the current account. In the financial

account, foreign direct investment reported lower net inflows. Portfolio investment posted net inflows, reversing a net outflow last year. The overall balance of payments surplus was 0.7% of GDP in H1 2024 compared to 1.1% in H1 2023.

Ample international reserves lent support to the external sector. Official reserves were $107.9 billion as of end-August, equivalent to 7.8 months of imports of goods along with services and income payments. The external debt to GDP ratio rose from 28.7% at the end of 2023 to 28.9% as of June 2024, mostly medium to long-term maturities. The Philippine peso depreciated by 1.5% against the US dollar in the year through August.

Prospects

Growth forecasts remain unchanged at 6.0% in 2024 and 6.2% in 2025 (Table 3.4.3). Growth is underpinned by broad-based domestic demand supported by a moderation in inflation and monetary easing (Figure 3.4.28). Sustained public investment, with its high multipliers, continues to lift growth.

Table 3.4.3 Selected Economic Indicators in the Philippines, %

Growth will remain robust, underpinned by broad-based domestic demand.

	2023	2024		2025	
		Apr	Sep	Apr	Sep
GDP growth	5.5	6.0	6.0	6.2	6.2
Inflation	6.0	3.8	3.6	3.4	3.2

GDP = gross domestic product.
Source: Asian Development Bank estimates.

Figure 3.4.28 Inflation

Moderating inflation and further monetary easing will support demand.

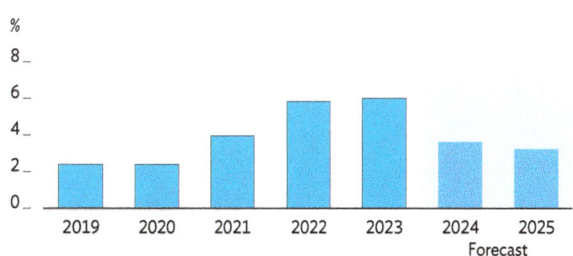

Sources: Philippine Statistics Authority; Asian Development Bank estimates.

Structural reforms, including market liberalization, open the economy to more foreign investment and trade, and support private investment.

Rising employment, higher remittance inflows, and lower interest rates will continue to support household spending. In July 2024, there were 3.1 million more jobs than a year ago. The services sector accounted for 70% of the increase in jobs, mostly in the wholesale and retail trades, accommodations and food services. Employment in agriculture also rose, while jobs in industry slightly declined. Despite the increase in new jobs, the number of unemployed was high at 2.4 million, 43% of which were youths aged 15–24 years. The youth unemployment rate was high at 14.8% in July 2024 compared with 14.2% in July 2023. Other challenges include the increase in elementary occupations and clerical jobs, which totalled a third of total employment in July 2024. Vulnerable jobs (own-account and unpaid family workers) also rose, comprising 36.3% of total employment. The 2023 "Trabaho para sa Bayan" Act (National Employment Master Plan) aims to support workers and businesses through industry-relevant upskilling and reskilling programs, active labor market programs including employment facilitation, and support to micro, small, and medium enterprises (MSMEs), for example, by increasing access to finance.

Manufacturing and construction prospects remain positive. The purchasing managers' index for manufacturing remained above the 50.0 threshold (steady at 51.2 in July and August), indicating continued expansion (Figure 3.4.29). Output and new orders expanded further, which led firms to raise purchasing and inventory along with adding new jobs. Manufacturing capacity utilization rose to 75.6% in July from 73.6% a year ago. High capacity utilization appeared in food processing, computers and electronic products, machinery, transport and electrical equipment. Infrastructure investment and public projects will underpin construction, while manufacturing will gain from an export recovery and robust domestic demand. Other positive indicators include sustained growth in passenger and commercial motor vehicle sales and lending to businesses in July such as manufacturing (7.9% growth year on year), and transportation and storage (20.6%).

Services, accounting for about 60% of GDP, should remain robust. Private consumption will underpin retail trade while growing international tourist arrivals will continue to benefit a range of services, notably hotels and restaurants, transport, and communication. International tourist arrivals rose by 10.8% year on year to 3.7 million in January to August 2024. The government is targeting at least 7.7 million for 2024, still below the 8.3 million arrivals in pre-pandemic 2019. In 2023, tourism accounted for 8.6% of GDP compared to 12.9% in 2019 (Figure 3.4.30). Tourism remains a key source of jobs, accounting for 12.9% of total employment in 2023 compared to 16.8% in 2019.

Figure 3.4.29 Manufacturing Purchasing Managers' Index

Leading indicators for manufacturing indicate continued expansion.

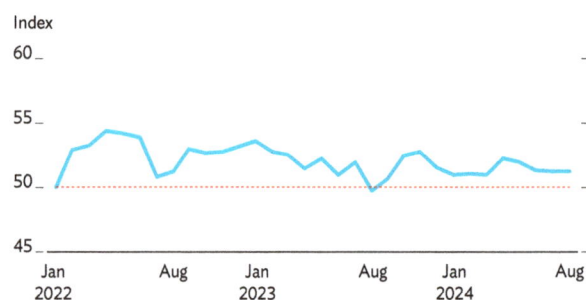

Note: A purchasing managers' index reading of <50 signals deterioration and >50 improvement.
Source: CEIC Data Company.

Figure 3.4.30 Tourism's Share of Employment and Gross Domestic Product

Tourism continues to recover but is still below pre-pandemic levels.

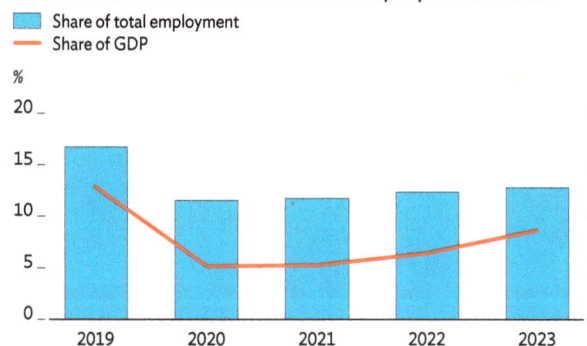

GDP = gross domestic product.
Source: Philippine Statistics Authority.

The proposed national budget for 2025 is 10.1% higher than in 2024, with one-third allocated for social services. Social programs include national health insurance, food stamps, nutrition and education programs, livelihood assistance, and conditional cash transfers to poor households. These programs aim to reduce poverty further. Poverty incidence declined to 15.5% of the population in 2023 from 18.1% in 2021. The number of poor declined to 17.5 million from 19.9 million in 2021, or lower by 2.4 million. The poverty rate fell across most regions, though in 2023 still high at 21.4% in the Visayas and 24.8% in Mindanao.

Public infrastructure spending, equivalent to 5.8% of GDP in 2023, is planned to be 5.0%–6.0% of GDP from this year through 2028. Infrastructure disbursements continued to rise at a double-digit pace through June (20.6% higher year on year in H1 2024). Under the government's infrastructure program, 66 projects are underway while another 31 have been approved for implementation as of August 2024. Most projects aim to improve physical connectivity through railways, bridges, and airports, or strengthen water management through irrigation, water supply, and flood control. Climate change mitigation and adaptation are priorities, as are digital connectivity, energy, and agriculture projects. The government has enhanced guidelines for project formulation, prioritization, and monitoring, as well as to expedite issuance of permits and licenses. The national budget also includes provisions for salary increases for government workers and support for holding midterm national and local elections in 2025.

The government is mobilizing more revenue to support higher investment while keeping within its fiscal consolidation goals. Under the government's medium-term fiscal framework, the fiscal deficit is programmed to narrow to 5.2% of GDP in 2025 and reach 3.7% of GDP by 2028. This is anchored on additional revenues. Proposed tax measures include a value-added tax on foreign digital service providers, an excise tax on single-use plastics, and rationalizing the mining fiscal regime. Digitalization programs are being ramped up to improve tax administration. Programs are also being undertaken to make spending more efficient. These include initiatives to right-size government bureaucracy and public financial management reform. The approval of the new government procurement law in July enhances project implementation and

procurement processes. These measures, from both the revenue and expenditure sides, will help manage government debt, which is programmed to fall below 60% of GDP in the medium-term. National government debt grew to 60.9% of GDP at the end of 2022 before declining to 60.1% at the end of 2023 (Figure 3.4.31). Debt composition remains favorable, with two-thirds denominated in Philippine peso, most of it medium or long-term. The country's investment-grade sovereign credit ratings were affirmed in 2024, supporting favorable international financing conditions.

Figure 3.4.31 Government Debt

Public debt relative to GDP, largely composed of domestic borrowing, rose substantially during the pandemic but edged down to 60.1% in 2023.

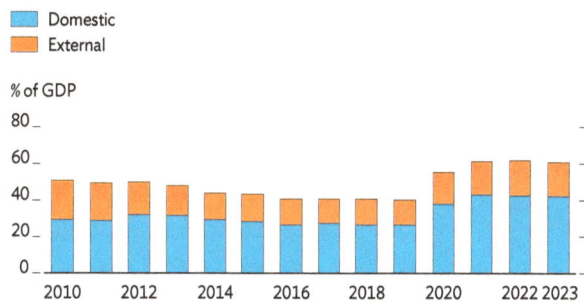

GDP = gross domestic product.
Sources: Bureau of the Treasury; CEIC Data Company.

Reforms are supporting private investment. Restrictions on foreign investor participation have been eased, opening up several sectors such as renewable energy, airports, telecommunications, railways, and expressways to full foreign ownership. These reforms complement the Philippines' ratification of the Regional Comprehensive Economic Partnership in February 2023. The Corporate Recovery and Tax Incentives for Enterprises Law, which reduced the corporate income tax rate from 30% to 25% (20% for MSMEs), is being refined to enhance investor incentives. The Public–Private Partnership Code that improved the regulatory framework for public-private partnerships also bodes well.

Inflation forecasts are lowered to 3.6% this year and 3.2% in 2025 with the moderation in food prices. Food price pressures are expected to continue to dissipate on the impact of reduced import duties on key staples. The government reduced rice duties to 15% from 35% for imports until 2028 subject to periodic review, and extended the reduced tariff rates on corn, pork, and mechanically-deboned meat. A sustained moderation in inflation could allow further monetary policy easing after a 25-basis point cut in the policy rate to 6.25% in mid-August. This was the first rate adjustment following the 450-basis point hike between May 2022 and October 2023.

The current account deficit will narrow this year supported by a recovery in merchandise exports and strong services exports. Tourism and business processing outsourcing should remain buoyant, while merchandise exports can recover with improved growth prospects in key markets like Japan and the euro area, which are among the top export destinations (Figure 3.4.32). Steady growth in remittances from overseas workers will continue to help lift the current account.

Figure 3.4.32 Merchandise Exports to Major Markets, 2023

Major advanced economies account for a significant share of exports.

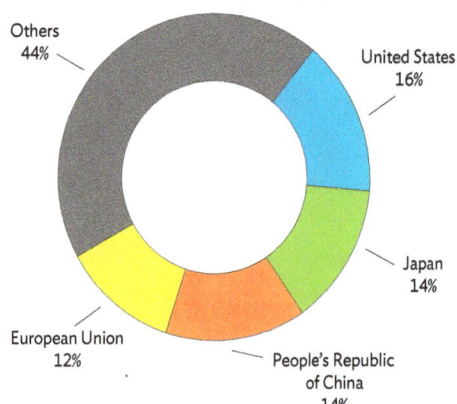

Others 44%
United States 16%
Japan 14%
People's Republic of China 14%
European Union 12%

Sources: Philippine Statistics Authority; CEIC Data Company.

Risks weigh on the outlook. Risk factors include a sharper slowdown in major advanced economies and the People's Republic of China, and financial volatility arising from US monetary policy decisions. Heightened geopolitical tensions and higher global commodity prices also pose risks. Severe weather events could elevate inflationary pressures.

Thailand

The growth forecasts from *ADO April 2024* have been lowered for 2024 and 2025, mainly due to weaker-than-expected public spending, private investment, and merchandise exports. Tourism and private consumption remain the main engines of growth. Headline inflation is forecast slightly lower. Risks to the growth outlook remain on the downside, most notably from global economic volatility, climate change, and high household and small- to medium-sized enterprise debt.

Updated Assessment

In the first half (H1) of 2024, the economy slowed from H1 last year due to a decline in public consumption and investment alongside a contraction in private investment. Real GDP expanded by 1.9% year on year. Exports of goods and services grew by 3.6% with a continued rise in international tourist arrivals. Total international tourists to Thailand increased by 35% to 17.5 million during H1 2024 compared to the same period in 2023. Goods exports remained the same as H1 last year at around B3.2 trillion. Exports of agricultural products, particularly rice, fruit, processed fruit, pet food, rubber, and processed chicken strengthened with rising external demand, mainly from the People's Republic of China (PRC) and the rest of Southeast Asia. However, exports of sugar and cassava dragged growth because of a supply shortage caused by El Niño. Exports of manufacturing products expanded moderately, primarily on exports of parts and telecommunication devices to the US and Hong Kong, China. Other major manufacturing exports, such as automotive parts, integrated circuits, electrical appliances, and chemical products contracted from lower exports to Australia, Europe, and the US. Imports of goods and services expanded by 2.8% from increasing Thailand's outbound tourism and other business service payments. Freight payments also increased as geopolitical tensions continued to escalate (Figure 3.4.33).

Private consumption expanded by 5.4% in H1, mainly from spending on tourism-related services. The labor market improved from higher employment in services and manufacturing. The unemployment rate at the end of June 2024 was a low 0.9%. However, consumer confidence in June 2024 fell to its lowest

Figure 3.4.33 Demand-Side Contributions to Growth

Strong tourism and private consumption supported economic growth in H1 2024.

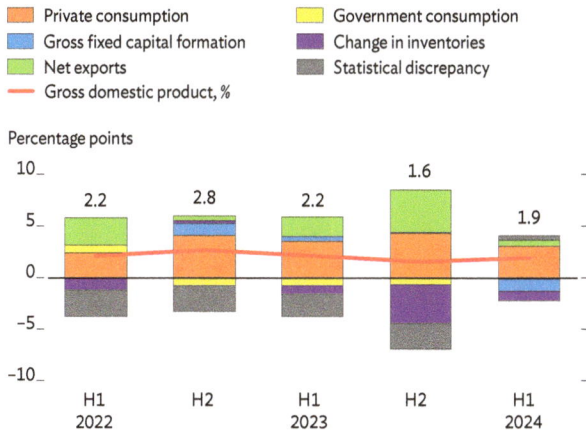

- Private consumption
- Gross fixed capital formation
- Net exports
- Gross domestic product, %
- Government consumption
- Change in inventories
- Statistical discrepancy

Percentage points

H = half.

Source: Office of the National Economic and Social Development Board.

H1 2024. Public investment started to increase in June, led by disbursements from the Irrigation Agency, while state-owned enterprise investment recorded small growth, led by projects in water pipeline construction, electricity distribution, mineral exploration, and communication network equipment. The public debt-to-GDP ratio remained manageable at 63.5% at the end of June 2024, up from 62.3% at the beginning of FY2024 (Figure 3.4.34).

Figure 3.4.34 Public Debt

Public debt increased slightly since the beginning of FY2024.

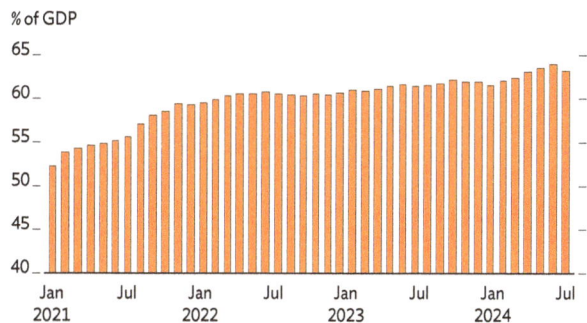

% of GDP

GDP = gross domestic product.

Source: Public Debt Management Office.

level since September 2023 due to concerns about an economic slowdown and political uncertainty. Household debt was a high 90.8% of GDP in the first quarter (Q1) of 2024. Still, the nonperforming loan ratio remained manageable at 2.8% in Q2 2024. Defaults on automobile and mortgage loans, however, particularly among low-income earners, increased prompting financial institutions to tighten loan conditions. Vehicle and residential property sales declined in H1 2024.

Private investment declined by 0.9% due to a contraction in Q2 2024. Investment in machinery and equipment declined as investment in the automotive sector fell, aligned with a drop in passenger car, truck, motorcycle, and bus sales. Construction investment also contracted for all types of residential buildings, particularly in Bangkok and its vicinity. Meanwhile, foreign direct investment has been rising since the end of last year, particularly in automobiles and parts, electrical equipment, chemical products, and rubber products.

Public consumption contracted by 0.9% in H1 2024 with investment contracting by 16.7%. The budget bill for fiscal year 2024 (FY2024 ending 30 September 2024) was enacted in March 2024, with the government beginning disbursements in May. Expedited disbursements during May and June 2024 could not avoid a spending contraction for all of

From July to August 2024, the government sped up efforts to push GDP growth by rolling out new stimulus measures. Notable were a tax deduction for domestic travel expenses in second-tier provinces, soft loans to small and medium-sized enterprises, and a massive digital cash handout (the so-called digital wallet scheme) worth B450 billion ($12.5 billion). Registration for the digital wallet scheme began on 1 August 2024. A B10,000 ($277) transfer to recipients via a smartphone application is slated for early Q4 2024, with the funds intended to be spent locally within 6 months. The cabinet approved B276 billion in additional borrowing for FY2024 to finance the digital wallet scheme. That would bring the total budget for FY2024 from B3.5 trillion ($95.6 billion) to B3.6 trillion ($98.9 billion). However, after the new prime minister assumed office on 16 August 2024, the scheme's conditions will be revised. The handout will now be partly distributed in cash with the transfer period possibly changed.

By sector, services performed well in H1 2024. Services grew by 3.3%, led by tourism-related activities. Agriculture declined by 1.9% as El Niño threatened major crop production such as off-season rice, sugarcane, cassava, palm oil, and fruit, especially durian. Manufacturing continued to decline by 1.4%. The contraction was mainly attributed to electronics, computers and peripheral equipment, integrated circuits and semiconductors, along with hard-disk drives due to slowing external demand. Construction contracted, mainly from a decline in public construction (Figure 3.4.35).

Headline inflation in H1 2024 fell to an average 0% compared to the same period last year, below the central bank target range of 1%–3%. Since *ADO April 2024*, the policy interest rate was maintained at 2.5% with expectations that inflation will turn positive and gradually return to the central bank target. The Thai baht weakened by 5.8% in H1 2024 from the same period last year as outflows continued from both stock and bond markets, attributed to global volatility pending US interest rate cuts (Figure 3.4.36).

Prospects

The economic recovery has been slower than forecast in *ADO April 2024*, particularly in merchandise exports, private investment, and public spending. Real GDP growth for this year is revised down from the 2.6% forecast in April to 2.3% (Table 3.4.4 and Figure 3.4.37). With global economic uncertainty and Thailand's structural problems in export-oriented manufacturing, the economy in 2025 is projected to grow slower than previously expected. Real GDP for next year is thus revised down from 3.0% to 2.7%.

Exports of goods is expected to recover slower than the previous forecast mainly due to structural problems and intensified geopolitical tensions, while exports of services are projected to continue to be robust. Although global trade volumes will likely accelerate in the forecast period, Thailand may not fully capitalize on the trend as several export products do not meet the global demand shift toward high-technology products. Geopolitical tensions and rising production costs, including increases in the daily minimum wage, energy and electricity prices, higher freight and surcharge costs, and a shortage of containers could also hamper merchandise export performance. Meanwhile, growth in services exports is projected to remain strong. This year, the number

Figure 3.4.35 Supply-Side Contributions to Growth

Services led growth in H1 2024, while agriculture declined due to the impact of El Niño.

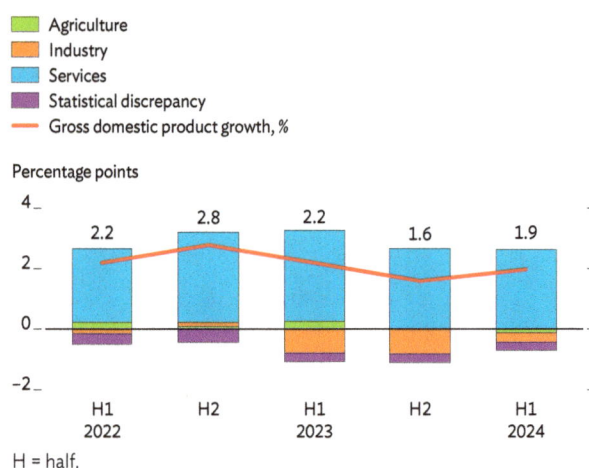

H = half.
Source: Office of the National Economic and Social Development Board.

Figure 3.4.36 Inflation and Policy Interest Rate

Low inflation persisted while the policy interest rate remained at 2.5%.

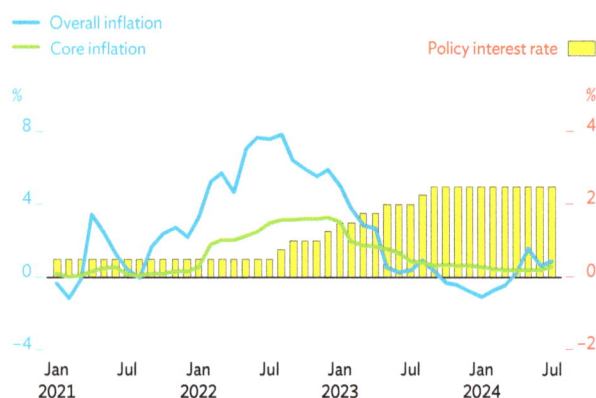

Source: CEIC Data Company.

Table 3.4.4 Selected Economic Indicators in Thailand, %

The economic recovery is below the April forecast due to weaker-than-expected export growth and private investment, and slow government disbursements.

	2023	2024		2025	
		Apr	Sep	Apr	Sep
GDP growth	1.9	2.6	2.3	3.0	2.7
Inflation	1.2	1.0	0.7	1.5	1.3

GDP = gross domestic product.
Sources: Office of the National Economic and Social Development Council; Asian Development Bank estimates.

Figure 3.4.37 Gross Domestic Product Growth

The growth forecast is revised down from 2.6% to 2.3% this year.

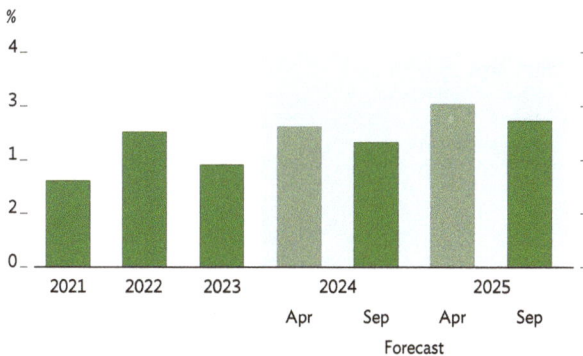

Source: *Asian Development Outlook* database (accessed 5 September 2024).

of international tourists is raised from 34 million to 35 million after Thailand announced the visa exemption extension period and increase the list of countries eligible for visa on arrival at immigration checkpoints. Imports of goods and services forecasts remain at 4.0% this year and 2.6% next year.

Private consumption is robust in 2024, but is likely to slow down next year due to tight financial conditions and continued weak consumer confidence. Even though spending on tourism activities could rise from the government tax incentive program and for those who work in tourism-related sectors and receive higher income from the rising number of international tourists, high household debt, weak consumer confidence, and stricter bank regulations could slow private consumption growth. In addition, there is concern over rising factory closures, which could hinder consumer purchasing power in the near term. The digital wallet program is expected to only have a small impact on private consumption as there are restrictions on location, retailer size, and types of products covered. Meanwhile, the private investment growth forecast is adjusted from 3.3% to 0.7% in 2024 due to the weaker-than-expected outturn in H1 2024, with growth for next year revised slightly from 3.5% to 3.2% due to growing investor concern over political uncertainty and policy continuity. In addition, a glut of cheap products, ranging from electronics, clothing and shoes, home decor items, and kitchen appliances, have been imported into Thailand from the PRC, likely affecting small and medium-sized enterprises as they lose price competitiveness.

Public spending is projected to accelerate after FY2024 budget got delayed for several months. Public consumption this year is below April expectations as growth contracted in H1 2024. Therefore, public consumption growth has been revised down slightly from the 1.5% forecast in April to 1.2%, with growth for next year maintained at 2.5%. Public investment is expected to accelerate in the remaining months of this year due to expedited disbursements after the FY2024 budget bill was enacted. However, it is not likely to compensate for the deep contraction in H1 2024. For next year, public agencies are expected to continue to speed up disbursements, particularly in projects that have been delayed since last year.

On the supply side, extreme weather events and weak merchandise exports could hamper agriculture and manufacturing growth, while services sector will remain strong. A shift from El Niño to La Niña is likely to affect Thailand from August into early next year, bringing more rain than usual, particularly to the northern and northeastern regions of the country. La Niña may ease drought severity from El Niño, but there may be a risk of flooding in these areas, affecting rice, fresh vegetables and some fruit production. Industrial growth this year is revised down as the merchandise export recovery is slower than expected. Industrial growth for next year remains at 2.7%. Growth in services is upgraded for 2024 in line with the rising estimated number of international tourists.

Inflation should remain low in 2024 and 2025. The headline inflation rate forecast is revised down from 1.0% in 2024 to 0.7% as inflation during H1 2024 was below April expectations (Figure 3.4.38). For 2025, the inflation forecast is also adjusted down from 1.5% to 1.3%. Prices of meat, fish, pork, aquatic animals, and fresh vegetables during H1 2024 were lower than expected due to ample market supply. Prices of these products are projected to gradually increase over the rest of 2024 and continue to increase in 2025 as unfavorable weather could reduce output. The government also retains energy prices cap and electricity tariffs to ease cost of living for households until the end of 2024.

Downside risks have deepened from *ADO April 2024* as the Thai economy will likely face increasing vulnerabilities and uncertainties. Extreme weather may affect agriculture production more than expected.

Figure 3.4.38 Inflation

Inflation is projected to remain low this year and next.

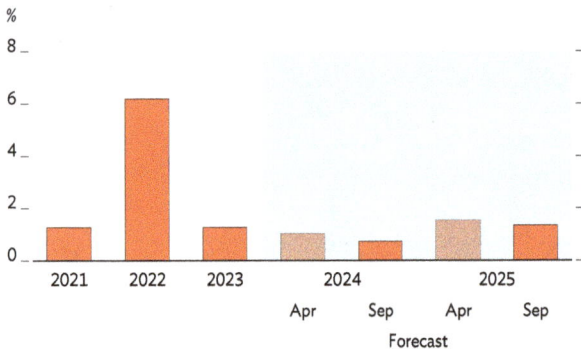

Source: *Asian Development Outlook* database (accessed 5 September 2024).

Figure 3.4.39 Supply-Side Contributions to Growth

All sectors performed strongly in H1 2024, particularly industry and construction.

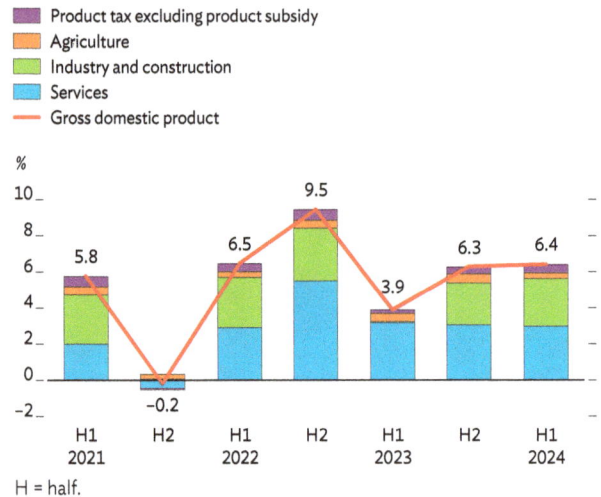

H = half.
Source: General Statistics Office.

Ongoing geopolitical conflict, elections in the US, and rising shipping costs could impact Thailand's exports more than expected. Increasing concerns about debt servicing among low-income households and small- and medium-sized enterprises is a key domestic risk. Furthermore, the domestic political situation should be closely monitored as it will directly impact implementation of big-ticket projects as well as consumer and investor confidence. Inflation pressures may emerge if energy and electricity price subsidies are further reduced in 2025 and global energy prices surge more than expected.

Viet Nam

The economy was robust in the first half (H1) of 2024, supported by improving industrial production and a strong recovery in trade. However, domestic demand remained sluggish, and subdued global economic prospects left some uncertainty. Projections for economic growth are unchanged at 6.0% this year and 6.2% in 2025. Inflation is expected to remain at 4.0% in both years due to persistent pressure from geopolitical tensions and disruptions in global supply chains. Significant downside risks—both domestic and external—highlight the need for accelerated institutional reforms to support the economy.

Updated Assessment

The economic recovery has strong momentum.
The economy expanded by 6.4% in H1 2024, almost double the 3.7% a year earlier (Figure 3.4.39). Industry

and construction grew by 7.5% compared with 1.1% in the same period last year. A resurgence in sectors such as rubber, metal products, electrical equipment, electronics, and computers boosted manufacturing by 8.7% relative to a low 0.4% a year ago. Services continued to grow at 6.6%, driven by a revival in tourism. Agriculture benefited from higher commodity prices, sustaining stable growth at 3.4%.

On the demand side, a strong trade bounce-back supported growth. Trade volumes recovered quickly, with exports up by 14.5% from last year's level while imports grew by 17%, leading to a trade surplus of $11.6 billion. However, this surplus was primarily driven by foreign direct investment (FDI)-led manufacturing, which contributed approximately $24 billion, while the domestic sector faced a trade deficit of $12.3 billion. Domestic demand revived slowly with a 5.8% expansion in final consumption with continued fiscal support, including the 2% value-added tax cut extension. Investment improved in H1 2024, with gross capital formation expanding by 6.7% after contracting 0.1% a year earlier.

Inward FDI continued to strengthen in H1 2024.
FDI disbursements increased to $10.8 billion, up 8.2% year on year, the highest for H1 in the last 5 years (Figure 3.4.40). In the same period, total FDI registrations reached $15.2 billion, a 13.1% increase

Figure 3.4.40 Foreign Direct Investment

Foreign direct investment continues to strengthen in 2024.

- New commitments
- Disbursements

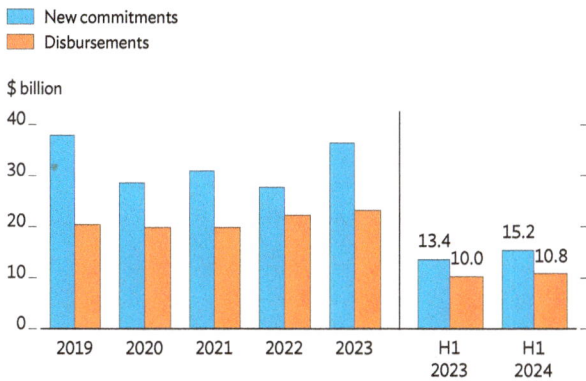

H = half.
Source: General Statistics Office.

Figure 3.4.42 Policy Interest Rates

The central bank maintained its pro-growth monetary policy in H1 2024.

- Discount rate
- Refinancing interest rate
- VND lending rate (average)

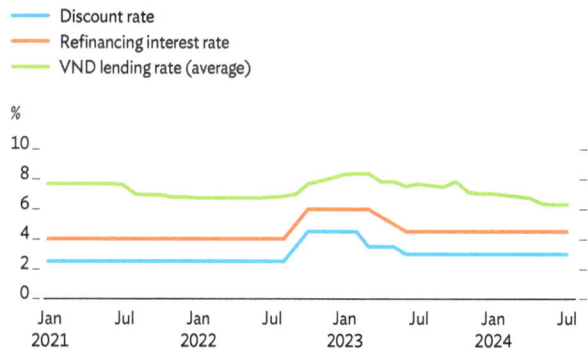

VND = Viet Nam dong.
Sources: State Bank of Vietnam; Asian Development Bank estimates.

year on year. Of the total, 71.6% was for manufacturing, particularly electronics, while about 20% went to real estate development.

Inflationary pressure inched up slightly. Inflation for H1 2024 averaged 4.1%, higher than the 3.3% the previous year, driven by higher foodstuff and domestic gasoline prices (Figure 3.4.41). Though month-on-month inflation was significant in January-February and July 2024, it largely stalled during the rest of the period, leaving prices up by 1.9% through August. A basic salary increase effective in July, currency depreciation, government-controlled fuel, electricity, education, and healthcare price adjustments also contributed to the overall inflation trend.

The State Bank of Viet Nam (SBV), the central bank, continued to pursue a flexible monetary policy to facilitate low-cost financing to support growth (Figures 3.4.42). It has extended the deadline

Figure 3.4.41 Monthly Inflation

Inflationary pressure inched up.

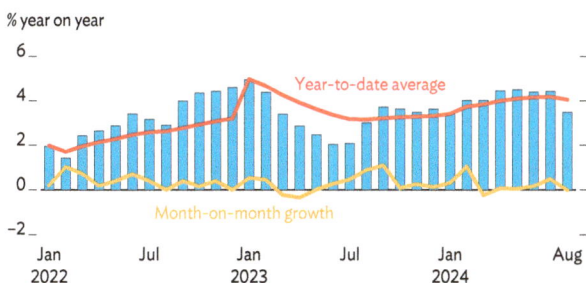

Source: General Statistics Office.

for adopting regulatory forbearance toward clients in difficulty until 31 December 2024. Accordingly, banks continued to restructure loans of clients in difficulty while retaining these loans in the same classification groups as before restructuring. Due to SBV's timely intervention in the foreign exchange market and in open market operations, the Viet Nam dong depreciated 5% against the US dollar in H1 2024, lower than some other regional currencies.

The corporate bond market recovered in H1 2024, compared to the low H1 base in 2023. Total issuance in the period amounted to an estimated VND115.5 trillion (equivalent to $4.7 billion), nearly 1.6 times of the issuance volume a year ago. Most of the issuance (around 64%) came from credit institutions that issued bonds to strengthen their prudential ratios and prepare for accelerating credit growth in the second half. Real estate bond issuance accounted for approximately 26% of total issuance. The slow real estate market recovery could not stimulate demand for raising capital through the corporate bond channel. Some real estate enterprises requested extensions and postponements of principal payments, easing immediate repayment pressures.

A gradual recovery in the global economy pushed up exports and imports. Export receipts in H1 2024 were $190 billion, up 14.5% compared to the same period in 2023. Improving demand was much more evident in Viet Nam's key markets, with exports to the US up by 22.1%, the European Union by 14.1%, and ASEAN by 12.9%.

The manufacturing revival drove an increase in imports of production inputs. Imports of many material goods increased sharply to serve domestic production, such as electronics, computers, and components. Total imports reached $178.4 billion, narrowing the trade surplus to $11.6 billion in the period. For H1 2024, the estimated current account surplus was 4.6% of GDP, lower than 6.1% a year earlier (Figure 3.4.43).

Figure 3.4.43 Balance of Payments Indicators

The current account balance is in surplus.

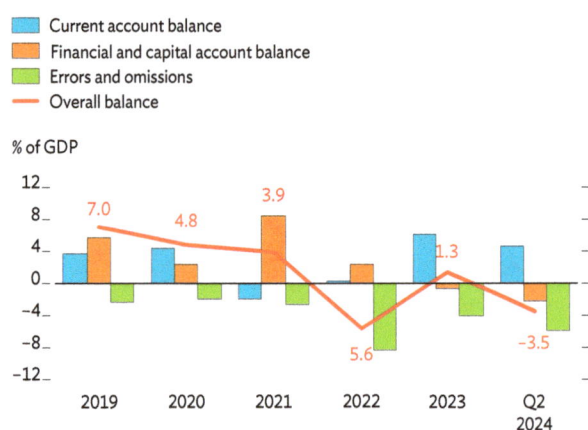

GDP = gross domestic product, Q = quarter.
Sources: State Bank of Vietnam; Asian Development Bank estimates.

Reduced capital inflows turned the financial and capital account into deficit, estimated at 2.2% of GDP in H1 2024 from a 0.8% surplus in H1 2023. The shrinking current account balance and financial and capital account deficit led the overall balance of payments into an estimated deficit of 3.5% of GDP in H1 2024. By the end of June 2024, foreign reserves were estimated to cover 2.8 months of imports, down from 3.3 months at the end of 2023.

State budget revenues increased due to the recovery of domestic production and robust trade activities. Budget revenues in H1 2024 reached VND1,021 trillion or 60% of the annual budget plan, up by 15.7% year on year. Budget expenditure decreased by 0.1%, with capital expenditure down by 8.8%, mainly due to limited public investment disbursements. The government is committed to disbursing VND670 trillion (equivalent to $27.3 billion) during the year. In the first 8 months of 2024, just 47.8% of the annual planned

public investment was disbursed. The budget surplus expanded to approximately 4.1% of GDP in H1 2024 from around 1.5% in H1 2023.

Prospects

Recent trends reinforce the *ADO April 2024* growth forecast. Economic growth is projected to expand by 6.0% in 2024 before improving to 6.2% in 2025 (Table 3.4.6). Inflation is also expected to remain benign at 4.0% in both years. The main forces impacting the economy have been the ongoing global economic slowdown, the continuing impact of Russia's war in Ukraine, and wider conflict in the Middle East and the Red Sea.

Table 3.4.5 Selected Economic Indicators in Viet Nam, %

Growth and inflation forecasts remain unchanged.

	2023	2024		2025	
		Apr	Sep	Apr	Sep
GDP growth	5.1	6.0	6.0	6.2	6.2
Inflation	3.3	4.0	4.0	4.0	4.0

GDP = gross domestic product.
Sources: General Statistics Office; Asian Development Bank estimates.

Export-oriented industries remain the main driver of growth. The gradual return of new orders and consumption revived manufacturing growth in H1 2024, with further momentum expected for the whole year. The manufacturing purchasing managers' index edged above 52.4 in August 2024, continuing to expand, indicating a recovery in consumption-led manufacturing (Figure 3.4.44). External demand for major electronics exports fueled industrial production. However, subdued global economic prospects leave some uncertainty. Industry is forecast to grow by 7.3% in 2024 and expand by 7.5% in 2025. Construction could further pick up if major infrastructure projects can be implemented as planned.

Other sectors are also expected to show modest growth. Services are expected to continue expanding by 6.6%, supported by revived tourism and the recovery of associated services. In August 2024, retail sales

Figure 3.4.44 Purchasing Managers' Index

The index gained in the year's second half, signaling a recovery.

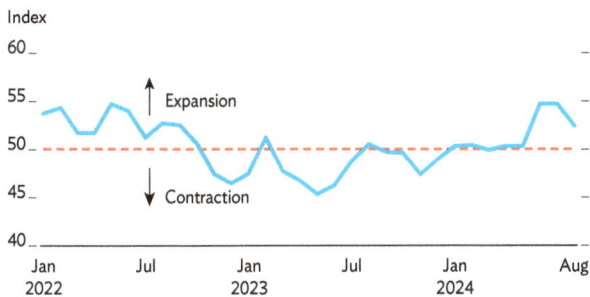

Note: A purchasing managers' index <50 signals deterioration, >50 improvement.
Source: IHS Markit.

improved by 7.9% year on year, lifting sales in the first 8 months of 2024 by 8.5% at current local prices (5.3% in real terms). This level remains lower than the 10.3% over the same period last year, showing sluggish domestic demand (Figure 3.4.45). Agriculture will benefit from rising food prices, and is now expected to expand by 3.4% in 2024.

On the demand side, fiscal expansion and monetary easing will continue to support consumption, which has remained subdued. Public investment will be crucial for economic recovery and growth in 2024. Continued fiscal support and substantial state investments will further stimulate demand during H2 2024. However, persistent corporate bond issuance continue to put downward pressure on the property sector, previously a key driver of domestic consumption. Domestic demand is expected to remain relatively weak through 2024–2025.

Figure 3.4.45 Retail Sales

Retail sales in the first 8 months of 2024 were lower than the same period in previous years, indicating sluggish domestic demand.

Source: General Statistics Office.

Trade recovery and positive FDI should be key growth drivers. Exports and imports in the first 8 months of 2024 showed strong rebounds of 15.8% and 17.7%, respectively, from the low 8-month base in 2023 (Figure 3.4.46). The uncertainty of the continued restructuring of global and regional supply chains hampers trade prospects. Imports and exports will likely grow by over 10% this year and slightly higher next year, with the gradual revival of external demand. Robust trade activity is expected to help maintain the current account surplus estimated at around 2.0% of GDP in 2024. As manufacturing activity returns, pushing up imports of production inputs, the current account balance is projected to narrow to 1.5% of GDP in 2025.

Figure 3.4.46 Trade Growth

Trade showed signs of recovery.

Source: General Statistics Office.

Shipments of mobile phones, computers, and electronic products have increasingly contributed to overall export growth. The proportion of these items in total export value has steadily grown. In 2011, they accounted for just 12% of total export turnover. By 2014, this share had doubled to 24% and almost tripled to 33% by 2023. The average growth rate of electronics products exports from 2011 to 2023 was 26.7%. This robust growth made it the largest export group for Viet Nam by 2023, with a value of $117.3 billion, accounting for 33% of the total export turnover (Figure 3.4.47).

By August 2024, total exports of computers, electronic products, and components reached $89 billion, representing 33.6% of total exports and a year-on-year increase of nearly 21%. This impressive growth not only indicates an expansion in

Figure 3.4.47 Exports of Electronics Products

Electronics have continued to support export growth.

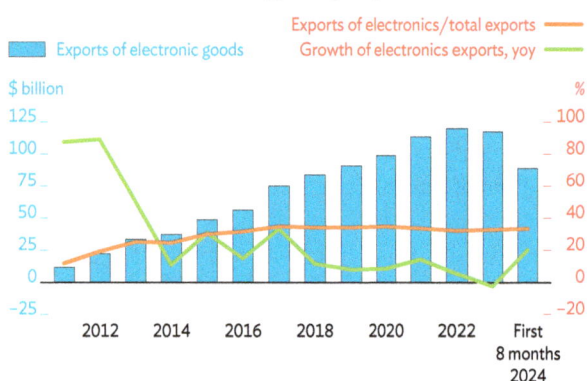

yoy = year on year.
Sources: Customs Vietnam; General Statistics Office.

scale but also showcases enhanced product quality, meeting the growing demand of the international market. This export performance led to $78.2 billion worth of imports, accounting for 31.8% of total imports, almost 26% higher than the same period last year. Additionally, the rise in Viet Nam's electronics exports underscores the global supply chain shift in high-tech products, with the country playing an increasingly significant role.

FDI continues to advance and support export growth. Registered FDI in the first eight months of 2024 reached $20.5 billion, a 7% increase compared to the same period in 2023. Of this total, $13.6 billion (77%) was directed toward export-oriented manufacturing, further bolstering export expansion.

The state budget is expected to shift into slight deficit toward the end of 2024. The National Assembly passed a continuation of the 2% reduction in the value-added tax effective until end-2024. The expansionary fiscal policy is expected to continue, although budget execution remains slow. Fiscal stimulus measures should be prioritized given Viet Nam's budgetary headroom. It should redouble efforts to accelerate disbursements of public investment. This will directly support industries such as construction and manufacturing and provide more employment opportunities.

The *ADO April 2024* inflation forecasts for Viet Nam are retained for 2024 and 2025. Despite a modest increase in inflation in H1 2024, the inflation

projection remains at 4.0% for both 2024 and 2025. The factors such as wage hikes and government-controlled price adjustments are expected to push inflation upward. However, monetary easing by the US Federal Reserve would help alleviate some inflationary pressure. By the end of August 2024, the consumer price index increased by 3.5% year on year. Average inflation for the first 8 months was 4.0% year on year, higher than the 3.1% a year earlier. Inflation is expected to ease during H2 2024, despite the effective basic salary increase in July.

Coordinated policies are thus crucial to support the economic recovery, considering relative price upticks and weak demand. In the near term, loosening monetary policy must be closely coordinated with implementing fiscal policy to effectively boost economic activity. Monetary policy will pursue the dual objectives of price stability and growth, even as policy space is limited. The heightened risk of nonperforming loans due to the economic down cycle limits the prospect of additional monetary easing.

There are significant uncertainties on the horizon. Domestically, the real economy continues to show weaknesses in its underlying structural foundations. Domestic demand will require stronger execution of fiscal stimulus measures. Externally, subdued global prospects could further hamper external demand, adversely affecting exports, manufacturing activity, and employment. Viet Nam's exports face increasing competition due to trade diversions from global value chain reconfigurations for products, such as garments, textiles, and electronics, as well as risks from heightened geopolitical tensions and rising protectionism. To maintain growth momentum through 2024 and 2025, preserving macroeconomic stability with a more balanced mix of monetary and fiscal policies is essential, complementing comprehensive governance reforms. Weaker than expected external demand would require further policy measures to spur business activities to stimulate domestic demand. While the SBV continues to pursue an accommodative monetary policy, its capacity to do so has become significantly constrained. Consequently, there is increased urgency for enhanced fiscal support, increased public investment disbursements, and further reforms in governance to alleviate the burden on monetary policy in bolstering the economy.

Other Economies

Brunei Darussalam

The April 2024 growth forecast remains unchanged given first quarter (Q1) data. GDP is projected to grow by 3.7% this year driven by strong oil and gas production. Prices overall fell slightly during the first half, leading to a lower inflation forecast for the year (Table 3.4.6).

Table 3.4.6 Selected Economic Indicators in Brunei Darussalam, %

Growth projections remain unchanged, with the inflation forecast for 2024 lowered and maintained for 2025.

	2023	2024		2025	
		Apr	Sep	Apr	Sep
GDP growth	1.4	3.7	3.7	2.8	2.8
Inflation	0.4	1.1	0.4	1.0	1.0

GDP = gross domestic product.
Sources: CEIC Data Company; Asian Development Bank estimates.

The strong Q4 2023 economic growth continued into Q1 2024, with GDP growing by 6.8% year on year. The uptick in economic activity was broad-based. On the demand side, public investment grew the most in Q1 2024 (48%), while private consumption contributed the most to overall growth (2.6 percentage points).

Developments in energy continue to underpin growth. The Salman oil field was commissioned in Q1 2024 with the oil and gas sector recovering strongly and steadily after contracting during the COVID-19 pandemic and the first three quarters of 2023. Still, the most recent quarterly oil and gas gross value added figures remain 18% below pre-pandemic levels. While some of this is due to depressed energy prices (especially of liquefied natural gas), it suggests there remains room for growth. As projected in April, oil production recovered to 101,000 barrels per day by end-2023, returning to its 2019 level. However, natural gas production was 783,000 British thermal units per day in Q4 2023, still about 22% lower than pre-pandemic production.

Expected trade and economic diversification complement the outlook for oil and gas. Expansions in investment and trade have boosted recent economic activity. Services growth continues to be strong, driven by trade, communications and business services. The past year has seen the launch of the first container shipping link with the People's Republic of China and ratification of the Comprehensive and Progressive Agreement for Trans-Pacific Partnership (in mid-2023). The first export container of halal foods was shipped to Sabah, Malaysia, in March 2024.

Growth forecasts are maintained considering the latest data, though the projections hold clear risks. While the high growth rate in Q1 is not sustainable for the rest of 2024 and 2025, continued investment in the country's traditional growth sectors will support public investment. The 2024 growth forecast remains at 3.7%. Growth will moderate to 2.8% in 2025 as energy production fully normalizes. Risks depend largely on external demand factors and global oil and gas markets. While geopolitical tensions pose downside risks through supply chain disruptions, expected strong energy demand in Asia in 2024 is a potential tailwind for trade and fiscal balances, which are expected to improve in 2024–2025.

The 2024 inflation forecast is adjusted downward due to consumer price trends through midyear, while the 2025 projection remains unchanged. Consumer prices deflated due to non-food items, particularly in transport, with year-to-date inflation at −0.3% through June. After high inflation during the COVID-19 pandemic, mild deflation appears to be returning as was common pre-pandemic. A base effect will likely restore some inflation later this year. The Brunei dollar has continued to appreciate against major trading partner's currencies since 2021 due to tightening by the Monetary Authority of Singapore. United States policy rate cuts in late 2024 would contribute to further appreciation and deflationary pressures.

Cambodia

The *ADO April 2024* growth forecasts remain unchanged. The projections, which use the new 2014 GDP base year, are based on the good performance of industry and services in the first half (H1) of 2024 (Table 3.4.7). Inflation projections are revised down this year before rising in 2025 to reflect the slow increase in food prices and decline in fuel prices in H1.

Table 3.4.7 Selected Economic Indicators in Cambodia, %

Growth projections remain unchanged, but inflation is now projected lower in 2024 before accelerating in 2025.

	2023	2024 Apr	2024 Sep	2025 Apr	2025 Sep
GDP growth	5.0	5.8	5.8	6.0	6.0
Inflation	2.1	2.0	0.5	2.0	2.5

GDP = gross domestic product.
Sources: National Institute of Statistics; Asian Development Bank estimates.

Industry will be the primary growth driver, with output forecast to grow by 8.0% in 2024 and 8.4% in 2025. Export growth in garments, footwear, and travel goods (GFT) rebounded strongly to 16.9% year on year in H1 2024 after declining 18.6% in the same period in 2023. Export growth of other manufactured products slowed to 1.3% year on year in H1 from 21.2% in H1 2023. Construction materials and equipment imports surged by 23.3% year on year in H1 on construction fueled by public infrastructure investment.

Agriculture will likely grow by 1.2% in 2024 and 1.3% in 2025. Despite drought due to El Niño, agriculture remains very much on track. Fertilizer imports increased by 14.6% year on year in H1 2024, while bank credit for agriculture surged by 22.3%, indicating increased production.

Services are forecast to grow by 5.4% in 2024 before tapering to 5.2% in 2025. Tourism continues to recover, with tourist arrivals rising by 22.7% year on year in H1 2024, reaching 94.8% of the pre-pandemic H1 2019 level. However, the share of air arrivals remains lower than land arrivals, suggesting more regional tourists with lower spending patterns. Domestic trade and transport performed well, with bank credit to trade up by 13.3% year on year and transportation services up by 25.2% in H1. Real estate remained subdued, with falling prices and fewer sales of homes and condominiums.

Inflationary pressure is less than anticipated. The economy experienced deflation in the first 2 months of 2024 at 0.5% year on year in January and 0.3% in February, primarily due to falling fuel and food prices. Inflation returned in April at 0.5% year on year and gradually increased to 0.7% in June, driven by food, clothing and footwear, and health product prices, which offset the drop in fuel prices. Overall, inflation is forecast at 0.5% in 2024, down from the 2.0% April projection, before rising to 2.5% in 2025.

Foreign direct investment declined somewhat in H1 2024. Foreign investment inflows are preliminarily reported to have decelerated by 6.7% year on year to $2.0 billion by the end of H1 2024, supported by growth in non-financial sectors, while financial sector investment declined significantly due to lower banking profits. Gross international reserves remained stable at $20.0 billion at the end of H1, up from $18.8 billion at the end of 2019.

Increased capital spending will delay fiscal consolidation in 2024. The general government budget deficit should reach $1.2 billion, equivalent to 2.5% of GDP. Revenue is budgeted at $7.7 billion, equivalent to 16.8% of GDP, with taxes accounting for 87.2% of revenues. To support an increase in infrastructure development, the budget was increased by $8.9 billion, equivalent to 19.3% of GDP.

The merchandise trade deficit, excluding gold, grew 14.9% year on year from $1.3 billion to $1.5 billion. Imports, excluding gold, rose by 12.8%, driven by increases in garment materials (21.2%), fuel (29.6%), and consumer durables (23.3%). Exports increased by 12.6% year on year, with GFT up 16.9% and non-GFT exports up 1.3%. The National Bank of Cambodia is expected to maintain the reserve requirement for both foreign currencies and the riel at 7.0% until the end of 2025.

The economic outlook remains subject to downside risks. These include potential slower growth in major economies like the US, Europe, and the People's Republic of China, high private debt, rising fuel prices, and more severe effects from extreme weather.

Lao People's Democratic Republic

The 2024 growth forecast remains unchanged, 2025 growth is revised down, while inflation projections for this year and next have gone up. Services and clean energy investments have supported economic growth. However, macroeconomic challenges from unsustainable public debt continue to constrain investment prospects and contribute to a loss of purchasing power that limits domestic consumption.

Economic recovery has been supported by tourism and transport services. The Visit Laos Year 2024 and holding the ASEAN Chairmanship boosted tourism. International tourist arrivals in the first half (H1) of 2024 reached 2.1 million, a 26% increase compared to H1 2023, but still 5% lower than pre-pandemic levels. The railway service between the Lao PDR and the PRC significantly boosted the country's attraction as a regional tourist destination and transit hub, with a 41.3% increase in passengers and a 31.9% increase in cargo in H1 2024.

Increased trade volumes resulted in a small trade surplus. The Lao PDR saw a small trade surplus of $2 million for the first 5 months of 2024. Official reserves were $1.8 billion in June 2024, including a $0.9 billion bilateral swap with the People's Bank of China, sufficient to cover 2 months of imports.

Public debt remains at critical levels. While public and publicly guaranteed debt declined from $13.9 billion in 2022 to $13.8 billion in 2023 (Figure 3.4.48), or from 112% to 108% of GDP, the ratio of external debt service to total government revenue jumped from 27% to 43%. To address liquidity challenges, the government continued to seek deferrals in scheduled loan service payments. External public debt service deferrals amounted to $1.9 billion between 2020 and 2023.

The kip continued its downward slide. External debt payments of Électricité du Laos (EDL)-Generation Public Company due in June coincided with a sharp depreciation of the kip (Figure 3.4.49). With debt service payments due in Thai baht, the kip sharply depreciated by 6.1% against the baht in the commercial market from 1 January to 30 August. In

Figure 3.4.48 Public and Publicly Guaranteed Debt

Total public debt remains at critical levels.

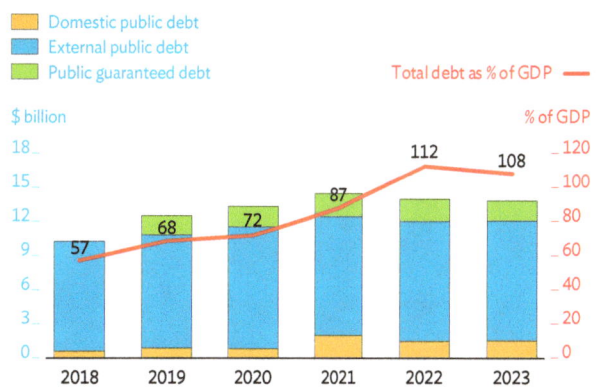

GDP = gross domestic product.
Source: Ministry of Finance.

Figure 3.4.49 Exchange Rate

Pressure on the Lao kip continues.

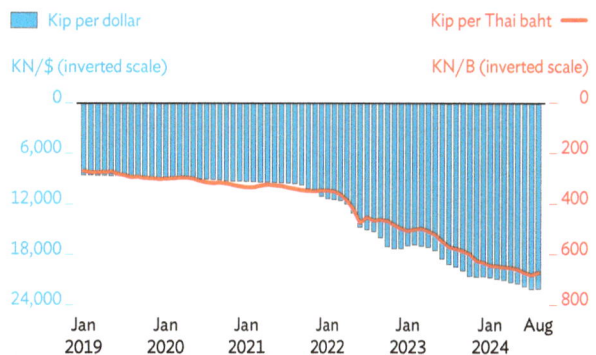

Source: Bank of the Lao PDR.

the same period, the kip depreciated by 7.5% against the US dollar in the commercial market and 4.6% in the parallel market, with the spread between the two markets rising to 9.1%. Despite the Bank of Lao PDR increasing its 1-week interest rate from 8.5% in February to 10.5% in August and tightening forex management, the kip has continued to depreciate.

Price instability persists, fueling inflationary expectations. Inflation increased by 24.3% year on year in August, with the 8-month average in 2024 at 25.3% (Figure 3.4.50). Shortages of skilled labor due to out-migration added pressure to domestic prices and wages. Businesses passed on these increased prices and wages to consumers, which further fueled inflationary expectations.

Figure 3.4.50 Components of Inflation

Food and non-alcoholic beverages constitute 48% of the consumer basket and drive inflation.

- Others
- Clothing and footwear
- Transport
- Overall inflation, % year on year
- Housing and utilities
- Restaurants and hotels
- Food and nonalcoholic beverages

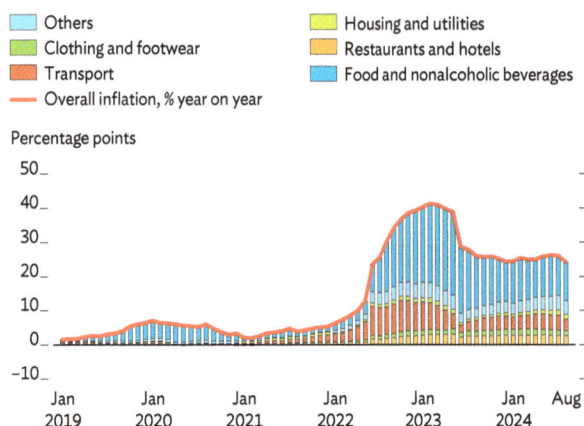

Source: Lao Statistics Bureau.

The *ADO April 2024* economic growth forecast for 2025 is revised down from 4.0% to 3.7%, while the 4.0% projection for 2024 is unchanged (Table 3.4.2). Growth prospects in 2024 are supported by a recovery in tourism and good rainfall. Continued limited refinancing options in 2025 amid considerable external debt maturities are expected to see public sector reliance on domestic markets for sourcing the foreign currency needed. This will limit the private sector recovery, depress household spending, and reduce business confidence.

Tourism and logistics services will boost growth. The country is striving to improve tourism, transport infrastructure, and hospitality services. The ASEAN Express freight train completed its first round trip from Malaysia through the Lao PDR to the People's

Table 3.4.8 Selected Economic Indicators in the Lao People's Democratic Republic, %

The 2025 growth forecast is revised down with inflation projections up significantly.

	2023	2024		2025	
		Apr	Sep	Apr	Sep
GDP growth	3.7	4.0	4.0	4.0	3.7
Inflation	31.2	20.0	25.0	7.0	21.5

GDP = gross domestic product.
Source: Asian Development Bank estimates.

Republic of China, with the 9-day journey offering 20% cost-savings compared to sea transport. The overnight Vientiane-Bangkok train, launched in July 2024, will further boost regional tourism.

Foreign direct investment and favorable rainfall will increase power generation and support agriculture. The direct and indirect effects of new 3 gigawatt investments in wind and solar power in 2024–2025 and the completion of the 600 megawatt Monsoon Wind Power Project in 2025 will support construction growth. The shift to La Niña in H2 2024 brings higher rainfall. The increased water in the hydropower dam will boost electricity output and power exports. Paddy and export crops will benefit from the increased rainfall, but the increased risk of floods could adversely affect agricultural productivity.

Inflationary pressures will persist. Consumer prices are projected to rise an average of 25% in 2024. An increase in the value-added tax from 7% to 10% and higher excise taxes for vehicles, alcohol, and cigarettes in May have further pushed up prices. Double-digit inflation is expected to persist at 21.5% in 2025.

Fiscal and monetary policy will remain tight amid debt stress. Reduced external borrowing and efforts to improve revenue collections and compress capital expenditure will help the government achieve a primary surplus over the next 2 years. However, with high debt service payments, the overall fiscal deficit is estimated at 2.5% of GDP for 2024 and 2025. Annual debt servicing needs are estimated at $1.3 billion during 2024–2028. And foreign exchange reserves at 2 months of import coverage as of March 2024, or $1.81 billion as of June 2024, is considered insufficient. To raise external financing, the government has announced issuance of bonds in July 2024 on the domestic market in Lao kip, Thai baht, and US dollars, equivalent to $320 million.

Risks to the outlook continue to center on resolving the country's debt distress. This will require coordinated efforts by the government and creditors and more transparent and sustainable public financial management.

Myanmar

The continuing conflict in Myanmar, combined with the weakening governance landscape, has a significant impact on the country's economic outlook. This situation creates considerable challenges and uncertainties for achieving economic stability and growth. Additionally, obtaining reliable and accurate economic data and information is also difficult due to the unstable situation in Myanmar. The economy remained sluggish from April through June 2024, highlighting the need for comprehensive measures to stimulate growth and improve conditions. Escalating conflict, especially at major border trade zones, along with exchange rate volatility, skyrocketing inflation, weaker investment and production, and macroeconomic instability hinder recovery. Consequently, this update lowers the real GDP growth forecast to 0.8% from 1.2% in *ADO April 2024* (Table 3.4.9).

Table 3.4.9 Selected Economic Indicators in Myanmar, %

Growth forecasts are revised down from April, with inflation now seen higher than the earlier projections.

	2023	2024		2025	
		Apr	Sep	Apr	Sep
GDP growth	0.8	1.2	0.8	2.2	1.7
Inflation	27.0	15.5	20.7	10.2	15.0

GDP = gross domestic product.
Note: Years are fiscal years ending 31 March of the following year.
Sources: Central Statistical Organization; Asian Development Bank estimates.

Multiple challenges limit growth. The manufacturing sector still faces persistent supply-side challenges constraining its growth. Factors limiting production include increasing input prices, longer delivery times for materials, unfavorable exchange rates, and a weaker labor market. Manufactured exports shrank by 11.7% in the first quarter of fiscal year 2024 (FY2024, ending 31 March 2025) compared to the previous year. There was also a sharp drop in capital imports, which contracted by 52.3%, indicating a substantial drop in private and public investment due to heightened uncertainty and instability across the country. Rising transportation costs and inflationary pressures, which reduce the purchasing power of the general population, pose downside risks to services, that depend heavily on domestic demand. Widespread conflict, security issues, and transportation disruptions will likely slow growth in travel and tourism along with retail trade due to movement constraints. The incentive of higher prices for agricultural products will be partially offset by higher input prices due to sharp currency depreciation, stringent price regulations, and rising trade disruptions from conflict areas, leading to lower-than-expected production. Recent severe flooding along the Ayeyarwady and Chindwin rivers have devastated croplands and economic activities in several areas.

External trade declined sharply. Trade contracted by 18.3% from April to June 2024 due to the disruptions in major border trade areas. Lower investment and production led to a 28.5% decrease in merchandise imports, largely caused by a sharp decline in capital imports. Merchandise exports also dropped by 5.9% in US dollar terms during the same period. Trade is expected to decrease even more with the ongoing instability. Foreign direct investment commitments in June 2024 reached $149.9 million, which, although higher than last year's $13.6 million commitment, remained 90.7% lower than pre-crisis levels (FY2020). Most of these commitments were directed toward manufacturing and telecommunications.

Inflation is now forecast higher than in *ADO April 2024*. Recent price trends show inflation will likely increase further in FY2024. The main reasons are currency depreciation and trade disruptions from conflicts. The market exchange rate depreciated sharply by an average of 26.1% from January to June 2024. This significant drop will increase near-term inflationary pressure from imports such as fertilizers and essential consumer products, including edible oils, medicines, and fuel. Instability along with disruptions in production and transportation will increase prices for food and non-food items especially in conflict areas. Due to the deteriorating governance landscape, the kyat is expected to continue to weaken, with persistent foreign exchange market instability. Scarce foreign exchange from lower inflows coupled with massive capital outflows and external migration continue destabilizing the foreign exchange market. Extreme weather events, such as cyclones and severe floods, pose adverse risks for agriculture production, subsequently affecting food prices.

Significant downside risks include continued political unrest, currency depreciation, and trade disruptions. Widespread armed conflicts across the country have led to an increase in internally displaced people and disruptions in livelihoods, resulting in an economic slowdown, high inflation, and increased poverty.

Singapore

Singapore's economy continued to grow steadily in the second quarter (Q2) of 2024. GDP grew in Q2 by 2.9% year on year, slightly down from 3.0% in Q1, resulting in 3.0% growth for the first half (H1). In Q2 2024, growth in services slowed to 3.7% as tourism normalized after a concert-driven boost in Q1. Meanwhile, transport benefited from increased port activity and a surge in deliveries from the People's Republic of China before tariffs from the US were imposed. Growth in finance, information, and communications improved. Manufacturing fell by 1.0%, less than the 1.7% contraction in Q1, driven by the drop in biomedical and precision engineering clusters, which outweighed gains in transport engineering, chemicals, electronics, and general manufacturing clusters. Construction remained robust, growing by 3.8% due to increased public sector projects. On the demand side, consumption increased, driven by higher public and private spending, while investment rose by 1.7%, a reversal from the 2.2% contraction in Q1, supported by higher private investment and robust public investment. Exports and imports in real terms were higher than the previous quarter.

Growth in H2 will benefit from the upturn in global electronics. Manufacturing will likely improve, primarily driven by recovery in electronics and better business sentiment. The manufacturing PMI remained in expansionary regime in July, higher than in June, while the electronics PMI has been expanding for 9 consecutive months. Business sentiment is upbeat, with 23% of firms expecting improvement in the next 6 months. Services will continue to drive growth H2 2024. In particular, trade should benefit from the global technology upturn, and modern services, particularly financial, strengthen as interest rates gradually fall. Travel-related industries will also continue to expand. However, tourism and direct domestic consumer services will likely slow, weighing slightly

on overall services growth. Domestic demand should support growth as consumer spending and investments rise in anticipation of lower interest rates. The improving external environment, with exports rising by 5.1% and imports by 8.1% in H1 2024, bolstered by the ongoing electronics upcycle, will also contribute to GDP growth. Thus, the *ADO April 2024* is slightly revised up to 2.6%, while the 2025 forecast remains the same (Table 3.4.10).

Table 3.4.10 Selected Economic Indicators in Singapore, %

The 2024 growth forecast has increased slightly, with inflation now lower than the April projection. Forecasts for 2025 remain unchanged.

	2023	2024		2025	
		Apr	Sep	Apr	Sep
GDP growth	1.1	2.4	2.6	2.6	2.6
Inflation	4.8	3.0	2.6	2.2	2.2

GDP = gross domestic product.
Sources: Ministry of Trade and Industry. Economic Survey of Singapore Second Quarter 2024; Asian Development Bank estimates.

Inflation continued to ease due to moderating imported inflation and reduced domestic cost pressures. In the first 7 months of 2024, headline inflation edged down to 2.8%, on average, with the July rate easing to 2.4% year on year. Core inflation, as followed by the Monetary Authority of Singapore, also decreased to 3.1%. The drop was primarily driven by lower private transport costs as prices fell for cars and motorcycles. Price increases for food, retail and other goods slowed while those for clothing and footwear fell more. Accommodation inflation edged down on modest increases in housing rents. In addition, the Singapore dollar appreciated against the US dollar by 2.0% in nominal effective terms during the first 7 months of 2024 as the Monetary Authority of Singapore maintained its exchange rate policy. The stronger nominal effective exchange rate should temper imported inflation in the months ahead. Core inflation will continue to moderate gradually during the rest of the year, declining further in Q4 2024 as import cost pressures recede. Consequently, the inflation forecast for 2024 is revised down to 2.6%, while the forecast for 2025 remains unchanged.

Risks to the economic outlook remain balanced.
Downside risks include fragile external demand, further escalating geopolitical tensions, potential disruptions in disinflationary momentum, and spillover effects from an economic slowdown in the People's Republic of China. Conversely, outlook could beat expectations if inflation declines faster than forecast, a more robust export rebound materializes and improving financial conditions provide additional support to investments.

Timor-Leste

Economic growth in 2024 has been hampered by slower-than-expected budget execution. As of 22 August 2024, public spending reached only 47.1% of the approved budget. This was mainly due to limited project readiness, delays in budget promulgation, slow public procurement, and institutional capacity constraints in implementing capital-intensive public sector projects. Capital spending on public works including preparatory works for high-level visits, such as the Pope's visit in September 2024, has increased since July. However, these expenditures will not offset the decline in public investment spending from the initial plan.

Growth momentum will continue but more moderately than forecast in *ADO April 2024*.
Increasing foreign tourists, personal remittances, government transfers, and consumer credits will help maintain the robust contribution of private consumption to growth. However, investment will be weaker than forecast in April in line with lower public capital spending compared to the approved budget. In addition, net exports in 2024 will drag on growth slightly less than the April forecast due to lower imports of goods and services. GDP growth in 2024 will accelerate from 2023 to 3.1% but remain below the April forecast (Table 3.4.11). The growth forecast for 2025 was revised down slightly to 3.9% due to lower budget spending than previously expected.

Inflation has moderated. Average inflation declined from 8.4% in December 2023 to 5.5% in July 2024 in part due to low non-tradables inflation, which averaged 1.6% as of July 2024. In addition, there was a continued decline in price increases of staple products and consumer durables mainly due to lower inflation among main trading partners. Finally, average food inflation moderated from 10.2% to 8.4%. While the inflation

Table 3.4.11 Selected Economic Indicators in Timor-Leste, %

Growth will be lower than the April forecast, and inflation will moderate.

	2023	2024		2025	
		Apr	Sep	Apr	Sep
GDP growth	1.9	3.4	3.1	4.1	3.9
Inflation	8.4	3.5	3.4	2.9	2.9

GDP = gross domestic product.
Sources: Asian Development Bank estimates; The National Institute of Statistics, Timor-Leste.

trend is consistent with *ADO April 2024* forecasts, the 2024 projection has been revised down slightly to 3.4% due to marginally lower domestic demand than previously estimated. The 2.9% inflation forecast for 2025 remains unchanged.

The sustainability of the Petroleum Fund requires policy shifts and avoidance of excessive withdrawals. Driven by investment income, the Petroleum Fund balance stood at $18.5 billion at the end of June 2024, rebounding by 2.2% year on year and marginally recovering from its recent trough of $17.4 billion in December 2022. However, the fund's sustainability and overall economic growth trajectory beyond 2024 will depend on two main factors. First, future investment income and development of the Greater Sunrise gas and condensate field. Second, public financial management reforms and policy shifts to avoid excessive withdrawals and ensure a more effective use of development finance opportunities. These policy shifts will be instrumental in tackling infrastructure and human capital development challenges, improving labor productivity, attracting foreign direct investment, promoting economic diversification and greater private sector contributions to growth, and boosting Timor-Leste's integration into the regional economy. Current account deficits will remain large but slightly smaller than forecast in April, mainly due to lower imports expected in both years in line with lower estimated budget spending for both 2024 and 2025 than the *ADO April 2024* forecast.

Several factors pose downside risks to the outlook.
These include low public capital investment spending, climate-related disaster risks, and the impact of external spillovers associated with prolonged geopolitical tensions on the terms of trade and domestic prices.

THE PACIFIC

The Pacific subregion is now forecast to grow slightly faster than projected in *ADO April 2024*. This is mainly attributable to higher growth in Fiji, the second-largest economy in the subregion, which more than offsets lower growth in Papua New Guinea (PNG), the predominant economy in the Pacific. The inflation forecast for 2024 has been revised down largely due to deflation in PNG during the first half (H1) of the year. The forecast for 2025 remains unchanged.

Subregional Assessment and Prospects

The subregion is forecast to grow by 3.4% in 2024 and 4.1% in 2025, yet limited fiscal space and high debt distress continue to exert pressure (Figure 3.5.1). The economic prospects of the Pacific are primarily determined by PNG and Fiji, collectively accounting for 90% of the subregion's GDP. Growth in PNG will likely be slightly lower than projected in April for both 2024 and 2025, primarily due to lower output in the resource sector. However, this has been more than offset by higher-than-expected growth in other economies, notably Fiji, where robust tourist arrivals exceeded expectations and government expenditure was higher than forecast.

Natural calamities and labor shortages persist as challenges to future growth. In addition, the Pacific faces challenges emanating from limited fiscal space and debt distress. Currently, seven of the 14 Pacific developing member countries (DMCs) are at high risk of debt distress—Kiribati, the Marshall Islands, PNG, Samoa, Tonga, Tuvalu, and Vanuatu. The remaining seven are at moderate risk—the Cook Islands, Fiji, the Federated States of Micronesia, Nauru, Niue, Palau, and Solomon Islands.

Figure 3.5.1 Gross Domestic Product Growth in the Pacific

Growth forecasts have been adjusted up, driven by continued strong growth in tourism and government stimulus, including higher public wages.

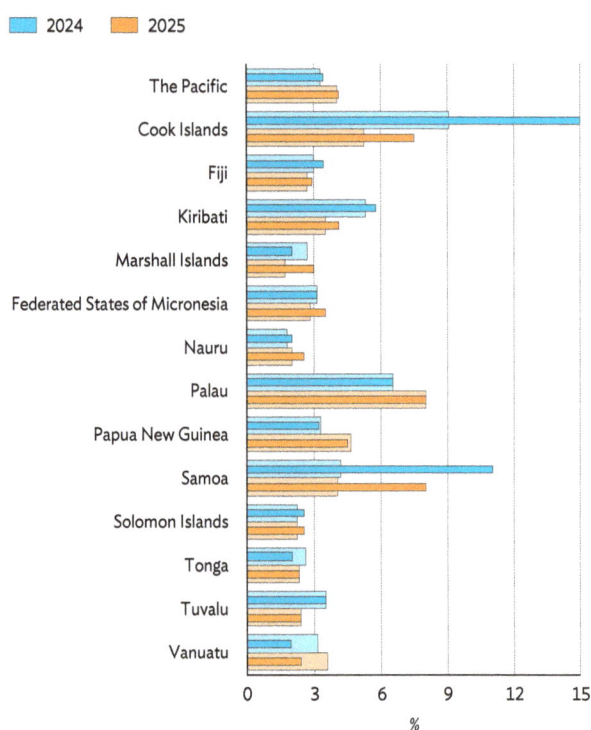

Note: Lighter colored bars are *Asian Development Outlook April 2024* forecasts.
Source: *Asian Development Outlook* database (accessed 5 September 2024).

The write-up on the Pacific was prepared by Kayleen Calicdan, Magdelyn Kuari, Kaukab Naqvi, Katherine Passmore, Cara Tinio, and Isoa Wainiqolo of ADB's Pacific Department (PARD); and Prince Cruz, Ana Isabel Jimenez, and Jennifer Umlas, PARD consultants.

Projected 2024 GDP growth for PNG is now 3.2%, slightly lower than the April 2024 forecast of 3.3%. The revision is mainly due to reduced production of liquefied natural gas (LNG), gold, and nickel in H1 2024. Looking ahead, the recovery of businesses affected by the 10 January 2024 social unrest, coupled with the 2025 planned start-up of the multibillion-dollar Papua LNG project will likely stimulate investment and economic growth. However, the subpar output in resource extraction continues to constrain growth. Consequently, GDP growth for 2025 is projected to reach 4.5%, compared to April's 4.6% forecast. In Fiji, visitor arrivals have been higher than forecast. And with fiscal stimulus provided in 2024 also expected to support economic activity, the economy is estimated to grow by 3.4% in 2024 compared to the 3.0% estimated in *ADO April 2024*. With continued growth in tourism, the economy is forecast to grow by 2.9% in 2025 compared to 2.7% envisaged in April.

Excluding Fiji and PNG, the other Pacific DMCs are projected to grow by 4.9% in 2024 and 4.1% in 2025. Growth in the Cook Islands, Kiribati, Nauru, Samoa, and Solomon Islands is now forecast higher than in April. For the Cook Islands, higher growth has been driven by tourism, while the increase in public wages in Kiribati had a substantially higher impact on domestic demand than forecast. Reactivating the Regional Processing Centre led to Nauru's higher forecast. Growth in Samoa should be bolstered by sustained growth in tourism and remittances, while in the Solomon Islands, the change reflects data revisions. In contrast, growth forecasts have fallen for Tonga in 2024, due to the impact of El Niño on agriculture, and Vanuatu, due to the adverse effects of the suspension of Air Vanuatu operations.

The inflation forecast in the Pacific has moderated in 2024, but remains unaltered for 2025 (Figure 3.5.2). Projected inflation for 2024 is now 3.6%, down from the April 2024 4.3% forecast. This deceleration is attributed largely to lower inflation in PNG during H1 2024. Reduced prices of alcoholic beverages, tobacco, betelnut, household equipment, and communications were significant in tempering the inflation outlook. However, the persisting upward trend in food prices, coupled with potential downside risks, such as fuel supply constraints and weather-related events associated with El Niño, threaten the current inflation trajectory. Also, local factors such as supply

Figure 3.5.2 Inflation in the Pacific

A lower subregional forecast in 2024 reflects lower than expected inflation in Papua New Guinea.

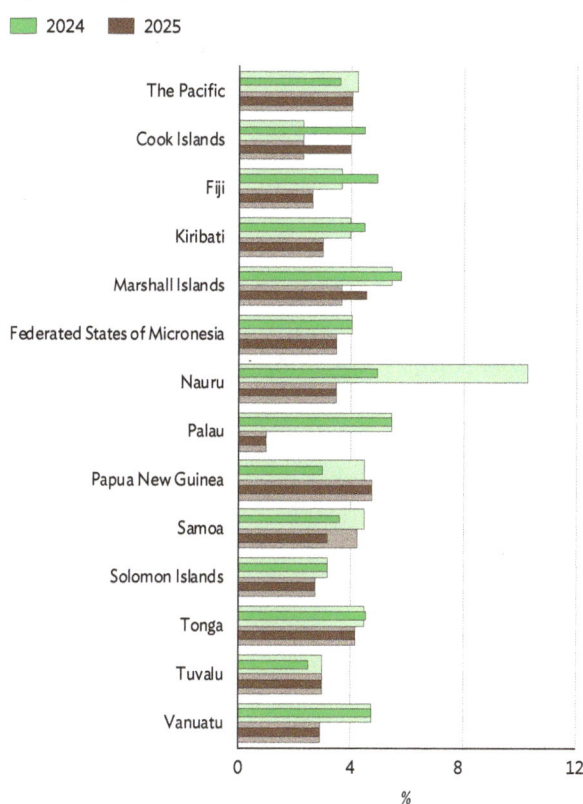

Note: Lighter-colored bars are forecasts in *Asian Development Outlook April 2024*.
Source: *Asian Development Outlook* database (accessed 5 September 2024).

chain disruptions and rising wages add inflationary pressure on smaller economies. Thus, inflation for PNG will likely rebound to 4.8% in 2025. Inflation in Fiji this year has been adjusted up due to the surge in food and fuel prices during H1 2024. Nonetheless, an anticipation of decelerating global prices in 2025 should keep inflation steady at 2.6% next year. Overall, the 2025 inflation forecast for the Pacific remains unchanged at 4.1%.

Fiji

Growth forecasts for 2024 and 2025 have been revised up due to stronger-than-expected tourism and increased government spending (Table 3.5.1). *ADO April 2024* assumed that limited hotel room inventory and high accommodation costs would slow tourism uptake. However, visitor arrivals in the first 7 months of 2024 grew by 6.7% compared to the same period in 2023, doubling initial projections. Fiscal spending was earlier projected to be restrained from fiscal year 2024 (FY2024 ended 31 July 2024) onwards. The government now plans a 10.9% increase in expenditure in FY2025, including salary increases for civil servants. This augmented fiscal stimulus, combined with a resilient tourism sector, is anticipated to support the growth outlook.

Table 3.5.1 Selected Economic Indicators in Fiji, %

Tourism-driven growth should continue despite a temporary spike in inflation.

	2023	2024		2025	
		Apr	Sep	Apr	Sep
GDP growth	7.5	3.0	3.4	2.7	2.9
Inflation	2.4	3.7	5.0	2.6	2.6

GDP = gross domestic product.
Source: Asian Development Bank estimates.

Tourism's steady growth has been led by arrivals from New Zealand and the US. Visitor arrivals from Australia—Fiji's largest source market, accounting for 47% of 2023 arrivals—increased by 2.5% in the first 7 months of 2024 while arrivals from New Zealand and the US rose by 7% and 12%, respectively. Arrivals from the US should be further boosted by the introduction of a non-stop Nadi-Dallas flight three times a week beginning December 2024.

Sector performance was mixed in H1 2024. While electricity and gold production increased, mineral water and timber production declined. Renewable energy generated two-thirds of electricity in the first quarter, and a new mine boosted gold production. Exports of taro, kava, and turmeric posted double-digit growth, indicative of annual production improvements. Cane and sugar production also increased by 12% and 21% in the first 11 weeks (period ended 19 August

2024) of the crushing season. Construction activity fell in the first quarter, but strong cement sales and increased building permits suggest a rebound later in the year.

Fiscal deficits narrowed. Lower government spending compared to revenue led to a narrower fiscal deficit in FY2024, equivalent to 4.0% of GDP, instead of the earlier forecast of 4.8%. The government aims to reduce the debt-to-GDP ratio to 60.0% by FY2040 from 78.0% in FY2024. To achieve the goal, the government plans to increase revenues driven by higher demand, improve tax compliance and collection, and review tax exemptions and incentives to offset rising expenditures.

Inflation forecasts for 2024 are revised up due to higher-than-expected price increases. Rising food and fuel prices drove consumer inflation in H1 2024. Higher minimum wages and civil servant pay will likely push prices up toward the end of the year. An expected slowdown in global prices next year may help stabilize inflation, leaving the 2025 inflation projection unchanged.

Papua New Guinea

Low resource extraction in the first half (H1) of 2024 reduces the growth forecast from *ADO April 2024* (Table 3.5.2). Production of liquefied natural gas (LNG), gold, and nickel were lower than expected. Maintenance at the LNG central processing facility and low supply from a matured gas field slowed LNG production, while bad weather reduced gold production particularly at the Lihir mine, with maintenance work affecting nickel output. Copper

Table 3.5.2 Selected Economic Indicators in Papua New Guinea, %

Weak resource extraction decreases the 2024 growth forecast, and subdued price pressures reduce the inflation projection.

	2023	2024		2025	
		Apr	Sep	Apr	Sep
GDP growth	2.0	3.3	3.2	4.6	4.5
Inflation	2.3	4.5	3.0	4.8	4.8

GDP = gross domestic product.
Source: Asian Development Bank estimates.

production was strong in the first quarter (Q1) of 2024 and will likely support mining growth. Production at the Porgera mine remains steady into H2 2024 following its resumption in February, despite the impact of the May 2024 landslide, and should reach near capacity in 2025, slower than expected in April. As a result, overall growth has been revised slightly down from the April forecast.

Growth in the non-resource sector is on track with April expectations, supported by spillover effects from the resumption of the Porgera mine, improved foreign exchange (FX) inflows, and higher cocoa prices. As projected, the resumption of operations at Porgera and a cocoa price increase contributed to higher FX receipts and more consumption spending. The improved FX also helped the central bank raise FX allocations, thereby lowering the backlog of outstanding FX orders at the end of Q2 2024.

The resolution of fuel supply for transport is helping to retain the outlook for the non-resource sector and the impact of the social unrest has stabilized. The positive outlook for transportation remains as Air Nuigini's re-fleeting program continues, improving both domestic and international travel. Flights also increased starting July between Port Moresby and Hong Kong, China from three to four flights a week. Travel and goods transport have gradually improved as fuel supplies, including aviation fuel, stabilized following restrictions imposed by Puma Energy, the major fuel supplier, in H1 2024. The increase in aviation fuel supply came from an agreement among the government, Oktedi Mining Limited, Pacific Energy Aviation Limited, and Air Nuigini, the national airline, to improve the supply chain of aviation fuel. The recovery of the shops affected by the impact of the social unrest on 10 January has been slow as expected, with most of the shops yet to be rebuilt. The central bank has been providing FX support to affected businesses and as of August, the government has provided K50 million to affected businesses, including wage support for employees.

Subdued inflationary pressures in H1 2024 bring down the inflation forecast from *ADO April 2024*, although prices of key consumer items continued to rise. The National Statistical Office

reported declines in the prices of alcoholic beverages, tobacco, and betelnut; household equipment; and communications, which led to prices contracting by 2.1% in Q1 2024 and by 0.7% in Q2 2024. Nonetheless, the price of key consumer items continues to increase, however, the increase was not as high as a year ago. Prices up by 5.0% or more include food and non-alcoholic beverages, household equipment, clothing and footwear, and healthcare. The inflation forecast for 2025 remains unchanged from the April forecast as exchange rate depreciation and FX restrictions continue.

Risks are tilted to the downside. These risks include (i) disruption to Porgera mine operations due to possible unrest in the area, (ii) law and order issues, (iii) fuel supply restrictions, and (iv) disaster and weather-related events. The final investment decision on the multibillion-dollar Papua LNG project should boost the economy, although it has been delayed until 2025.

Solomon Islands

Growth forecasts have been revised upwards, for both 2024 and 2025, but growth is still expected to be lower than in 2023 (Table 3.5.3). Official revisions to GDP estimates for the past 3 years suggest that services and industry have been playing a more important role in the economy than previously thought (Box). Accordingly, forecasts for growth in 2024 and 2025 have been raised but are still lower than 2023, which was boosted by spending and investment related to hosting of the Pacific Games.

Table 3.5.3 Selected Economic Indicators in Solomon Islands, %

GDP forecasts for 2024 and 2025 are raised given the higher growth in services and industry, while inflation projections remain unchanged.

	2023	2024		2025	
		Apr	Sep	Apr	Sep
GDP growth	3.0	2.2	2.5	2.2	2.5
Inflation	5.1	3.2	3.2	2.7	2.7

GDP = gross domestic product.

Sources: Solomon Islands National Statistics Office; Asian Development Bank estimates.

Box National Accounts in Solomon Islands

The Solomon Islands National Statistics Office released gross domestic product data indicating expansions of 2.6% in 2021 and 2.4% in 2022. This contrasts with estimates of a contraction by the Central Bank of Solomon Islands and other development partners, including ADB. The reported 2021 expansion was mainly driven by growth in communications (37.9%) and education (14.4%), while the reported 2022 growth was due to hotel and restaurants (28.8%), construction (19.8%), and communications (19.2%). This update raises the estimated growth for 2023 from 2.5% in *ADO April 2024* to 3.0%. The government has indicated that recent data releases remain subject to review.

Source: Solomon Islands National Statistics Office.

As mentioned in *ADO April 2024*, the budget deficit is expected to narrow. Government spending was 13.5% lower in the first half (H1) of 2024 compared to the same period in 2023. This was due to reduced expenditure following the 2023 Pacific Games and the caretaker government period prior to the 2024 general election. Capital expenditure fell by almost 50%, while revenues fell by 8.0%, including an 80.0% decrease in grants. This was likely due to grant deferrals during the caretaker government period.

A new government is in place following a peaceful April election. The new government has released a 100 Days Program focused on economic recovery. Reported initiatives include a Citizenship by Investment program, meeting the target of 8,000 workers deployed under labor mobility schemes in Australia and New Zealand in 2024, finalizing a value-added tax bill to be tabled in Parliament, and reviewing fishing revenue arrangements.

Government debt has continued to rise as expected. By June 2024, overall debt had increased to 20.7% of GDP from 19.9% at the end of 2023. External debt was 12.1% of GDP and domestic debt 8.6% in June 2024. External debt was up by 5.1% from the end of 2023, largely due to loan disbursements for a donor-financed infrastructure project. While domestic debt was up by 2.4%, its growth has slowed.

Lower gold production contributes to a decline in mineral exports. Gold production was down by 7.8% to 29,635 ounces in H1 2024 compared to H1 2023, with exports of minerals down by 11.6% over the same period. While log output was up 8.7% to 914,000 cubic meters, the log and timber export value increased by only 4.4% with the average price of timber down by 11.4%. Fishing performed well, with fish catch-up by 15.9% to 14,966 metric tons, and the value of exports up by 26.6%. However, crop production was mainly down with cocoa falling by 50.1%, copra by 39.9%, and palm oil by 6.2%.

In line with *ADO April 2024*, lower infrastructure spending has led to lower imports. After rapidly expanding due to the 2023 Pacific Games, imports decreased by 15.1% in H1 2024, led by lower imports of fuel (down 27.2%) and machinery and transport equipment (down 24.5%). Imports of food, however, rose by 29.1%. Gross foreign reserves continued to decline to SI$5.6 billion in June 2024 from SI$5.8 billion at the end of 2023. It is still sufficient to cover 10.4 months of imports and well above the minimum 6-month threshold of import cover.

The inflation forecast is maintained in both 2024 and 2025. After rising to 4.6% in the first quarter (Q1) 2024, inflation decreased to 3.4% in Q2. Lower inflation in H2 2024 will likely come from lower price increases for food and alcohol and tobacco (mainly due to betel nut prices). The price of betel nut increased by 65.8% in Q1 2024, before easing to 25.4% in Q2. Rice inflation also eased from 8.0% in Q1 2024 to 5.9% in Q2 2024. With inflation expected to ease further, the central bank shifted to an accommodative monetary policy stance in September. This is expected to support growth in the short- to medium-term.

Vanuatu

Economic growth forecasts are down with the suspension of Air Vanuatu operations in May 2024. Providing crucial domestic and international air links, Air Vanuatu has played a critical role in the country's development. Domestically, it linked the capital Port Vila to major tourism destinations Santo and Tanna and other areas via 26 airports on 19 islands. Internationally, it was used by 75% of passengers in 2023. With the airline under administration, GDP growth is now forecast to be substantially lower in both 2024 and 2025 (Table 3.5.4).

Table 3.5.4 Selected Economic Indicators in Vanuatu, %

GDP growth forecasts for 2024 and 2025 are revised down mainly due to the impact of the suspension of Air Vanuatu operations.

	2023	2024		2025	
		Apr	Sep	Apr	Sep
GDP growth	1.0	3.1	1.9	3.6	2.4
Inflation	11.2	4.8	4.8	2.9	2.9

GDP = gross domestic product.
Sources: Vanuatu Bureau of Statistics; Asian Development Bank estimates.

Tourism-related services growth will likely slow. Other international airlines quickly stepped in to restore international links to Port Vila in May and to Santo in July, but domestic connectivity remains constrained. A few domestic Air Vanuatu flights were restored in August and some chartered flights are operating. With tourism-related industries still reeling from the effects of the pandemic and disasters in 2020 and 2023, Air Vanuatu's suspension will mainly affect accommodation and restaurants, wholesale and retail trade, and transportation. Relative to Port Vila and Santo, the impact on tourism in outer islands will be more extensive as long as domestic flights remain limited.

Visitor arrivals by air remained below pre-pandemic levels even before Air Vanuatu came under administration. Arrivals by air were 56% of pre-pandemic levels from January to April 2024. By contrast, cruise ship arrivals were 135% of pre-pandemic levels during the same period. Data on visitors by air from Australia and New Zealand, the two largest source markets, indicate that arrivals in May 2024 dropped to 62% of pre-pandemic levels from 111% in January to April. Arrivals from New Caledonia, the third largest source market, remained well below pre-pandemic levels.

A reduction in seasonal workers is expected to lead to lower remittance growth. There were 6,216 seasonal workers in Australia in June 2024, 21% lower than the 7,888 in June 2023. Although the Air Vanuatu suspension should not significantly impact seasonal worker deployment to Australia and New Zealand, the plan to expand recruitment from outside Port Vila and Santo will be affected. The decline will likely lead to a slowdown in remittance growth in 2024, which, combined with lower honorary citizenship program (HCP) revenues and tourism receipts will reduce foreign reserves.

The Air Vanuatu suspension adds to the fiscal crunch, but the projected deficit will be smaller than anticipated in the 2024 budget. The 2024 budget—dubbed "the capital budget"—was approved in April and focused on capital investment. It projected a deficit equivalent to 10.2% of GDP. The budget includes capital expenditure reaching 19.1% of GDP, up from 6.4% in 2023 and current spending at 35.5% of GDP, up from 32.7%. However, the massive increase in capital spending will unlikely be met given the delays and a low execution rate.

Revenues will be less than anticipated, particularly through the declining HCPs. The 2024 budget projected nontax revenues to rise to 14.1% of GDP from 9.4% in 2023, of which HCP revenue was equivalent to 6.9% of GDP. Actual nontax revenue collected in the first half of 2024 was less than 30% of the annual target largely due to the sharp fall in HCP revenue. This was in anticipation of the European Union decision to revoke visa-free entry for Vanuatu passport holders in June 2024. Value-added tax collection—the largest revenue source—was less than 40% of the annual budget target.

Inflation forecasts remain unchanged in both 2024 and 2025. Actual 2023 inflation was 11.2%, lower than the *ADO April 2024* estimate of 13.5%. Consumer prices rose 5.6% in the first quarter (Q1) of 2024 but are expected to decline over the rest of the year as supply stabilizes. Food inflation fell from 24.8% in

Q2 2023 to 10.1% in Q1 2024, while transport inflation fell from 14.5% in Q1 2023 to 0.0% in Q1 2024. Inflation for housing utilities also fell from 6.0% in Q1 2023 to –9.2% in Q1 2024.

Monetary policy tightened further in September. While inflation has eased, it remained above the Reserve Bank of Vanuatu's target range of 0% to 4%. Monetary authorities raised the policy rate from 2.25% to 2.75%, while the Capital Adequacy Ratio was raised from 10.0% to 12.0%.

In May, constitutional amendments were accepted by voters in a landmark step toward strengthening political parties. Political instability has long been a risk to growth, contributing to slow fund disbursement, delayed resolution of key issues, and distracting from stable governance.

Central Pacific Economies

Growth forecasts for Tuvalu remain as in April, but higher public wages in Kiribati and the reactivation of Nauru's Regional Processing Centre raised GDP projections for these economies. Higher wages should also lead to increased inflation in Kiribati in 2024, while lower communication costs in Nauru and lower food prices in Tuvalu are expected to reduce inflation below earlier forecasts. Projected inflation for 2025 is unchanged for all Central Pacific economies.

Kiribati

GDP growth projections are adjusted upward. The 38% increase in public sector wages have had a substantially higher impact on domestic demand than was forecast in *ADO April 2024*. Accordingly, growth projections for both 2024 and 2025 have been raised (Table 3.5.5).

The fiscal deficit is expected to widen in 2024. The increase in public sector wages will drive up expenditures to 126% of GDP in 2024 from 102% in 2023. Revenues will rise more slowly, from 101% of GDP in 2023 to 103% in 2024. The fiscal impact has been greater than expected earlier in the year and the deficit in 2024 is now expected to be equivalent to

Table 3.5.5 Selected Economic Indicators in Kiribati, %

Stronger domestic demand prompts higher growth and inflation forecasts for 2024.

	2023	2024		2025	
		Apr	Sep	Apr	Sep
GDP growth	4.2	5.3	5.8	3.5	4.1
Inflation	9.3	4.0	4.5	3.0	3.0

GDP = gross domestic product.
Sources: International Monetary Fund Article IV Staff Report; Asian Development Bank estimates.

about 22% of GDP compared with an earlier estimate of 9.7%, covered by cash reserves and a withdrawal from the Revenue Equalization Reserve Fund.

Inflation is forecast higher for 2024 but remains unchanged for 2025. Besides directly increasing domestic demand, the rise in public sector wages could also spill over to private sector wages and contribute to higher inflation. But inflation should moderate in 2025 as the impact of the wage increase dissipates, thus the April forecast is unchanged.

Risks to the outlook remain tilted to the downside. Global inflation could raise the cost of imported inputs to public investment projects. In addition, fishing license revenues face continued risks from ocean temperature changes and impacts on fish stocks while natural hazards can disrupt project implementation.

Nauru

Growth forecasts are raised for fiscal year 2024 (FY2024 ended 30 June 2024) and FY2025 (Table 3.5.6). The Australian-financed Regional Processing Centre (RPC) moved to an enduring capability mode in July 2023, ensuring it remains potentially operational even when there is no activity. However, following the arrival of several groups of "transferees" in late 2023 and early 2024, the RPC returned to active status with an associated increase in support from the Australian government. In June 2024, there were 101 transferees in the RPC. Higher RPC revenues have boosted government spending and investment leading to the higher growth forecasts.

Table 3.5.6 Selected Economic Indicators in Nauru, %

GDP growth forecasts are raised as the Regional Processing Centre is reactivated, while the inflation forecast for 2024 is reduced.

	2023	2024		2025	
		Apr	Sep	Apr	Sep
GDP growth	1.6	1.8	2.0	2.0	2.5
Inflation	5.2	10.3	5.0	3.5	3.5

GDP = gross domestic product.
Note: Years are fiscal years ending on 30 June of that year.
Sources: Nauru budget documents; Asian Development Bank estimates.

Capital and current spending increased significantly. Three supplementary budgets for FY2024 pushed government spending up by 19.4% from the original budget, which was used in *ADO April 2024*. While current expenditure was up 16.6%, capital expenditure expanded by 64.6% (mainly for the 2026 Micronesian Games and Higher Grounds Initiative). The increased current expenditure budget was mainly allocated for vocational training and education under the Alternative Pathways Program, RPC operations, and personnel costs.

The spending increase is financed by larger grants and revenues from RPC operations. Compared to the original budget for FY2024, tax revenues increased 67.3%—business profit and nonresident withholding taxes—and nontax revenues rose 12.1%, mainly associated with the RPC. Fishing license revenues rose 12.5% while grants increased by 20.2%. Overall, the fiscal surplus is estimated to have expanded to 27.7% of GDP in FY2024 compared to 13.6% in the original budget. The government's contribution to the Nauru Intergenerational Trust Fund increased by 8.7%.

Further growth in spending is projected in FY2025 with the RPC reactivation. The passage of the FY2025 budget was delayed until August as the government adjusted its spending priorities. Overall expenditure is higher by 12.1%, greater than the 6.3% increase in FY2024. Compared to the FY2024 budget, allocations for personnel costs are up by 20.3%, social benefits by 16.4%, and capital spending by 16.4%. With expected revenues rising by only 1.2%, the overall fiscal surplus is projected to ease to 15.3% of GDP in FY2025.

The inflation forecast for FY2024 is reduced as communication costs decline. The index for food and nonalcoholic beverages will still likely increase by double-digit rates, but communications inflation—the key driver for the original forecast—is projected to ease. In August 2024, the state-owned Cenpac Corporation signed an agreement with Starlink to provide fee-based public access which should reduce internet costs and fundamentally shift the communications landscape. The inflation forecast for FY2025 is unchanged.

Tuvalu

GDP growth forecasts are unchanged from *ADO April 2024* (Table 3.5.7). Growth is being driven by development partner-supported construction such as ongoing coastal adaptation projects, boat harbor development, school construction, and housing initiatives. Capital expenditure in the first half (H1) of 2024 reached A$5.1 million, at par with spending for the entire 2023. Visitor arrivals also boosted economic activity. The 853 visitors in the first quarter (Q1) of 2024 were 31.8% higher than in Q1 2023 and mainly from Fiji, Australia, and New Zealand.

Table 3.5.7 Selected Economic Indicators in Tuvalu, %

Growth forecasts remain unchanged, but the inflation forecast is lowered for 2024.

	2023	2024		2025	
		Apr	Sep	Apr	Sep
GDP growth	3.9	3.5	3.5	2.4	2.4
Inflation	7.2	3.0	2.5	3.0	3.0

GDP = gross domestic product.
Sources: Tuvalu Central Statistics Division; Asian Development Bank estimates.

Government spending will continue to drive growth in 2025. The fiscal year 2025 (FY2025) budget is the first budget to reflect the change in the government's financial year, which now ends 30 June instead of 31 December. In November 2023, a budget was approved covering the first 6 months of 2024. Total expenditure for FY2025 is estimated to drop to 90.3% of GDP from 112.4% in 2023 and 116.9% of GDP in H1 2024. The decline in expenditure largely reflects a decline in government revenue, led by fishing license revenues which is anticipated to fall from 49.5% of GDP in H1 2024 and 46.7% of GDP in 2023 to 36.3% in FY2025.

The fiscal balance moves toward deficit in FY2025. From a surplus equivalent to 5.4% of GDP in 2023 and 5.1% in H1 2024 (partial figure on the transition to fiscal year), the budget projects a deficit of 3.7% of GDP in FY2025. The deficit is expected to be financed through a withdrawal from the Consolidated Investment Fund.

The inflation forecast is revised down for 2024 but retained for 2025. The revision is due to the lower-than-expected 4.5% inflation in H1 2024. Average prices of food items increased by 4.8%, telecommunications by 46.9% and cooking and fuel prices by 4.8%, while transport costs fell 6.2%. Inflation is expected to slow further in H2 2024.

Downside risks remain. Disasters triggered by natural hazards, revenue volatility, delays in infrastructure project implementation, and an increase in global commodity prices continue to pose risks to development.

North Pacific Economies

Growth projections for the Marshall Islands are adjusted over the forecast horizon, while those for the Federated States of Micronesia (FSM) and Palau remain unchanged. Financial assistance through the renewed Compacts of Free Association (COFAs) with the US will notably enhance growth and fiscal prospects. Domestic price pressures are expected to keep inflation elevated in the Marshall Islands and the FSM, while trends in international commodity prices will likely continue to moderate price growth in Palau.

Marshall Islands

Growth projections are adjusted to account for recent developments (Table 3.5.8). Although fisheries, construction, and hosting the Micronesian Games should still drive economic growth in fiscal year 2024 (FY2024, ending 30 September 2024 for all three North Pacific economies), the 2024 forecast is revised down because the economy is now estimated

Table 3.5.8 Selected Economic Indicators in the Marshall Islands, %

Recent developments, including renewed financial assistance from the US, change the growth and inflation outlook.

	2023	2024		2025	
		Apr	Sep	Apr	Sep
GDP growth	−0.6	2.7	2.0	1.7	3.0
Inflation	7.3	5.5	5.8	3.7	4.6

GDP = gross domestic product.
Note: Years are fiscal year ending on 30 September of that year.
Sources: Graduate School USA Economic Monitoring and Analysis Program; Asian Development Bank estimates.

to have contracted in FY2023. High inflation and the end of financial support in response to the coronavirus disease pandemic have had a stronger negative effect on economic activity than was first thought during the previous fiscal year. In addition, concerns over the sustainability of the Bikini resettlement funds affected the operations of the Kili Bikini Ejit local government, constraining consumption and government employment. Financial assistance under COFA, which began in the fourth quarter of FY2024, should have a greater impact starting in FY2025.

Inflation projections are revised up from April. Prices, mainly of food, grew faster than initially estimated in FY2023. However, inflation is still expected to moderate in FY2024 and FY2025, in line with international commodity price trends.

Renewed COFA grants significantly brighten fiscal prospects. The government began to receive COFA grants late in FY2024, which could result in a fiscal surplus higher than the 0.2% of GDP projected in April. In addition, these grants make another fiscal surplus likely for FY2025, compared with the deficit projected in April. By the end of FY2024, public debt will likely be equivalent to 18.3% of GDP, down from 21.6% at the end of FY2023.

Federated States of Micronesia

The growth forecast for FY2025 is revised up on the anticipated impact of financial assistance under the renewed COFA (Table 3.5.9). The FSM economy is expected to continue growing in FY2024, driven by a continued recovery in tourism and

Table 3.5.9 Selected Economic Indicators in
the Federated States of Micronesia, %

Growth is now forecast higher in FY2025.

	2023	2024		2025	
		Apr	Sep	Apr	Sep
GDP growth	0.8	3.1	3.1	2.8	3.5
Inflation	6.2	4.1	4.1	3.5	3.5

GDP = gross domestic product.
Note: Years are fiscal year ending on 30 September of that year.
Sources: Graduate School USA Economic Monitoring and Analysis
Program; Asian Development Bank estimates.

Table 3.5.10 Selected Economic Indicators in Palau, %

Growth and inflation forecasts are unchanged from April.

	2023	2024		2025	
		Apr	Sep	Apr	Sep
GDP growth	-0.2	6.5	6.5	8.0	8.0
Inflation	12.4	5.5	5.5	1.0	1.0

GDP = gross domestic product.
Note: Years are fiscal year ending on 30 September of that year.
Sources: Graduate School USA Economic Monitoring and Analysis
Program; Asian Development Bank estimates.

construction. Financial assistance under the renewed COFA began late in FY2024 and will likely boost growth significantly from FY2025 onwards. This led to the increased growth forecast for that year. However, out-migration remains a major downside risk given the importance of labor to sectors driving growth.

Inflation remains on track. As mentioned in *ADO April 2024*, increased demand from continued economic expansion helped keep inflation high, with higher wages for federal government employees and for employees of the Chuuk and Pohnpei state governments exerting additional price pressures. Also, the FSM has grappled with the impacts of El Niño on local food and water supply over most of FY2024. Salary increases in other States may also contribute to inflation, compounded by higher domestic demand potentially driven by the new COFA grants.

COFA grants are improving the fiscal outlook.
The new grants should help create a fiscal surplus in FY2024, rather than the deficit projected in April. In FY2025, COFA grants should also offset continued increases in recurrent spending—particularly on state payrolls—and higher capital expenditure, and result in a deficit smaller than the 3.0% of GDP forecast in April. Debt should still be equivalent to 15.9% of GDP at the end of FY2024.

Palau

Economic growth remains on track (Table 3.5.10).
The economy is showing signs of recovery. Tourist arrivals will likely return to pre-pandemic levels by FY2025 barring any major external shocks or natural calamities. The economy is expected to receive a boost

at the beginning of FY2025, due to election-related expenditures in the latter part of FY2024. Moreover, a resurgence in construction is anticipated as new public infrastructure projects are implemented, which along with COFA grant-funded projects, should also support economic growth.

As of May, international visitor arrivals were up a substantial 96.8% for FY2024. The majority of visitors came from the People's Republic of China; North America; and Taipei,China. Arrivals from Taipei,China have increased in the past few months, following the increase in flight frequency by the flagship airline from two to three weekly flights since April. In contrast, arrivals from Japan and the Republic of Korea—two of Palau's main tourist markets before the pandemic—remain low. Although arrivals for the current fiscal year until May were only 57.0% of the FY2019 level, the rising influx of tourists indicates a steady recovery of tourism.

Inflation forecasts remain unchanged. The *ADO April 2024* forecast remains unchanged. Prices for all goods and services—except food and non-alcoholic beverages, household utilities, and healthcare—have continued to increase although not as fast as in FY2023. Transportation prices grew fastest, driven by rising fuel costs.

Fiscal surpluses are likely as COFA grants start coming in. In terms of the economic recovery and availability of additional COFA funds, a fiscal surplus of 3.4% of GDP for FY2024 and 1.9% of GDP for FY2025 is projected, consistent with the April forecasts. The recently signed COFA on 9 March 2024 has improved Palau's finance and macroeconomic prospects. The additional resources will bolster the government's capacity to extend productive investments and foster widespread economic growth. COFA is projected to significantly augment fiscal space, enabling Palau to alleviate the debt incurred during the pandemic and build up cash reserves while maintaining budgetary surpluses in the medium term. Nonetheless, challenges may persist due to capacity constraints to effectively utilize these additional resources. Also, potential risks of fiscal strain may emerge from tax refunds and implementing the June supplementary budget.

South Pacific Economies

Visitor arrivals continue to grow across South Pacific economies. The increase drives up growth projections for the Cook Islands and Samoa. The growth forecast for Tonga is reduced due to the impacts of El Niño on agriculture. Inflation has moderated significantly from recent highs, although weather disruptions and supply chain issues prompt higher inflation forecasts for the Cook Islands.

Cook Islands

Growth exceeded April projections, driven by stronger than expected tourism (Table 3.5.11). An almost 30% increase in visitor arrivals in fiscal year 2024 (FY2024, ended 30 June 2024 for all four South Pacific economies) was largely due to improved air connectivity with key source markets. Growth is still expected to moderate in FY2025 as arrivals increase more slowly, but the forecast is adjusted up to account for elevated base effects. Labor shortages, project implementation delays, and natural hazards remain key downside risks to the outlook.

Inflation in FY2024 is estimated to have been higher than forecast in April, and the FY2025 forecast has also increased. Prices grew faster than expected across most of the consumer price basket, driven by factors including weather disruptions and supply chain issues (particularly in the case of food, non-alcoholic beverages) and transport costs. The inflation projection for FY2025 is adjusted upward to account for estimated higher inflation in FY2024 but should still moderate over the fiscal year, aligned with international commodity price trends and anticipated slower inflation in New Zealand, the Cook Islands' main source of imports.

ADO April 2024 forecast a fiscal deficit, but the government realized a surplus estimated to be equivalent to 0.8% of GDP. Higher tax receipts contributed to a 16.7% increase in revenue. Conversely, expenditure grew by 7.2% with both capital and current spending lower than expected. In contrast, a deficit equivalent to 0.1% of GDP is now expected in FY2025 compared with the 1.8% surplus forecast earlier. This in part reflects the May 2024 announcement of an extensive infrastructure spending plan emphasizing critical projects in transportation—including expanding the Rarotonga International Airport—telecommunications, and public utilities. Public debt was estimated to be equivalent to 34.3% of GDP at the end of FY2024.

Samoa

The economy grew faster than forecast in FY2024 (Table 3.5.12). Growth in FY2024 was substantially higher than projected in *ADO April 2024*. This was largely because of a 40.9% increase (year on year) in visitor arrivals that significantly boosted services

Table 3.5.11 Selected Economic Indicators in the Cook Islands, %

Growth and inflation have been stronger than expected.

	2023	2024 Apr	2024 Sep	2025 Apr	2025 Sep
GDP growth	14.0	9.1	15.0	5.2	7.5
Inflation	13.2	2.3	4.5	2.3	4.0

GDP = gross domestic product.
Note: Years are fiscal years ending on 30 June of that year.
Sources: Cook Islands Statistics Office; Asian Development Bank estimates.

Table 3.5.12 Selected Economic Indicators in Samoa, %

Economic growth was stronger and inflation more moderate than April forecasts.

	2023	2024 Apr	2024 Sep	2025 Apr	2025 Sep
GDP growth	8.0	4.2	11.0	4.0	8.0
Inflation	12.0	4.5	3.6	4.3	3.2

GDP = gross domestic product.
Note: Years are fiscal years ending on 30 June of that year.
Sources: Samoa Bureau of Statistics; Asian Development Bank estimates.

output. Arrivals from main source markets, New Zealand and Australia, were up by 37.9% and 47.5% year on year, respectively. In addition, agriculture and fisheries expanded more rapidly than expected. Growth will still likely moderate in FY2025 as the increase in tourist arrivals slows somewhat, but the forecast is adjusted up to account for higher starting point from FY2024. Stimulus from Samoa's hosting of the Commonwealth Heads of Government Meeting (CHOGM) in October 2024 is expected to boost growth during FY2025.

Inflation slowed more than projected in *ADO April 2024* and the FY2025 forecast is revised downward. Among the major components of the consumer price basket, prices of food and alcoholic beverages grew much more slowly, and those of transport and housing and utilities contracted compared with the previous fiscal year. Inflation year on year for June 2024 was 0.9%, the lowest since May 2021. The forecast for FY2025 is adjusted down on expectations that inflation will continue to moderate following international commodity price trends. The central bank announced that it will take steps to return the policy rate from near-zero (where it has been since 2008) to a "neutral" 2%–3% to absorb large amounts of excess liquidity in the financial system, but not to adopt a tighter monetary policy stance. As of June 2024, the policy rate stood at 0.23%.

A fiscal surplus equivalent to 0.1% of GDP is estimated for FY2024 compared with a projection of 4.7% in *ADO April 2024*. The lower surplus reflects a decline in revenues as collections of value-added tax and import duties fell with moderating prices and were lower than projected in the FY2024 budget, while expenditures increased on higher public service wages—driven by the ongoing implementation of a cost-of-living adjustment (COLA)—and consumption of goods and services. The surplus is expected to still widen to 1.4% of GDP in FY2025, but well below the earlier 6.0% forecast, largely due to higher expenditure related to the hosting of CHOGM and implementation of the final phase of the COLA.

Tonga

The economy continues to grow driven by disaster reconstruction and the tourism recovery. GDP growth projection for FY2024 is downgraded while FY2025 is unchanged from *ADO April 2024* (Table 3.5.13). As expected, visitor arrivals were up 64.2% in FY2024, which supported wholesale and retail trade, accommodation and food services, transport, and other services. However, agricultural production was weaker-than-expected due to the impacts of El Niño.

Table 3.5.13 Selected Economic Indicators in Tonga, %

Economic growth forecast for 2024 is downgraded due to the impact of El Niño on agriculture, while inflation is revised slightly higher.

	2023	2024		2025	
		Apr	Sep	Apr	Sep
GDP growth	2.2	2.6	2.0	2.3	2.3
Inflation	9.7	4.5	4.6	4.2	4.2

GDP = gross domestic product.
Note: Years are fiscal years ending on 30 June of that year.
Sources: Tonga Statistics Department; Asian Development Bank estimates.

Government fixed asset investment drives strong construction growth. Capital spending expanded by 59.8% in FY2024, higher than the 41.9% increase in FY2023. Projects include the reconstruction and rehabilitation for housing, roads, bridges, wharves, and airports after the January 2022 volcanic eruption and tsunami. Current spending, however, was virtually unchanged in FY2024 from a year earlier. With revenue up by 4.4%, and overall expenditures higher by 9.9%, a fiscal surplus of 3.1% in FY2024 was in line with the projection in *ADO April 2024*.

As projected in April, construction will continue to drive growth. The newly approved FY2025 budget increases capital spending by 50.9%, while current expenditure rises by 22.9%. Development projects focus in strengthening agriculture, tourism, and fisheries. Higher expenditure will mainly be funded by a 10.4% increase in tax revenue and 14.7% rise in development partner grants. The FY2025 budget projects a fiscal surplus of 3.4% of GDP, higher than expected in *ADO April 2024* but needed due to higher debt service obligations.

Inflation continued to moderate as increases in food and fuel prices eased. As predicted, inflation was significantly lower than in FY2023 and below the National Reserve Bank of Tonga's reference rate of 5.0%. Although food price inflation—accounting for 39.8% of the consumer price basket—eased from 10.1% in FY2023 to 7.4% in FY2024, it remained relatively elevated due to the impacts of El Niño on agriculture. Inflation for transport—16.4% of the basket—fell to 5.4%. The index for housing, water, electricity, and gas—10.8% of the basket—fell to a deflation of 4.7% in FY2024 from a 20.0% inflation in FY2023.

Accommodative policy will continue as inflation eases further. Inflation is expected to remain below the 5.0% reference rate in FY2025 (forecast unchanged from *ADO April 2024*) as global food and fuel prices ease and supply bottlenecks are reduced. The impact of El Niño on agricultural production is also expected to diminish. The monetary policy stance announced in September remained accommodative, with the Statutory Reserve Deposit ratio at 15% (since May 2023). Foreign reserves increased 2.5% to T$924.3 million at the end of June 2024 from end-2023, enough to cover 11.9 months of imports.

The impact of disasters is a risk to the economy. Aside from the impact of El Niño on GDP and inflation, other disasters continue to pose risks. In June, volcanic activity once again damaged the submarine cable severing internet connections. Other risks include a more rapid fall in remittances and continued labor shortages. After growing by an average 15.3% from FY2021 to FY2023, remittance inflows decreased by 2.1% in FY2024. Remittance inflows were around 39% of GDP in FY2024, about five times the receipts from tourism.

Niue

The economy likely improved in FY2024 as visitor arrivals and spending continued to grow. Tourist arrivals as of January 2024 were the highest post-pandemic. In addition, the 50th Constitution Day celebrations in October 2024 should provide further economic stimulus in FY2025. This positive outlook is balanced by an expected decrease in business activity after completion of the airport and road projects.

The fiscal position is expected to move into deficit in FY2025. In FY2024, the government had a budget surplus estimated to be equivalent to 0.8% of FY2022 GDP. The FY2025 national budget projects a deficit of NZ$12.8 million, equivalent to 35.4% of FY2022 GDP. Structural challenges include maintaining population growth and addressing the growing fiscal impacts of climate change. Although overall expenditure has been kept under control, expected public sector costs and new infrastructure projects will lead to increased spending in the medium term. Efforts to enhance customs and taxation revenue collection continue, along with initiatives to tap into non-tax revenue sources beyond tourism.

Inflation picked up slightly in FY2024. Average inflation was estimated at 5.5% in June 2024, up from 5.1% the previous year. Prices of food and non-alcoholic beverages rose by 11.5% (year on year), and those of alcohol and tobacco increased by 6.6% because of higher import costs. However, prices are expected to moderate in FY2025 following easing prices in New Zealand.

4

STATISTICAL APPENDIX

STATISTICAL NOTES AND TABLES

This statistical appendix presents economic indicators for the 46 developing member economies in the Asian Development Bank (ADB) in three tables: gross domestic product (GDP) growth, inflation, and current account balance as a percentage of GDP. The economies are grouped into five subregions: the Caucasus and Central Asia, East Asia, South Asia, Southeast Asia, and the Pacific. The tables contain forecasts for 2024–2025 and historical data for GDP and inflation from 2021 and for the current account balance from 2019. Updated historical data are lacking for Niue, which precludes forecasts.

The data are standardized to the degree possible to allow comparability over time and across economies, but differences in statistical methodology, definitions, coverage, and practice make full comparability impossible. National income accounts are based on the United Nations System of National Accounts, while data on the balance of payments use International Monetary Fund (IMF) accounting standards. Historical data are variously based on official sources, statistical publications and databases, and documents from ADB, the IMF, and the World Bank. Projections for 2024 and 2025 are generally ADB estimates based on quarterly or monthly data as available, though some projections are from governments.

Most economies report by calendar year. The following report all variables by fiscal year: Afghanistan, Bangladesh, Bhutan, India, Nepal, and Pakistan in South Asia; Myanmar in Southeast Asia; and the Cook Islands, the Marshall Islands, the Federated States of Micronesia, Nauru, Palau, Samoa, and Tonga in the Pacific.

Regional and subregional averages are provided in the three tables. Averages are weighted by purchasing power parity (PPP) GDP in current international dollars. PPP GDP data for 2021–2022 were obtained from the IMF World Economic Outlook Database, October 2023 edition. Weights for 2022 are carried over to 2025.

The following paragraphs discuss the three tables in greater detail.

Table A1: Gross Domestic Product Growth Rate, % per year. The table shows annual growth rates of GDP valued at constant market prices, factor costs, or basic prices. GDP at market prices is the aggregate value added by all resident producers at producers' prices including taxes less subsidies on imports plus all nondeductible value-added or similar taxes. Most economies use constant market price valuation. Pakistan uses constant factor costs, and Fiji basic prices. A fluid situation permits no forecasts for 2024–2025 for Afghanistan.

Table A2: Inflation, % per year. Data on inflation rates are period averages. Inflation rates are based on consumer price indexes. The consumer price indexes of the following economies are for a given city only: Cambodia is for Phnom Penh, the Marshall Islands for Majuro, and Sri Lanka for Colombo. A fluid situation permits no forecasts for 2024–2025 for Afghanistan.

Table A3: Current Account Balance, % of Gross Domestic Product. The current account balance is the sum of the balance of trade in merchandise, net trade in services and factor income, and net transfers. The values reported are divided by GDP at current prices in US dollars. A fluid situation permits no data for 2021–2023 for Afghanistan.

Table A1 Gross Domestic Product Growth Rate, % per year

	2021	2022	2023	2024 Apr	2024 Sep	2025 Apr	2025 Sep
Developing Asia	**7.4**	**4.3**	**5.1**	**4.9**	**5.0**	**4.9**	**4.9**
Developing Asia excluding the PRC	**6.4**	**5.5**	**5.1**	**5.0**	**5.1**	**5.3**	**5.2**
Caucasus and Central Asia	**5.8**	**5.3**	**5.3**	**4.3**	**4.7**	**5.0**	**5.2**
Armenia	5.8	12.6	8.3	5.7	6.0	6.0	6.0
Azerbaijan	5.6	4.6	1.1	1.2	2.7	1.6	2.6
Georgia	10.6	11.0	7.5	5.0	7.0	5.5	5.5
Kazakhstan	4.3	3.2	5.1	3.8	3.6	5.3	5.1
Kyrgyz Republic	5.5	9.0	6.2	5.0	6.3	4.5	5.8
Tajikistan	9.4	8.0	8.3	6.5	6.5	6.5	6.5
Turkmenistan	5.0	6.2	6.3	6.5	6.5	6.0	6.0
Uzbekistan	7.4	5.7	6.0	5.5	6.0	5.6	6.2
East Asia	**8.0**	**2.9**	**4.7**	**4.5**	**4.6**	**4.2**	**4.2**
People's Republic of China	8.4	3.0	5.2	4.8	4.8	4.5	4.5
Hong Kong, China	6.5	–3.7	3.3	2.8	2.8	3.0	3.0
Republic of Korea	4.6	2.7	1.4	2.2	2.5	2.3	2.3
Mongolia	1.6	5.0	7.4	4.1	5.5	6.0	6.0
Taipei,China	6.6	2.6	1.3	3.0	3.5	2.7	2.7
South Asia	**8.8**	**6.5**	**6.8**	**6.3**	**6.3**	**6.6**	**6.5**
Afghanistan	–2.1	–20.7	–6.2	...	...	...	...
Bangladesh	6.9	7.1	5.8	6.1	5.8	6.6	5.1
Bhutan	4.4	5.2	4.0	4.4	5.5	7.0	7.0
India	9.7	7.0	8.2	7.0	7.0	7.2	7.2
Maldives	37.7	13.9	4.1	5.4	5.0	6.0	5.4
Nepal	4.8	5.6	2.0	3.6	3.9	4.8	4.9
Pakistan	5.8	6.2	–0.2	1.9	2.4	2.8	2.8
Sri Lanka	4.2	–7.3	–2.3	1.9	2.6	2.5	2.8
Southeast Asia	**3.6**	**5.6**	**4.1**	**4.6**	**4.5**	**4.7**	**4.7**
Brunei Darussalam	–1.6	–1.6	1.4	3.7	3.7	2.8	2.8
Cambodia	3.1	5.1	5.0	5.8	5.8	6.0	6.0
Indonesia	3.7	5.3	5.0	5.0	5.0	5.0	5.0
Lao People's Democratic Republic	2.3	2.5	3.7	4.0	4.0	4.0	3.7
Malaysia	3.3	8.7	3.6	4.5	4.5	4.6	4.6
Myanmar	–5.9	2.0	0.8	1.2	0.8	2.2	1.7
Philippines	5.7	7.6	5.5	6.0	6.0	6.2	6.2
Singapore	9.7	3.8	1.1	2.4	2.6	2.6	2.6
Thailand	1.6	2.5	1.9	2.6	2.3	3.0	2.7
Timor–Leste	2.9	4.0	1.9	3.4	3.1	4.1	3.9
Viet Nam	2.6	8.0	5.1	6.0	6.0	6.2	6.2
The Pacific	**–1.7**	**8.1**	**3.4**	**3.3**	**3.4**	**4.0**	**4.1**
Cook Islands	–25.5	10.5	14.0	9.1	15.0	5.2	7.5
Fiji	–4.9	20.0	7.5	3.0	3.4	2.7	2.9
Kiribati	8.5	3.9	4.2	5.3	5.8	3.5	4.1
Marshall Islands	1.1	–0.7	–0.6	2.7	2.0	1.7	3.0
Federated States of Micronesia	3.0	–0.9	0.8	3.1	3.1	2.8	3.5
Nauru	7.2	2.8	1.6	1.8	2.0	2.0	2.5
Niue	–6.2	...	...	...	...	...	...
Palau	–13.0	–1.7	–0.2	6.5	6.5	8.0	8.0
Papua New Guinea	–0.8	5.2	2.0	3.3	3.2	4.6	4.5
Samoa	–7.1	–5.3	8.0	4.2	11.0	4.0	8.0
Solomon Islands	2.6	2.4	3.0	2.2	2.5	2.2	2.5
Tonga	–1.3	0.0	2.2	2.6	2.0	2.3	2.3
Tuvalu	1.8	0.7	3.9	3.5	3.5	2.4	2.4
Vanuatu	–1.6	2.0	1.0	3.1	1.9	3.6	2.4

... = not available, PRC= People's Republic of China.

Note: The current uncertain situation permits no forecasts for Afghanistan in 2024–2025.

Table A2 Inflation, % per year

	2021	2022	2023	2024		2025	
				Apr	Sep	Apr	Sep
Developing Asia	**2.6**	**4.4**	**3.4**	**3.2**	**2.8**	**3.0**	**2.9**
Developing Asia excluding the PRC	**4.2**	**6.7**	**6.3**	**5.1**	**5.1**	**4.4**	**4.5**
Caucasus and Central Asia	**9.6**	**12.9**	**10.5**	**7.9**	**6.9**	**7.0**	**6.2**
Armenia	7.2	8.6	2.0	3.0	0.8	3.5	2.5
Azerbaijan	6.7	13.9	8.8	5.5	2.1	6.5	3.8
Georgia	9.6	11.9	2.5	3.5	2.5	4.0	3.5
Kazakhstan	8.0	15.0	14.5	8.7	8.5	6.3	6.1
Kyrgyz Republic	11.9	13.9	10.8	7.0	6.8	6.5	6.2
Tajikistan	8.0	4.2	3.8	5.5	5.5	6.5	6.5
Turkmenistan	19.3	11.2	5.9	8.0	5.0	8.0	5.0
Uzbekistan	10.7	11.4	10.0	10.0	9.5	9.5	9.0
East Asia	**1.1**	**2.3**	**0.6**	**1.3**	**0.8**	**1.6**	**1.3**
People's Republic of China	0.9	2.0	0.2	1.1	0.5	1.5	1.2
Hong Kong, China	1.6	1.9	2.1	2.3	1.8	2.3	2.3
Republic of Korea	2.5	5.1	3.6	2.5	2.5	2.0	2.0
Mongolia	7.1	15.2	10.4	7.0	6.8	6.8	7.2
Taipei,China	2.0	2.9	2.5	2.3	2.3	2.0	2.0
South Asia	**5.8**	**8.0**	**8.4**	**7.0**	**7.0**	**5.8**	**6.1**
Afghanistan	5.8	7.8	10.8	...	...	...	...
Bangladesh	5.6	6.2	9.0	8.4	9.7	7.0	10.1
Bhutan	7.3	5.6	4.2	4.5	4.6	4.2	4.2
India	5.5	6.7	5.4	4.6	4.7	4.5	4.5
Maldives	0.5	2.3	2.9	3.2	2.8	2.5	2.3
Nepal	3.6	6.3	7.7	6.5	5.4	6.0	5.5
Pakistan	8.9	12.2	29.2	25.0	23.4	15.0	15.0
Sri Lanka	6.0	46.4	17.4	7.5	3.8	5.5	5.5
Southeast Asia	**2.0**	**5.2**	**4.2**	**3.2**	**3.3**	**3.0**	**3.2**
Brunei Darussalam	1.7	3.7	0.4	1.1	0.4	1.0	1.0
Cambodia	2.9	5.3	2.1	2.0	0.5	2.0	2.5
Indonesia	1.6	4.1	3.7	2.8	2.8	2.8	2.8
Lao People's Democratic Republic	3.8	23.0	31.2	20.0	25.0	7.0	21.5
Malaysia	2.5	3.3	2.5	2.6	2.4	2.6	2.7
Myanmar	3.7	27.2	27.0	15.5	20.7	10.2	15.0
Philippines	3.9	5.8	6.0	3.8	3.6	3.4	3.2
Singapore	2.3	6.1	4.8	3.0	2.6	2.2	2.2
Thailand	1.2	6.1	1.2	1.0	0.7	1.5	1.3
Timor–Leste	3.8	7.0	8.4	3.5	3.4	2.9	2.9
Viet Nam	1.8	3.2	3.3	4.0	4.0	4.0	4.0
The Pacific	**3.2**	**5.2**	**3.0**	**4.3**	**3.6**	**4.1**	**4.1**
Cook Islands	1.8	3.6	13.2	2.3	4.5	2.3	4.0
Fiji	0.2	4.3	2.4	3.7	5.0	2.6	2.6
Kiribati	2.1	5.3	9.3	4.0	4.5	3.0	3.0
Marshall Islands	2.2	2.9	7.3	5.5	5.8	3.7	4.6
Federated States of Micronesia	1.8	5.0	6.2	4.1	4.1	3.5	3.5
Nauru	1.7	1.5	5.2	10.3	5.0	3.5	3.5
Niue	3.4	3.1	8.6	...	...	...	...
Palau	−0.5	13.2	12.4	5.5	5.5	1.0	1.0
Papua New Guinea	4.5	5.3	2.3	4.5	3.0	4.8	4.8
Samoa	−3.0	8.8	12.0	4.5	3.6	4.3	3.2
Solomon Islands	0.8	5.4	5.1	3.2	3.2	2.7	2.7
Tonga	2.3	8.2	9.7	4.5	4.6	4.2	4.2
Tuvalu	6.7	12.2	7.2	3.0	2.5	3.0	3.0
Vanuatu	2.3	6.7	11.2	4.8	4.8	2.9	2.9

... = not available, PRC= People's Republic of China.

Note: The current uncertain situation permits no forecasts for Afghanistan in 2024–2025.

Table A3 Current Account Balance, % of Gross Domestic Product

	2019	2020	2021	2022	2023
Developing Asia	**0.8**	**1.9**	**1.5**	**1.3**	**1.3**
Caucasus and Central Asia	**−2.9**	**−4.8**	**−0.4**	**3.8**	**−3.2**
Armenia	−7.1	−4.0	−3.5	0.3	−2.3
Azerbaijan	9.1	−0.5	15.1	29.8	11.5
Georgia	−5.4	−12.3	−10.3	−4.5	−4.4
Kazakhstan	−3.9	−6.4	−1.4	3.1	−3.3
Kyrgyz Republic	−12.0	4.5	−8.0	−42.1	−50.4
Tajikistan	−2.2	4.1	8.2	15.6	−0.7
Turkmenistan	...	...	6.5	7.1	5.9
Uzbekistan	−5.6	−5.0	−7.0	−3.5	−8.6
East Asia	**1.5**	**2.6**	**2.9**	**3.0**	**2.1**
People's Republic of China	0.7	1.7	2.0	2.5	1.4
Hong Kong, China	5.9	7.0	11.8	10.2	9.3
Republic of Korea	3.4	4.3	4.4	1.4	1.9
Mongolia	−15.2	−5.1	−13.8	−13.4	0.7
Taipei,China	11.0	14.5	15.3	13.3	13.9
South Asia	**−1.3**	**0.4**	**−1.3**	**−2.6**	**−0.9**
Afghanistan	11.7	11.2	...	...	...
Bangladesh	−1.3	−1.3	−1.1	−4.0	−2.6
Bhutan	−12.9	−13.0	−20.1	−31.2	−25.2
India	−0.9	0.9	−1.2	−2.0	−0.7
Maldives	−25.9	−35.8	−8.7	−16.3	−21.3
Nepal	−6.9	−0.9	−7.7	−12.5	−0.9
Pakistan	−4.2	−1.5	−0.8	−4.7	−1.0
Sri Lanka	−2.1	−1.4	−3.7	−2.0	1.8
Southeast Asia	**1.7**	**2.8**	**1.0**	**0.9**	**2.0**
Brunei Darussalam	6.6	4.3	11.2	19.6	12.9
Cambodia	−8.2	−2.6	−30.1	−19.2	1.3
Indonesia	−2.7	−0.4	0.3	1.0	−0.1
Lao People's Democratic Republic	−12.2	−6.6	−2.3	−4.2	−2.5
Malaysia	3.5	4.2	3.9	3.2	1.5
Myanmar	0.4	−2.5	−1.3	−3.4	−5.5
Philippines	−0.8	3.2	−1.5	−4.5	−2.7
Singapore	16.0	16.6	19.8	18.0	19.8
Thailand	7.0	4.2	−2.0	−3.2	1.3
Timor−Leste	7.9	−17.7	9.7	16.3	−20.0
Viet Nam	3.7	4.3	−2.0	0.3	6.0
The Pacific	**8.2**	**6.5**	**5.3**	**4.7**	**11.5**
Cook Islands	31.7	9.6	−16.1	−7.0	5.1
Fiji	−4.9	−13.6	−12.4	−17.2	−9.5
Kiribati	49.5	20.0	28.4	31.9	34.9
Marshall Islands	−31.3	15.0	22.5	17.5	...
Federated States of Micronesia	15.9	3.3	0.6	...	...
Nauru	4.6	2.5	3.1	−0.6	3.5
Niue	...	...	...	...	...
Palau	−30.6	−43.9	−41.0	−48.8	−41.2
Papua New Guinea	14.4	14.4	12.6	14.4	20.9
Samoa	2.5	0.5	−14.5	−11.3	−3.4
Solomon Islands	−9.5	−1.6	−5.1	−14.0	−11.0
Tonga	−4.0	−7.5	−6.2	−6.3	8.4
Tuvalu	−22.2	16.3	24.1	4.6	2.2
Vanuatu	7.8	−6.1	−7.7	−13.0	−2.8

... = not available.

www.ingramcontent.com/pod-product-compliance
Lightning Source LLC
Chambersburg PA
CBHW050243220326
41598CB00048B/7490